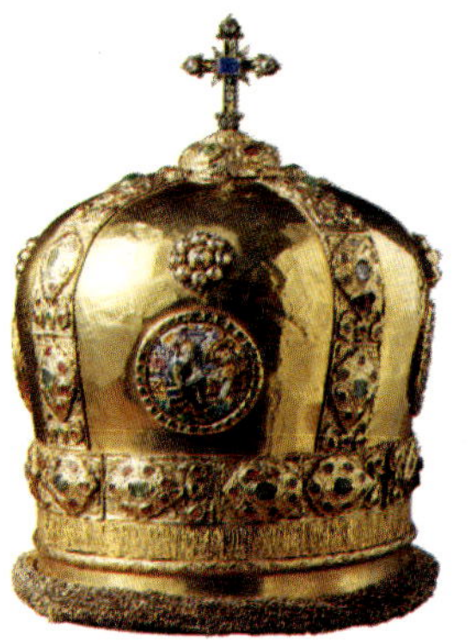

SECRET TREASURES OF RUSSIA

One Thousand Years of Gold and Silver from the State History Museum Moscow

Published by Art Exhibitions Australia Limited
(Australian Company Number 008 554 550)
98 Cumberland Street, The Rocks, Sydney
New South Wales, Australia, 2000

National Library of Australia Cataloguing-in-Publication entry:

Secret treasures of Russia.

Bibliography.
ISBN 1 875460 03 9.

1. Gosudarstvennyĭ istoricheskiĭ muzeĭ (Moscow, R.S.F.S.R.)—Catalogs. 2. Jewelry—Russian S.F.S.R.—Moscow—Catalogs. 3. Jewelry—Soviet Union—Catalogs. 4. Goldwork—Soviet Union—Catalogs. 5. Silverwork—Soviet Union—Catalogs. I. Art Exhibitions Australia.

739.270947074094

First edition
Reprinted 1992

Photography by Nikolai Alekseev, State History Museum, Moscow

Designed by Minale, Tattersfield, Bryce and Partners Pty Limited
Colour separation by Enticott Ultra, Melbourne
Typesetting by Typographix, Brisbane
Printed by Lithocraft Graphics, Melbourne

Acknowledgements

The planning and development of this exhibition necessitated the advice, assistance and special efforts of a number of individuals in Moscow. Particular thanks are due to Professor Konstantin Levykin, Director, and Dr Tamara Igumnova, Deputy Director, Research and Scientific Department, State History Museum; Professor Elvin K. Kalinin, Chairman of the Board, Vjacheslav P. Sergeev, Deputy Director, and Natasha Makarova, Exhibitions Manager, of The Russian Charitable Foundation "Intellect"; and Dr Alekxander I. Shkurko, First Deputy Minister of Culture of the Russian Soviet Federative Socialist Republic.

Art Exhibitions Australia also wishes to thank the many organisations and individuals in Australia who have contributed to the project, especially:

Loti and Victor Smorgon
Yuri and Irene Sokol of Dilankex Pty Limited
Queensland Art Gallery, Doug Hall, *Director*
The Australian Government, in particular the Department of the Arts, Sport, the Environment and Territories, the Department of Foreign Affairs and Trade and the Department of the Prime Minister and Cabinet
Intourist Australia Limited

Indemnified by
The Australian Government through the Department of the Arts, Sport, the Environment and Territories

Australian Tour

March–October 1992

Sponsored by

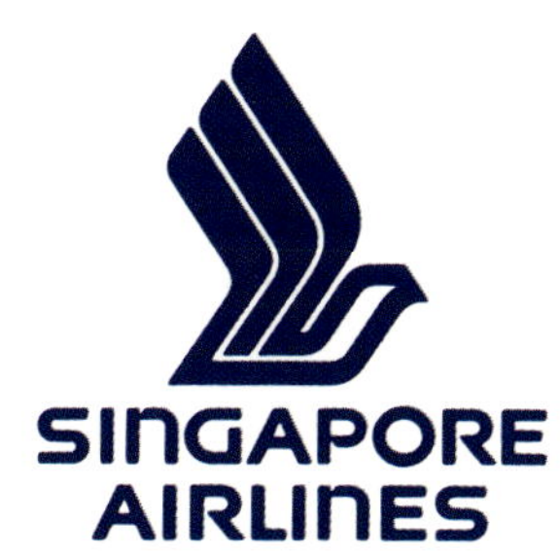

Australian Airlines EXPRESS

AUSTRALIAN AIRLINES

STATEMENT FROM THE HONOURABLE P.J. KEATING, M.P. PRIME MINISTER OF AUSTRALIA

This exceptionally fine exhibition of Russian artistry over more than one thousand years offers all Australians rare insights into a rich culture with a long and fascinating history.

That history is, of course, still evolving. The Russian Federation now stands at the centre of the newly formed Commonwealth of Independent States as the former Soviet Union undergoes dramatic economic, social and political changes.

The changes present opportunities to build and extend relationships. I hope this exhibition marks the beginning of a wider cultural exchange between Australia and the Russian Federation.

I would especially like to thank the Government of the Federation for making the exhibition available to tour Australia, and in particular the Director and staff of Moscow's State History Museum for their efforts and expertise in selecting and assembling the exhibition.

The works in the exhibition are eloquent ambassadors for the Russian people, telling us of their depth of tradition, their achievement of artistic excellence over many centuries, the inextinguishable flame of Orthodox Christianity, the strength and resilience of a people who could revive their national culture and unique artistic expression after periods of foreign domination.

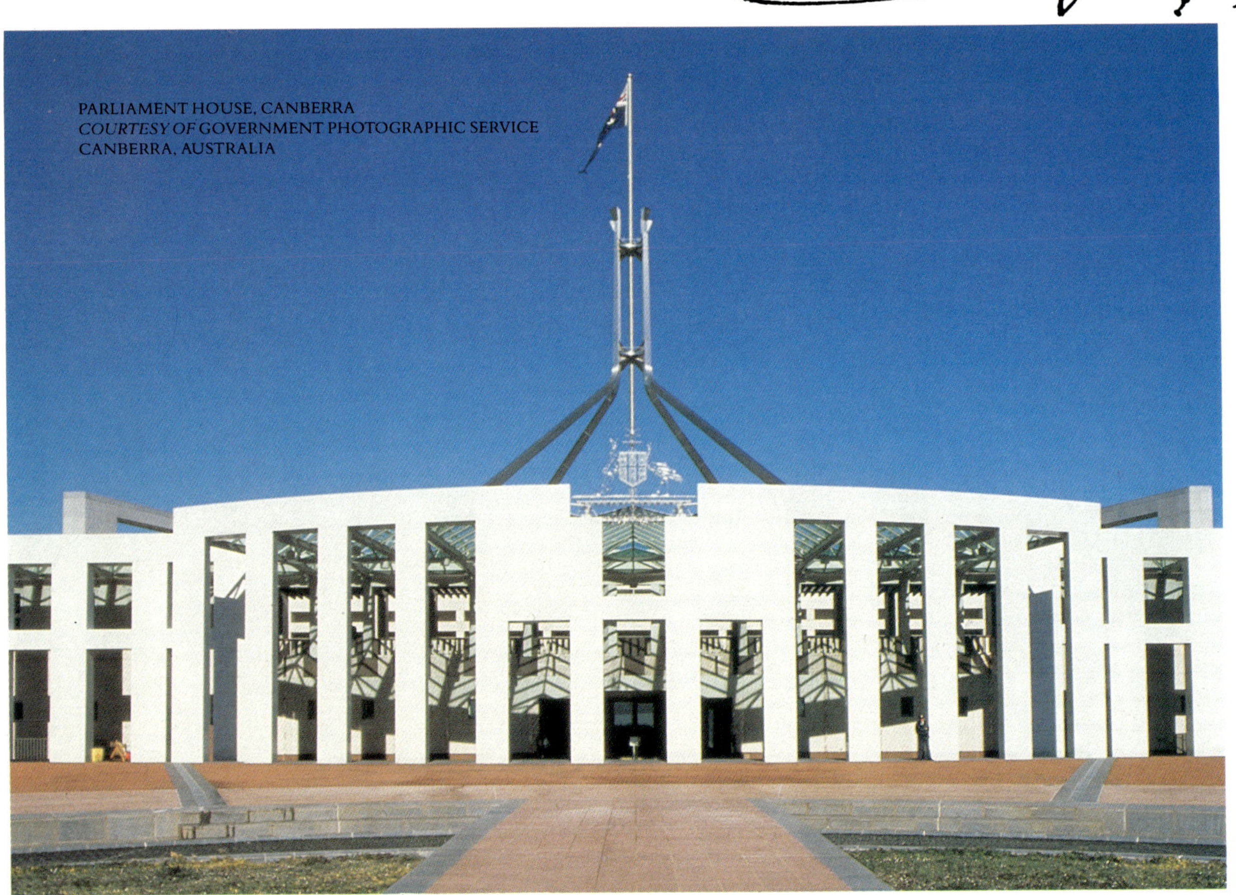

PARLIAMENT HOUSE, CANBERRA
COURTESY OF GOVERNMENT PHOTOGRAPHIC SERVICE
CANBERRA, AUSTRALIA

STATEMENT FROM GENNADY E. BURBULIS
STATE SECRETARY, FIRST DEPUTY OF THE PRESIDENT OF THE RUSSIAN FEDERATION GOVERNMENT

As the new Russia undergoes social, economic and political changes, we are striving to develop contacts with other countries for mutual benefit.

This exhibition, *Secret Treasures of Russia,* visits Australia as the first exchange to represent sovereign, independent Russia.

Russian culture, which developed in a vast territory over a period of one thousand years, has always been distinguished by originality and by readiness to interact with other civilisations of the world.

In this exhibition, the principal periods of Russian history are shown through the evolution of the art of jewellery. Many exhibits are individually connected with historical figures.

We hope that *Secret Treasures of Russia* will encourage Australians to become more closely acquainted with Russia, despite the great distance between our countries, enabling us to develop and extend our long-standing cultural and business contacts.

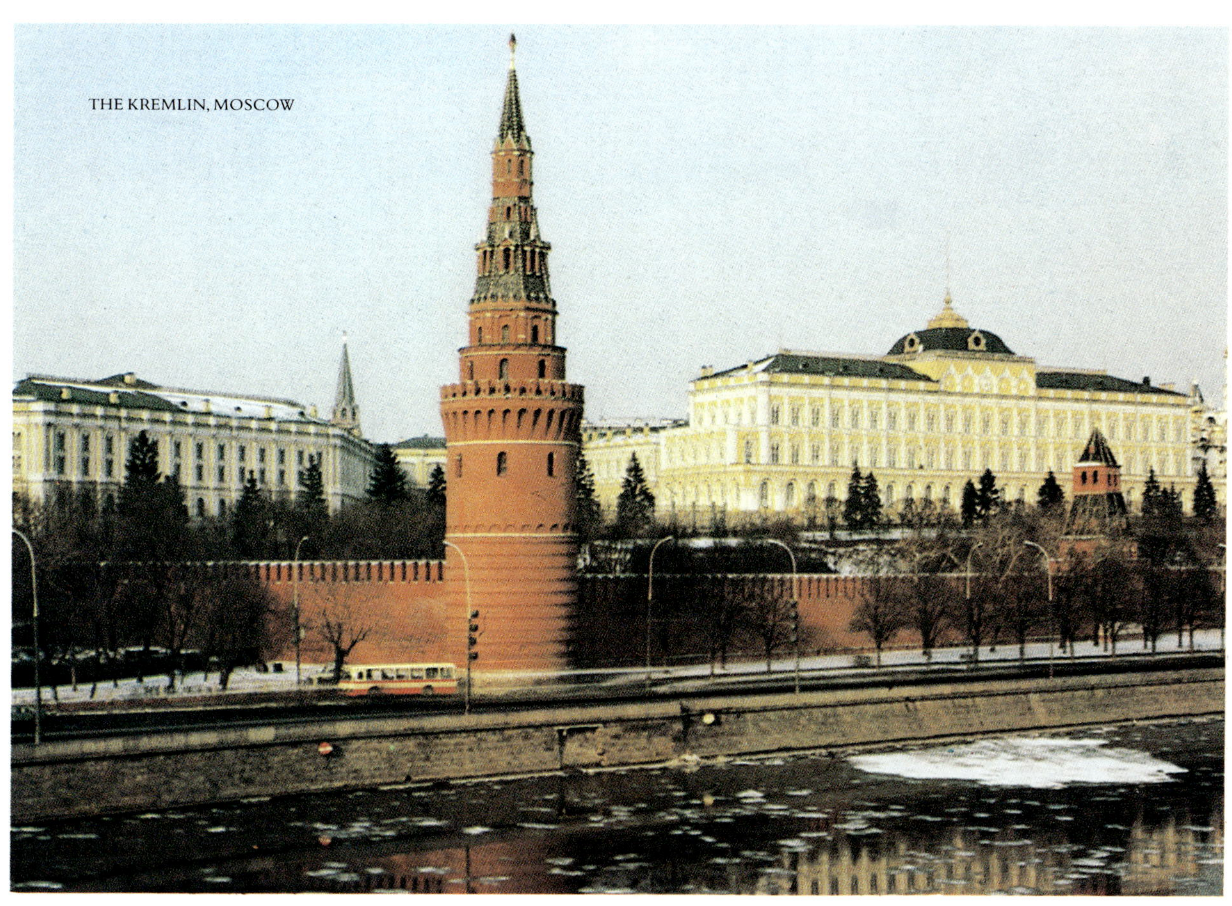
THE KREMLIN, MOSCOW

FOREWORD

This exhibition, the 39th organised by our company since 1980, grew from extraordinary circumstances.

The breathtaking speed of change within the former Soviet Union has swept in a new openness to the rest of the world and in the process has provided a unique opportunity for all Australians.

The quality of this display perfectly exemplifies the purpose for which our company was established: the enrichment of Australian life through significant exchanges with the great cultures of the world.

As the International Cultural Corporation of Australia Limited, and since 1991 as Art Exhibitions Australia Limited, our company has brought to Australia an unprecedented range of exhibitions drawn from the world's cultural heritage, including displays from Asia, Europe, North and South America, Great Britain and the Middle East.

In partnership with the Australian Government, with a broad array of corporate sponsors and with lending and exhibiting museums, Art Exhibitions Australia has made a substantial contribution to the cultural life of the nation. Our exciting plans for the 1990s promise to continue and extend this productive role.

Secret Treasures of Russia has been made possible through the generosity of the Government of the Russian Federation.

I would also like to express our appreciation to Professor Konstantin Levykin and Dr Tamara Igumnova, the Director and Deputy Director of Moscow's State History Museum, for their professional co-operation.

We are grateful to the staff at the Embassy of the Commonwealth of Independent States in Canberra, and at the Australian Embassy in Moscow, for their invaluable assistance.

I would especially like to acknowledge the generosity of Loti and Victor Smorgon of Melbourne. This exhibition has been made possible through their personal financial support.

Specialised transportation services are, of course, crucial for all Art Exhibitions Australia projects. For this exhibition, the carriers are also our supporters; Singapore Airlines is our main sponsor and Australian Airlines has contributed domestic transport. The continuing role of these airlines provides outstanding service and has enabled us to plan an ambitious series of exhibitions.

Major undertakings such as this exhibition would not be financially viable without the support of the Australian Government; indemnification is provided through the Department of the Arts, Sport, the Environment and Territories and security by the Australian Protective Service.

I am sure that this exhibition will deepen understanding and friendship between the people of Russia and Australia. It will also contribute to the momentum for a growing program of cultural exchange between our countries.

James B. Leslie, A.O., M.C.
Chairman
Art Exhibitions Australia Limited

PREFACE

Over recent times the world community has watched with amazement and disbelief as the rigid authoritarian regimes of the former Soviet Union and Eastern Bloc countries have given way to a series of sovereign states, each committed to democracy and free-market economies.

The raising of the notorious Iron Curtain has revealed an incredible wealth of heritage material unseen by recent generations. Among the treasures now available for international display are those preserved in the strongrooms of the State History Museum on Red Square in the heart of the great metropolis of Moscow.

The collection of 297 unique objects of Russian gold and silver selected to tour in Australia includes some of the most significant examples of the art yet available to a world audience. Australians are privileged to have a special opportunity to view this material and gain insights into Russian art and its relationship with the ever-changing society in which it was created.

The objects in the exhibition span one thousand years of turbulent history. They are of unique artistic and historical significance; their forms and ornamentation attest to the distinctive nature of Russian applied arts and their links with the rich traditions extending back to the very origins of the country. The collection comprises secular and ecclesiastical pieces of untold beauty, created in various artistic centres throughout Russia, including the famous workshops of the Moscow Kremlin.

The project has been the means of establishing close personal links between specialists in the State History Museum and Art Exhibitions Australia Limited. The complex arrangements for the Australian tour have also been assisted by the generous support of the Russian Ministry of Culture, the Russian Charitable Foundation "Intellect" and Dilankex Pty Limited of Sydney. The interaction between all these agencies has made it possible to bring together a superb exhibition for Australia.

Secret Treasures of Russia is a spectacular exhibition about a subject with wide public appeal from a country which dominates the world news at a time of dramatic change. The Australian tour will create a new awareness of the ancient, varied and rich heritage of a great nation. It also will be a significant contribution to engendering closer friendship and co-operation between the peoples of the Russian Federation and Australia. I trust this exhibition will be the first of a continuing series of cultural exchanges between Australia and Russia.

Robert Edwards, A.O.
Chief Executive and Director
Art Exhibitions Australia Limited

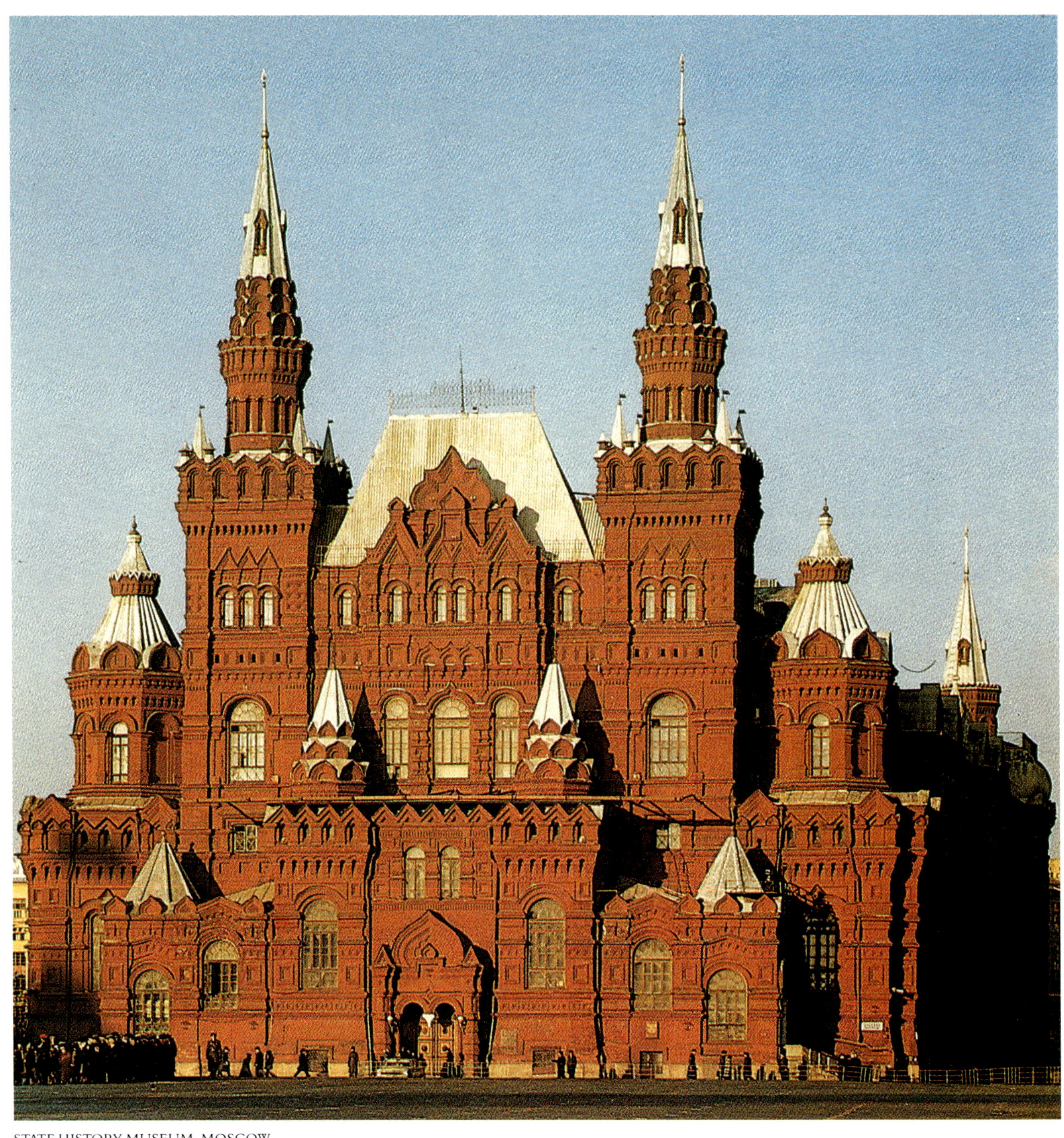

STATE HISTORY MUSEUM, MOSCOW.

> *“Museums are one of the major means by which the people can attain a national consciousness; this is the highest aim of history as a science.”*

K.N. Bestuzhev-Ryumin

INTRODUCTION

The idea of establishing a national museum first emerged in Russia in the early 19th century but was not implemented until much later. The institution was founded in 1872 and officially inaugurated in 1883 as the Imperial Russian History Museum. The group responsible for founding and establishing the Museum was led by some outstanding historians and scholars, the pride of Russian historical science, including A.S. Uvarov, I.E. Zabelin, K.N. Bestuzhev-Ryumin, S.M. Solovyev, V.O. Klyuchevsky and F.I. Buslayev.

The Statutes of the Museum stated in 1874 that the Museum "aims to serve as a visual aid to understanding the major epochs of the country and to promote knowledge of Russia's national history". This determined the Museum's display and collection policies, which through their scope had to demonstrate the Museum's broad charter: "to reflect and portray a thousand years of Russia's national history through visual images".

The Museum's first acquisitions comprised exhibits from the Sebastopol Section of the 1872 Polytechnic Exhibition as well as the collections of the Moscow Archaeological Society and the Ministry of National Properties. Other museums, academies, libraries, institutions and private collectors contributed generously to the Museum's collections. In 1908, a total of 900 private collectors donated to the Museum.

Of particular note was the donation in 1908 by Peter Ivanovich Schukin, a merchant and famous collector. At first Schukin collected books and engravings, later progressing to ancient Russian items including armoury, tableware, kitchenware, embroidery, samovars and jewellery — objects which illustrated the lives of people in almost every stratum of society from the 16th to the 19th centuries. This collection began with one of the works from the exhibition, the silver ladle "granted by the Empress Elizabeth Petrovna to the Ataman (Cossack chieftain) of the Yaik Regiment, Feodor Andreev, the son of Borodin, in the year of 1761".

Fine work in gold and silver has played a great role over a thousand years of Russian history. The art first emerged in Kievan Rus and underwent various periods of development, reaching its peak during the more prosperous periods of the country's history and experiencing temporary decline during times of war and depression. The style which gradually emerged was inimitable in its beauty, ornamentation, form and essence, qualities inherent in Russian gold and silver.

In contrast to the collections of the Armoury Chamber and the Hermitage Museum, the Department of Precious Metals of the State History Museum possesses an extraordinarily wide range of works; as well as those made by craftsmen of the Armoury Chamber and other holders of the Imperial Warrant, the collection includes objects belonging to the Russian Tsars and the Court. Indeed, vast breadth is the main distinguishing quality of the collection; Russian gold and silver work is shown in its development of national forms, ornamentation, motifs and variety of techniques. The collection represents almost all the centres of jewellery-making, including items that belonged to the Boyars, nobility, wealthy mercantile community, middle class and peasants.

This unique collection, from which *Secret Treasures of Russia* has been drawn, has turned the Department of Precious Metals into the centre for the study of Russian jewellery art.

Professor Konstantin Levykin
Director
State History Museum

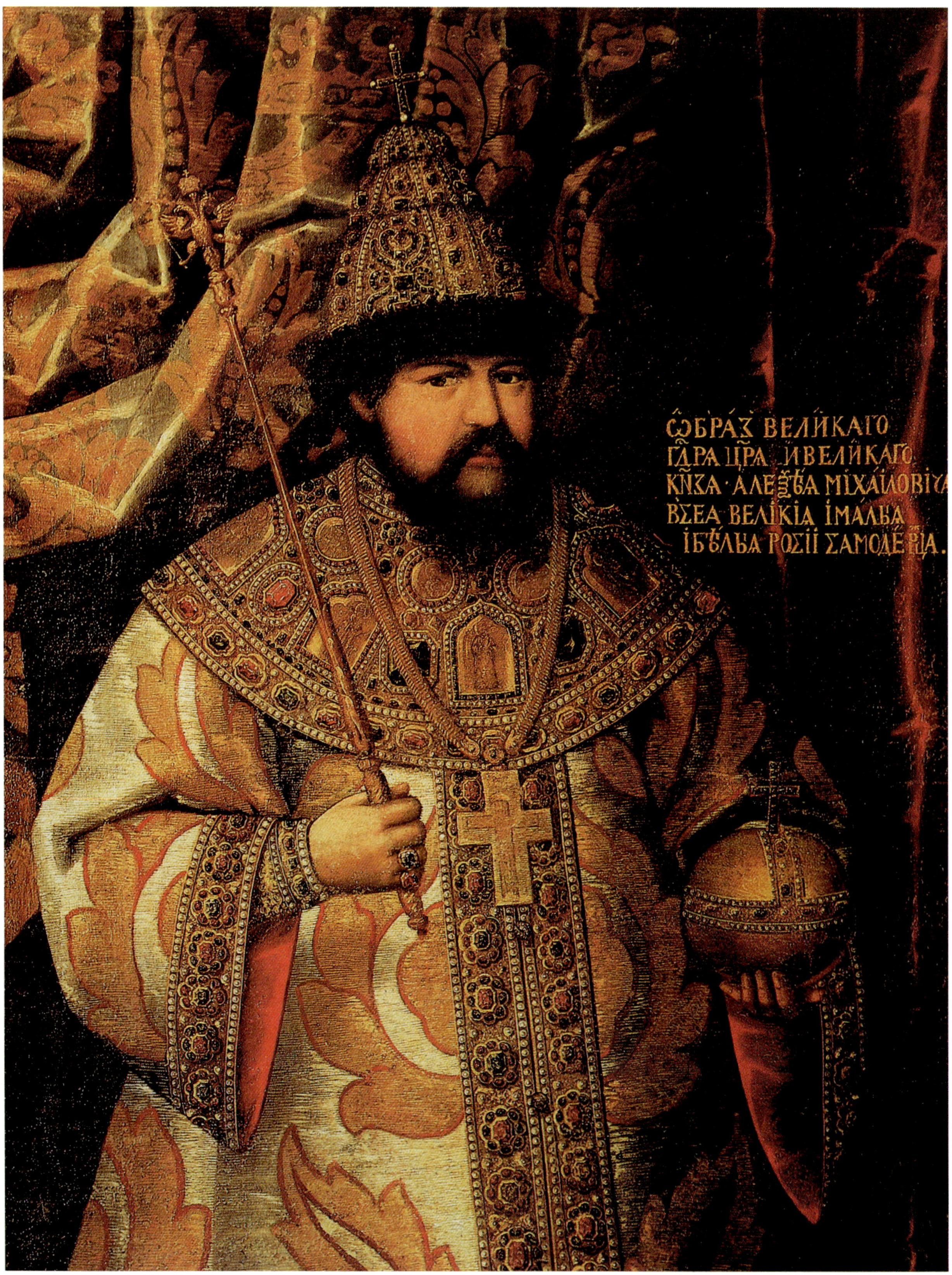

TSAR ALEKSEI MIKHAILOVICH (1629–76)

I

BEFORE THE TARTAR YOKE

Gold and Silver of Old Russia

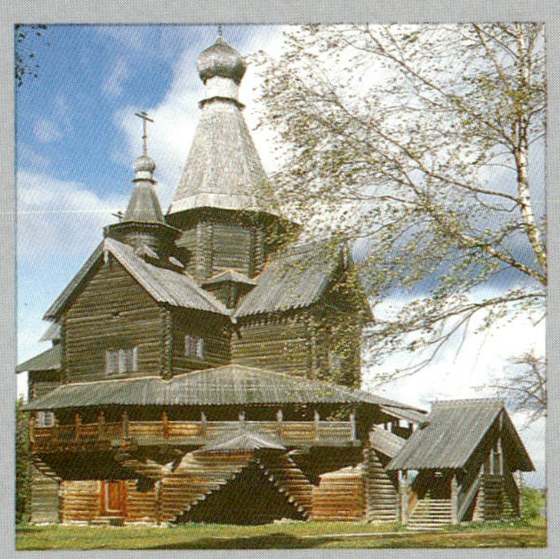

Early Russian culture is usually associated with Kievan Rus, the first state of the eastern Slavs, founded at the end of the 10th century by the merging of a large number of Slavic tribes. Rus soon became the largest state in eastern Europe, possessing an original, brilliant culture and craft skills of a very high standard. Christianity, introduced to Kievan Rus from Byzantium in 988, gave a further impetus to the cultural development of Old Russia.

The development of urban crafts led to the creation of delicate ornaments, using very complicated techniques. The main centre for such work was Kiev, the capital of the first Russian state. In the mid 12th century, however, Kiev lost its exclusive status as sole centre of innovation in jewellery-making. The period of feudal disunity resulted in the split of Kievan Rus into a number of independent princedoms, leading in turn to the flourishing of local schools.

This exhibition includes artefacts from various centres of Old Russia, including Kiev, Chernigov, Vladimir and Old Ryazan. Having inherited the best traditions of the craftsmen of the Dnieper region, the jewellers of these towns made their own unique contributions to the further development of Russian jewellery-making.

The Archaeological Department of the State History Museum boasts the richest collections of works from this early period, discovered in excavations of settlements and barrows of the 10th to 13th centuries. They represent, however, only a small part of the works of the Old Russian craftsmen. Their rarity increases the historical value of these artefacts, which illustrate the characteristics of Russian applied arts before the Tartar invasion and provide insights into the spiritual life of the Old Slavs and the surprising skills of the Russian craftsmen.

Most of the pieces exhibited were found in treasure-troves created by wealthy Russians, mainly in the 12th and early 13th centuries, when threatened at various times by war, social upheaval, assaults by nomadic tribes and the Mongol invasion, which shook Russia in the mid 13th century. Ornaments found in these treasure-troves belonged to the Kievan nobility and were made in royal workshops. Their design reflects the nobility's refined tastes and pursuit of exquisite luxury.

For example, grivnas (necklaces), the favourite adornment of Russian women of the time, made of silver or bronze hoops of twisted wire and plates, are frequently found in rich urban and rural barrows. Dress for festive occasions included barms (necklaces) made of several round ornamented segments. Individual segments of such barms, bearing images of the Virgin or the cross, are also included in the exhibition.

The decoration of these ornaments indicates the richness and magnificence of dress of the princes and boyars of Old Russia. Elaborate headdresses were adorned with gold and silver three-beaded temple rings with fine filigree wire and granular decoration, as well as by kolts (temple pendants) with enamel inlay and miniature granular or nielloed decoration. These were attached to the headdress with bands or chains.

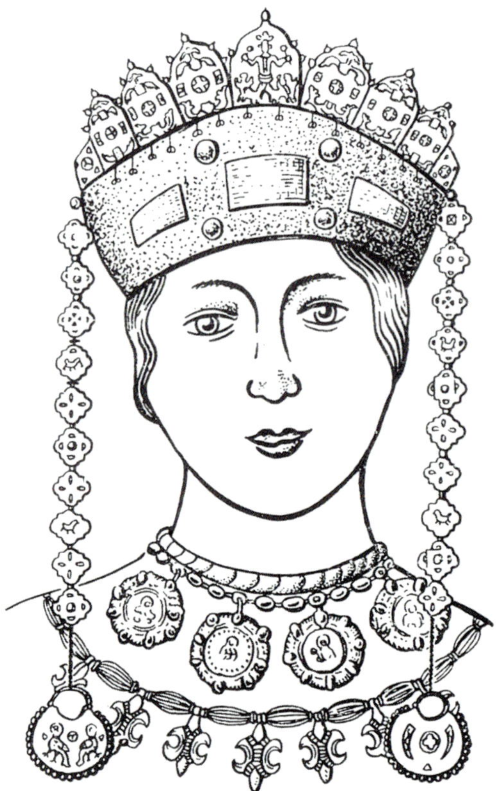

COSTUME OF WEALTHY RUSSIAN WOMAN, 12th–13th CENTURY

Bracelets demonstrate the height of the craftsmen's proficiency. Of particular interest are the bracelets formed by wide, gilded, engraved and nielloed hoops. Their design shows Byzantine influence, but the decoration applied by Russian craftsmen is completely original. Mythical images of griffins and birds are encircled by floral patterns. Nielloed images of creatures on Russian ornaments sprang from the

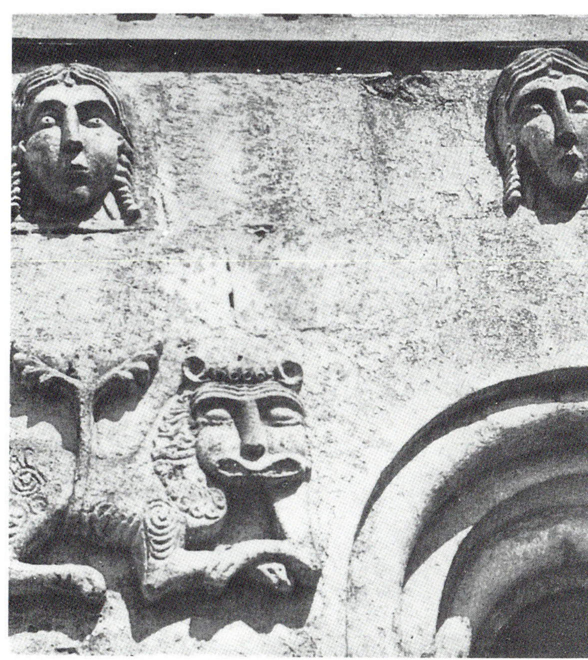

DETAIL OF WESTERN FACADE, POKROV CHURCH, NERLI, 1164

oriental cultural tradition; the elements of this style can also be seen in illuminations in Slavic manuscripts.

The wide-band bracelets vividly illustrate the vitality of the Russian pagan cultural tradition, which also manifested itself in applied art and the ornamentation of ancient edifices. Holiday dress was adorned with beads and various pendants, lily shapes being among the most popular. Treasure-troves often contained finger rings of various shapes, plain and twisted, occasionally with engraved or nielloed patterns on the bezel.

Metalwork in Old Russia attained high technical and artistic standards. Almost all techniques and methods of metal treatment, especially of precious metals such as silver and gold, were employed. These craftsmen mastered casting, forging, soldering and twisting as well as far more sophisticated techniques. In this exhibition one can see the finest examples of the jeweller's art: polychrome enamel, nielloed patterns, miniature metallic granules and filigree wire lace, all created by anonymous Russian craftsmen.

The oldest exhibit is the earring found near Kiev, which dates from the 10th or early 11th century (cat. no. 1).

Filigree wire technique was well-known and widely used by the early craftsmen. This technique exploits the ductile properties of precious metals. The extruded

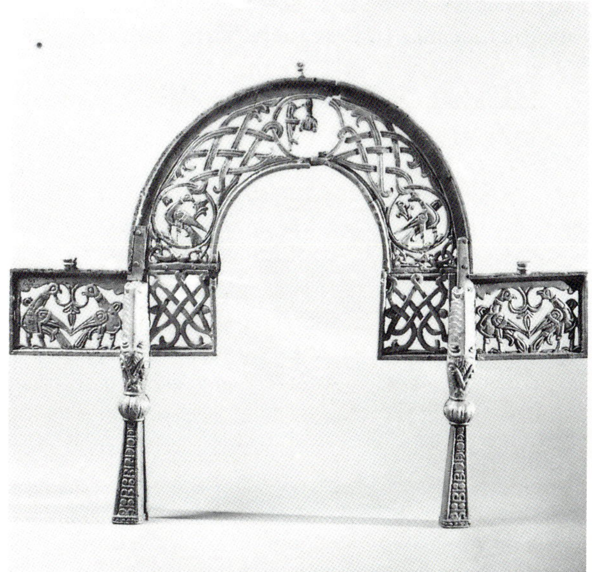

12th CENTURY BRONZE ARCH, CHERNIGOV PROVINCE

wire is used to create metal lacework, which can be either open or on a substrate formed by a metal plate. In the fretwork pattern the wire itself forms the framework of the ornament. This technique predominates in the decoration of three-beaded temple rings, where the fretwork pattern of the beads is formed by a web of thin wire, creating an effect of transparency and weightlessness. Beads, knots and aigrettes in the exhibition are lavishly decorated with filigree patterns, often supplemented with granular decorations composed of miniature gold and silver balls, each soldered on to either the wire frame or the plain surface of the ornament. This technique is characteristic of three-beaded temple rings, where filigree wire and metal granules are used in a wide range of combinations. Kolts, made by Kievan jewellers, are striking examples of artefacts decorated with granules. The entire surface of one kolt is covered with rows of soldered miniature grains. Several hundred metallic granules were used for the ornamentation of such pendants.

During the second half of the 11th century, enamel was introduced to Kiev, the capital of Old Russia, resulting in artefacts perfect in both technique and design. Although cloisonné enamel technique was brought over from Byzantium, Russian craftsmen not only mastered this complex method but created innovative ornaments.

Most of the earliest enamelled pieces were discovered in Kiev, where the first enamel workshop of the

12th century was probably founded. Kolts and aigrettes with images of birds are believed to have been made there.

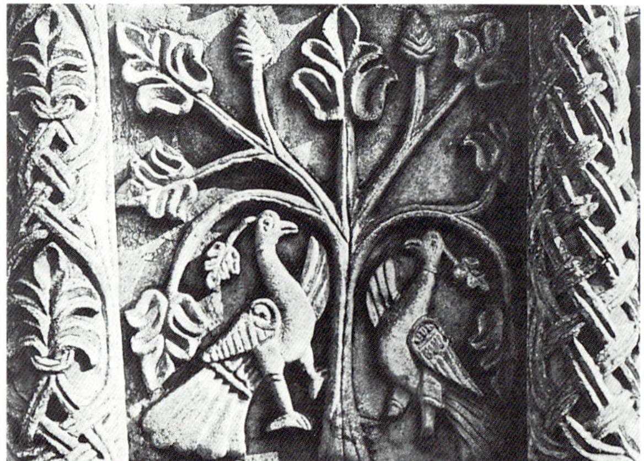

DETAIL OF NORTHERN FACADE, DMITRI CHURCH, VLADIMIR, 1194–97

The cloisonné enamel technique, used mainly for the decoration of gold artefacts, is extremely complex and demands special skills. In creating a kolt, for instance, the pattern was first embossed into the thin gold plate to form a bed for the enamel, inside which were soldered thin gold wires. The bed was then filled with enamels of different colours and baked in the furnace. The molten enamel powder was thus firmly bonded to the metallic base and polishing completed the operation. The roundel with the image of Christ extending his arm in blessing (cat. no. 11) was made with this technique.

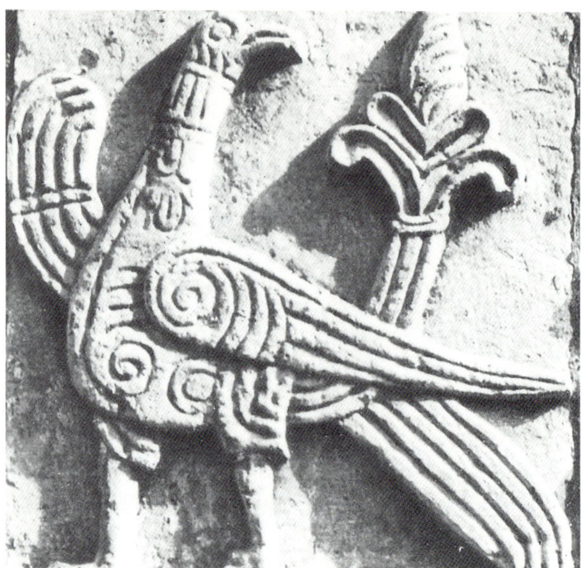

DETAIL OF NORTHERN FACADE, DMITRI CHURCH, VLADIMIR, 1194–97

Silver ornaments, such as kolts, bracelets and finger rings, were decorated with nielloed patterns. Enamelled gold ornaments (kolts, barms and aigrettes) were mainly worn at festive occasions. Silver nielloed artefacts, preferred for daily wear, show a stronger influence of folk art and its pagan roots.

Although the first nielloed pieces appeared in Russia in the late 11th century, the real flowering of this technique occurred during the 12th century. Again, Kiev led the way. Ornaments with nielloed patterns from Kiev, Chernigov and Vladimir are included in the exhibition.

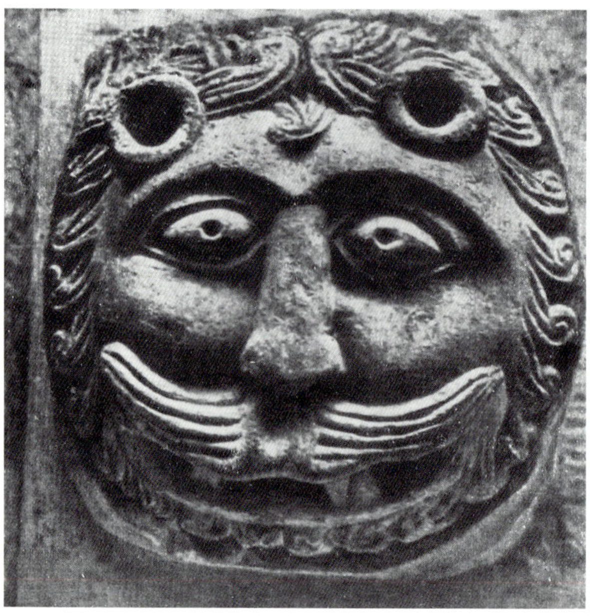

DETAIL OF NORTHEN FACADE, USPENSKY CHURCH, VLADIMIR, 1168–60

Niello was used in two different ways: it could either underline the contour of the pattern against a light background or serve as a background itself, thus creating a positive image. Before nielloing, the pattern was chased or die-stamped into the silver plate. The background of the high relief pattern was then treated with a cutting tool to ensure a better adhesion between the silver substrate and niello. The background was filled with niello powder mixed with water. The whole was then baked in the furnace, ensuring a strong bond between the molten mass and the silver substrate.

The unique artistry, technique and skill of the craftsmen of Old Russia did not vanish into obscurity. Their traditions were developed further and improved by their successors.

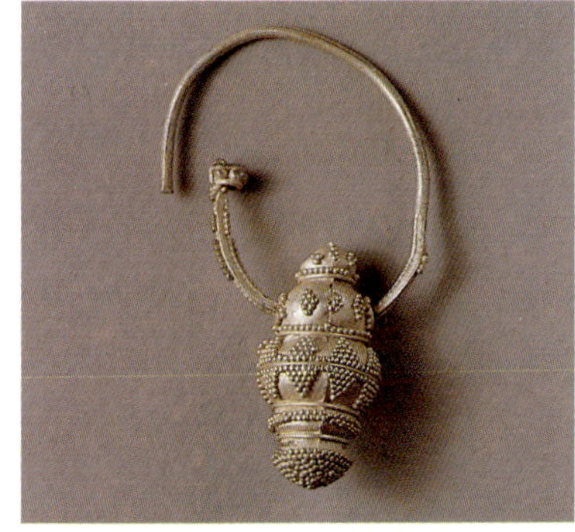

1

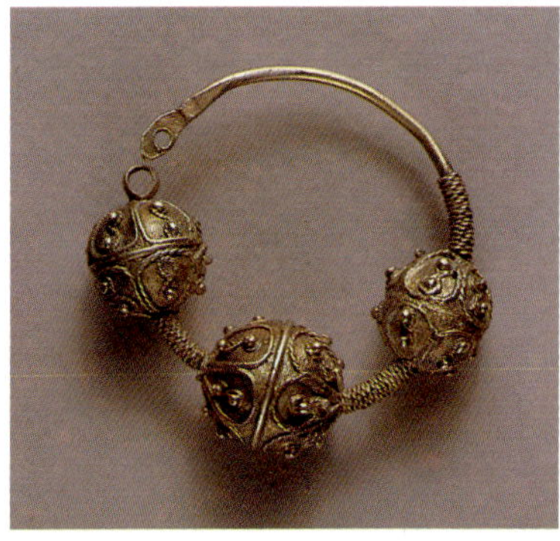

2

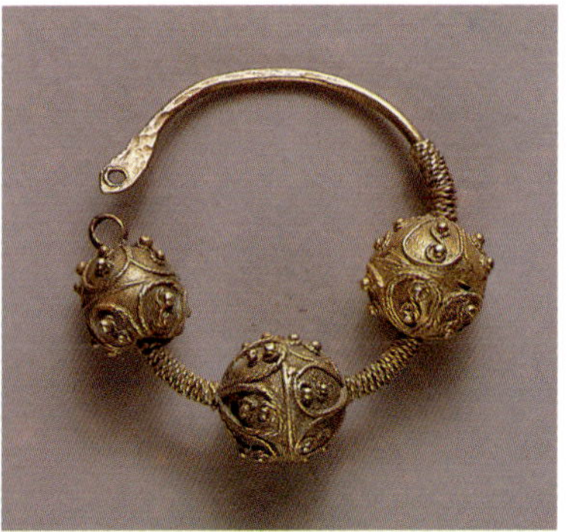

3

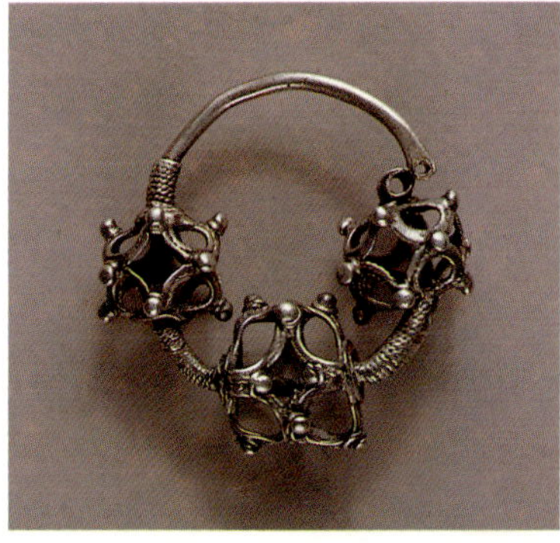

4

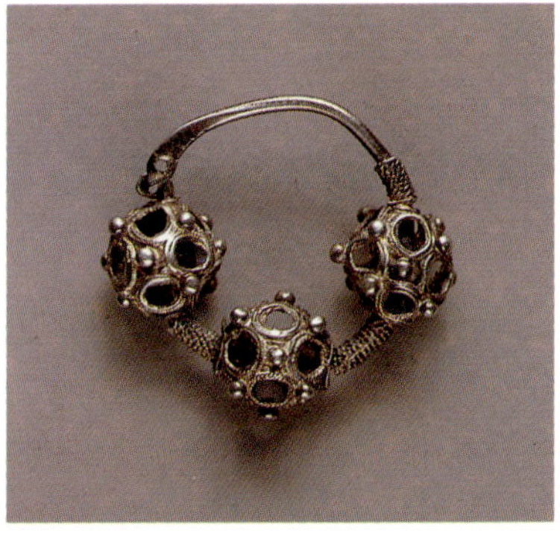

5

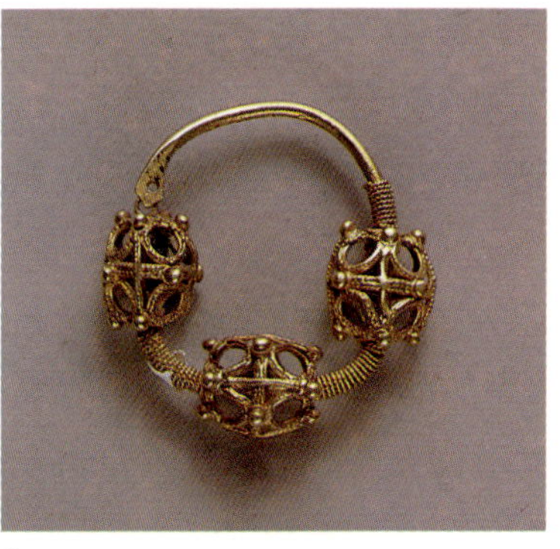

6

1. Earring
Dnieper region,
second half of 10th–early 11th century
silver, 6.0 x 3.2 cm
formerly collection:
P.I. Schukin
16472; 1948/1

Woman's earring comprising a hollow bead and top section decorated with finely-soldered silver granules arranged in a pattern of equilateral triangles and rhombuses. Although the exact location of its discovery is unknown, it is typical of earrings from the western and south-western territories of Old Russia.

2. Three-beaded temple ring
Kiev, 11th–12th century
silver gilt, filigree
diameter: 4.8 cm
43078, 1734/4

Rings of this type would originally have been attached with bands to a woman's headdress and suspended at temple level. The round, hollow beads are decorated with filigree and silver granules. Types of temple rings varied between the territories of Old Russia. While the exact location of the discovery of this ring is unkown, three-beaded pendants were characteristic of southern regions.

3. Three-beaded temple ring
probably Kiev, 11th–12th century
silver gilt, filigree
diameter: 4.8 cm
accessioned 1906
43079; 1734/5

The form and technique of this ring are similar to those of cat. nos 1 and 2. The exact location of its discovery is unkown.

See Vasilenko, fig. 103

4. Three-beaded temple ring
probably Kiev, 12th century
silver, filigree
diameter: 4.0 cm
formerly collection:
D.Ya. Samokvasov
76990; 1673/91

Ring featuring a filigree fretwork bead frame and pattern of silver granules, found during the excavation of the ancient settlement of Knyazya Gora, near Kiev.

See Vasilenko, fig. 96

5. Three-beaded temple ring
probably Kiev, 12th century
silver, filigree
diameter: 3.8 cm
formerly collection:
D.Ya. Samokvasov
76990, 1673/100

Ring with a filigree fretwork bead frame and granular decoration, found at Knyazya Gora.

See Vasilenko, fig. 101; Ribakov (2), fig. 89

6. Three-beaded temple ring
probably Kiev, 12th century
gold, filigree
diameter: 3.8 cm
formerly collection:
D.Ya. Samokvasov
76990; 2211/9

The frame of each bead is formed by a thin filigree wire, ornamented with a granular design. Although made of gold, this ring is similar in shape to cat. no. 5 and was also unearthed at Knyazya Gora, near Kiev.

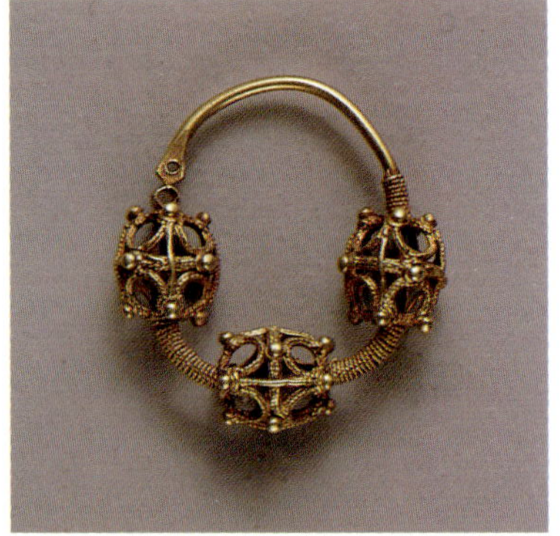
7

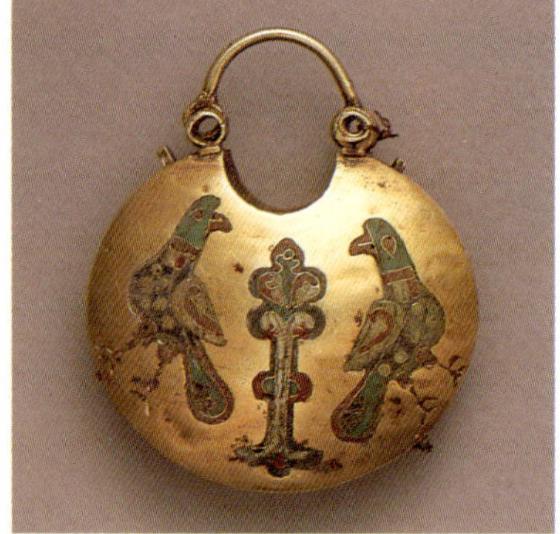
8

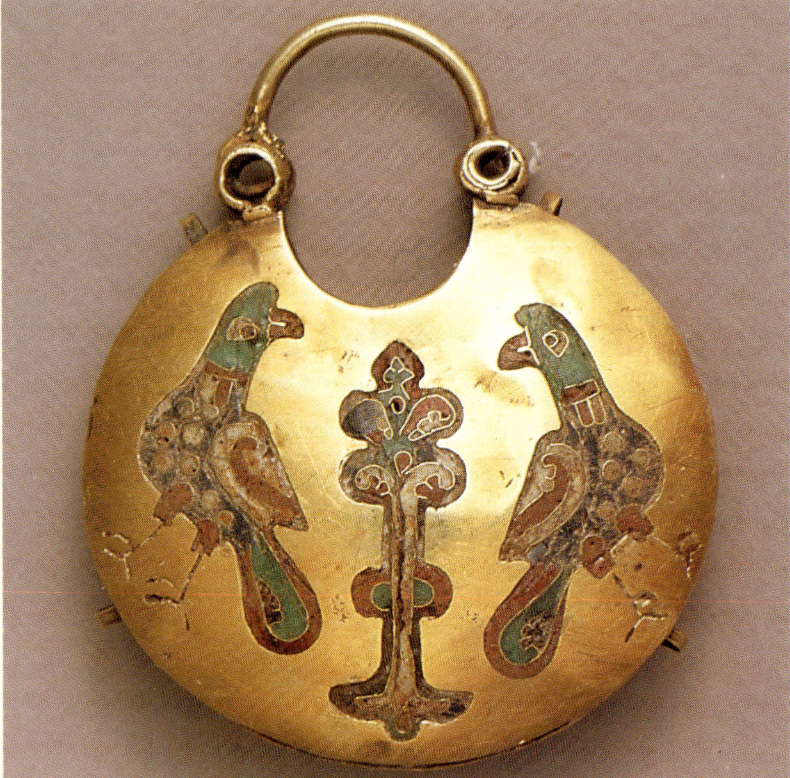
9

7. Three-beaded temple ring
probably Kiev, 12th century
gold, filigree
diameter: 4.0cm
formerly collection:
D.Ya. Samokvasov
76990; 2211/10

Identical in shape and technique to cat. no. 6. Found at Knyazya Gora, near Kiev.

8. Kolt (temple pendant)
Kiev, 12th century
gold, cloisonné
4.0x3.6cm
53091; 2200/2

Kolt identical to cat. no. 9.

9. Kolt (temple pendant)
Kiev, 12th century
gold, cloisonné
4.0x3.6cm
53091; 2200/1

Kolts, or temple pendants, formed part of the headdress of wealthy women. Along the rib of the kolt are loops to secure pearl beads which have not survived. The obverse bears an image of two birds on either side of a tree, while the reverse is decorated with a geometric pattern. The blue, red, green and white enamel inlays have retained their original surface and sheen.

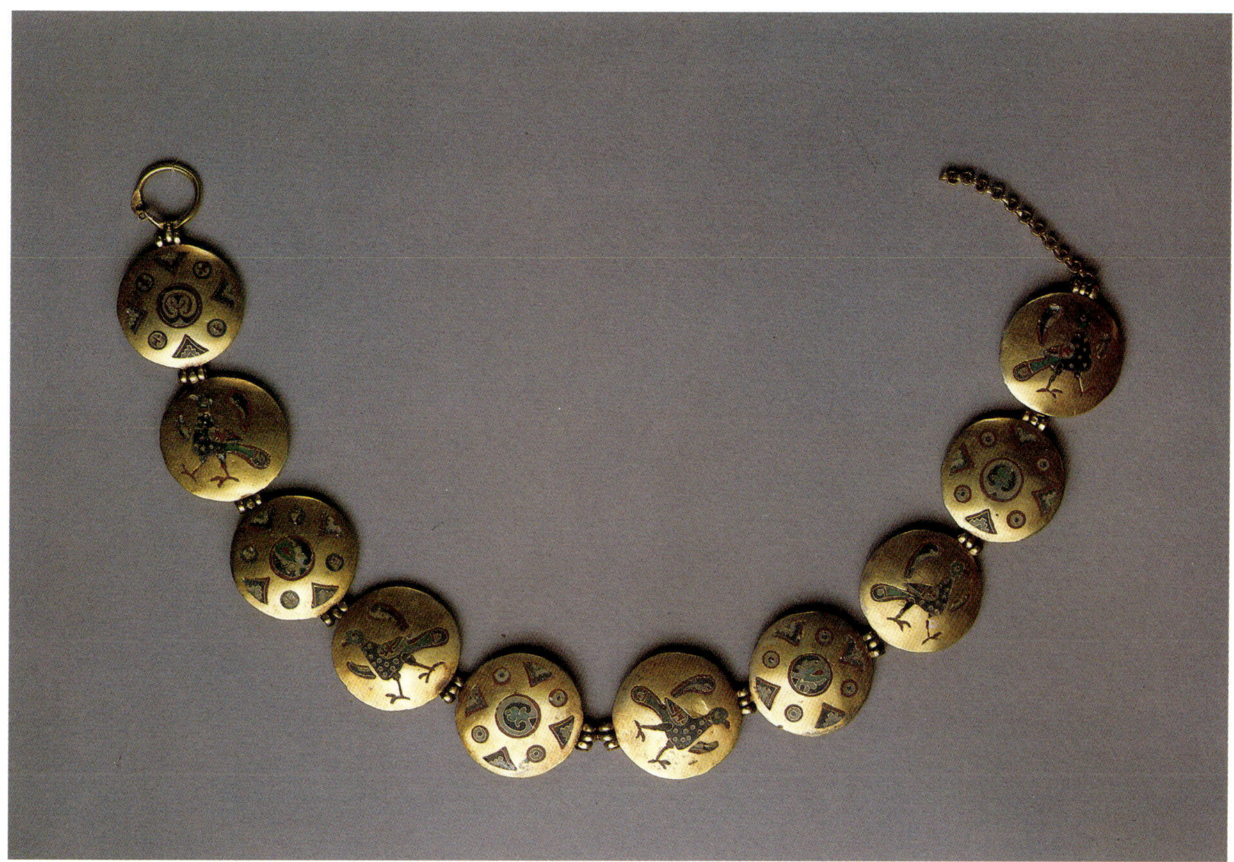

10

10. Chain
Kiev, 12th century
gold, cloisonné
diameter of lockets: 2.8 cm
53090; 2200/3

As with cat. nos 8 and 9, this chain would have formed part of the headdress of a wealthy woman. The chain was presumably used to hang kolts (temple pendants) but could also have been used as a necklace. Each locket consists of two soldered round plates. The obverse of each is decorated with blue, red, green and white enamel, while the reverse is plain. Five lockets bear bird images; each of the remainder is decorated with a unique geometric pattern. The unity of design and colour indicate that cat. nos 8, 9 and 10 were created as a set. They were found in a treasure-trove discovered in Kiev in the 1840s.

See Uvarov, enamels nos 1 and 2; Korzukhina, p. 107, item 65; Makarova (1), tables 3, 14, 15, 6, 1, 2, p. 104, cat. 19–20, p. 107, cat. 52; Vasilenko, p. 116; Bocharov, p.49

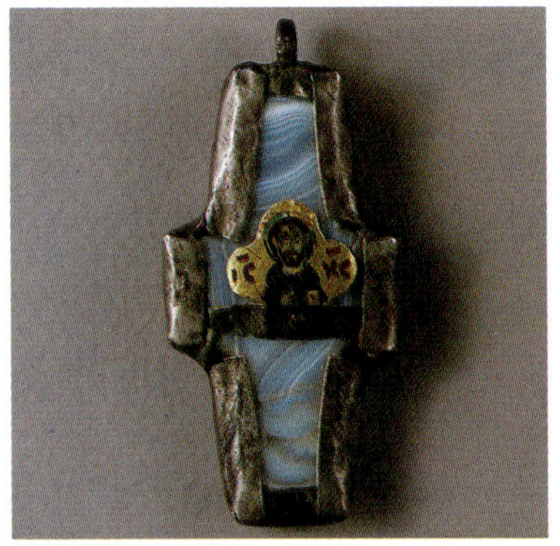
11

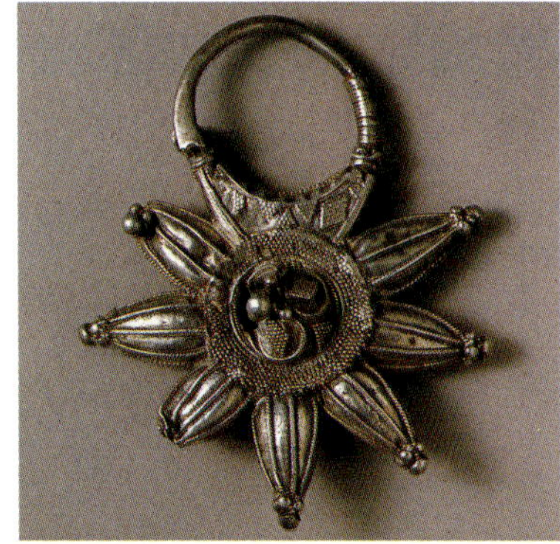
12

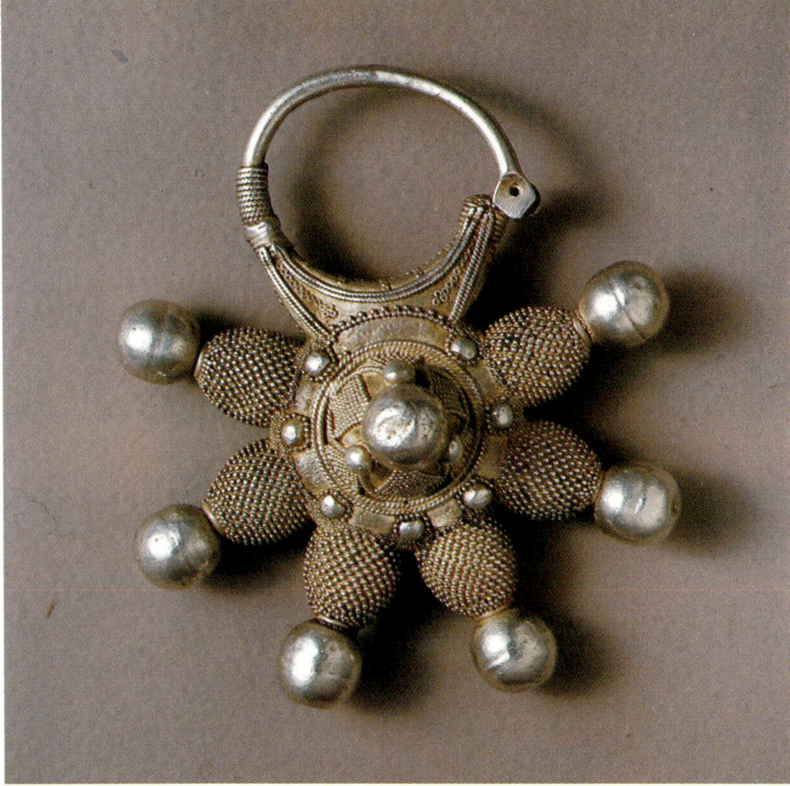
13

11. Roundel
Kiev, 12th–13th century
gold, cloisonné, tin, agate
1.7 x 1.7 cm
75042/9309

Forged cloisonné roundel bearing an image of Christ with arms extended in blessing. The roundel is attached to an agate cross of a later date, in a tin setting. Such pieces were used originally to ornament bookcovers and ecclesiastical robes.

See *Russian Enamel Catalogue,* no. 20; Makarova (1), p. 123, cat. 133, table 13–8

12. Kolt (temple pendant)
Kiev, 12th–early 13th century
silver, filigree
7.0 x 6.0 cm
49876, 1091/49

Pyramids made up of large silver granules decorate the central section and the ends of the seven arms of the pendant. The arms are also ornamented with longitudinal filigree scrolls, while the central parts of the obverse and reverse are decorated with fine, randomly arranged granules. The middle of the obverse side and the upper part of the kolt bear a pattern of triangles and rhombuses made of silver granules.

13. Kolt (temple pendant)
probably Kiev, 12th century
silver, filigree
7.0 x 7.5 cm
purchased 1903
41426; 1952/1

The central section and each of the six arms of this pendant are decorated with plain hollow balls. The kolt is ornamented on both sides; the entire surface of the arms is decorated with a pattern of silver granules, while the middle of the obverse side features a pattern of granular triangles and the reverse and top of the kolt are ornamented with circles of filigree. The exact location of the discovery of this piece is unknown.

See Vasilenko, fig. 106

14. Kolt (temple pendant)
Kiev, 12th–early 13th century
silver, engraving, filigree, niello
diameter: 5.8cm
49876; 1091/3

Ribbed kolt with 24 arms, decorated with filigree and linked by a pseudo-filigree plait. The inlays in the centre of the kolt bear images of a wild beast, engraved in the nielloed background.

15. Aigrette
Kiev, 12th–early 13th century
silver, filigree
5.0 x 4.5cm
49876; 1091/25

Although resembling a buckle, this ornament would have formed part of a headdress. Each of the three beads is decorated with circles, the radii of which are formed of twisted wire. The centre of each circle is formed by a silver ball; the ends of the pendant are flattened and rolled into tubes.

16. Aigrette
Kiev, 12th–early 13th century
silver, filigree
5.5 x 4.5cm
49876; 1091/26

This piece is identical in shape and ornamentation to cat. no. 15.

17. Pectoral cross
Kiev, 12th–early 13th century
silver, glass
4.8 x 3.3cm
49876; 1091/23

The middle and the straight, plain arms of the cast cross bear studs of brown and blue glass of which only three remain intact.

18 Bead
Kiev, 12th–early 13th century
silver, filigree
length: 3.0cm
49876; 1091/20

Oval bead ornamented with geometric patterns of regular filigree circles, inside each of which is a rhombus surrounded by four small triangles formed by silver balls. The ends of the bead are covered with filigree scrollwork.

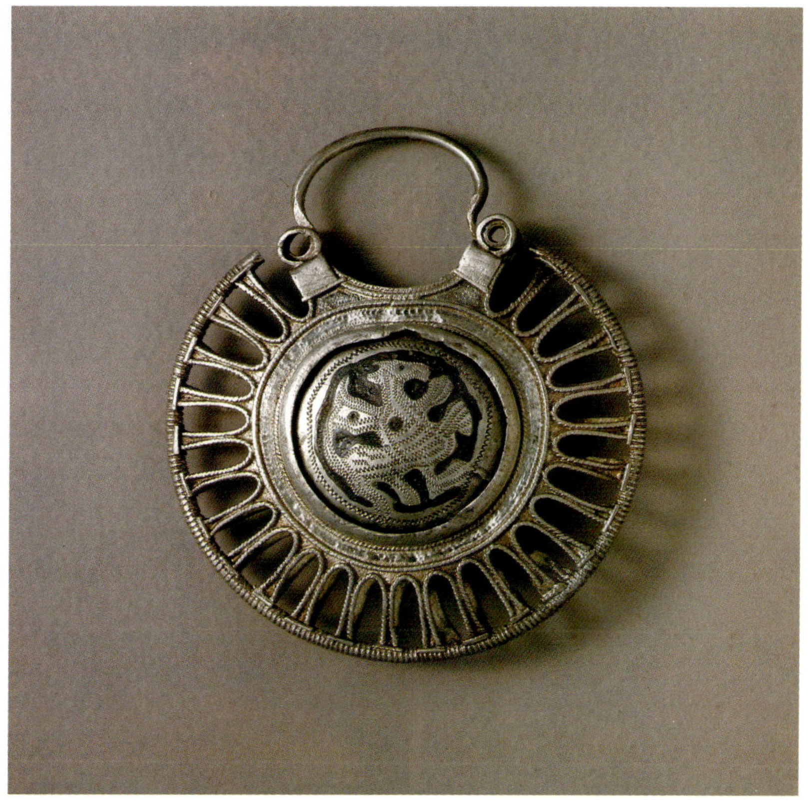

14

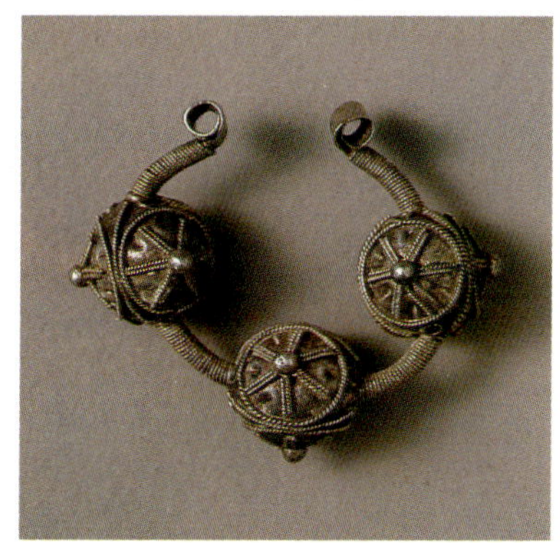

15

16

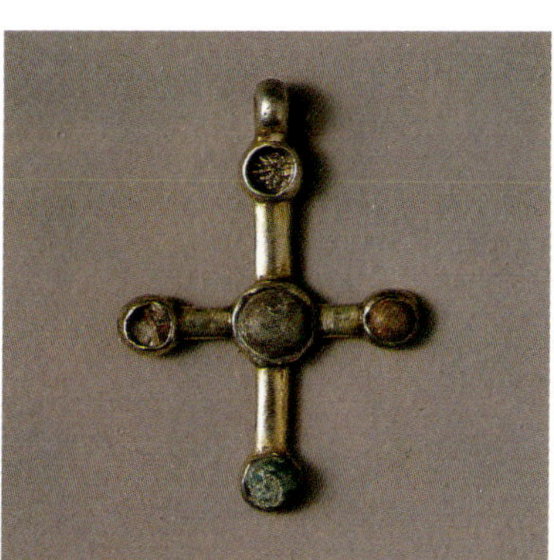

17

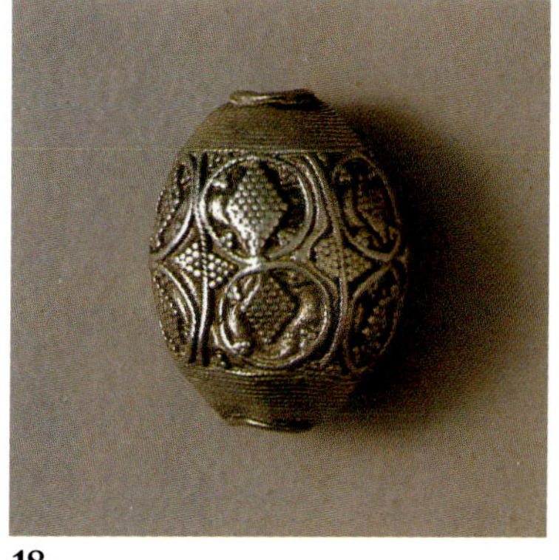

18

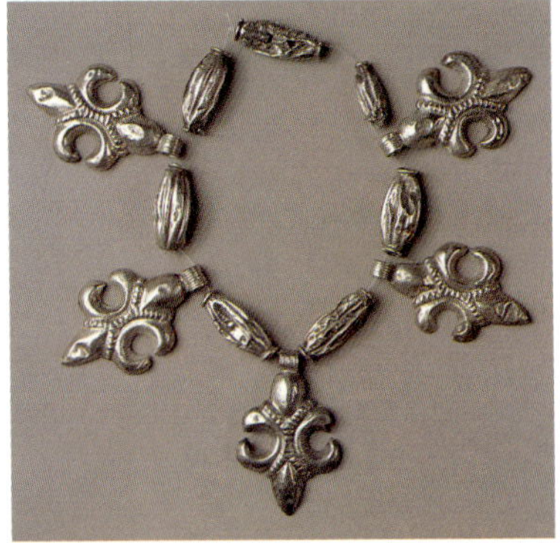

19

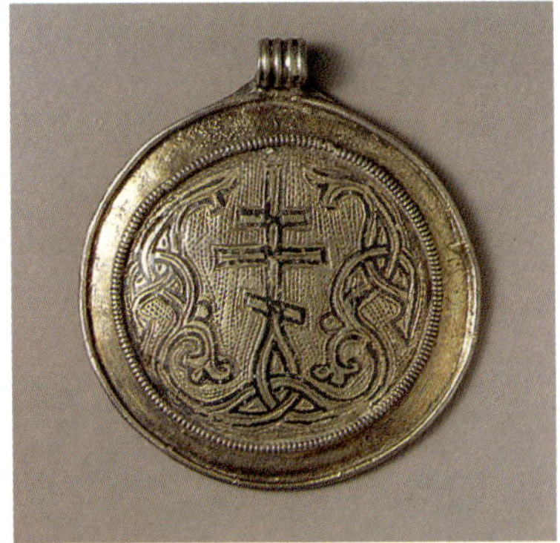

20

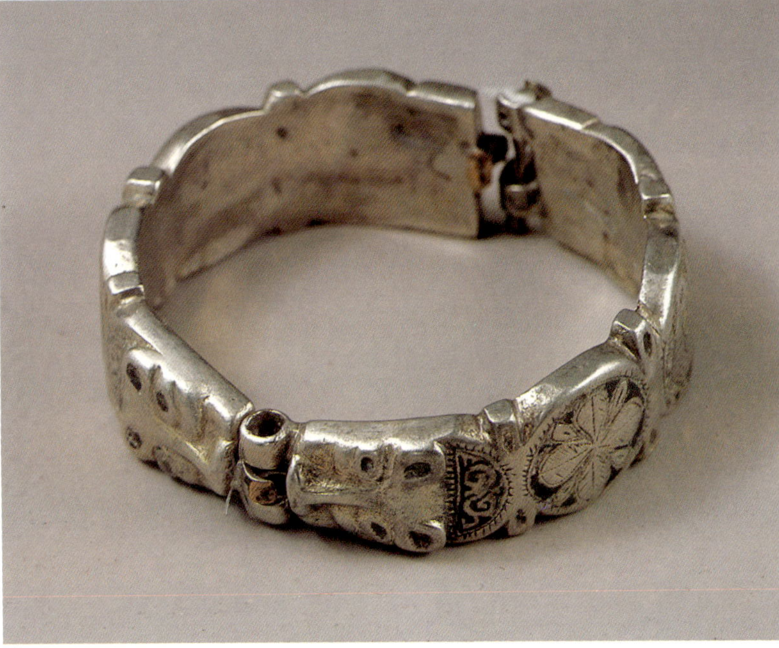

21

19. Necklace
Kiev, 12th–early 13th century
silver, die-stamped pattern
pendants: 4.5 x 2.6 cm;
beads: 2.0–2.5 cm long
49876; 1091/5

The seven beads of the necklace are oval in shape with ribs. Each of the five pendants is made up of two soldered silver plates, the lower plain, the upper bearing a die-stamped design. The lily shape of the pendants is common to artifacts found in the rich treasure troves and settlements of Old Russia and was widely used in the applied arts of the time.

20. Locket
Kiev, 12th–early 13th century
silver gilt, niello, engraving
diameter: 5.0 cm
49876; 1091/78

Round silver locket with a gilt centre, bordered by two soldered wire scrolls, the outer plain and the inner imitation filigree. The centre bears an image of a cross with nielloed contours against an engraved background.

Lockets such as this were worn on necklaces by princes on gala occasions.

21. Bracelet
Kiev, 12th–early 13th century
silver, niello, engraving
diameter: 6.5 cm;
width: 2.0 cm
49876; 1091/16

Bracelet with a die-pressed pattern and hinged on a pivot. Each end bears the image of a lion mask with traces of niello for the eyes and ears. Each half of the bracelet consists of three round sections with an engraved pattern on the nielloed background. One half features a "krin", a bird with its head turned towards its tail and another krin. The images on the other half are a four-petalled rosette, a bird and a krin.

Bracelets such as this probably served as talismans. Lion masks were widely used in the decoration of the white stone cathedrals of Vladimir-Suzdal Rus.

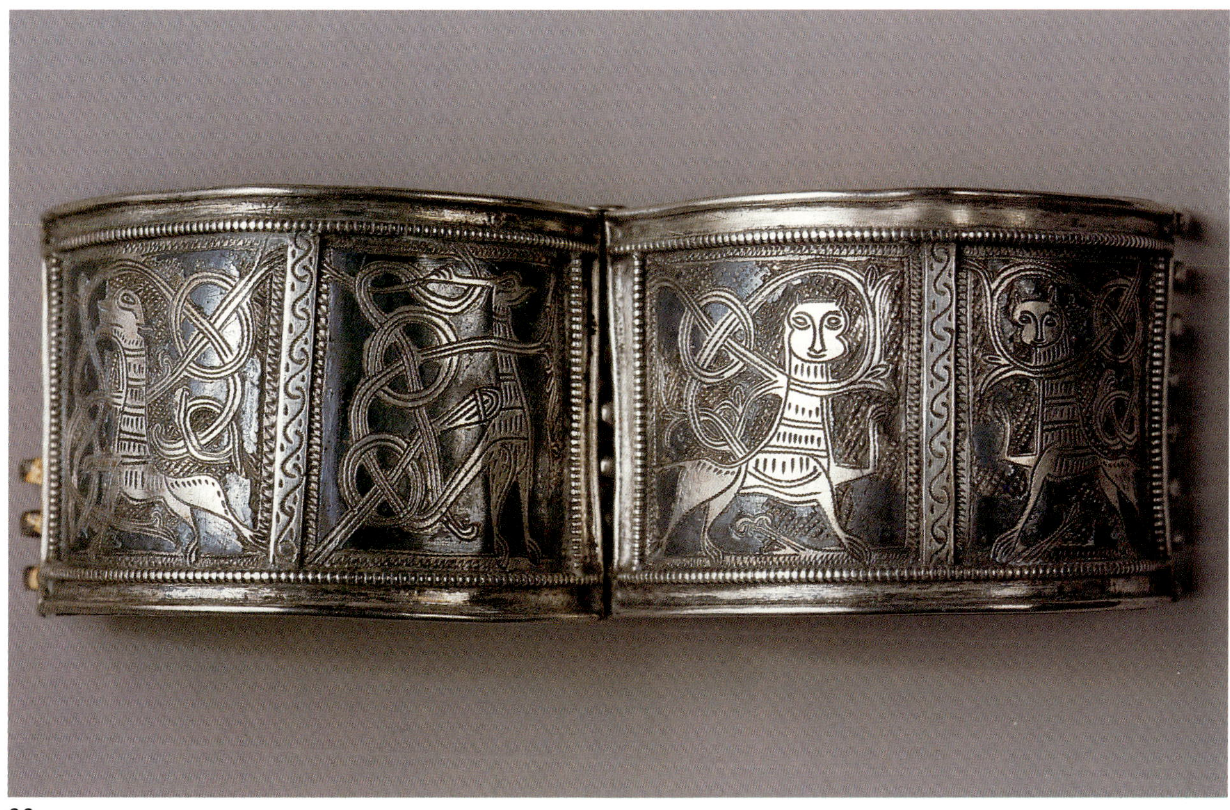

22

22. Bracelet
Kiev, 12th–early 13th century
silver, niello, engraving
diameter: 7.5 x 6.0 cm;
width: 5.2 cm
49876; 1091/12

The two halves of this bracelet are hinged on a pivot. Each half has an edging of two rollers; the outer plain, the inner with an imitation granular pattern. Each half of the bracelet is decorated with images of beasts engraved on a nielloed background. Where the niello is missing the original background, with its gnarled grid, is visible.

Although the design of this bracelet shows strong Byzantine influence, the decoration is uniquely Russian.

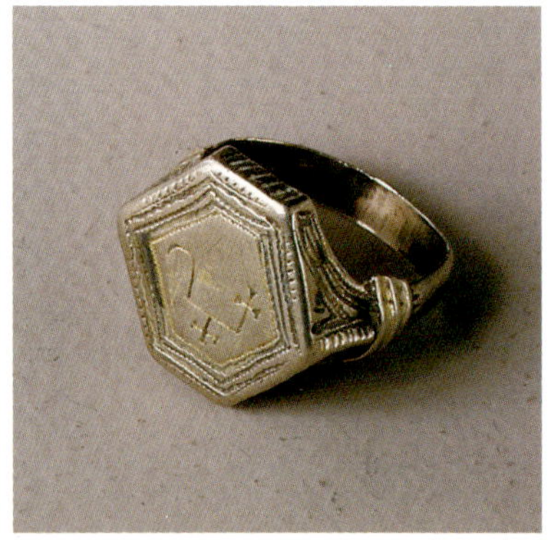
23

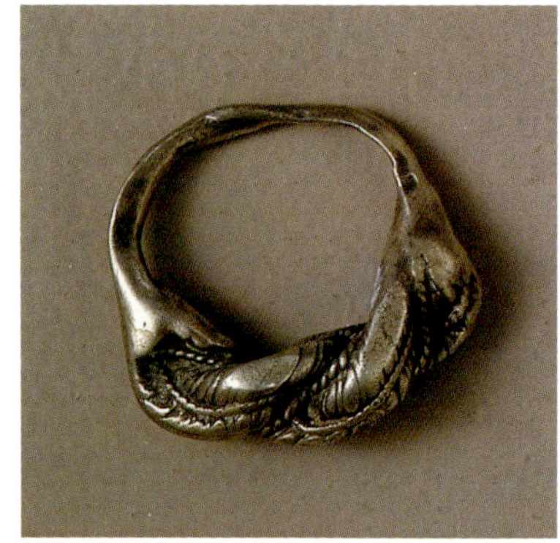
24

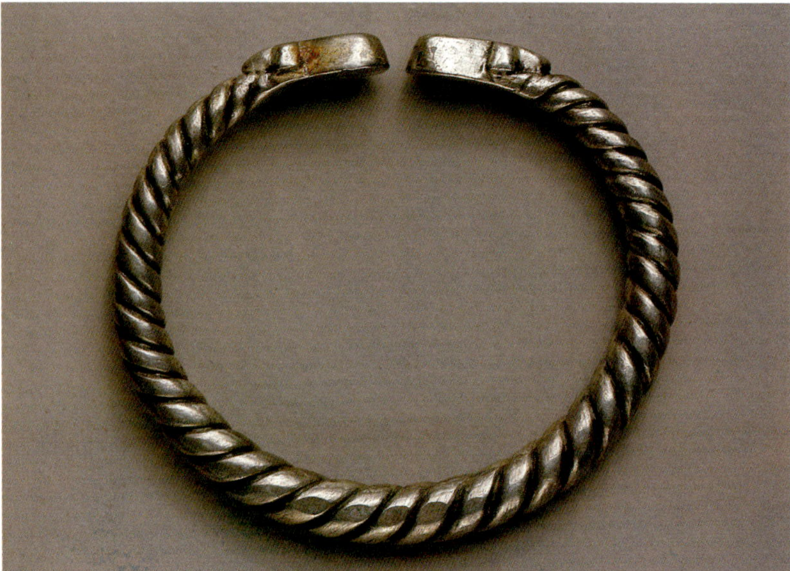
25

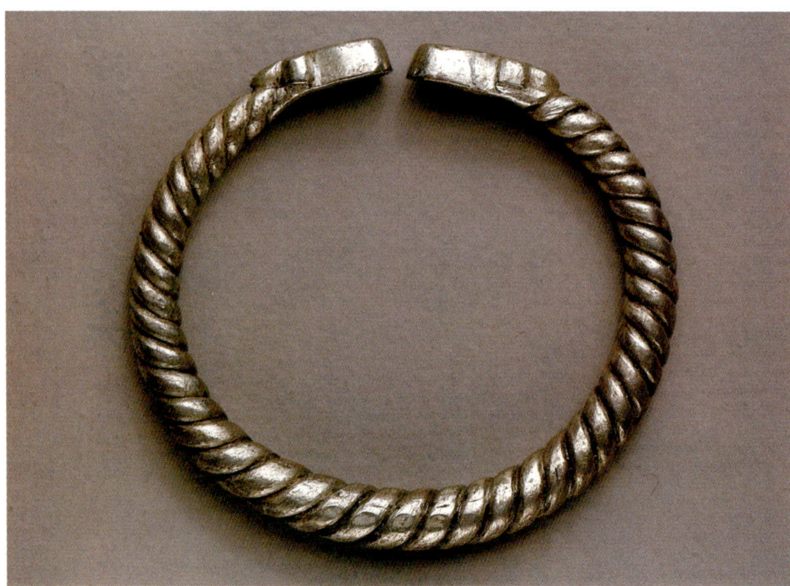
26

23. Finger ring
Kiev, 12th–early 13th century
silver, niello, engraving
diameter: 2.0 cm;
bezel: 2.2 x 2.2 cm
49876; 1091/50

The sides of the hexagonal hollow bezel and the contour of the ring are decorated with nielloed lines. The centre of the bezel bears a prince's insignia.

24. Finger ring
Kiev, 12th–early 13th century
silver, twisted wire
diameter: 2.6 cm
49876; 1091/53

The massive, twisted central section is made up of thin twisted scrolls. This shape of finger ring was common in both rural and urban handicrafts in Old Russia. Cat. nos 12 and 14–24 were found in 1903 in a treasure trove uncovered in Kiev during construction work on the wall of a monastery. Most of the treasure uncovered was acquired by the State History Museum in Moscow in 1916; the remainder is held by the Historical Museum in Kiev.

See Ribakov (2), fig. 59 b; Ribakov (1), p. 415, fig. 202, 4; Ribakov (3), fig. 109; Korzukhina, p. 120–122, item 103, table 12, 4; Vasilenko, fig. 130; Makarova (2), fig. 16, 38, 53, p. 131, 142, 149, cat. no. 80, 225, 286

25. Twisted bracelet
Kiev, 12th–early 13th century
silver, twisted wire, solder, engraving
diameter: 7.3 cm
54746; 2214/5

26. Twisted bracelet
Kiev, 12th–early 13th century
silver, twisted wire, solder, engraving
diameter: 7.2 cm
accessioned 1920s
54746, 2214/6

The bracelets (cat. nos 25 and 26) have soldered almond-shaped ends with an engraved design. A large number of similar bracelets have survived, of which the ends are not only engraved but also nielloed. These were introduced at the end of the 11th century and became widespread in the 12th and 13th centuries.

Both bracelets were unearthed in Kiev in the 19th century, in a treasure-trove which came to light during the excavation of the site of the Tithe church.

See Korzukhina, p. 108, item 66

27. Grivna (twisted necklace)
Chernigov region, 11th–12th century
silver, twisted wire
22.5 x 20.5 cm
55631; 2232/1

Grivna made up of several twisted scrolls, the ends of which are flattened and rolled into tubes.

Grivnas occur frequently in Old Russian treasure troves, indicating that they were an integral part of a noblewomen's dress. Twisted grivnas have sometimes been found in the rich barrows of village cemeteries.

28. Kolt (temple pendant)
Chernigov, second half of 12th century
silver, niello, engraving
8.5 x 8.5 cm
46043; 1118/1

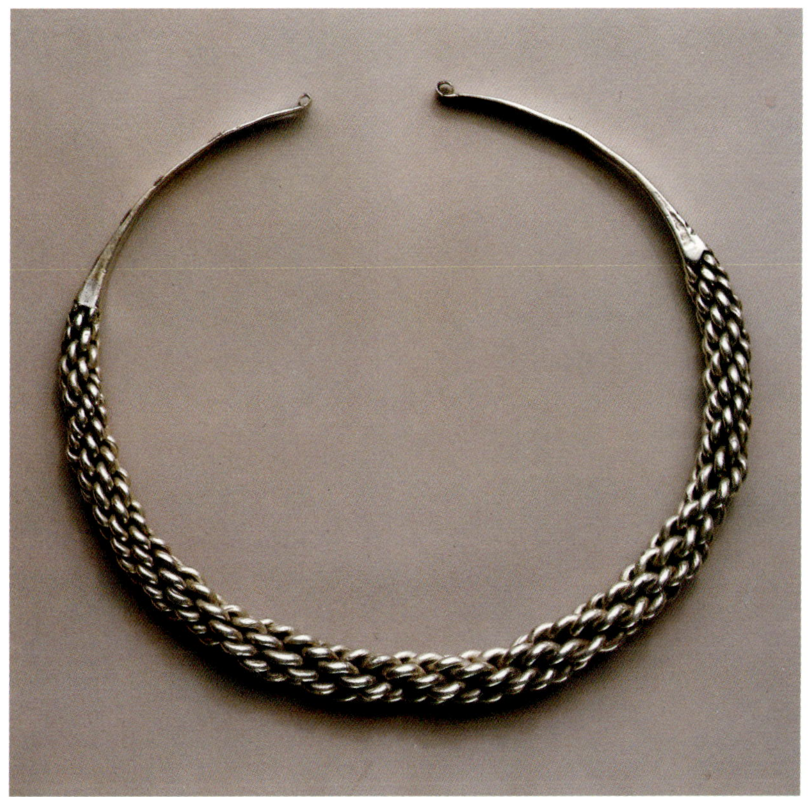

27

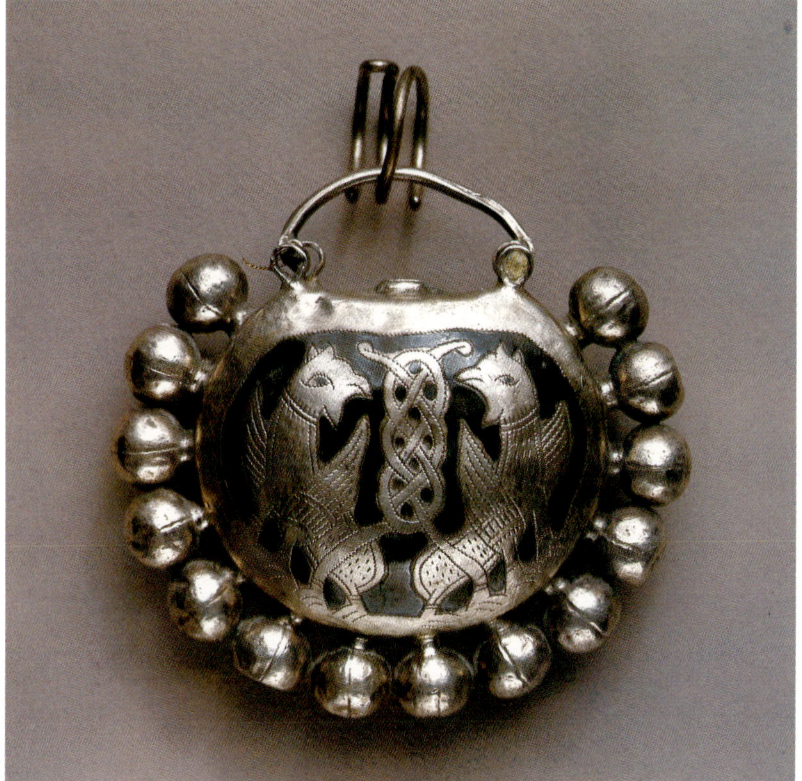

28

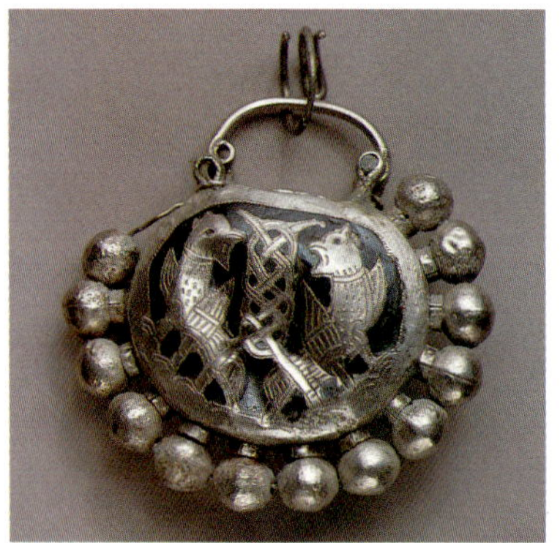
29

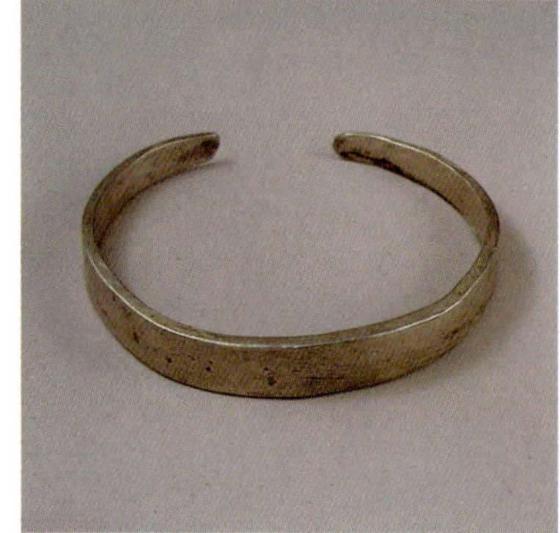
30

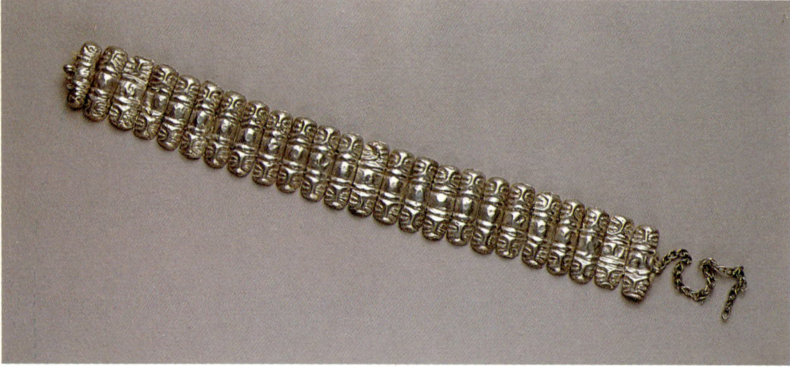
31

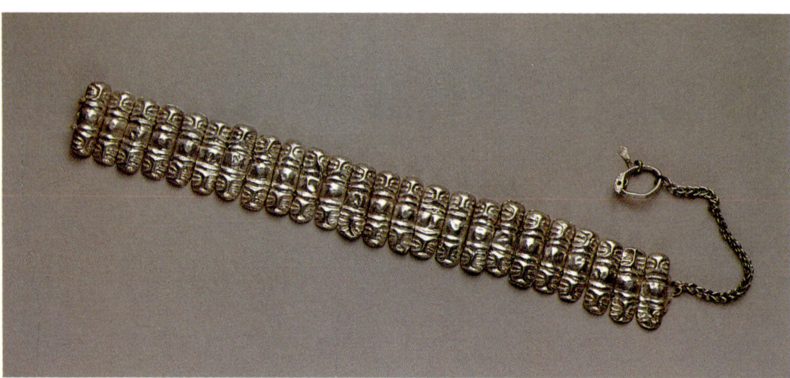
32

29. Kolt (temple pendant)
Chernigov, second half of 12th century
silver, niello, engraving
8.7 x 9.0 cm
46043; 1118/2

The matching kolts, cat. nos 28 and 29, would have formed part of a woman's holiday headdress. Each hollow kolt is made up of two soldered plates, bordered by tiny silver balls fixed on pins and decorated on both sides with a symmetrical composition of two griffins back to back with their heads turned to the central design, symbolising the tree of life, all on a niello background.

30. Bracelet
Chernigov, second half of 12th century
forged silver
diameter: 6.7 cm
46043; 1118/26

Bronze ornaments, similar in shape to this plain lamellate bracelet with tapered ends, were very common in both urban and rural handicrafts in Old Russia before the Tartar Yoke.

31. Chain
Chernigov, second half of 12th century
silver, die-stamped pattern, solder
length: 18.5 cm;
each link: 2.3 x 0.7 cm
46043; 1118/29

32. Chain
Chernigov, second half of 12th century
silver, die-stamped pattern, solder
length: 18.4 cm;
each link: 2.3 x 0.7 cm
46043; 1118/30

Cat. nos 31 and 32 consist of rectangular paired rings. Each link is made of two plates; the lower plain and the upper ornamented with a die-stamped pattern. These chains were probably used to suspend kolts from a headdress.

33. Bracelet
Chernigov, second half of 12th century
silver, twisted wire, solder, niello
diameter: 8 cm
46043; 1118/24

Twisted bracelet with almond-shaped tips (one missing) decorated with a nielloed pattern.

34. Finger ring
Chernigov, second half of 12th century
silver gilt, engraving, niello
diameter: 2.3 cm; bezel: 1.7 cm
46043; 1118/20

In a nielloed frame in the centre of the square bezel is the engraved insignia of a prince. The shoulders of the ring are decorated with fretwork.

Cat. nos 28–34 were found in a treasure trove uncovered in 1908 near the village of Nizovka (Holy Lake) in the Chernigov region. The archaeologist D.Ya. Samokvasov purchased the entire collection and donated it to the State History Museum in 1910.

See Ribakov (2), p. 316, fig. 82, 83b; Korzukhina, p. 138–139, article 152; Vasilenko, fig. 91, 104; Makarova (2), p. 52, fig. 13, 15, 18; cat. no. 7, 64, 132–133

35. Bracelet
probably Vladimir, mid 12th century
silver gilt, engraving
diameter: 6.4 cm; width: 4.5 cm
54746; 2103/1

The two sections of this bracelet are hinged on a pivot, each section divided into two parts by a vertical line. The images are on two levels; in the upper part of the right-hand section are images of men and women; in the lower part is a regular pattern. In the upper part of the left-hand section are images of birds and hares; the lower features a miniature floral design. All these elements are engraved, while the animals, birds and people as well as the ribs and dividing lines are gilt. The ornamentation of the bracelet reflects the pagan traditions and

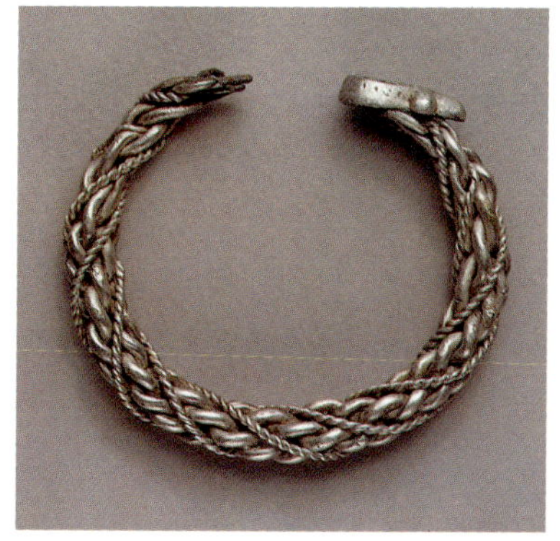

33

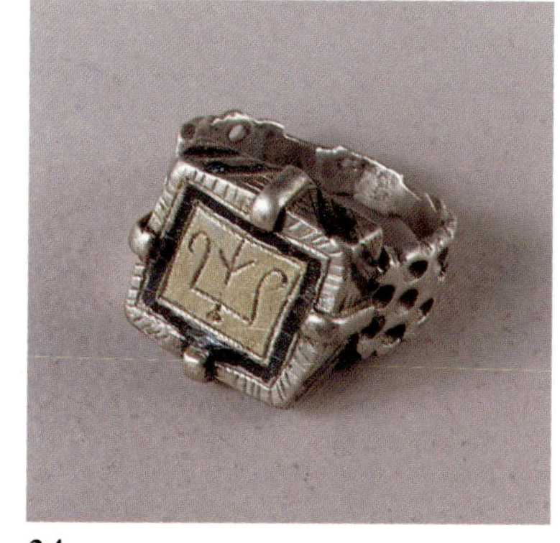

34

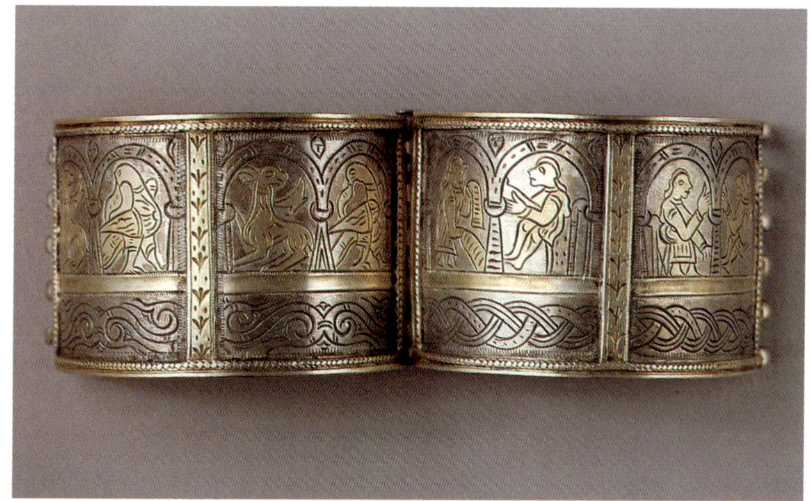

35

beliefs which were long preserved in the culture and art of Old Russia.

The exact location of this find is not known. There are two identical bracelets in the collection of the State History Museum.

See Ribakov (2), p. 267, fig 60; Vasilenko, pp. 302–303, fig. 133, 134; Bocharov, pp. 143–147, fig. on p. 147; Makarova (2), cat. no. 208, fig. 29, 30

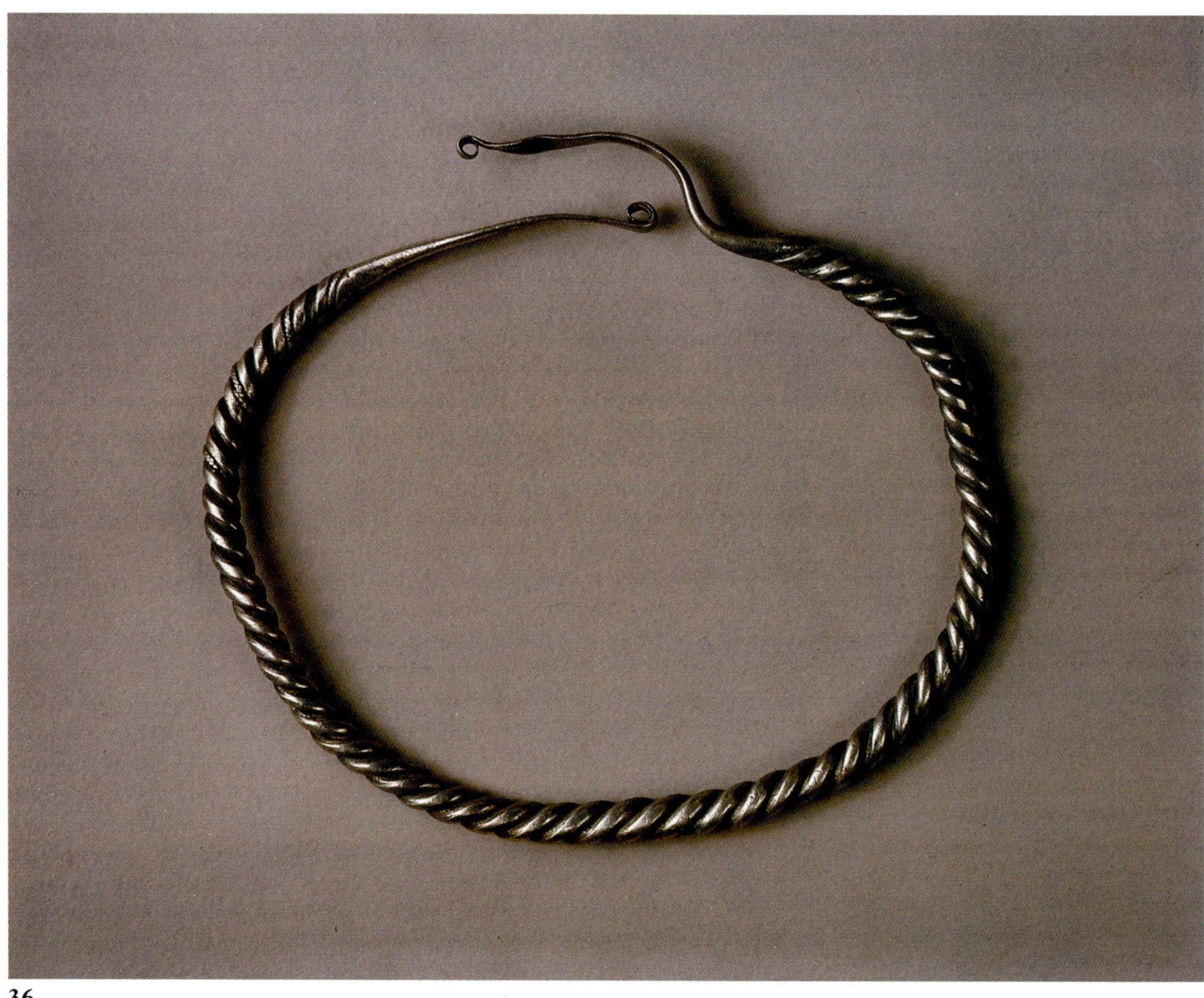

36

36. Grivna (necklace)
Vladimir, 12th–13th century
twisted silver wire
14.5 x 15.3 cm
accessioned 1898
36209; 1089/17

Grivna made up of three twisted wires decorated with a thin wire scroll. The lamellate ends are soldered to the main section.

Ornaments of this shape were common throughout Old Russia. This example was found in a treasure trove unearthed in Vladimir in 1896.

See Korzukhina, pp. 146–147, article 168

37. Locket
Vladimir, 12th–early 13th century
silver gilt, engraving, niello
diameter: 6.0 cm
accessioned late 19th century
78605; 1088/1

Round silver gilt locket bordered by two soldered imitation filigree scrolls. The figure of the Virgin is in the centre of the engraved and nielloed image.

38. Locket
Vladimir, 12th–early 13th century
silver gilt, engraving, niello
diameter: 5.2 cm
accessioned late 19th century
78605; 1088/3

On the outer rim of the round locket is a border of notched imitation filigree. The centre bears an engraved and nielloed cross.

Cat. nos 37 and 38 are from the one set.

39. Kolt (temple pendant)
Vladimir, 12th–early 13th century
silver, filigree
diameter: 8.5 cm
accessioned late 19th century
78605; 1088/16

The central section and the ends of four of the six arms of the pendant are decorated with plain conical beads. The entire surface of the kolt, both obverse and reverse, is ornamented with fine filigree and silver granules.

Cat. nos 37–39 were all found in the one treasure trove in Vladimir in 1837.

See Korzukhina, pp. 145–146, article 166; Makarova (2), fig. 49, 53, p. 148, cat. no. 279, p. 150, cat. no. 297

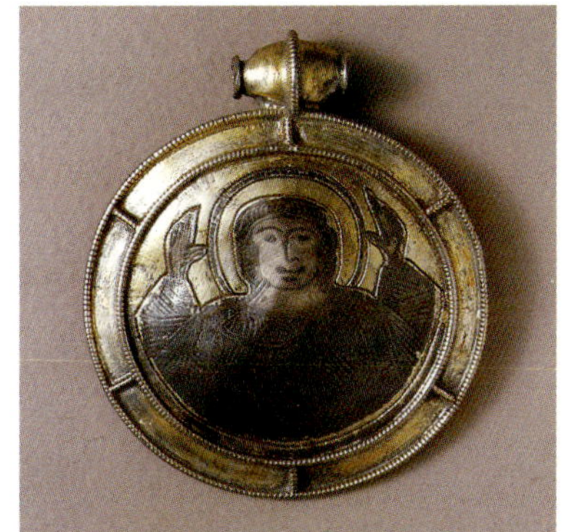

37

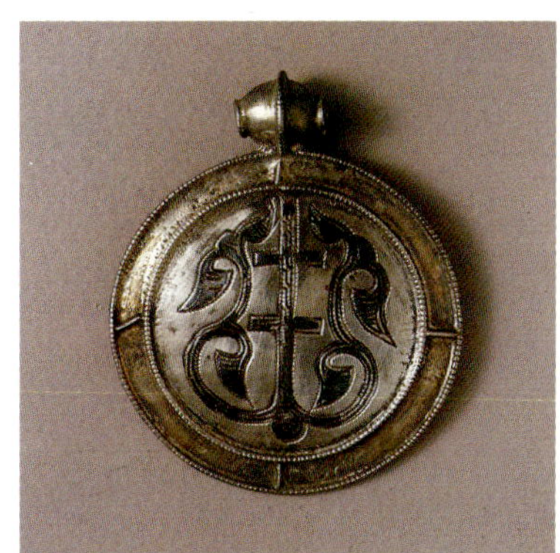

38

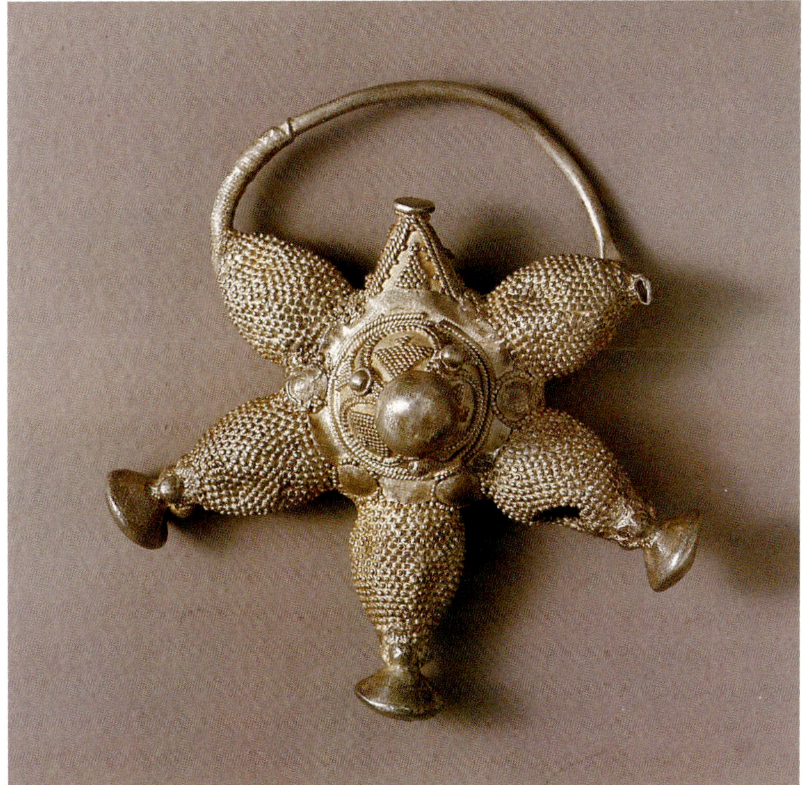

39

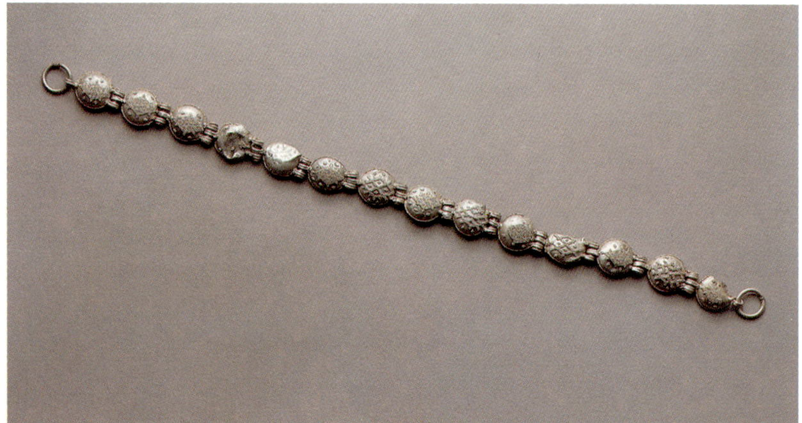

40

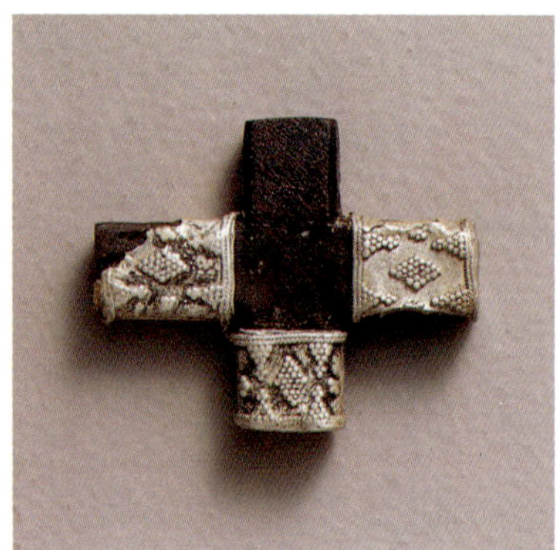

41

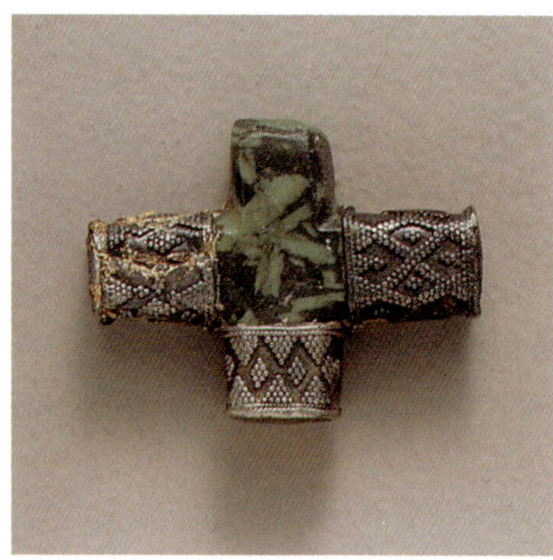

42

40. Chain
Old Ryazan, 12th–13th century
silver
length: 32.2 cm;
diameter of each link: 1.5 cm
80241; 1593/2

Chain consisting of 14 semispherical links, connected by pivots.
The overall design is formed by the alternation of rhombuses and a grid of silver grains.

The chain was found in the ancient settlement of Old Ryazan.

See Mongait, fig.118, 1

41. Pectoral cross
Old Ryazan, first quarter of 13th century
stone, silver
3.4 x 2.6 cm
83881; 1200/14

The arms of the stone cross are set with silver. The obverse is decorated with silver grains.

42. Pectoral cross
Old Ryazan, first quarter of 13th century
Serpentine, silver, filigree
4.0 x 3.0 cm
accessioned 1952
83881; 1200/13

Cross made of serpentine, a semi-precious dark green stone.
The arms are set with silver and the obverse is decorated with silver grains and filigree.

Cat. nos 41 and 42 were found in 1950 in a treasure trove in Old Ryazan.

See Korzukhina, p. 145, article 165; Mongait, p. 149, fig 118, 4

II

MEDIEVAL RUSSIA

Gold and Silver of the 13th–15th Centuries

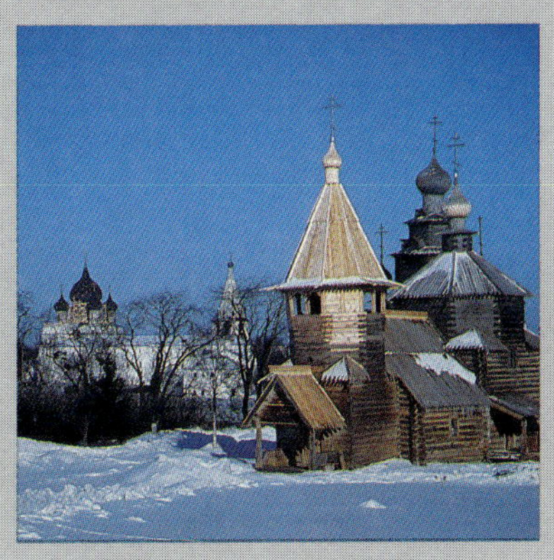

The monk and scribe Theophilus noted in the celebrated treatise *Diversarum Artium Schedula* that Russian jewellery was equal to that of the Byzantine empire, the Middle East, Italy, France and Germany. Goldsmiths and silversmiths working in the 13th–16th centuries, a period rich in momentous events, had earned such praise.

In 1132 the Old Russian State came to an end. The disintegration of this powerful nation that had occupied such a prominent place among European countries was accompanied by desperate internecine struggle. The negative consequences of this process were greatly aggravated by border hostilities with the Swedes and Germans to the west and the Mongol-Tartars to the east. The yoke of the Golden Horde, which lasted for nearly two-and-a-half centuries, became the strongest impediment to Russia's economic, political and cultural development.

The destruction of craft centres and the collapse of trade relations with Europe and the east, the sources of Russian gold and silver (local deposits were not discovered until around 1700), resulted in a noticeable decline in jewellery production. Most of the more intricate techniques were forgotten for many decades; cloisonné enamel, for example, the secrets of which had been passed down from father to son, was not mastered again until the 19th century. All this caused a general deterioration that lasted until the middle of the 14th century; the number of articles decreased, quality suffered and the production of secular objects almost ceased.

Jewellery-making was not completely interrupted, however, and the strengthening and isolation of feudal principalities positively favoured the formation of regional centres. The work of masters living during the 13th–16th centuries in Moscow, Novgorod, Tver, Pskov, Vladimir and other towns is notable for distinct peculiarities of style, pattern and technical execution. The examples of small objects from this period which are included in the exhibition, such as precious sacred images, panagias and crosses, demonstrate this.

The making of small works is a unique aspect of Russian applied arts. The level of participation of gold and silver craftsmen in the creation of these articles varied from complete authorship to the manufacture of precious frames which, from playing a rather modest role in the early period, had acquired more importance by the 15th century. Frames for carved icons, crosses and panagias were characterised by their diversity; they were in the shape of smooth forged strips revealing the natural beauty of pure metal, decorated with precious stones and ornamented with carving, filigree, enamel or niello.

Small-scale plastic art was practised on a large scale in Russia. A cross worn next to the skin was an accessory of every Orthodox Christian; miniature icons, especially those depicting patron saints, played the role of protectors. Quite often crosses and miniature icons were hung on the most revered icons in temples. These wonderful works were manufactured in all large Russian towns and in monasteries. They are notable for their diversity of subject matter. The adherence of certain artistic centres to particular styles and patterns can be used to determine a work's origin.

Carving and zern (decoration using small grains of metal) were favourite devices of decoration among jewellers of the 12th–15th centuries. According to archaeological data, niello had been employed as early as the 9th century, but thereafter was rarely used as the main device in the decoration of precious works until the end of the 14th century. The encolpion or pectoral cross in this exhibition (cat. no. 46) is an example. It is one of the oldest types of encolpion—a cross cast in two halves, joined at the top—the form of which is closely related to the Byzantine tradition that played a leading role in Russia for 500 years. Archaeological data and chronicles indicate that Byzantine masters including builders, icon-painters and jewellers worked in the Kiev area at the turn of the 10th century. The imported encolpions became indigenous; richly decorated crosses, bearing the local name "moshch viki" (relics) were a compulsory part of Tsarist regalia up to the reign of Peter the Great (1672–1725). The example on display is an expressive and characteristic example of Russian applied art of the turn of the 14th century.

The notions of divine patronage, good and evil, life and death were clearly expressed in icon painting, monumental art and small plastic art of the period. The influence of church canon grew noticeably weaker in icon painting as it increased in the applied arts; images of purely Russian origin appeared—those of locally revered and newly created saints. At the same time, powerful patriotic tendencies began to manifest themselves in the arts. The encolpion (cat. no. 46) shows a carved and gilded traditional image of the crucifixion with Mary and John the Baptist in the foreground. Originally, there was a pearl-edging around the cross, which has since been lost. Of special interest is the reverse, where an anonymous artist has depicted, in niello, saints whose relics were supposed to have been put into the cross: John, Nicholas, Demetrius, George, Sergius and John Climacus. The selection of these saints was not random; it reflects the basic world view and philosophical notions widely spread in the 14th–15th centuries, when Russia was building up energy to overthrow the Tartar-Mongol regime.

St Nicholas was especially revered as the patron of Christians, the defender of Russian towns against foreign oppressors and the protector of widows and orphans. Demetrius and George personified military feats and successful struggle against a strong and insidious enemy. Important ideas were connected with the images of St Sergius; the creator of cat. no. 46 was probably referring to Sergei Radonezhsky (1321/22–92), an outstanding church and public figure of the Russian middle ages, an adherent of princely power and the fight against foreign oppression. Having high moral authority over the people and the nobility, the revered Sergei more than once played the role of conciliator between hostile Russian princes and consistently lobbied for the unification of the states around Moscow. In 1380 he blessed the Great Moscow Prince Dmitri Ivanovich, later called Donskoi (1350–89), and his army on their way to the Battle of Kulkov, which resulted in the defeat of the Golden Horde's main forces, thus beginning the liberation of Russia from the Mongol-Tartar yoke.

Sergei Radonezhsky was the founder and Father Superior of the Troitsky Monastery, situated 30 kilometres to the north of Moscow, which holds a special place in the spiritual and cultural life of the Russian people. Wonderful monuments to literature and art were created there. The talent of the great icon painter Andrei Rublev was developed in the Troitsky Monastery; his creative work represents one of the peaks of icon painting. Sergei was a monastic reformer and taught many hermits including Pafnuty, Father Superior of the Borovsky Monastery, from where the encolpion Pafnuty was acquired by the State History Museum.

Images of saints, delicately worked in niello, are stern and concentrated. The young face of George is full of inner force. The gesture of his hand, holding the cross of a martyr, is especially expressive, resembling as it does a hand grasping a sword. Half-length images of saints, due to their harmony and natural disposition in space, are reminiscent of monumental fresco painting.

The level of artistic execution of the cross proves that its creator was a master of the technique of niello, notable for its beauty and unusual durability, which in Russia was widely used for centuries.

The 14th-century silver frame of the 15th-century icon, cat. no. 47, is an outstanding example of niello art; images of Christ, archangels and saints are finely delineated in a pale, nearly grey colour. They are characterised by a harmony of pose and gesture, plasticity and flexibility, the key features of the Paleologue Renaissance. The effects of this movement reached Russia via the accomplished painter Theophanes the Greek (c.1340–after 1405) and by masters from Constantinople who came to Moscow half-a-century later together with Zoya (Sofia) Paleologue, a niece of the last Byzantine Emperor Konstantine XI. She became the wife of the Great Moscow Prince, the first Sovereign of All Russia, Ivan III (1462–1505). Their grandson was Ivan the Terrible, one of the most famous Russian rulers. In the imagery of the silver frame of cat. no. 47, one can feel a direct connection with Moscow miniatures of the 14th–15th centuries in the reserved and harmonious drawing and the gentleness of the silhouettes. There is also a stylistic similarity with Muscovite and Middle-Russian icons of Andrei Rublev's epoch (c. 1365–c.1430).

In medieval Russia and Europe, monasteries, as well as princely courts, frequently became centres of culture; chronicles, devotional books and various literary collections were written, icons were painted and outstanding examples of the decorative arts, including jewellery, appeared. The Troitsky Monastery was the largest artistic centre of the 15th century. Here, at the time of Father Superior Kir Zinoviy (1432–45), a special spiritual climate was created, which stimulated the production of a number of unique examples of gold and silver work. They were made by masters who left Moscow because of the feudal war during the second quarter of the 15th century, when many valuables in the Great Prince's treasury and precious church relics were lost through fire and plunder. Behind the safe walls of the monastery, a Moscow silversmith created a panagia (cat. no. 49), which could be ascribed to the rare, early type of episcopal panagias with cast images on the lid.

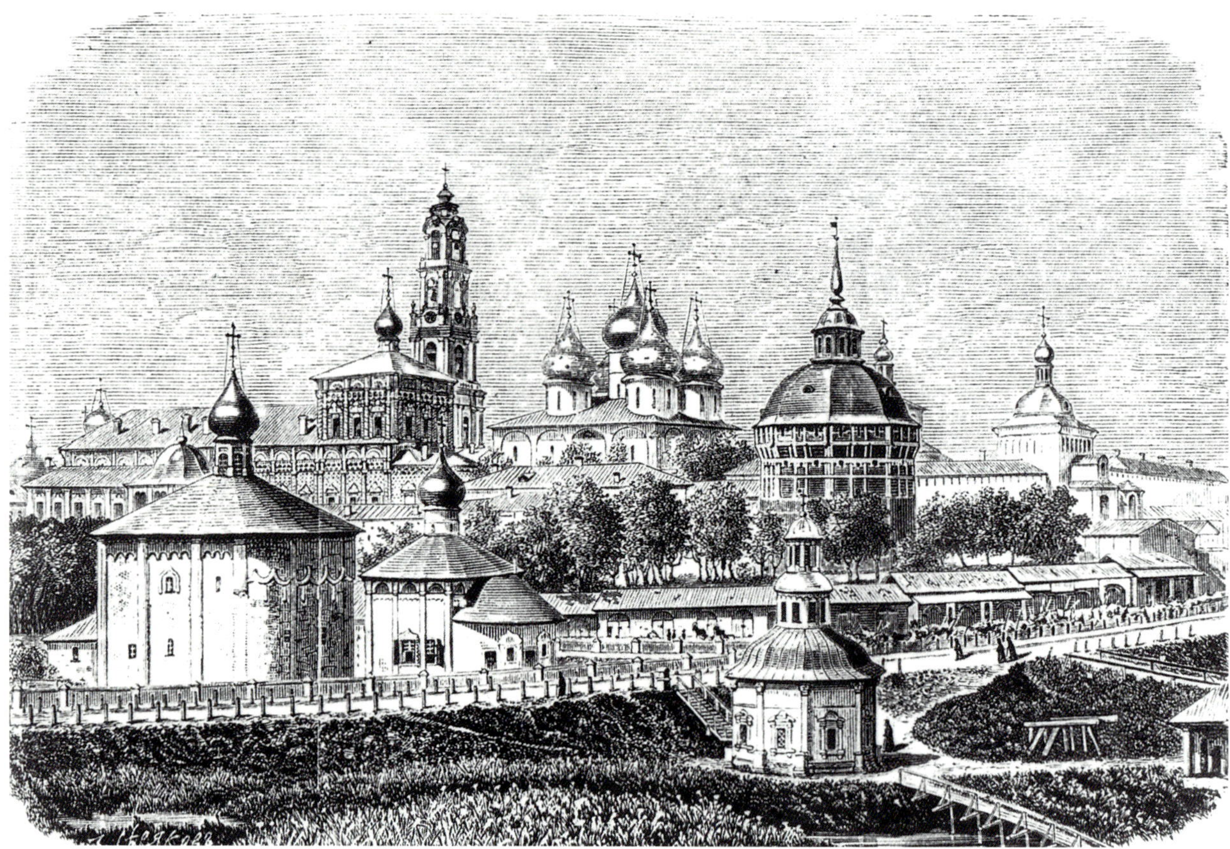

SERGEEV MONASTERY

Similar objects are known only in Moldova and Valashia of the middle ages, where, in contrast to Russia, they were preserved only from the turn of the 15th century. The outside of the panagia has carved images of Christ and the Disciples. On the inside are traditional compositions, masterfully captured by a light but steady engraving of the Virgin of the Sign and the Trinity. The decoration is organically supplemented with a delicate stylised grass pattern on a background of dark-green enamel. The panagia reveals a refined understanding of aesthetics as well as taste and technique, and reveals its creator as one of the most talented masters.

In conclusion, it can be seen that gold and silver work received a powerful impetus from the liberation of Russia in the late 15th century and the foundation of a united state with Moscow as its capital.

43. Icon: St Demetrius of Thessalonica
Russia, 11th–12th century
slate, beaten silver
6.2 x 5.5 cm
74467 OK 9111

One side of the small two-sided icon bears a carved image of St Demetrius of Thessalonica; the other a carved, low relief image of St Nicholas and the Seven Righteous Adolescents.

44. Icon: Archangel Michael
Russia, 12th–13th century
cast silver gilt
7.7 x 5.7 cm
3120 OK 9237

Small icon cast in the lost wax method. One side features a high relief image of the Archangel Michael; the other a low relief image of John the Baptist.

45. Icon: St George the Victorious
Novgorod, 14th century
stone, beaten silver
5.0 x 4.2 cm
54626 OK 9223

The small icon bears two carved relief images; on one side St George the Victorious and on the other a multifigured composition of the Holy Sepulchre.

46. Encolpion (pectoral reliquary cross)
Russia, 14th–15th century
silver gilt, niello, chasing
11.0 x 7.0 cm
67510 OK 6044

On the obverse of the cross is chased a crucifixion scene. The reverse is decorated with nielloed chasings of half-length portraits of St Nicholas the Miracle Worker, John the Baptist, St Demetrius of Thessalonica, St George, St Sergius and St John Climacus.

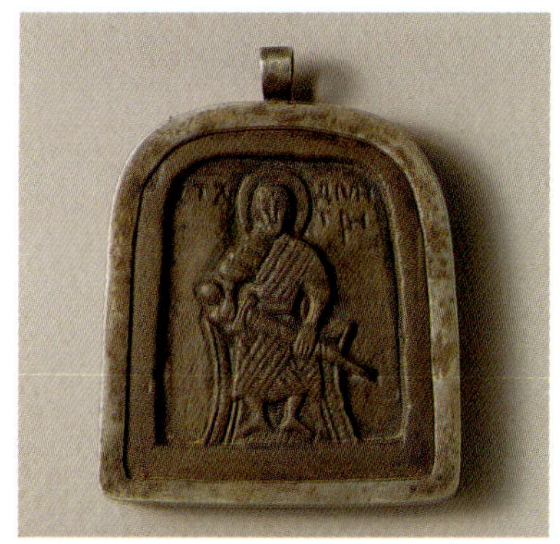

43

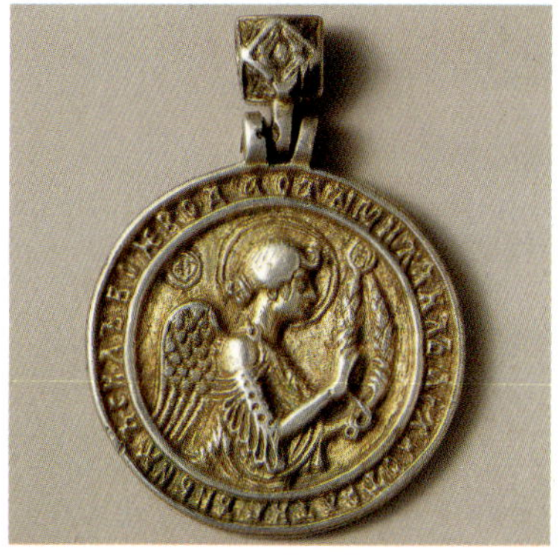

44

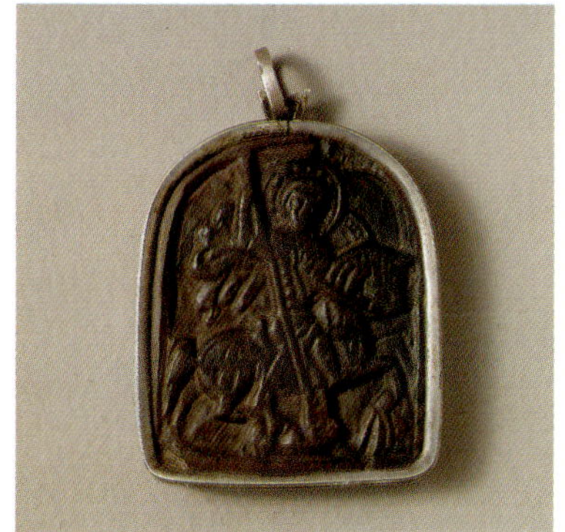

45

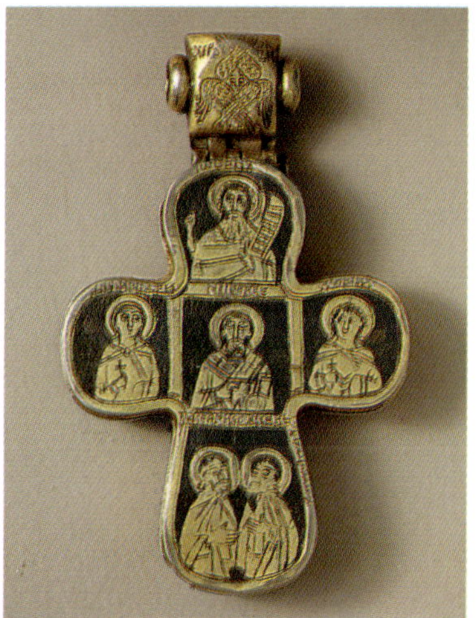

46

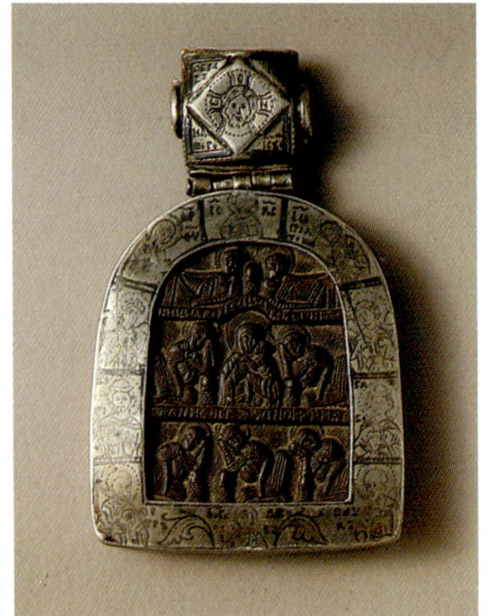
47

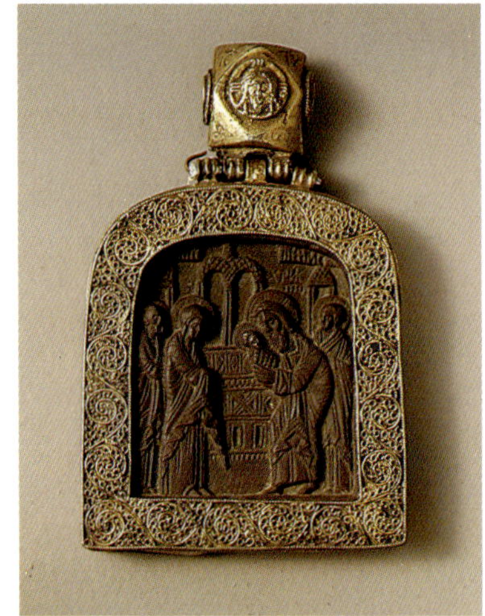
48

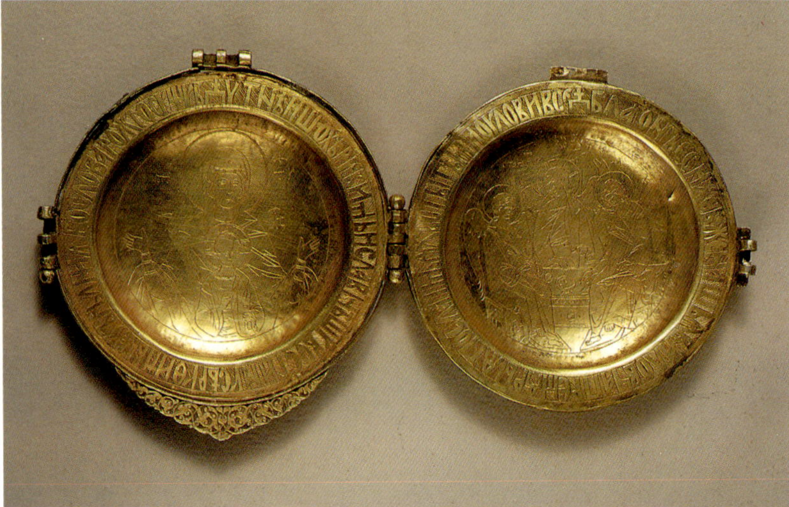
49

47. Icon: Tender Mother of God
Russia, icon: 18th century; frame: early 15th century
slate, silver, niello
10.2 x 6.3 cm
18155 OK 9132

The obverse features a relief composition of the Tender Mother of God and the Seven Adolescents of Ephesus; the reverse, the legend of St Nicholas the Miracle Worker in 15 rectangular sections. The smooth frame is decorated on the obverse with nielloed half-length portraits of Christ, the Virgin, John the Bapist, two Archangels, Saints Boris and Gleb, the Apostles Peter and Paul and St Jacob.

48. Icon: The Holy Meeting
Russia, probably Moscow, 14th century
slate, embossed silver, filigree
10.5 x 6.6 cm
54626 OK 9120

49. Panagia (pectoral image)
Russia, 1430–50
silver gilt, enamelled chasing
11.2 x 21.2 cm
80761 OK 13352

A composition of The Virgin of the Sign and the Trinity is chased on the interior. These images are bordered by a liturgical inscription chased into the engraved background.

III

MOSCOW

and the Major Centres of Jewellery Art 16th–17th Centuries

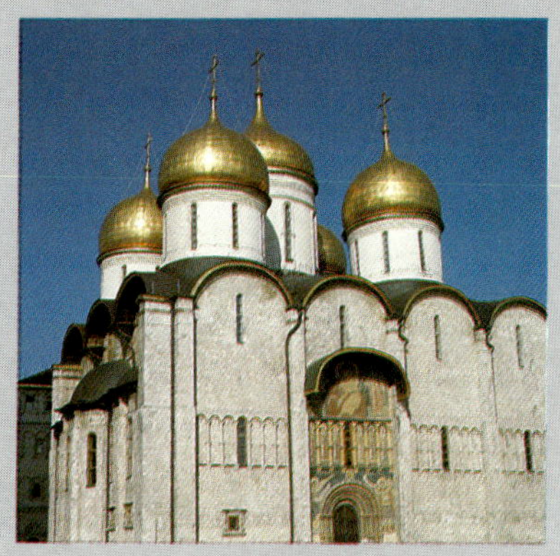

During the last quarter of the 15th century, the long process of unifying the medieval principalities of the territory of Russia into one state was coming to an end. This process affected every aspect of life in the emerging nation, including the development of the arts. The making of gold and silver jewellery, closely connected to Russia's historical development, progressed from the 15th to 17th centuries along two main lines: externally, with the emergence of more centres of art; and internally, as craftsmen, building on their rich heritage, mastered new techniques of ornamentation and design.

Craftsmen moved to Moscow, the new Russian capital, from all over the nation—Novgorod, Smolensk, Kostroma, Yaroslavl and other towns—as well as from other countries including Poland, Sweden, France, Germany, Italy and Greece.

To meet the growing demand for jewellery, utensils, armour and ornamental harnessware, particularly from the Royal Court, increasing numbers of craftsmen were required. The splendour of the Moscow court in the 16th and 17th centuries was noted by contemporaries and foreigners living in Russia, such as Sigizmund Heberstain, an ambassador of the Holy Roman Empire; Jerom Horsey, an English business representative; and Jacob Reitenfels, an observing ambassador of the Duke of Tuscany.

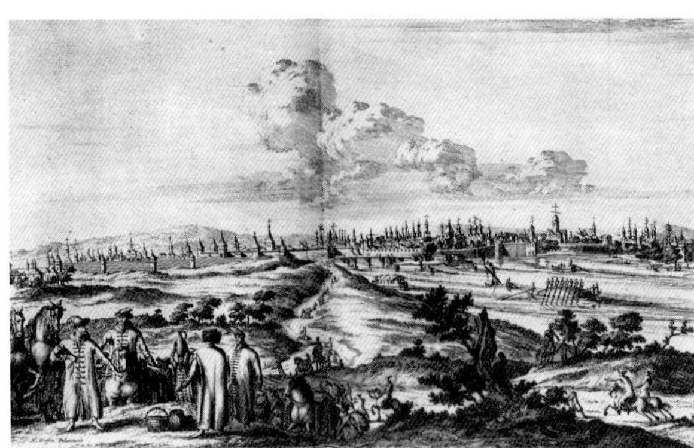

VIEW OF NOVGOROD

New chapels being constructed in the capital and other cities and towns required numerous precious liturgical vessels and utensils. Jewellers from the workshops of the Moscow Kremlin, freelance craftsmen from other centres and silversmiths working in the large monasteries were engaged in their production. The works in the exhibition, from the 15th, 16th and 17th centuries, are of great artistic value and demonstrate the high standard of craftsmanship prevalent at the time. The objects are distinguished by the pronounced national style which was characteristic of the development of gold and silver work throughout the period.

Moscow, Novgorod and other towns on the Volga and in northern Russia played an important role in this developmental process. Novgorod, known as "Novgorod the Great", was founded in the mid 9th century. Christianity was introduced simultaneously to Novgorod and the principality of Kiev. For more than three centuries Novgorod was the capital of the Boyards' Republic and one of Russia's major political, economic and trading centres. It held an important place in the cultural life of the Middle Ages.

Because Novgorod had not been destroyed by war, in contrast to many other Russian towns, and had not experienced the hardships of the Tartar-Mongol Yoke, the city reigned as one of the most important centres of jewellery-making in Russia for a considerable period. Archaeological finds suggest that workshops existed on the site of the town from the 11th to 13th centuries, producing copper, brass and silver ornaments, tableware and liturgical items. These finds show that Novgorod craftsmen had mastered the techniques of casting, basma (hand-stamping), chasing and cloisonné. Their work has a distinct local flavour. The Novgorod masters promoted new styles, while preserving the old artistic traditions which combined Slavic, Byzantine and Scandinavian elements.

The favourite decorative technique was filigree. In the late 15th and 16th centuries the most common filigree pattern was large, raised hearts made up of double spiral locks against a background of small, often gilt, circles. Examples can be found in the finger crosses and altar crosses in the exhibition, made by Novgorod craftsmen. In the second half of the 16th century, in Novgorod and other centres, filigree was combined with cloisonné. The colouring of the cloisonné was subtle and generally limited to three main colours. The diptych featuring relief images of the Chosen Saints and the scene of the Nativity of John the Baptist (cat. no. 52) testifies to the taste and skills of this Novgorod master. The silver frame is highlighted with poly-chromatic cloisonné against a floral filigree pattern. The same technique was used for the decoration of the unique panagia or pectoral image dating from the late 16th or early 17th century (cat. no. 61).

The real masterpiece of Novgorod's jewellery tradition is the frame of the icon: Our Saviour (cat. no. 53). The fine filigree patterning of the twining stalks, buds and fancy leaves is decorated by enamel painted in the characteristic colours of Novgorod: blue, green and aqua. This traditional restraint in colouring enhances, rather than diminishes, the effect produced by the combined work of the painter and the jeweller. This piece is distinguished by the combination of nobility and harmony unique to medieval jewellery production in "Novgorod the Great".

Silver utensils, used by different sections of the population, also demonstrate the originality and skills of the Novgorod craftsmen. One scholar of Old Russia has remarked: "Silver and even gold tableware was, after icons, one of the most important elements of a room's interior, being the substitute for works of fine art... Such tableware was also a sign of wealth, and was therefore exhibited on suitable occasions". (I.E. Zabelin, *Family Life of the Russian People in the 16th–17th Centuries,* 3 vols, Moscow, 1990, Vol. 1, p. 216) Novgorod craftsmen were equally successful in making ladles, loving cups and stopas (wine glasses) which featured the distinctive national forms and decoration. According to available documentation, the first silver ladle was made in Novgorod in the 14th century. In the 17th century, local craftsmen as well as jewellers from the other major centres sometimes demonstrated their skills by decorating the surfaces of articles imported from western Europe, such as smooth silver cups with hinged lids. Such articles were not produced within Russia until the 1690s. The exhibited example, a tankard made in Tallinn (cat. no. 62), has been entirely covered with a delicate complicated floral pattern of locks and leaves, combined with figures of animals, birds and fish. This type of decoration, reflecting man's new attitude to art and reality, was further developed in the first quarter of the 17th century.

One exquisite example of the work of a Novgorod silversmith is the tiny cast Korchik (cat. no. 58), the shape of which originated from the form of an ancient ladle. The ornamentation of this article is remarkable for its unique combination of traditional and innovative details, demonstrating that Novgorod craftsmen were familiar with the creations of their western European counterparts. The outstanding achievement of the Novgorod silversmiths from the late 15th to 17th centuries—the development of new decorative techniques with precious metals—greatly influenced the development of jewellery in Moscow and the towns of the Volga region and northern Russia.

The city of Moscow led the complex process of Russia's cultural development in the 16th and 17th centuries. Moscow had played the principal role in the unification of all Russian lands in the late 15th century and became the capital of the unified national state. This was a decisive factor in the development of gold and silver production in the city.

Moscow craftsmen drew on the rich heritage of the local art schools, but they also introduced new styles and designs, soon taking the lead in jewellery manufacture. Moscow jewellers perfected all the techniques of production and decoration of gold and silver articles. During this period, filigree especially flourished. The mount of the double-sided pectoral plate with the carved image of the Virgin of the Sign (cat. no. 60) was probably made by the masters of filigree during this period. Small zern—a special technique for making patterns from metal grains—add to the subtlety of the delicate filigree frame. The filigree threads form the open-work stylised floral pattern on each side of the mount.

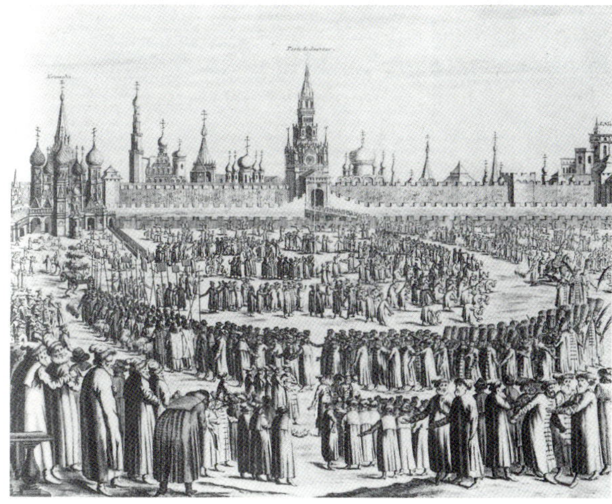

SOLEMN PROCESSION IN RED SQUARE, MOSCOW, 17th CENTURY

The late-16th century altar cross (cat. no. 54) is an excellent example of the growing interest among Moscow jewellers in chasing as a highly expressive decorative technique. The front of the cross is chased with a typical pattern of twining herbs and flowers, borrowed from traditional folk motifs common in wood carving and early illuminations and illustrations. The chased composition, formed by the images of the crucifixion with two interceding and two flying angels, occupies the centre of the cross. Despite the flashes of the semi-precious stones, the pattern is characterised by its graphic style.

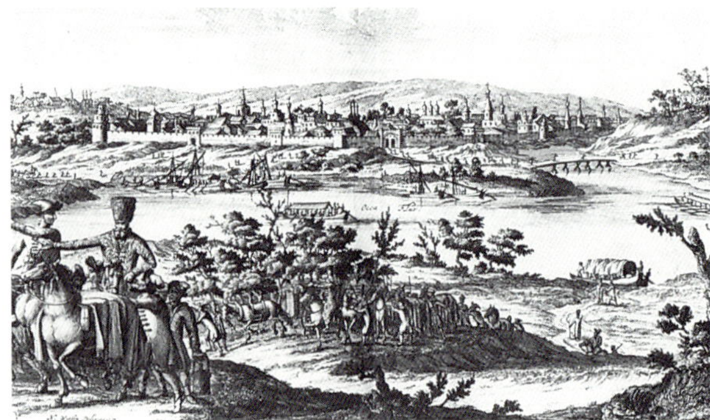

VIEW OF KOLOMNA

The technique of basma, the hand-stamping of images and patterns onto thin sheets of metal, was used in the 16th and 17th centuries in Moscow, in parallel with chasing. Basma became widespread in Russia from the 12th century, as it does not require large quantities of valuable raw materials and is highly decorative in effect. It was often used on the covers of religious books and icon mountings. Gold and silver jewellery-making flourished in the capital during the late 16th and 17th centuries, largely because of the activity of the Moscow Kremlin workshops, particularly the Armoury Chamber, the first official record of which appears in the "Royal Book" in 1574. The best Russian and foreign jewellers worked here, mainly for the Royal Court, creating unique masterpieces of decorative and applied arts. One such masterpiece is the 1652 altar cross (cat. no. 57) donated by Tsar Aleksei Mikhailovich and his first wife Tsarina

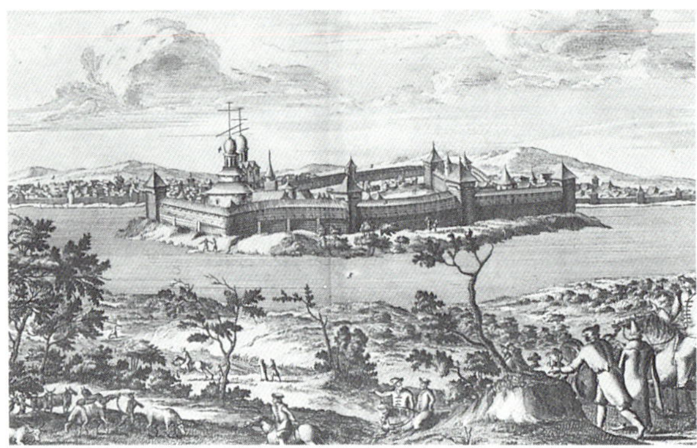

VIEW OF TVER

Maria Ilynishna. The tradition of donating valuable church utensils, icons and books to churches, monasteries and convents dates back to the beginning of Russian Christianity. Donors included Tsars, boyards, representatives of high clergy, gentry, merchants, craftsmen and even peasants. Reasons for donation included the celebration of military victories, coronations, weddings, the conception of a child (especially an heir), recovery from illness and the consecration of new churches.

The cross (cat. no. 57) was made by the Kremlin masters on the order of the second Tsar of the Romanov family, Aleksei Mikhailovich, the father of the future emperor Peter the Great, for the Court Church of the Nativity of the Blessed Virgin, built on the order of Elena Dmitrievna Donskoi, the widow of the Grand Prince of Moscow, Dmitri Donskoi. This piece demonstrates the outstanding skill of the Moscow jewellers. It is remarkable for its beauty and unity of style. The materials used for the decoration speak of the special status of the jewellers who worked in the Kremlin workshops in the vicinity of the Royal Court. They had the benefit of a wide choice of precious and semi-precious stones, local and imported enamels of many colours, and precious metals. All this promoted the rapid development of the art of jewellery in Moscow. For example, only in Moscow was enamel used in combination with gold.

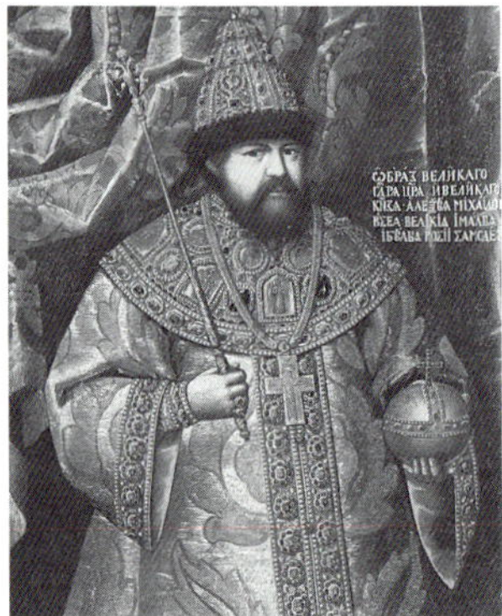

TSAR ALEKSEI MIKHAILOVICH 1670

The obverse of the cross of Tsar Aleksei is typical of the mid 17th century in its degree of elaboration. The pure, cold colours of the cloisonné filling the spaces in the filigree floral design combine harmoniously with the gleam of the adorning gems — pale emeralds, rubies and sapphires — the favourite stones of the Moscow Tsars since the reign of Ivan the Terrible (1530–84). The semi-precious stones, five of which are partly faceted, are set in high casts, the chiselled gold surfaces of which are decorated with enamel. The gilt, slightly recessed, background enhances the colourful combination of the gems, enamel, glittering pearls and silver filigree. One can imagine the effect this cross would have produced in the Orthodox Church during the Liturgy, surrounded by hundreds of burning candles, beautiful icons in gold and silver frames, elaborate books, shining vessels and priests in colourful robes. The domination of enamel in the decoration of the cross indicates that, from the mid 17th century, enamel became the favourite decorative technique on gold and silver articles, corresponding to the aspiration of the applied arts of the time to a highly elaborate effect known as "uzorochie".

In the last decade of the 17th century, bright, colourful enamels were used by Moscow craftsmen to decorate the smooth surfaces of gold, or thickly gilt silver, articles. An example is the setting of the 1681 icon, St Feodor Stratilatus and St Agafya (cat. no. 66). The enamel work in masterpieces such as this rivals diamonds, rubies and emeralds in beauty and glitter.

During the last decades of the 17th century, covering the reigns of Tsars Aleksei Mikhailovich, Theodor Alekseevich and Princess Sofia — the regent during the childhood and adolescence of Peter I and his brother Ivan — a rich flourishing and remarkable progress took place in gold and silver work with the emergence of new techniques and an increase in the number of craftsmen, particularly foreign jewellers.

The style and ornamentation of Russian jewellery of the time is strongly influenced by oriental art: a mixture of Turkish, Moslem and Greek Athenian styles. The ornamentation of silver incorporates authentic oriental elements, such as carnations, garnets and large fans. This tendency is also evident in the frequent combination of rubies, emeralds and diamonds, which is of oriental origin. The same influence can be seen in the Russian masters' attraction to bright green enamels. Examples include cartouches and cloisonné fragments of various shapes and sizes, used to decorate large gold and silver articles.

The exhibited mitre (headgear for the high clergy in the Orthodox Church) is decorated with such fragments (cat. no. 73). This stunning gold mitre was made in the workshops of the Moscow Kremlin in 1685 and presented by Tsars Ivan Alekseevich (1666–96) and Peter I (1672–1725) with their elder sister, Princess Sofia (1657–1704), to Prince Gideon Svyatopolk-Chtevertinsky, Metropolitan of Kiev, who was the first to submit entirely to the religious and political power of Moscow. Four round enamel cartouches with relief images of the Evangelists and their insignia, outlined by glittering emeralds, stand out against the cast glowing surface of the mitre. Above each fragment is a rosette of diamonds and white enamel. The whole is crowned with a sapphire cross, signifying the ownership of the Metropolitan.

In addition to enamel articles, Moscow silversmiths became justly famous for their niello work. From the mid 16th century this technique began to flourish in Moscow, peaking by the mid 17th century. The cover of the gospel (cat. no. 68), printed in 1657 in Moscow, is one of most beautiful examples of niello work. Following the Byzantine style, in which the front is covered with precious floral-patterned fabrics, the Russian master has imitated a woven or embroidered surface in silver. A delicate niello pattern of flowering herbs twines fancifully against the gilt background. This pattern has much in common with the ornamentation of the reign of Ivan the Terrible. The decoration is enhanced with traditional compositions of chasing and smooth semi-precious stones, testifying to the creator's skill in niello, and resulting in a successful combination of several decorative techniques.

The niello images and elaborate floral pattern on the altar cross contributed by Russian Tsar Feodor Alekseevich are quite different (cat. no. 63). The smooth, seven-pointed cross has unusual symbols and ornamentation. The images surrounding the crucifixion on the front of the cross first appeared in Russian applied art in the second half of the 17th century; they are analogous to the symbols of the earlier religious monuments of Russia's southern and western neighbours, the Ukraine and Byelorussia.

In the second half of the 17th century the development of these cultures was closely connected with that of Russia. The beautiful floral pattern of the reverse of the cross is stylistically related to the ornamentation in books of the time, particularly grammar and spelling texts. This characteristic reflects the taste of Tsar Feodor Alekseevich, a talented and educated governor, whose tutor was Simeon Polotsky (1629–80), an outstanding Byelorussian, Russian citizen and man of the church. A talented polemicist, teacher, poet and playwright, Polotsky was one of the initiators of the

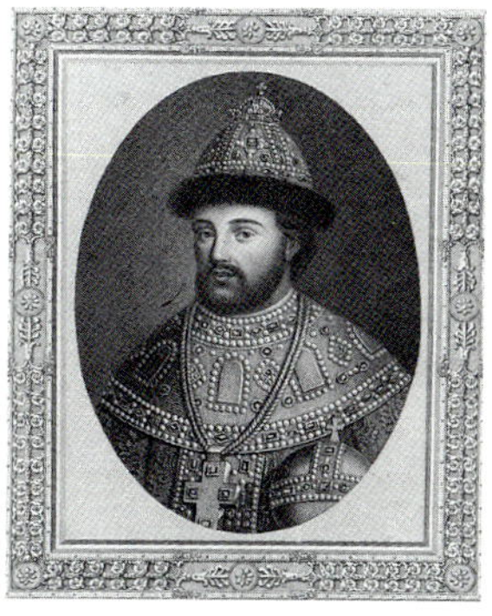

TSAR IVAN ALEKSEEVICH 1817

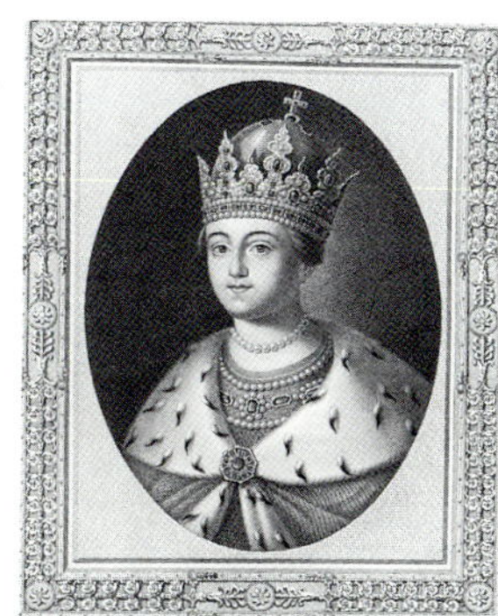

TSARINA SOFIA ALEKSEEVNA 1817

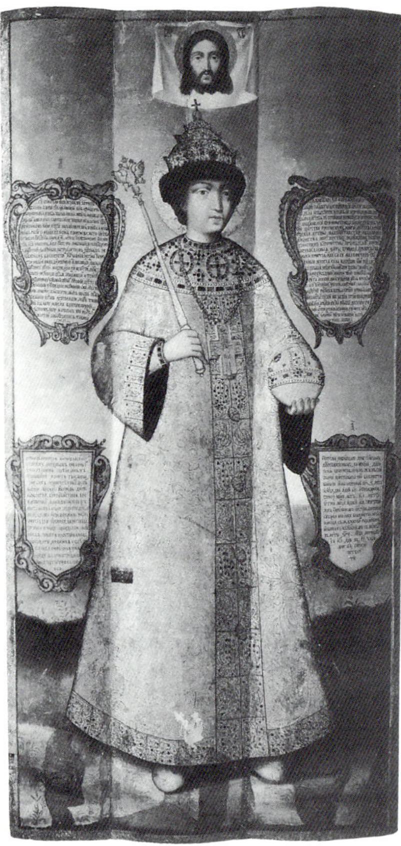

TSAR FEODOR ALEKSEEVICH 1685–86

Royal Slavic-Greek-Latin Academy, the first University in Moscow, which opened in 1687.

The exhibited chalice (cat. no. 69) was made in 1686 by the master of the Kremlin Silver Chamber, by order of Vasily Golitsyn, one of the most important figures of the day. Golitsyn, the head of the Department of Foreign Affairs at the time and a favourite of Princess Sofia Alekseevna, pursued a policy of strengthening contact with western and central Europe. This trend was characteristic of Russian foreign policy during the last decades of the 17th century.

The chalice contributed by Vasily Golitsyn is a wonderful monument, enhanced by the new artistic ideas originated by Russian jewellers under the influence of Turkish and western European art. The bold combination of new with traditional decorative techniques and national shapes creates an impressive result. The uniquely vivid colours of the chalice come from the combination of the background, covered with a thick niello pattern of herbs and flowers of oriental design and technique, with authentically Russian carved Christian symbols and large carved flowers, curls and garlands, typical of northern baroque ornamentation.

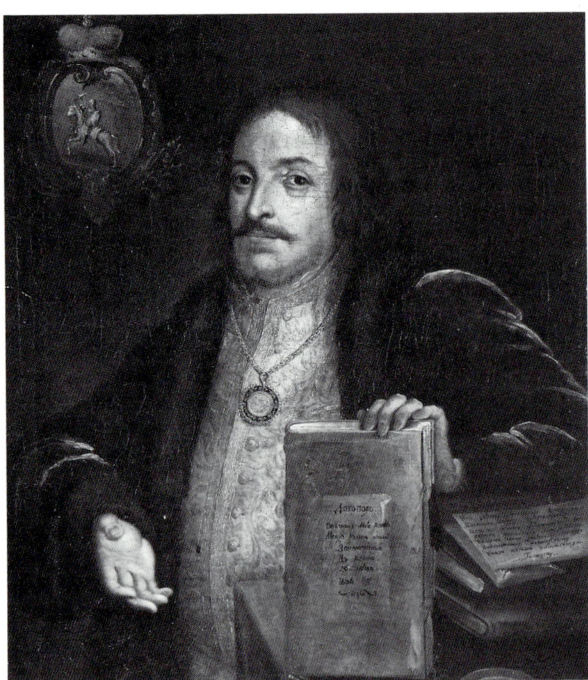

PRINCE VASILY GOLITSYN, SECOND QUARTER OF THE 18th CENTURY

Among the various masterpieces of ecclesiastical art created by Moscow craftsmen in the last decade of the 17th century, a cup for holy water (cat. no. 70) and a hanging cup (cat. no. 71) are particularly remarkable, reflecting the dominant motifs of the end of the century. The skill of manufacture and artistic perfection which these cups display probably source them to Moscow Kremlin craftsmen.

No stylistic innovations were made in the area of niello work in Moscow in the early 18th century. This was a period of development of existing aesthetic principles. A special area of creativity of Moscow jewellers of the 16th and 17th centuries was the production of the valuable drinking vessels required in great number by the royal court and nobility. The large collection of silver articles in this exhibition carries the traditional folk elements of decoration: a wide variety of forms and delicate ornamentation. The collection is particularly valuable as many of the articles belonged to well-known historical figures. A cast, boat-shaped ladle (cat. no. 74) was modelled on a wooden prototype dating back more than 2000 years to the Slavic tribes. Valuable ladles of the 14th century are described in the wills of the Grand Moscow Princes.

In the 15th century, Moscow masters created a new, simple but elegant variant of the ladle. Cat. no. 74, dating back to the late 16th or early 17th century, carries all the indications of Moscow workmanship; it is low, with thin sides, a broad bottom and light handle. Although not decorated, it looks festive and testifies to the ability of the creator to convey the intrinsic beauty of silver.

As well as ladles, various loving cups — almost spherical vessels with or without a short foot — were produced, also based on ancient wooden or clay prototypes. Loving cups were used in rituals inherited from ancient times, feasts to drink the health of the Tsar, and the rite of fraternisation, in which those who drank from one cup were considered to be joined as brothers. Loving cups filled with a mixture of water and honey were also put on graves. The first written record of loving cups dates from the beginning of the 16th century, but only later examples survive. Cups varied in size and decorative techniques, which included engraving, chasing, niello, enamel and filigree.

In the mid 17th century the masters of the Kremlin Silver Chamber made a small loving cup with a cloisonné floral pattern framed in filigree against a delicately gilt background (cat. no. 77). This loving cup is remarkable for the elaboration achieved with only a few colours by a simple technique of highlighting the enamel surface with spots of contrasting colour. Such innovations demonstrate that the Moscow masters of enamel were constantly searching for new methods, even when applying traditional techniques.

The jewellers of the 17th century often used chasing and engraving to decorate silver tableware. The combination of these techniques creates a magnificent effect. An example is the early 17th century loving cup (cat. no. 75) which belonged to Princess Marfa Mikhailovna Suleshova (née Saltykova). A beautiful design of twined flower stalks with leaves and sprouts covers the entire surface of the cup and lid. These motifs are borrowed from ancient Byzantine patterns widely used by Moscow jewellers in the late 15th and 16th centuries. The inscription, stating that the cup belongs to Princess Marfa Suleshova, adds to the noble design of the whole. This inscription is made in the ancient style, known as "vyaz", in which all the letters are connected to form an even, unbroken pattern. Such patterns sometimes served as the sole, but very expressive, form of decoration.

Similarly, six gilt motifs shaped like unfurled scrolls, together with the title and name of the owner, enliven the smooth surface of a silver beaker of the 16th century (cat. no. 78). This vessel belonged to the prince who became Tsar Feodor Ivanovich (1557–98), the last Russian sovereign from the Ryuriks and the son of Ivan the Terrible.

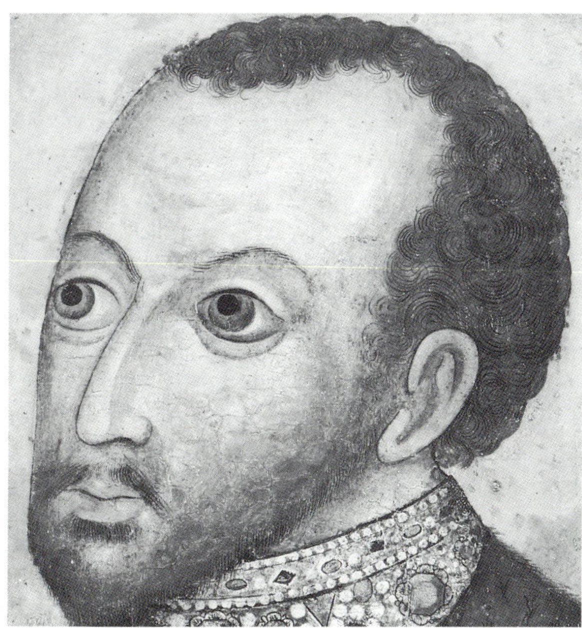

TSAR FEODOR IVANOVICH, SECOND HALF OF 17th CENTURY

The gilt beaker with spherical feet made by Moscow masters in the late 17th century (cat. no. 81) also bears an inscription indicating that it belonged to a prince:

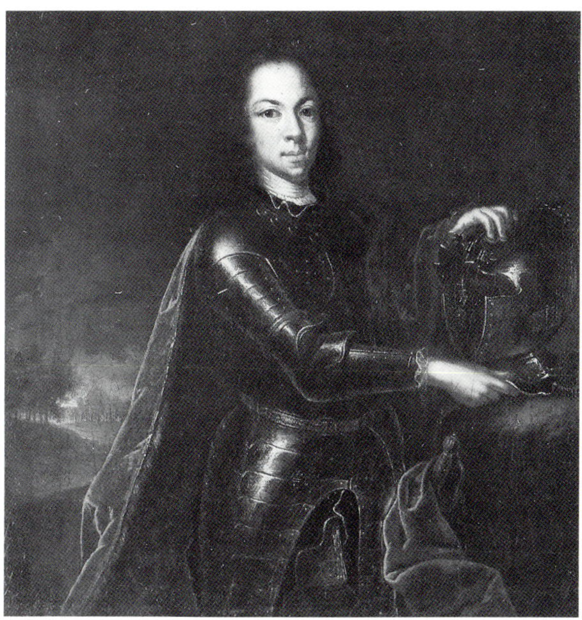

TSAREVITCH ALEKSEI PETROVICH, 1710

Aleksei Petrovich, elder son of Peter the Great. This article is one of very few surviving objects connected with the tragic fate of Prince Aleksei. An opponent of Peter's reforms, he was convicted in court and sentenced to death. He died in prison.

The inscription engraved in gold on the loving cup which belonged to Prince Ivan Borisovich Cherkassky (an active political figure in Russia in the first half of the 17th century) is a true masterpiece of Moscow decorative art. This loving cup (cat. no. 76), made in 1634, is distinguished by the artistry of the inscription, the virtuosity of technique, perfect proportions and the harmonious combination of a floral pattern with engraved fantastic animals in gilt cartouches. It is an outstanding example of 17th-century Russian decorative and applied art, an extremely important century in the development of Russian culture.

The 17th century was the transitional period during which Russia learned to appreciate contemporary European culture. During the closing decades of the century, contact grew between Russia and the nations of Europe. An engraved tankard made by Vasily Andreev (cat. no. 84) is in indication of the results of this exchange. The smooth, massive silver cup was made in Talinn in the late 17th or early 18th century. From Talinn it was taken to Moscow, to Vasily Andreev, who worked in the Armoury Chamber. Andreev, born in the Ukraine, studied in Moscow under Afanasy Trukhmensky, a peerless engraver in copper and silver. Working in the Armoury Chamber under Trukhmensky's guidance, Andreev became the best metal engraver of his time. Among the surviving articles by Andreev, two cups from the State History Museum are of special interest. They are engraved with images from a Bible illustrated by Nicolas Piskator, in 1650. The magnificent composition in silver demonstrates the unprecedented scope of the creative imagination and skills of the Russian silversmith. It is equal to anything made by western jewellers.

The craftsmen from the Volga River region hold a unique place in Moscow jewellery. The town of Yaroslavl was the major centre of jewellery-making in the region. The town, founded in the 11th century, was originally the main Russian port on the Volga River and played a key role in the promotion of trade and exchange, inside and outside Russia. The wealthy citizens, who made up a considerable part of the town's population, built new houses and erected numerous churches, filling them with gorgeous colourful and original pieces of ecclesiastical art marked by pronounced national characteristics and the influence of folk art. Unfortunately, the great fire of 1658 almost completely destroyed all the wooden houses, churches and monasteries of Yaroslavl. Many articles made of precious metals from the 15th century to the first half of the 17th century were also destroyed by the fire. The majority of the surviving masterpieces of Yaroslavl jewellery date from the second half of the 17th century, when the town was being rebuilt and demanded more valuable articles. Each creation of the local masters is highly original; there are no ordinary or inexpressive objects.

The originality of gold and silver work in Yaroslavl lies in the frequent use of elaborate, high-relief chasing rather than the more common techniques of niello, enamel and engraving. Yaroslavl silversmiths, inhabitants of the woodlands, were inspired by the wonderful three-dimensional carvings decorating the iconostases, the houses of merchants and manufacturers and the fantastic images of folklore. Another source of Yaroslavl uzorochie (high elaboration) was a book-print, the influence of which is seen in the ornamentation of chased mountings of icons, including those exhibited: The Nativity of the Virgin and Christ in Glory (cat. nos 92 and 93).

In the 17th and 18th centuries, icon frames were often enhanced by the addition of crowns, the unique shapes of which serve as a faultless indicator of Yaroslavl origins. Elaborate chasing combined with delicate shadowless engraving are typical of the Yaroslavl silver utensils. An example is the donated ladle of 1685 (cat. no. 95).

The art of silver chasing also flourished in Kostroma, another merchant town on the Volga River and as old as Moscow. Cat. no. 97 is a gospel printed in Moscow, with a cover made in Kostroma in 1677. This cover is decorated with a beautiful pattern of inter-twining stalks with flowers and leaves. Against this background, the images of God in Sabaoth, the Deisus, saints and the evangelists stand out in relief.

In the 16th and 17th centuries, gold and silver work also flourished in the towns of northern Russia. The development of crafts and icon painting in this region was closely linked to the Stroganovs, a family of merchants and manufacturers who played a key role in the development of the rich but wild areas of Siberia and the north. The family, remarkably wealthy and well-educated for its time, established a number of artistic workshops, employing talented architects, bone-carvers, embroiderers and jewellers. The works produced are distinguished by the beauty, finesse and delicacy of each design or image.

The study of Russian art includes the definition "Stroganovsky", which refers to items such as icons and embroidery and indicates a time and place of production as well as a characteristic stylistic unity. The originality of style which distinguished Stroganovsky masters is the result of a combination of natural talent and the creative comprehension of the best pieces of Russian, and particularly Novgorod, applied art in addition to western European designs. The influence of Novgorod art is evident in the icon which belonged to Nicholas Stroganov, The Legend of St Nicholas the Martyr (cat. no. 95), in the use of blue, green and pale-blue enamels—the favourite colour combination of Novgorod jewellers in the late 16th century—and also in the filigree design of twining stalks.

The towns of Solvychegodsk, Veliky Ustyug and Vyatka, surrounded by the harsh northern landscape, produced silversmiths with a surprisingly colourful perception of the world around them. They expressed their vision principally through enamel decoration. In the last quarter of the 17th century the Solvychegodsk masters of enamel originated the technique which grew to dominate their work; colourful ornamentation was painted against a white background covering the entire inner surface of a silver object. Large tulips, irises, sunflowers and carnations with expressively twined stalks, as well as people, animals and birds, were favourite motifs. These designs were executed in bright colours, generally different shades of yellow, red, blue and green. The most common technique of decoration of the outer surfaces was a filigree design, delicately framed with painted cloisonné against a silver or gilt background. A bowl, small box and charochka (wine-tasting cup) are examples in the exhibition. In making various decorations and body-crosses, Solvychegodsk craftsmen often used a complex technique of covering cast objects with enamel, without the use of filigree (cat. nos 100, 101 and 102).

As the town of Solvychegodsk began to lose its economic importance in the early 18th century, local crafts fell into decline. The second large centre of Stroganov trade and manufacture after Solvychegodsk was Veliky (Great) Ustyug. In the early 18th century it also became the main cultural centre in northern Russia. Solvychegodsk, close to Veliky Ustyug and the centre of gold and silver work, strongly influenced the creative activity of Veliky Ustyug's craftsmen, arousing their interest in the art of enamel. Cat. no. 94 is the only dated piece from Veliky Ustyug from the last quarter of the 17th century. This icon, St Prokopy and St John of Ustyug, is set in a particularly beautiful silver gilt frame featuring an exquisite combination of coloured enamels. The carved frame of the pectoral icon, The Ascension (cat. no. 103), is decorated with enamels of the same colours and has the same pattern of intertwining leaves, sprouts and locks.

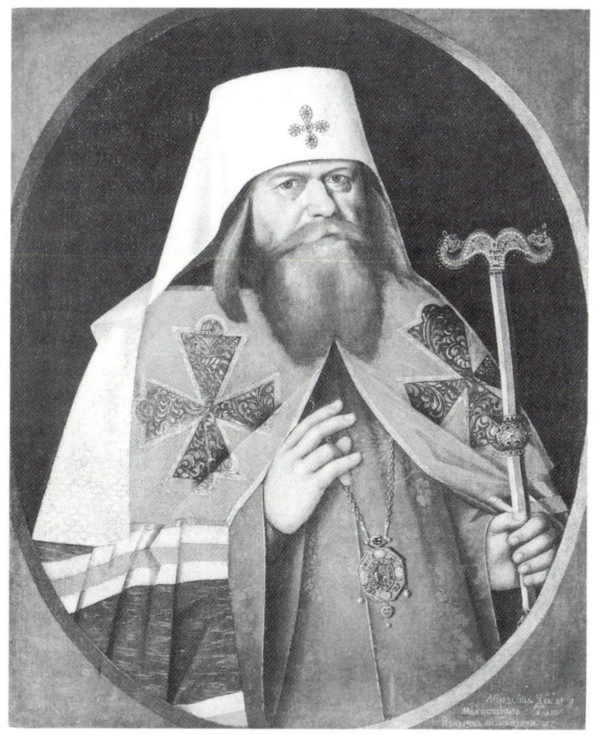

PATRIARCH ADRIAN, 1650

Unfortunately, masterpieces of jewellery from northern Russia were not widely distributed. Being rare and valuable, they were kept among the treasures of Tsars, Patriarchs of the Russian Orthodox Church and members of noble families.

The works of 16th and 17th century Russian jewellers are supreme masterpieces, distinguished by a high level of artistic skill, unprecedented scope of imagination and a constant striving for perfection. The forms and ornamentation of these pieces are characterised by originality and the influence of national traditions. The source of this creative activity was the spiritual and daily life of the Russian people.

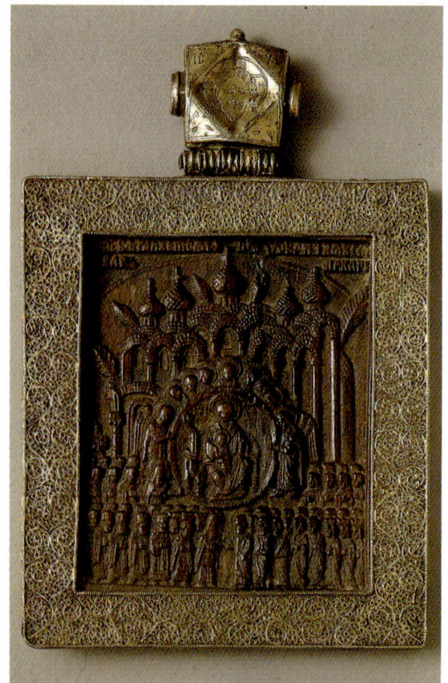
50

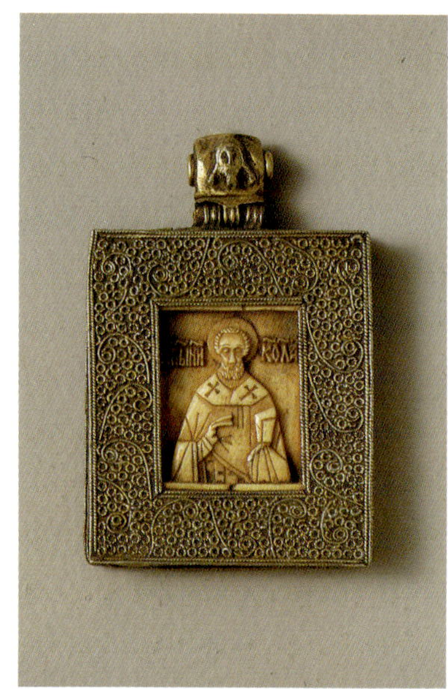
51

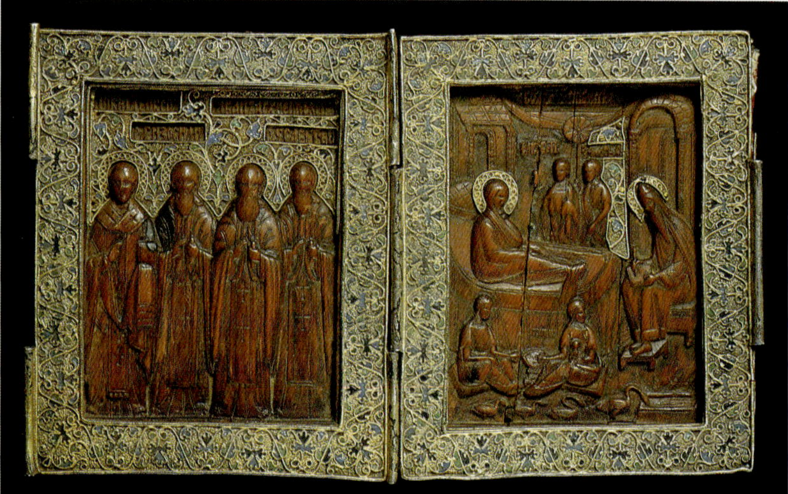
52

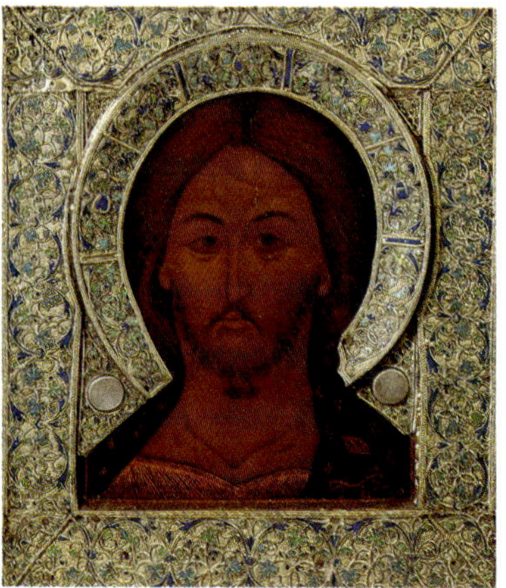
53

50. Icon: Rejoice in Thee
Moscow–Novgorod,
16th century
wood, silver gilt, filigree
13.6 x 8.9 cm
16416 OK 11511

51. Icon: St Nicholas
Novgorod, 16th century
bone, embossed silver gilt, filigree, basma
7.2 x 4.6 cm
3239 OK 11507

52. Devotional diptych
Novgorod, 16th century
cypress, velvet with gold thread, silver gilt, filigree, enamel
13.7 x 22.0 cm
3357 OK 9170

Two carved relief wooden icons featuring portraits of saints and the Nativity of John the Baptist. The frame is decorated with polychrome enamel over filigree floral ornament.

53. Icon: Our Saviour
Novgorod, 16th century
tempera on wood panel, textile, silver gilt, enamel, filigree
30.3 x 25.0 cm
74822 OK 8127

Icon frames made of precious metals and decorated with precious stones first appeared in Russia before the Tartar-Mongol invasion. Until the 17th century the frames were generally made of strips of silver, sometimes gilt, embossed or covered with basma, which concealed the edges and part of the background of the icon. From the 17th century onwards the frame almost completely covered the icon, with only the faces and hands visible.

54. Altar cross
Novgorod, late 16th century
cast silver gilt, glass, filigree
29.0 x 15.3 cm
2401 OK 6907

55. Pectoral cross
Novgorod, late 16th century
silver, gilt, filigree
11.2 x 7.8 cm
6979 OK 43

56. Altar cross
Moscow, 1594
embossed silver gilt, sapphires, emeralds, pearls, almandites, chasing
35.0 x 16.4 cm
75471 OK 8656

Chased into the reverse of the cross are inscriptions of blessings and a record of the donation of the cross by Boyar Dimitry Ivanovich Godunov to the patrimonial Ipatyevsky Monastery.

57. Altar cross
Moscow, 1652
cast gold, silver, emeralds, rubies, sapphires, pearls, enamel, filigree, chasing
39.7 x 17.2 cm
OK 6906

Cross made by order of Tsar Aleksei Mikhailovich and Tsarina Maria Ilynishna as donation to the palace church of the Nativity of the Blessed Virgin in the Moscow Kremlin.

58. Korchik
Novgorod, late 16th century
embossed silver, chasing
7.0 x 11.5 x 6.8 cm
64058 OK 8167

59. Panagia (pectoral image)
Russia, early 17th century
cast silver, carnelian, carving
4.5 x 11.0 cm
3107 OK 7370

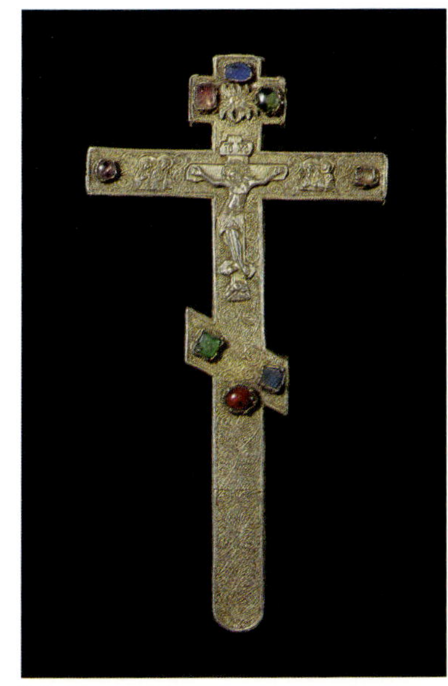

54

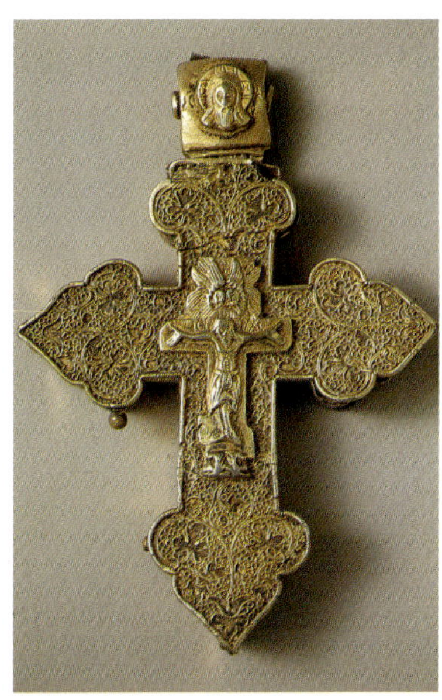

55

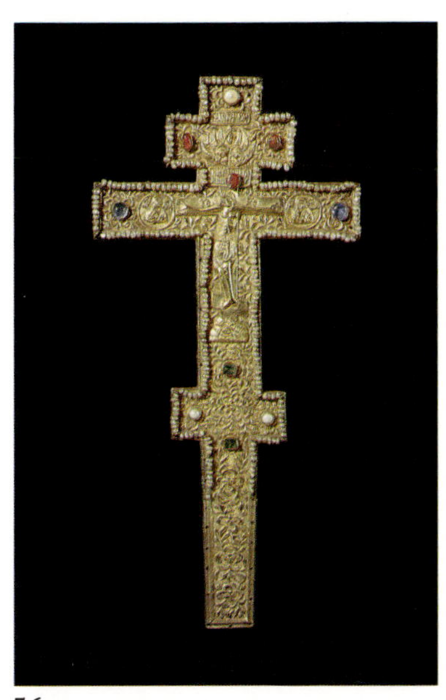

56

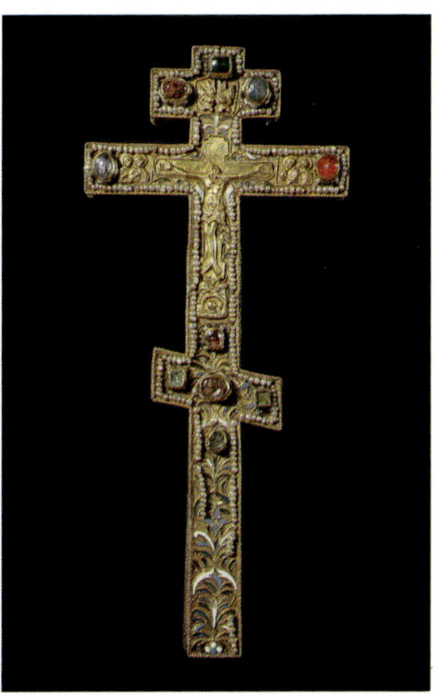

57

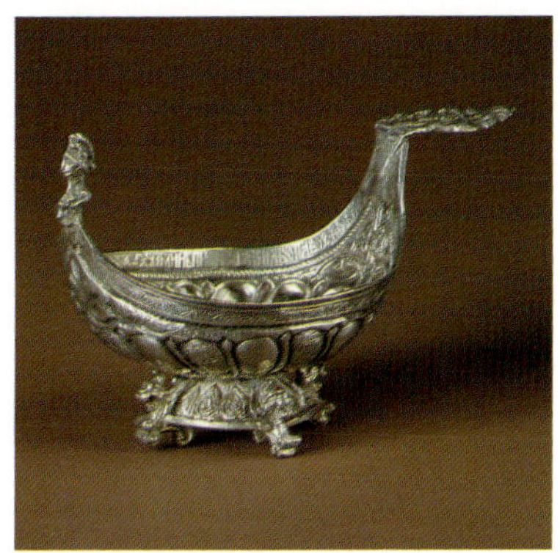

58

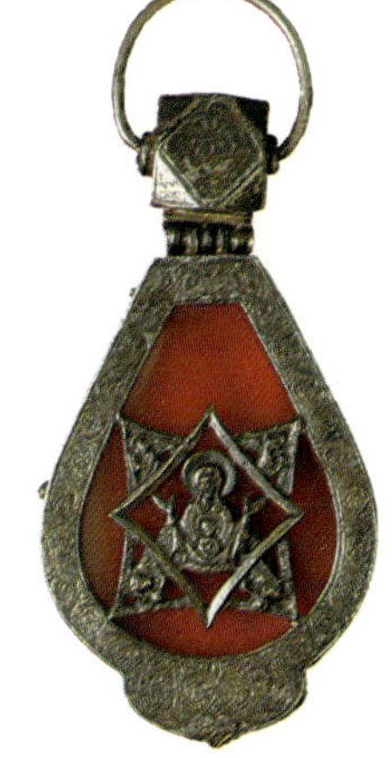

59

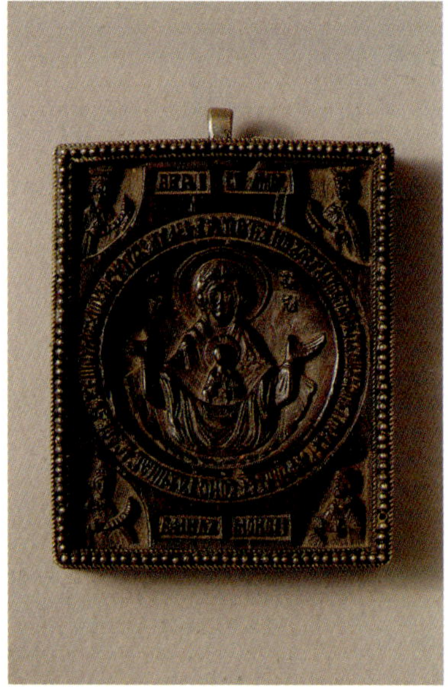
60

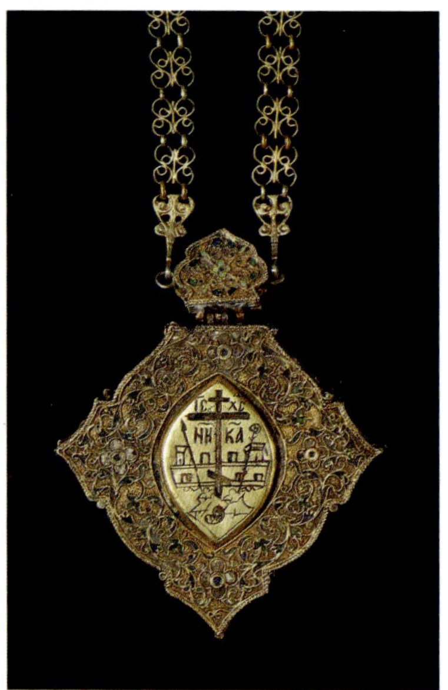
61

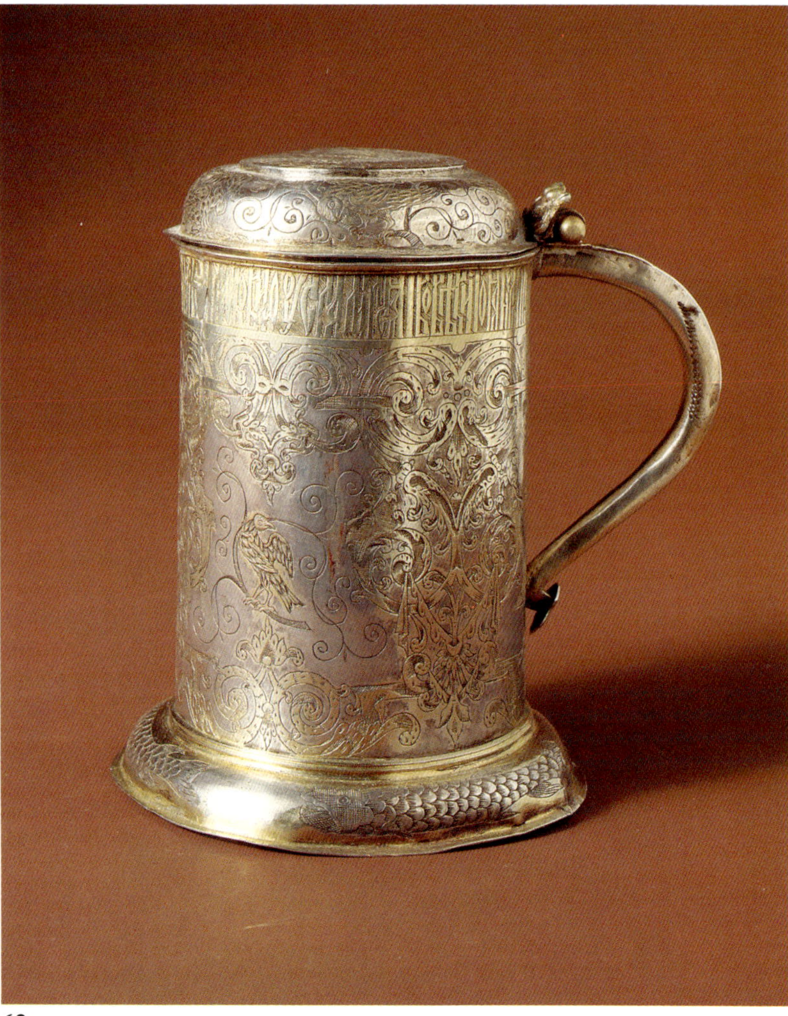
62

60. Icon: The Virgin of the Sign
probably Moscow, 16th century
wood, silver, filigree
8.0 x 6.0 cm
73284 OK 7733

The obverse of this small double-sided icon bears a carved image of The Virgin of the Sign enclosed in a circle with liturgical inscriptions and images of four prophets. On the reverse are carved the calvary and eight half-length portraits of saints.

61. Panagia (pectoral image) on a chain
Novgorod, late 16th–early 17th century
silver gilt, enamel, filigree, pouncing, chasing
12.6 x 9.1 cm
78747 OK 11388

62. Tankard
Novgorod–Tallinn, last quarter of 17th century
silver gilt, chasing
14.7 x 11.1 cm
379 OK 627

63. Altar cross
Moscow, 1679
silver, niello
36.5 x 20.2 cm
80253 OK 12379

The handle bears a nielloed engraving stating that the cross was made by order of Tsar Feodor Alekseevich for donation to one of the Moscow Kremlin Palace Churches.

Tsar Feodor Alekseevich (30 May 1661–27 April 1682), enthroned in 1676, was the son of Tsar Aleksei Mikhailovich from his first marriage to Maria Miloslavskaya. He was an outstanding personality and a talented ruler who initiated a number of important reforms. He conducted an active foreign policy and successfully concluded the conflict with Turkey, thus contributing to the liberation of a considerable part of the Ukraine from Turkish domination.

Feodor Alekseevich was a highly-educated individual, fluent in foreign languages, interested in music and a composer of religious poetry. He supported the establishment of the Slavonic-Greek-Latin Academy, the first university in Russia.

64. Altar cross
Moscow, late 17th century
embossed silver gilt, jewels, wood, niello
21.5 x 39.0 cm
67739 OK 7050

65. Icon: The Descent into Hell
Russia, late 16th–early 17th century
tempera on wood panel, embossed silver gilt, textile, enamel
48.2 x 37.2 cm
75428 OK 8451

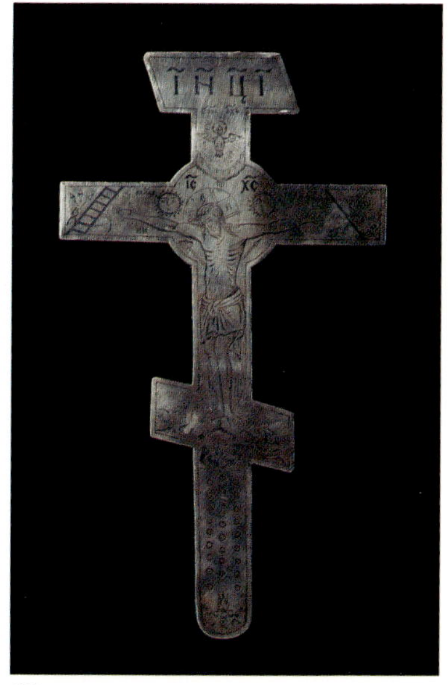

63

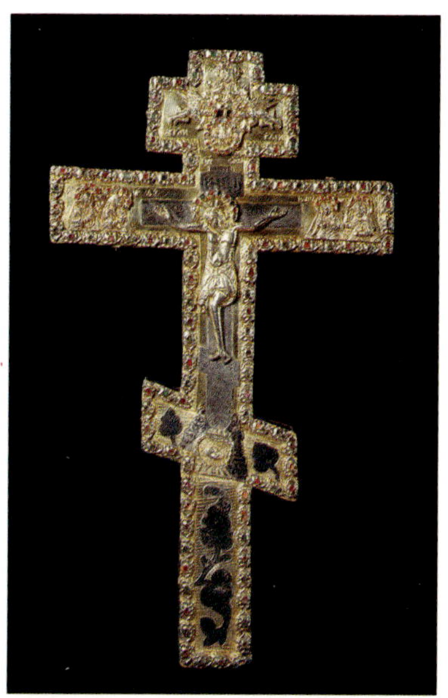

64

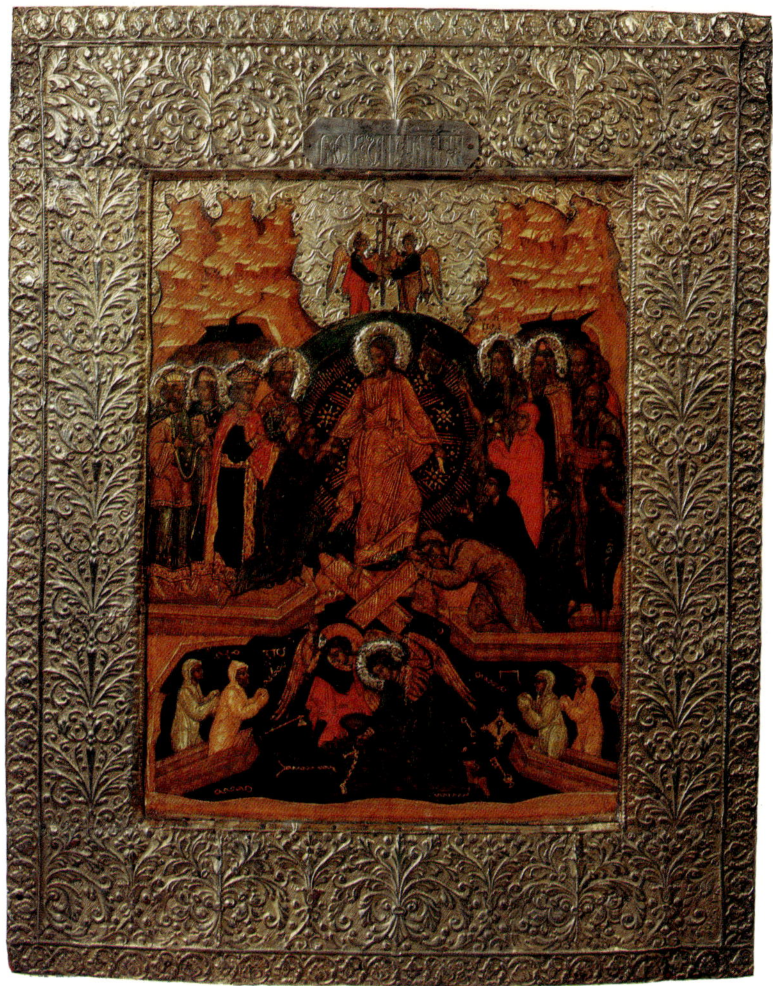

65

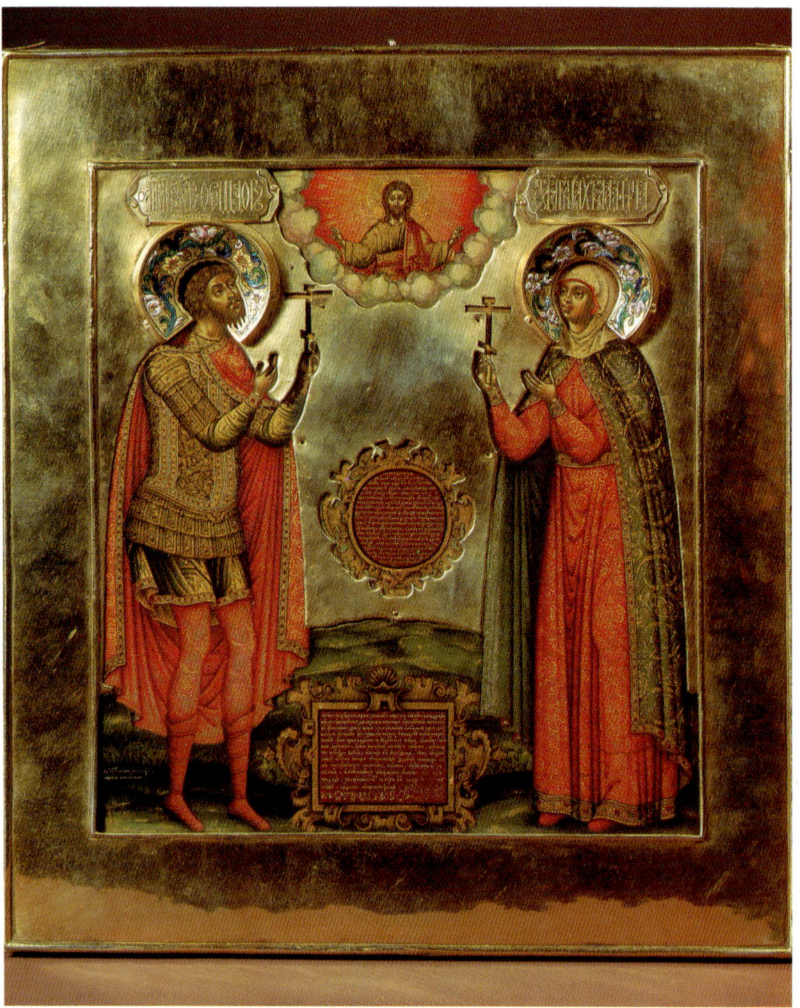

66

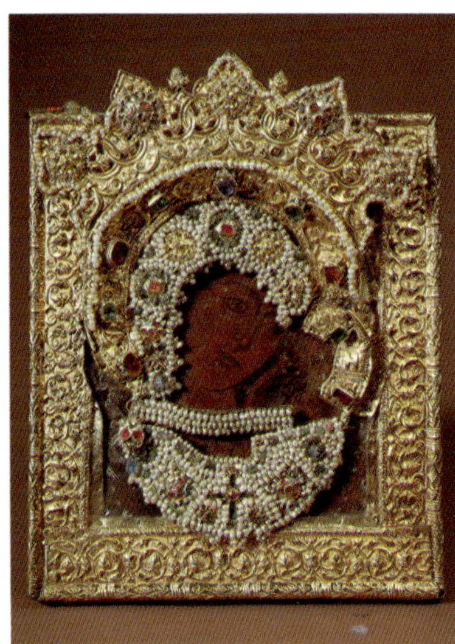

67

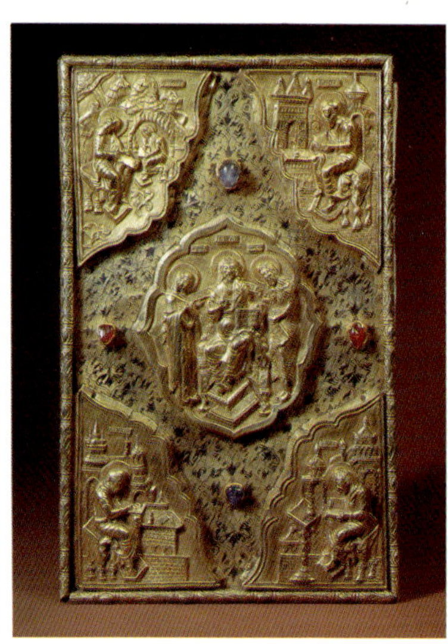

68

66. Icon: St Feodor Stratilatus and St Agafya
Moscow, 1681
tempera on wood panel, gold, silver gilt, enamel
37.2 x 32.4 cm
68965 OK 7398

Icon probably painted on the occasion of the wedding of Tsar Feodor Ivanovich and Agafya Grushetskaya in 1681.

67. Icon: The Virgin of Kazan
Moscow, second half of 17th century
tempera on wood panel, embossed gold, silver, copper, mica, emeralds, rubies, diamonds, sapphires, pearls, amethyst, glass, enamel
33.5 x 25.0 cm
57129 OK 3657

68. Gospel with cover
Moscow, early 17th century
embossed gold, silver gilt, sapphires, paper, leather, velvet, niello, chasing
9.5 x 38.8 x 23.8 cm
68931 OK 6160

Gospel printed in Moscow in 1657 and bound in a cover of an earlier date.

69. Chalice
craftsmen of the Kremlin Silver Chamber, Moscow, 1686
embossed silver gilt, niello, engraving
height: 32.5 cm;
diameter of bowl: 16.4 cm
99867 OK 16241

The lower edge of the base bears an engraved inscription of the donation of the chalice by the Boyar Prince Vasily Vasilyevich Golitsyn (1643–1714) to the Church of Christ's Holy Resurrection. From 1676 to 1679 Golitsyn was the head of the "Posolsky" (Department of Foreign Affairs) and other important state bodies. One of his diplomatic successes was the signing of the "Eternal Peace" with Poland in 1686. Highly-educated, he favoured the broadening of Russia's international relations. He was a favourite of Princess Sofia, regent during the infancies of Ivan and Peter I.
After the accession of Peter I he was exiled to the north.

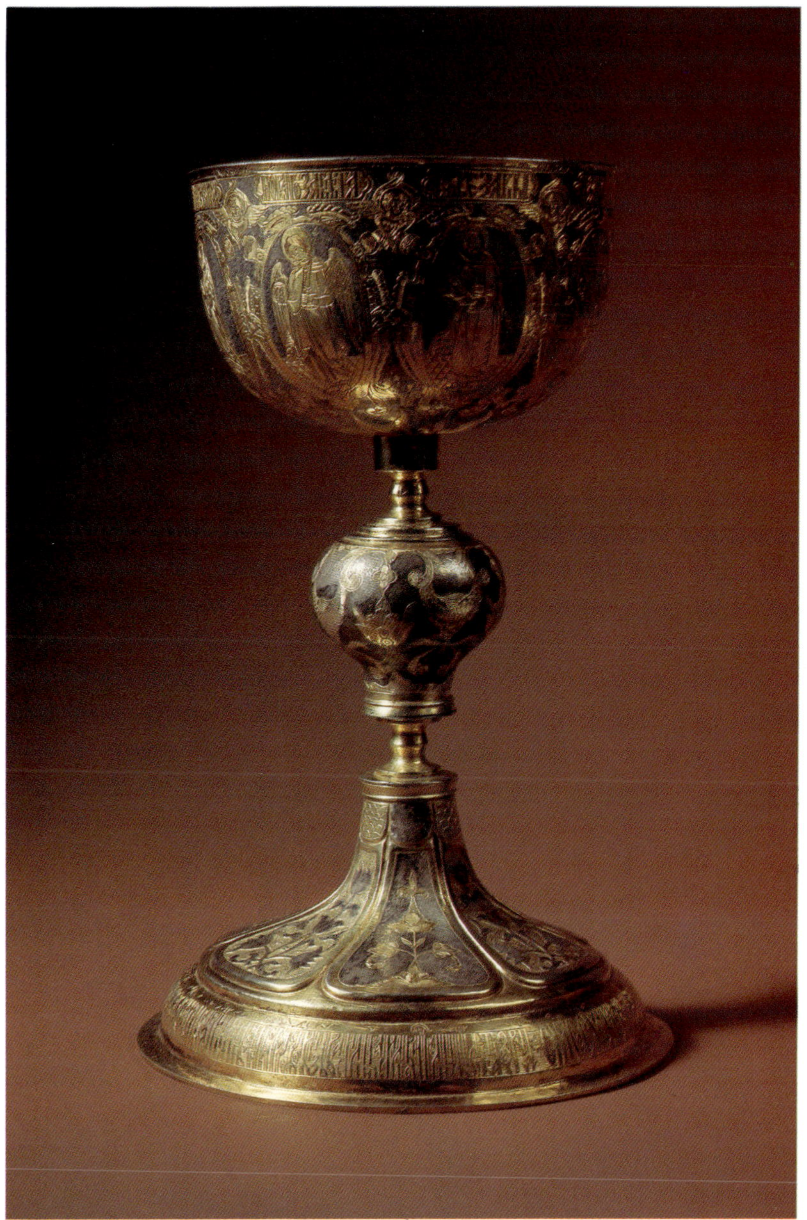

69

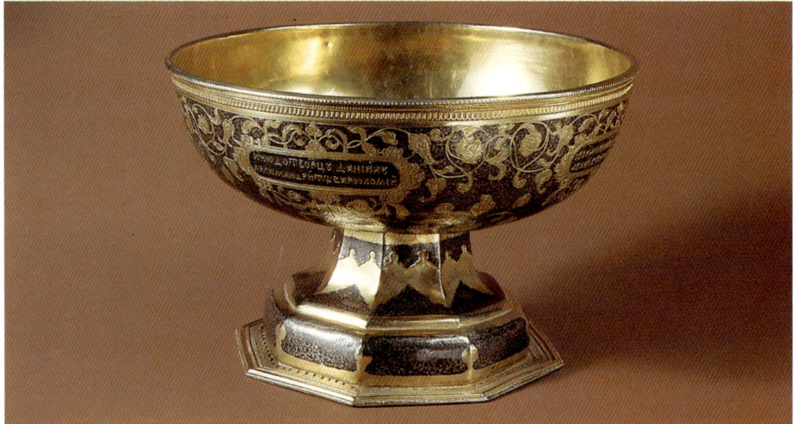

70

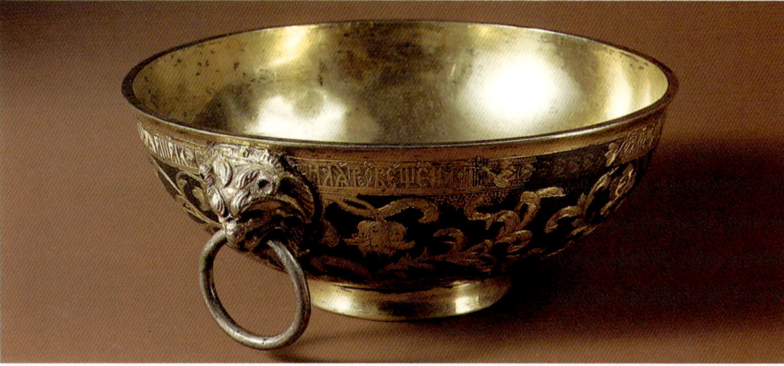

71

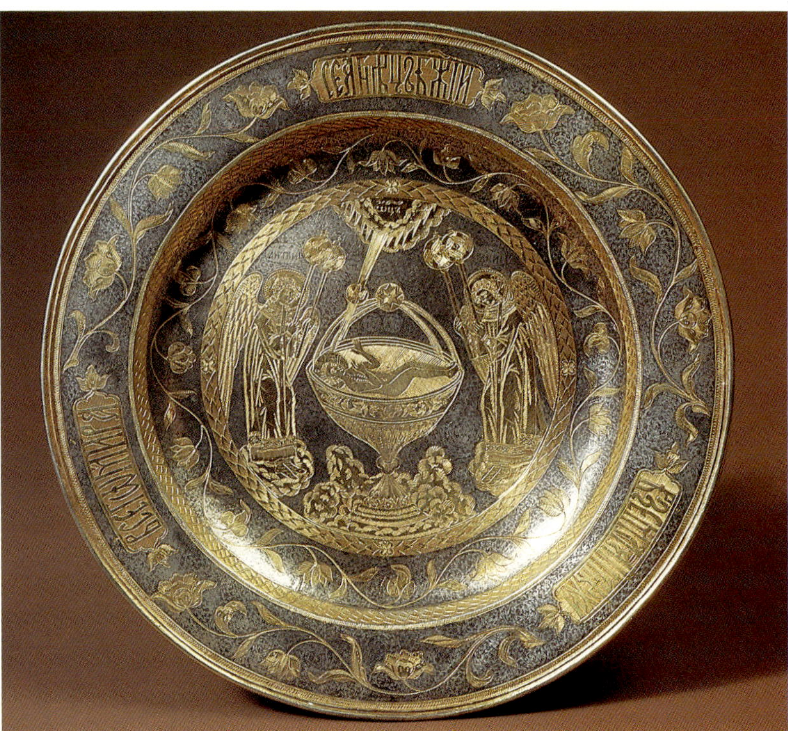

72

70. Cup for holy water
Moscow, 1693
silver gilt, niello, chasing
height: 15.0 cm;
diameter: 22.0 cm
104606/2 OK 22732

Engraved in the four medallions is an inscription recording the donation of the bowl by Archimandrite Bartolomeos to Danilov Trinity Monastery (founded in Pereyaslavl-Zalessky in 1508).

71. Hanging cup
Moscow, 1699
silver, gilt, niello, chasing
8.0 x 20.4 x 20.4 cm
54823 OK 1171

The upper part has four marks with engraved inscriptions stating that the cup belongs to the Metropolitan Trifily of Nizhny Novgorod.

72. Discos
Moscow, 1686
silver gilt, niello, chasing
diameter: 27.5 cm
99866 OK 16244

Discos or liturgical dish of the Orthodox Church used during the sacrament of the Eucharist.

73. Mitre
Kremlin workshops, Moscow, 1685
cast and beaten silver, gold, diamonds, rubies, emeralds, enamel
height: 30.0 cm
81538 OK 13692

On the lower part of the mitre are a silver fringe and an engraved inscription: "By the grace of God, we, the Lord Sovereigns and Grand Dukes Ivan Alekseevich, Peter Alekseevich and the Tsarina Grand Duchess Sofia Alekseevna, Autocrats of all the Great and Small and White Russias, grant this to the devout and holy Gideon, Metropolitan of Kievan, Galician and Little Russias".

The mitre was granted to Prince Gideon Svyatopolk-Chtevertinsky (d. 5 April 1690), who was enthroned as Metropolitan in Moscow on 8 November 1685.

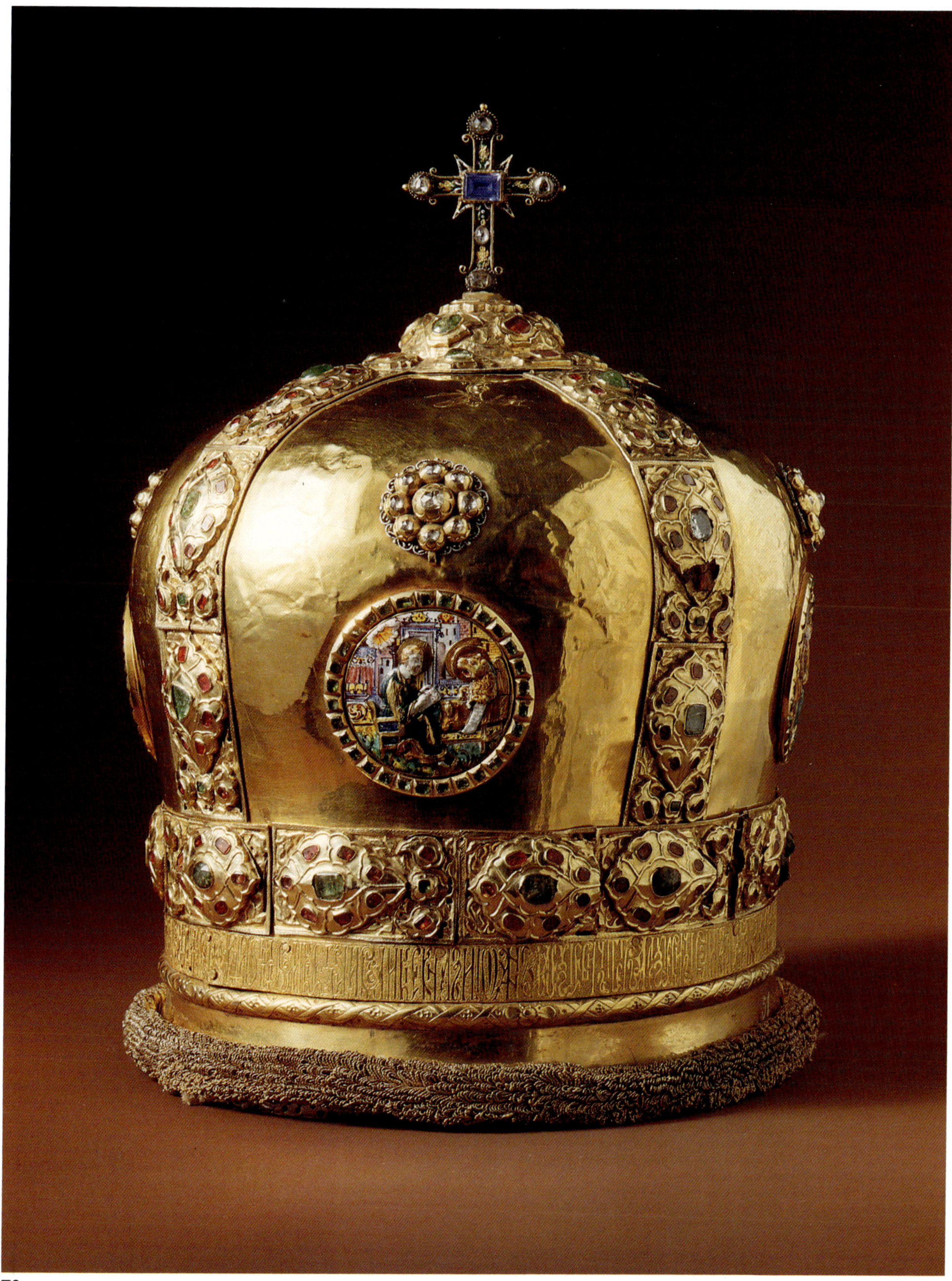

73

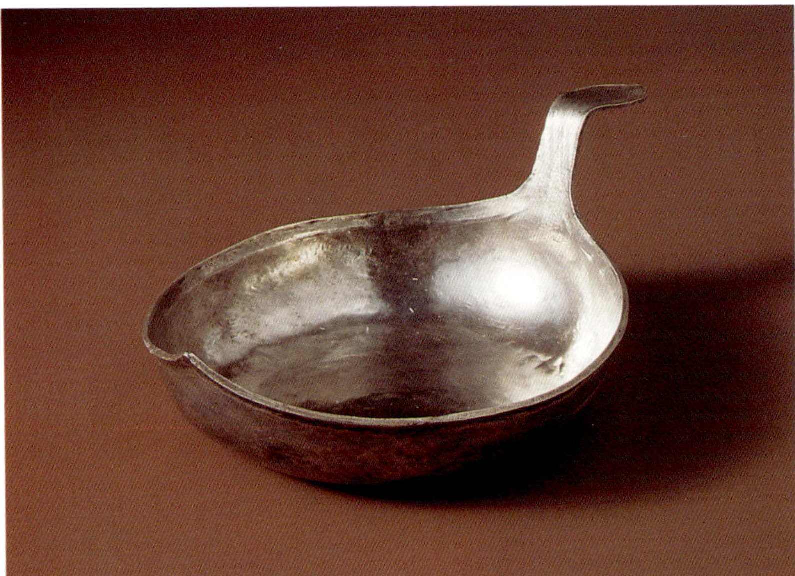

74

74. Ladle
Russia, late 16th–early 17th century
beaten silver
7.3 x 19.3 x 14.2 cm
49031 OK 33

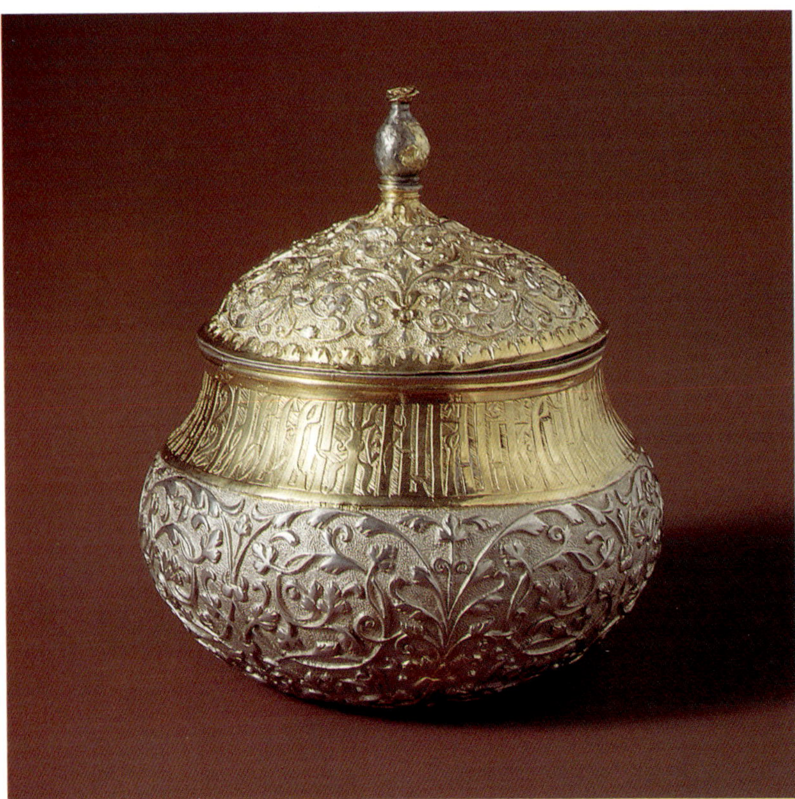
75

75. Covered bratina (loving cup)
Moscow, first quarter of 17th century
embossed silver gilt, engraving
height: 13.3 cm;
diameter: 8.9 cm
2 OK 1046

The engraved inscription states that the bratina belongs to Princess Marfa Mikhailovna Suleshova (née Saltykova). The lid decoration has been lost.

76. Bratina (loving cup)
Kremlin workshops, Moscow, 1634
embossed silver gilt, engraving
height: 15.7 cm; diameter: 20.5 cm
72740 OK 6772

The upper part of the goblet is decorated with a linked inscription stating that it belongs to Prince Ivan Borisovich Cherkassky, an active participant in Russian political life in the first half of the 17th century. He was at various times head of the Streletz Department, the Department of Public Expenses and the Treasury Department.

77. Bratina (loving cup)
craftsmen of the Kremlin Silver Chamber, Moscow, mid 17th century
silver gilt, enamel, filigree
height: 9.0 cm; diameter: 6.8 cm
53497 OK 1053

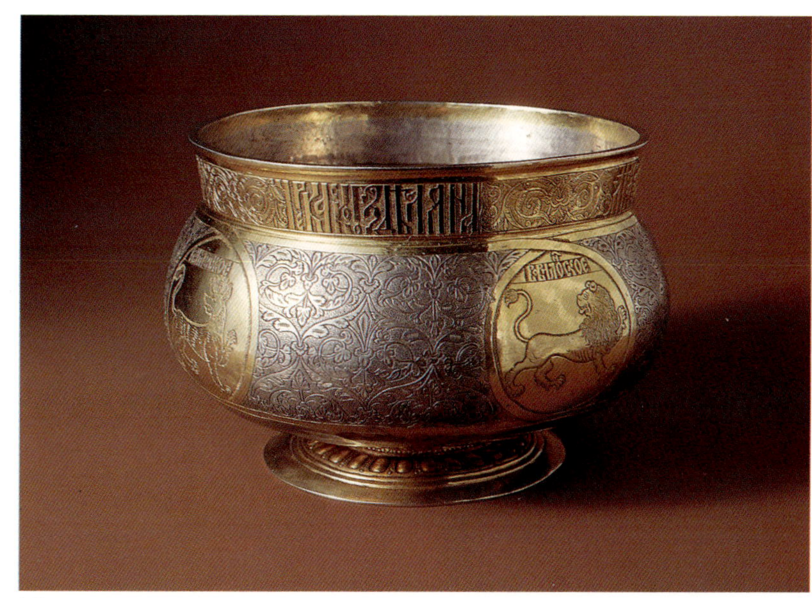

76

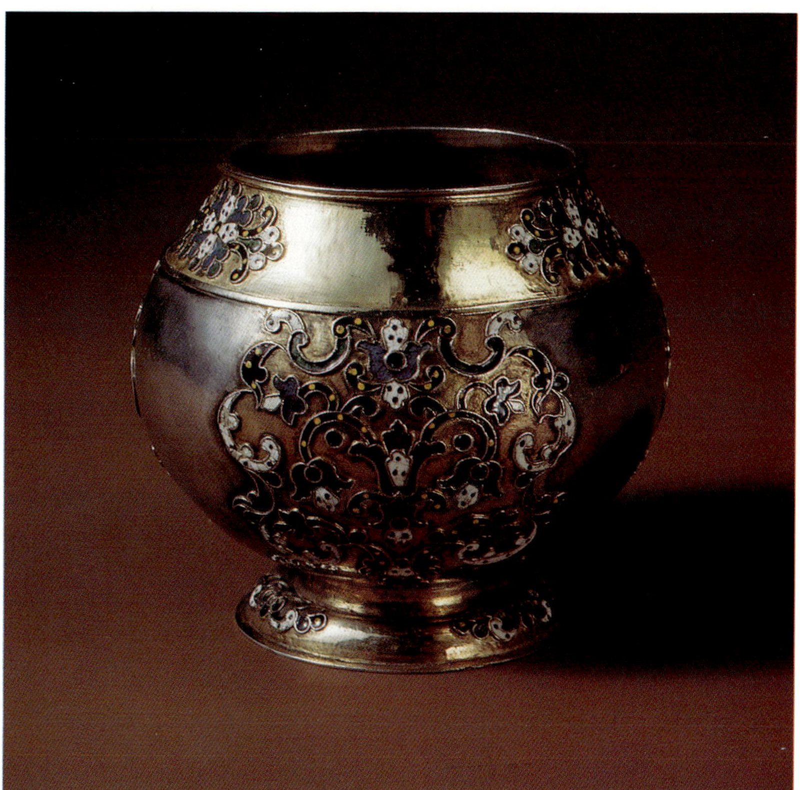

77

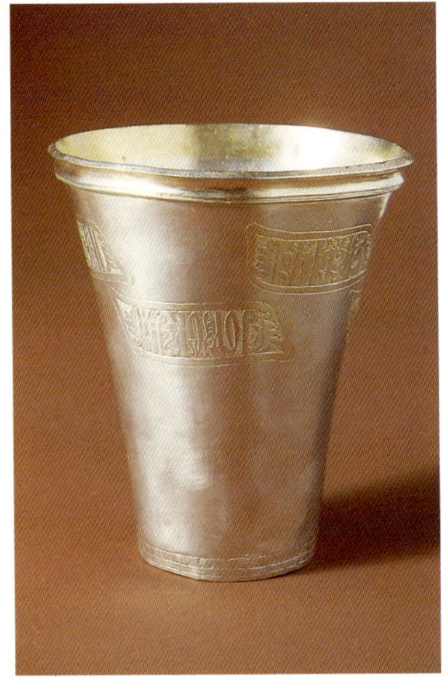

78

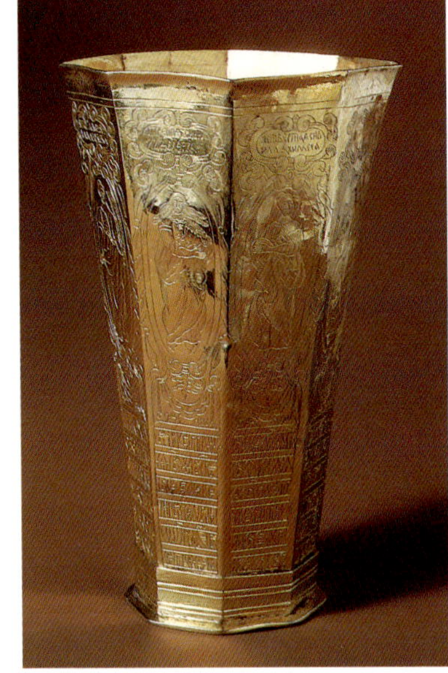

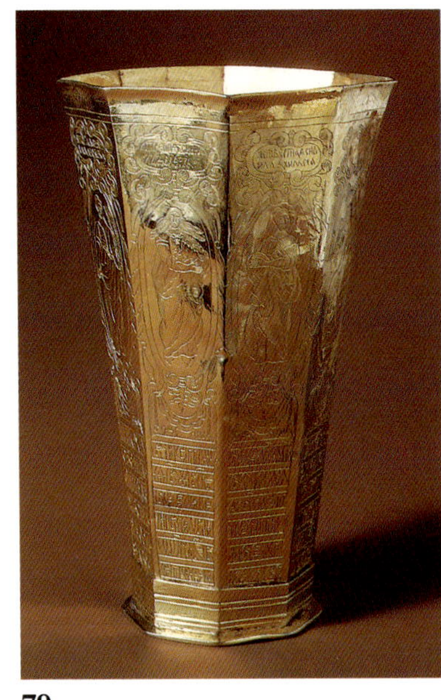

79

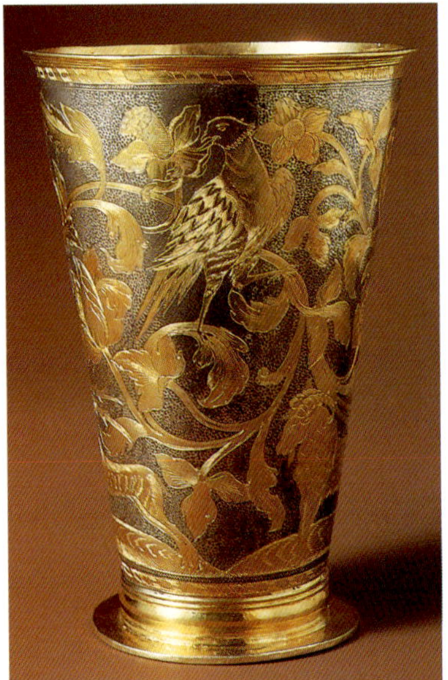

80

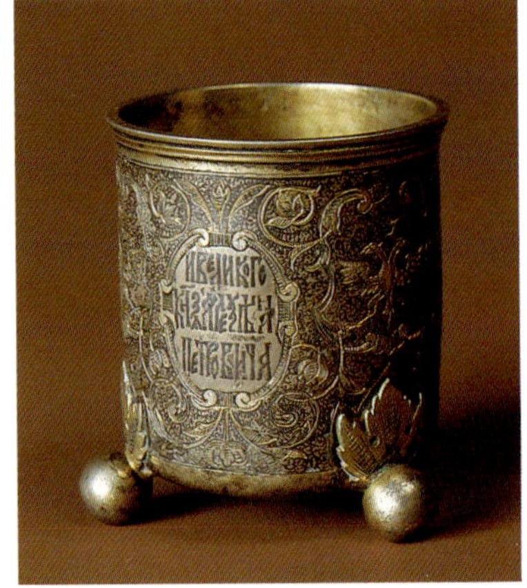

81

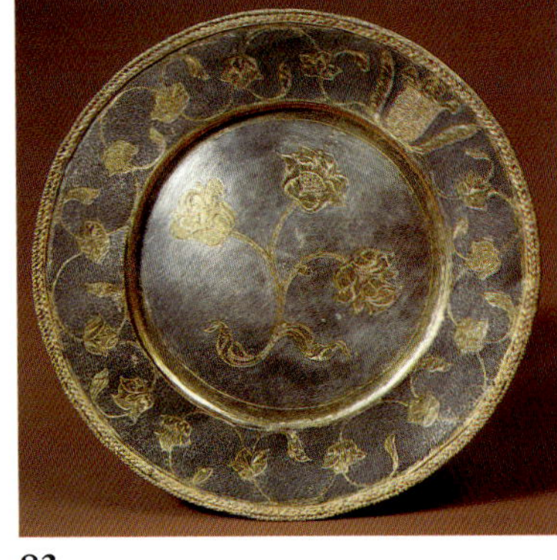

83

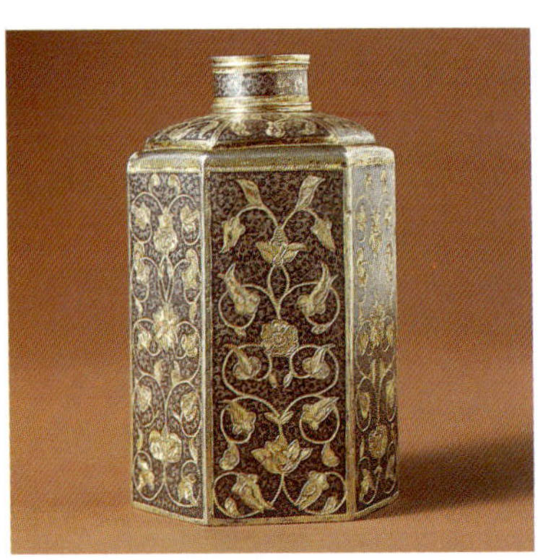

82

78. Beaker
Moscow, 1560–84
silver gilt, chasing
13.8 x 12.3 x 12.3 cm
83711 OK 14163

Beaker once the property of Feodor Ivanovich (1557–98), the son of Ivan the Terrible and the last Tsar of the House of Ryurik. After Feodor's death the beaker was probably given to the Sacristy of the Pskov Cathedral and later to the State History Museum.

79. Tankard
Moscow, 1690–91
silver gilt, chasing
height: 21.8 cm;
diameter: 12.8 cm
50146 OK 1021

An inscription on the upper part of the tankard reads "Moscow 1690–91".

80. Tankard
Moscow, 1696–97
silver gilt, niello, chasing
height: 19.2 cm;
diameter: 13.1 cm
82417 OK 13996

The tankard bears the inscription "Moscow 1696–97".

81. Beaker
Moscow, late 17th–early 18th century
silver gilt, niello, chasing
8.1 x 7.0 x 7.0 cm
30414 OK 1096

Enclosed within the three figured cartouches is an inscription stating that the beaker belonged to the son of Peter the Great, Tsarevich Aleksei Petrovich (1690–1718). An opponent of the reforms of Peter I, Aleksei was convicted in court and sentenced to death. He died in prison.

82. Quarter vessel
Moscow, 17th century
silver gilt, niello, chasing
height: 13.2 cm
350 OK 1194

Travelling vessel with a screw-in stopper for holding liquid or powdered substances.

83. Dinner plate
Moscow, late 17th century
silver gilt, niello, engraving
diameter: 21.1 cm
428 OK 888

Until the end of the 17th century, plates, when used as part of the tableware, were mostly decorative. They were made of precious metals, enamelled and nielloed. In the 18th century silver plates were incorporated into the dinner service.

84. Tankard
Vasily Andreev, Kremlin Armoury, Moscow–Tallinn, late 17th–early 18th century
silver gilt, embossing, chasing, engraving
22.5 x 17.7 cm
42003 OK 615

85. Tankard
Moscow, late 17th–early 18th century
silver gilt, embossing, niello, chasing
22.5 x 16.3 cm
50324 OK 634

86. Wine-tasting cup
Moscow, mid 17th century
embossed silver gilt, casting, engraving
4.9 x 8.3 cm
6793 OK 849

87. Dinner spoon
probably Moscow, mid 17th century
silver gilt, niello, chasing
length: 14.6 cm
6266 OK 502

The earliest dinner spoons made by Russian craftsmen date back to the early 17th century. Russian spoons can be dated not only by variations in ornament, but also by the length of the handle; in the first half of the 17th century handles were short, in the late 17th century long and straight, and in the 18th century flat and usually dilated.

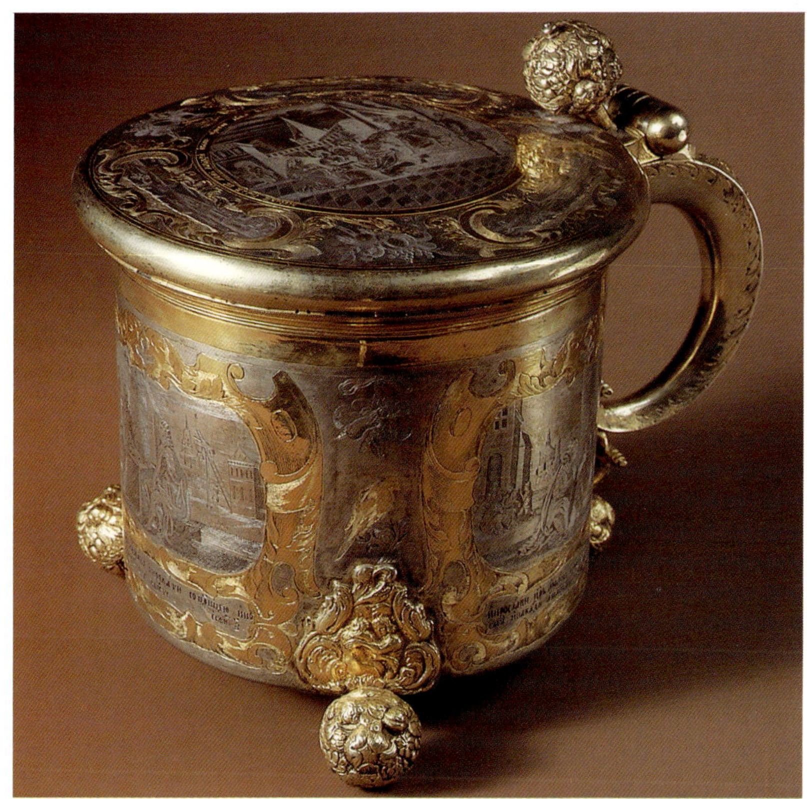

84

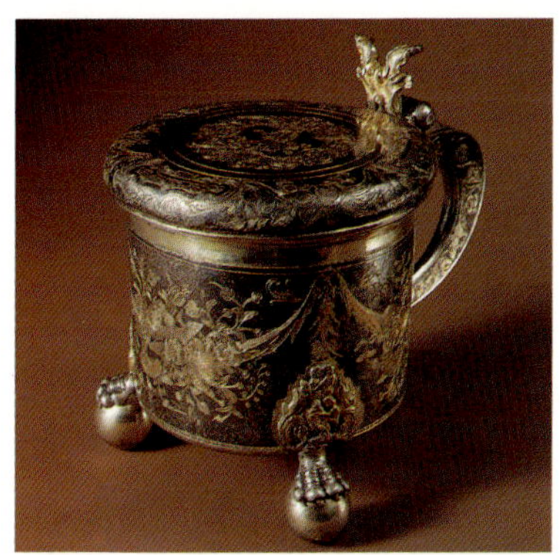

85

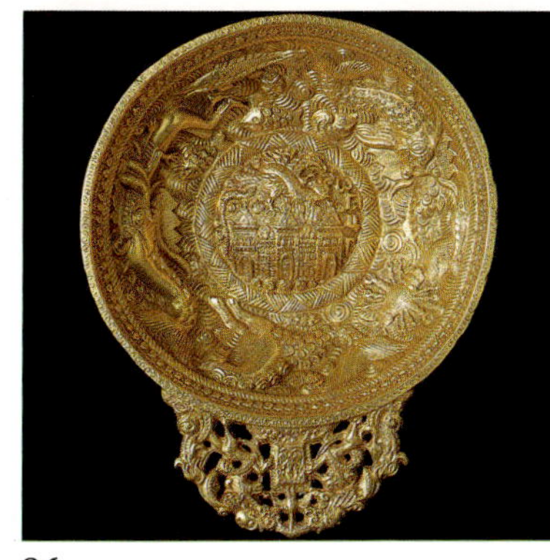

86

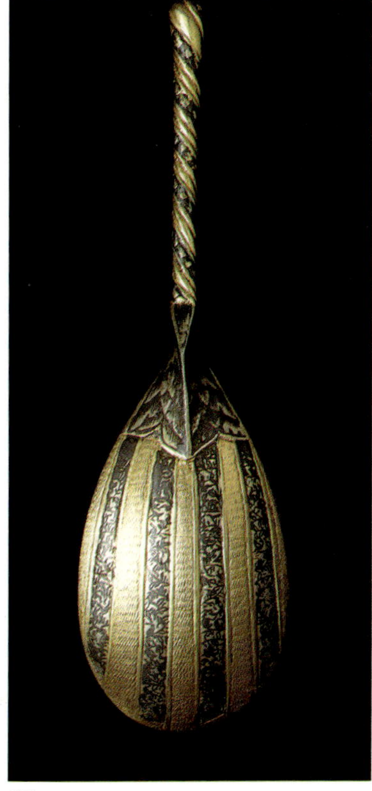

87

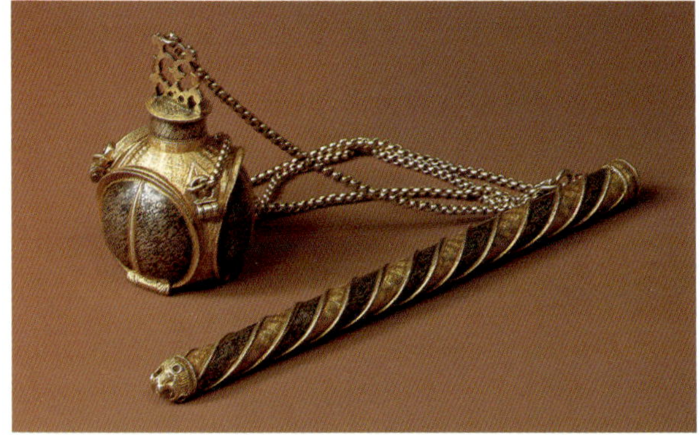

88

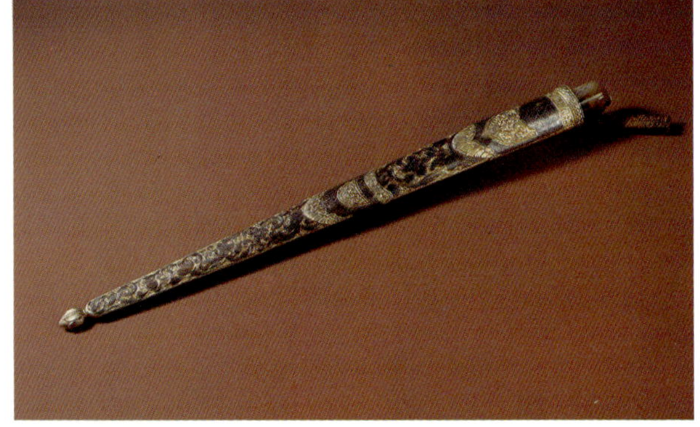

89

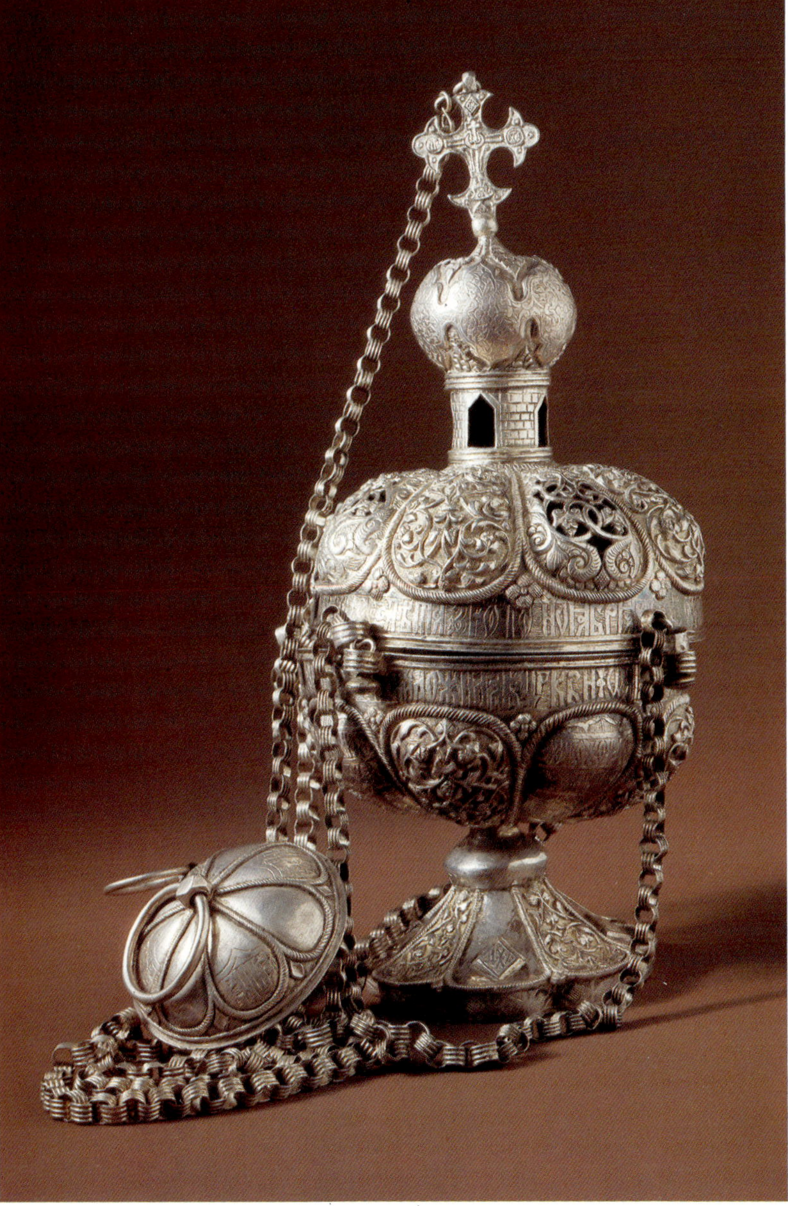

90

88. Desk set
Peter Ivanov, Kremlin Silver Chamber, Moscow, late 17th–early 18th century
silver gilt, niello, engraving
inkwell: 9.0 x 5.5 x 5.5 cm; length of penstand: 20.9 cm
18397 OK 650

Unique example of a desk set made from precious metal. Only individual items from this type of set exist in Russian collections. These include the State History Museum, the Armoury Chamber and the State Hermitage.

89. Knife and scabbard
Moscow, 1697
embossed silver gilt, agate, niello, velvet, leather, chasing
length of scabbard: 36.4 cm; length of knife: 36.2 cm
9883 OK 7024

Knife and scabbard probably belonged to Duke Osyp Ivanovich Scherbatov, a member of the nobility during the reign of Peter I.

90. Censer
Yaroslavl, 1661
embossed silver
height: 31.4 cm
1510 OK 6498

Censer given to the Church of St John Chrysostom of the Yaroslavl Kremlin.

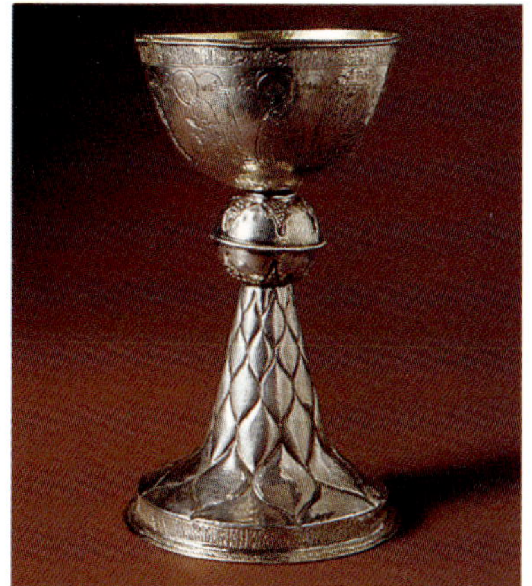

91

91. Chalice
Yaroslavl, last half of the 17th century
silver gilt, embossing, chasing
height: 19.7 cm
4200 OK 6227

Chalice donated by a merchant, Foma Gurjev, to the Chapel of the Last Judgement, Church of the Epiphany, Yaroslavl.

92. Icon: The Nativity of the Virgin
probably Yaroslavl, mid 17th century
tempera on wood panel, embossed silver gilt
32.4 x 28.0 cm
54627 OK 8113

93. Icon: Christ in Glory
probably Yaroslavl, second half of 17th century
tempera on wood panel, embossed silver gilt
39.4 x 38.3 cm
76322 OK 9184

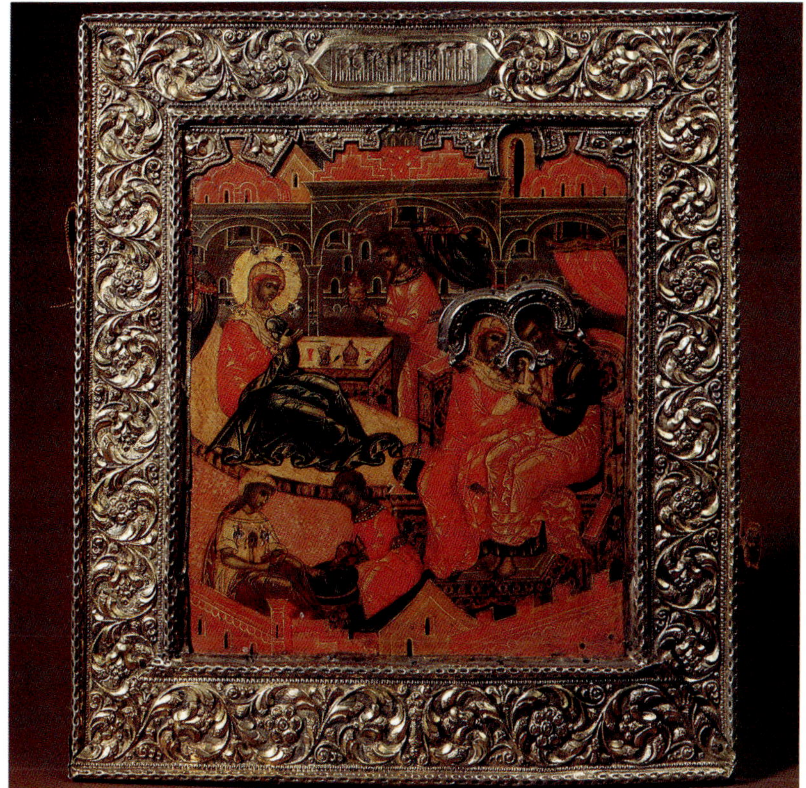

92

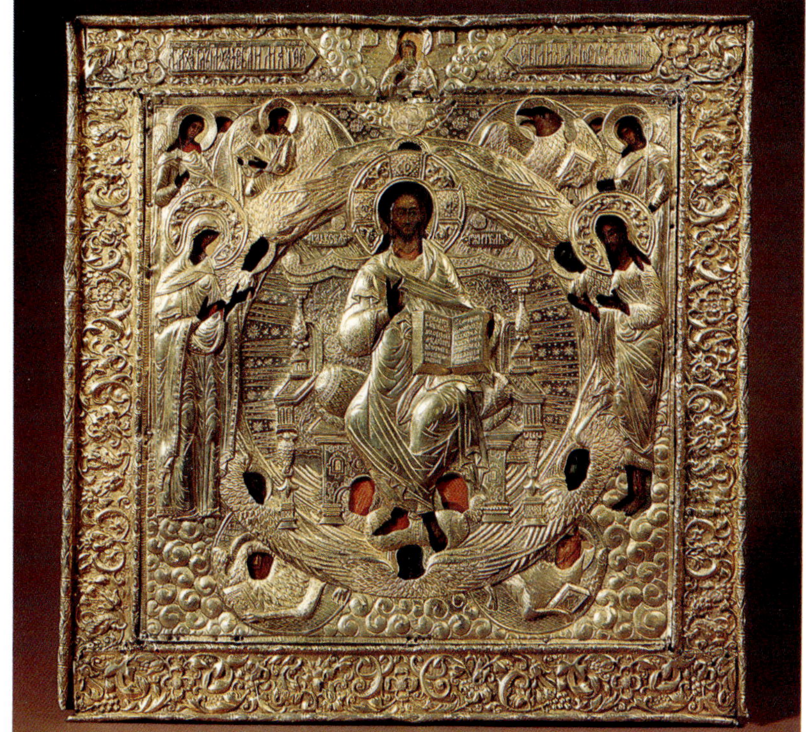

93

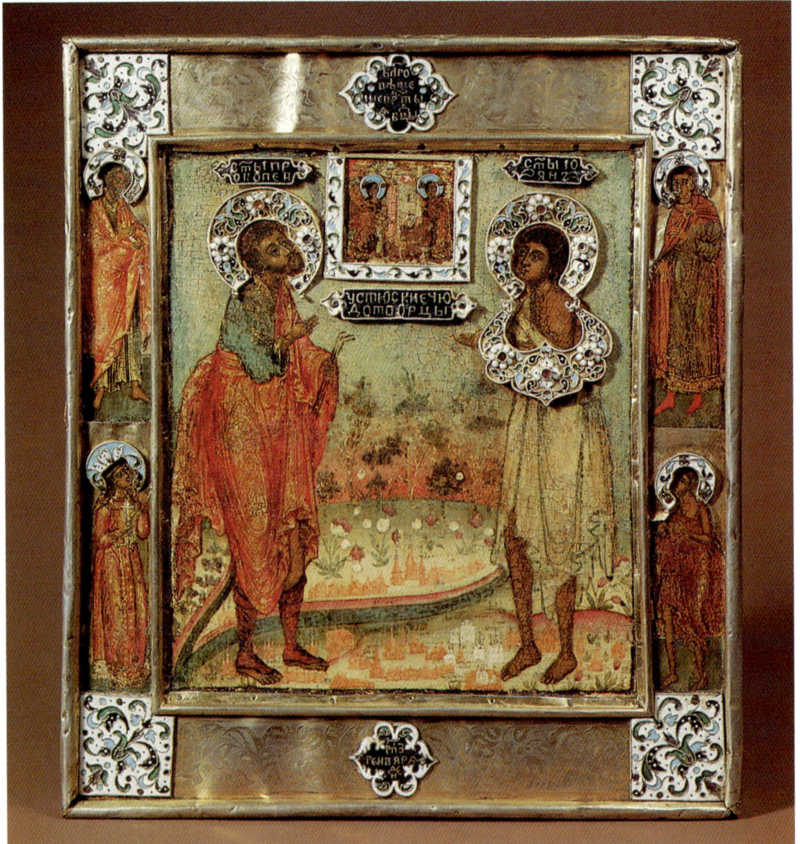

94

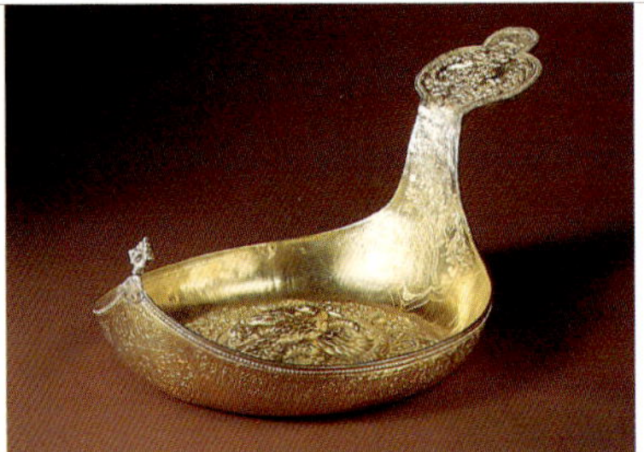

95

94. Icon: St Prokopy and St John of Ustyug
Veliky Ustyug, icon: 1677; frame: 1679
tempera on wood panel, silver gilt, enamel, filigree, engraving
35.0 x 30.5 cm
57520 OK 13367

At the feet of the full-length portraits of the patron saints of Veliky Ustyug, Prokopy and John of Ustyug, is a depiction of the town quarters. The inscription states that the icon was made by order of the "God-loving" Peter Lukyanovich Kuchukov, a citizen of the town.

95. Ladle
Yaroslavl, 1685
embossed silver gilt, chasing
15.0 x 38.7 x 23.0 cm
19 OK 895

Ladle presented by Tsars Ivan and Peter Alekseevich to Stefan Ivanovich Kuchumov, head of the Yaroslavl Vineyards, in recognition of loyal service and profit to the Treasury.

96. Folding diptych: The Legend of St Nicholas the Martyr
Solvychegodsk, 1598
tempera on wood panel, embossed silver gilt, enamel, niello, filigree, basma
33.0 x 13.6 x 1.8 cm
74873 OK 6065

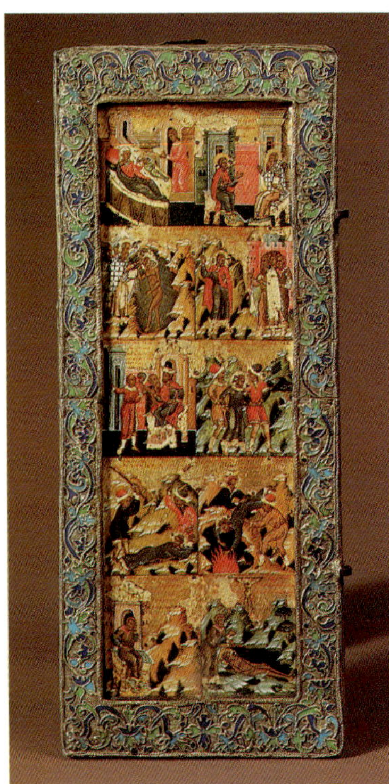

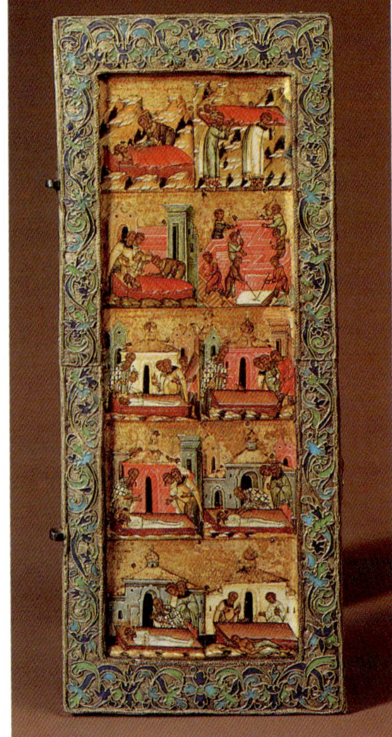

96

97. Gospel in cover
Kostroma, 1677
embossed silver gilt, wood, paper, copper
39.9 x 25.5 cm
OK 8617

Gospel printed in Moscow in 1657 and bound in a cover made in Kostroma.

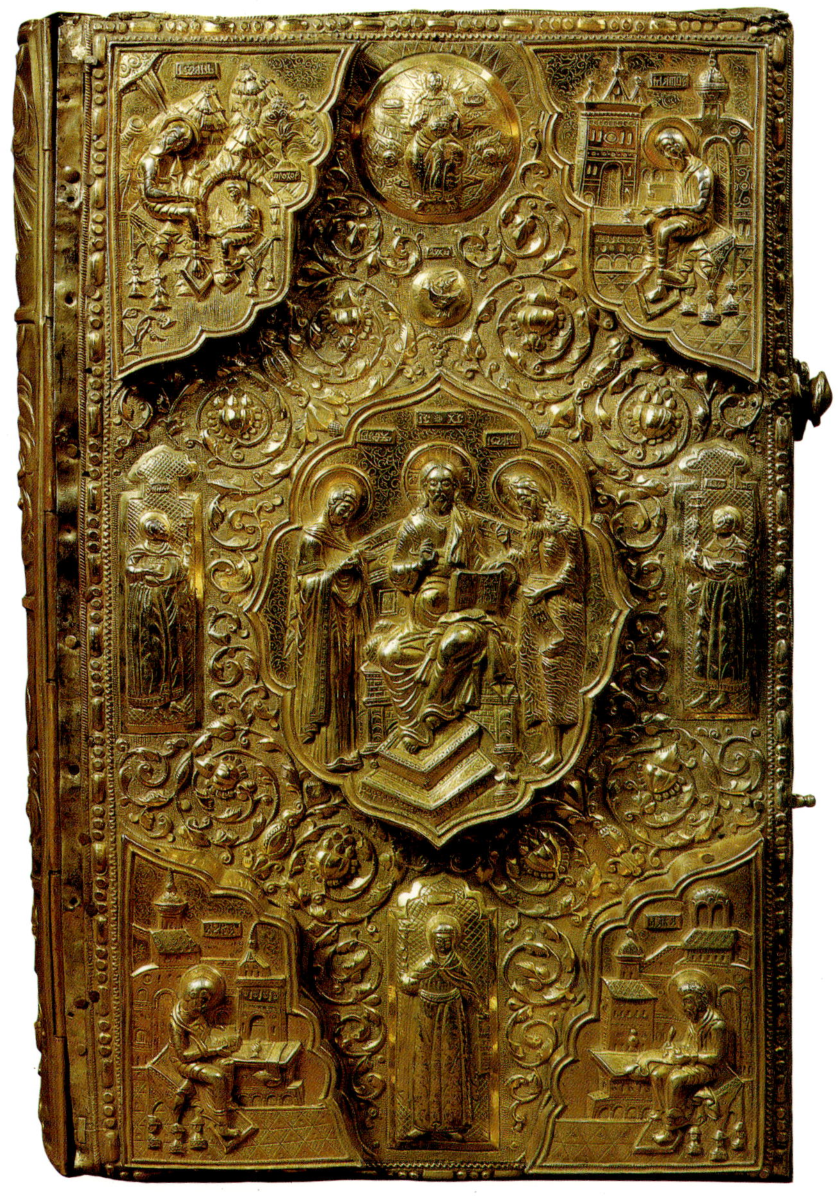

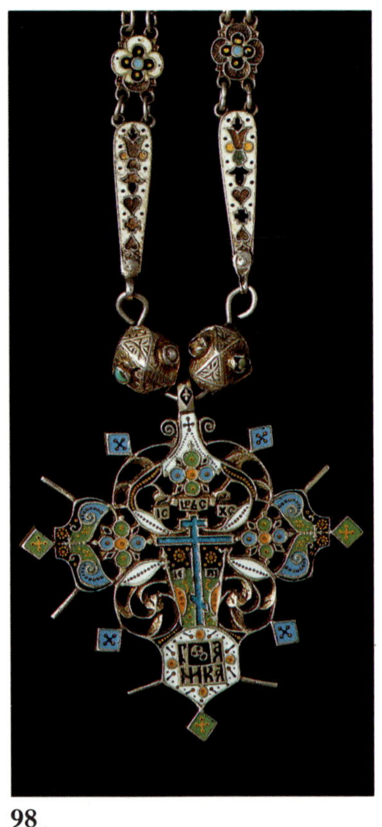

98

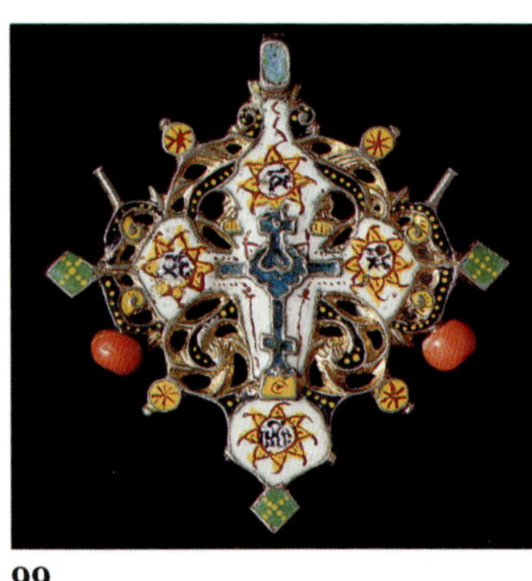

99

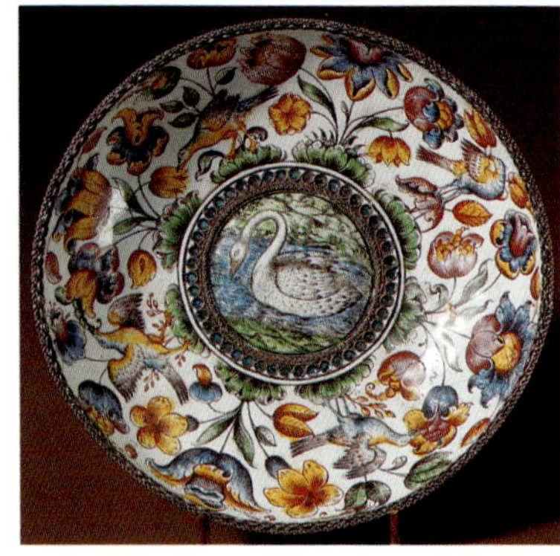

100

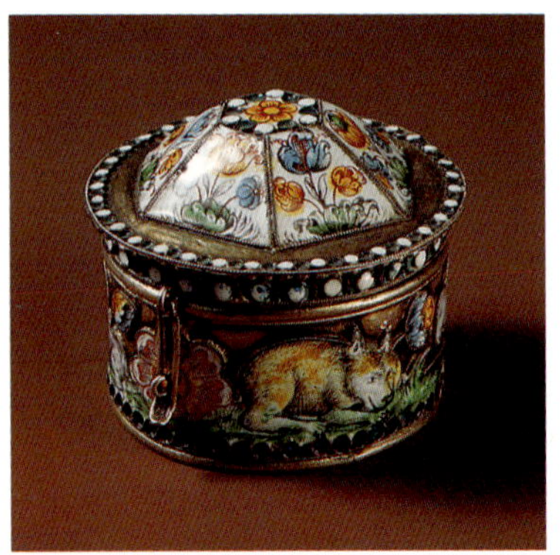

101

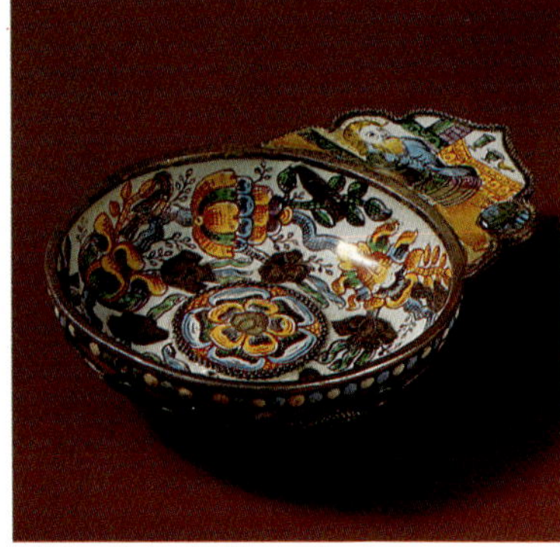

102

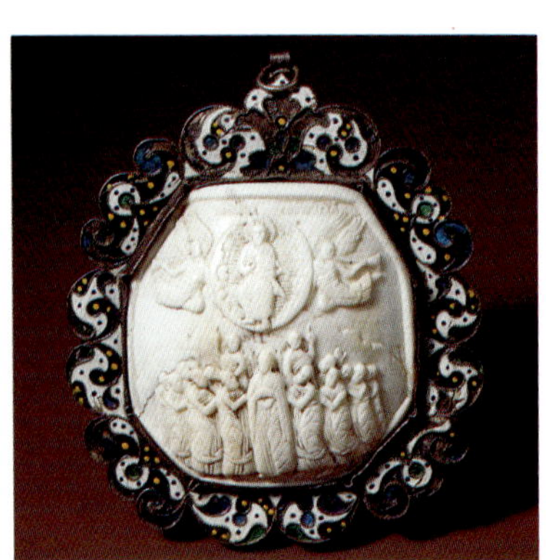

103

98. Pectoral cross (tel'nik) with chain
Veliky Ustyug, second half of 17th century
cast silver gilt, enamel, pearls, jewels, filigree
6.5 x 7.5 cm
4952 OK 6917

99. Pectoral cross (tel'nik)
Stroganov craftsmen, Solvychegodsk, last quarter of 17th century
cast silver, coral, enamel
6.5 x 7.0 cm
3427 OK 6918

100. Bowl
Solvychegodsk, last quarter of 17th century
silver, painted enamel, filigree
height: 4.8 cm;
diameter 16.3 cm
695 OK 710

101. Small box
Stroganov craftsmen, Solvychegodsk, last quarter of 17th century
silver gilt, filigree, painted enamel
5.2 x 5.7 x 5.7 cm
1504 OK 723

102. Charochka (wine-tasting cup)
Stroganov craftsmen, Solvychegodsk, last quarter of 17th century
cast silver gilt, filigree, painted enamel
3.0 x 8.2 x 8.2 cm
237 OK 719

103. Icon: The Ascension
Veliky Ustyug, late 17th century
shell, silver, enamel, filigree
10.7 x 9.0 cm
64054 OK 9230

IV

NEW TRADITIONS

Gold and Silver of the Russian Empire

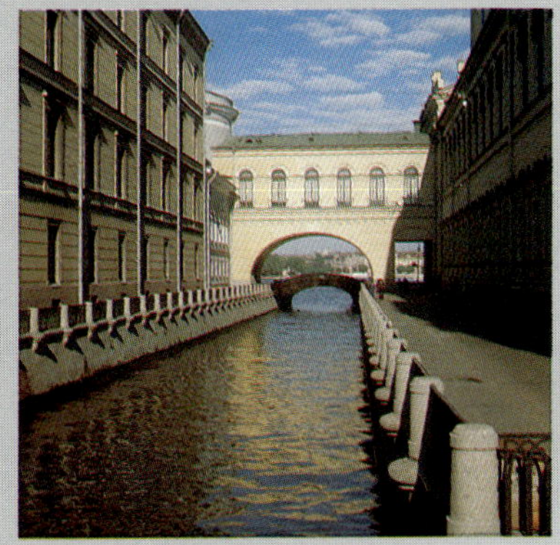

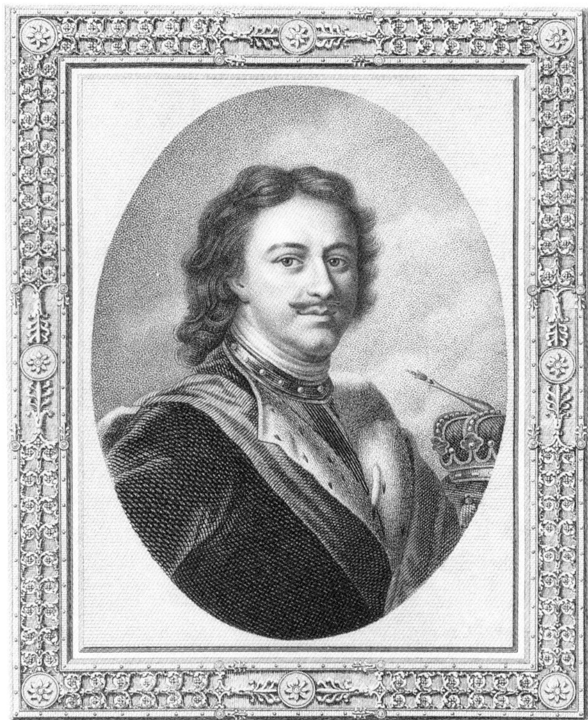

PETER THE GREAT, 1817

Around the turn of the 17th century, Russia underwent a complex but very important transition, from a medieval church culture to a kind of Enlightenment. From this new rationalism during the reign of Peter the Great arose new architectural styles, forms of decorative arts and genres in the fine arts. The economics, politics and culture of the old way of life had been transformed and the outlook of the new Russia found expression in the applied arts.

Because of the great cost of Peter's reforms, jewellery production was placed under state supervision and the sale of gold and silver was strictly controlled. It was prohibited to put a thick layer of gold on manufactured articles or to use it to decorate ornaments and portraits. This attitude was dictated by the basic ethos of the the time: expediency and practicality.

Peter's ukases (decrees) limiting the use of precious metals resulted in a significant reduction in jewellery production, so only a few gold and silver articles from his reign have survived. Articles made by masters of the Armoury Chamber and Silver Row (an organisation of Moscow master-jewellers which produced and sold silver articles during the 17th and 18th centuries) retain the traditional shapes and motifs of the decorative style of the late 17th century. Goblets, vessels, ladles and tankards made at the turn of the century are considerably smaller but varied in shape.

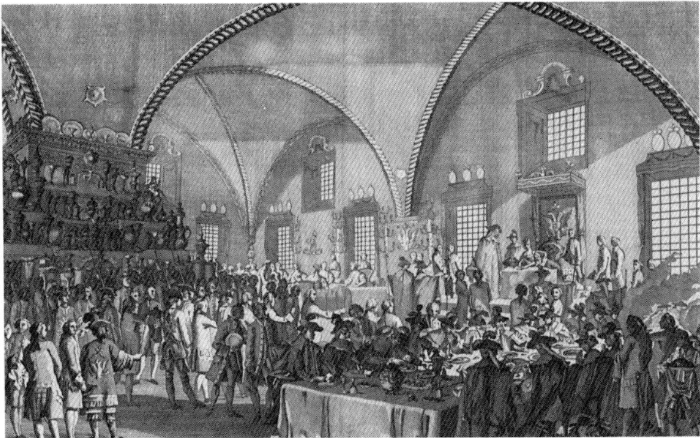

DINNER IN THE GRANOVITAYI CHAMBER (HALL OF FACETS), 1790s

They are decorated with low relief carving, chasing and nielloing. The ornamentation is frequently in the form of flowers, fruit, berries and leaves, sometimes attached to ribbons or twisted into garlands. The articles of the period were usually small so that they did not require much precious metal, of which the source—disused foreign gold and silver coins and silver objects—was limited.

The wide-ranging reforms implemented by Peter I at the beginning of the 18th century led to changes in the Russian way of life. Gradually, with the proliferation of the new applied arts, the old objects disappeared; goblets acquired the shape of cups and mugs were placed on saucers. Wine glasses were originally used only by the aristocracy; bowls were in use among the upper echelons of society as wine vessels and as sideboard ornaments and gifts. Until about 1600 bowls had been mainly imported, but during the 17th century samples of Russian work began to appear and

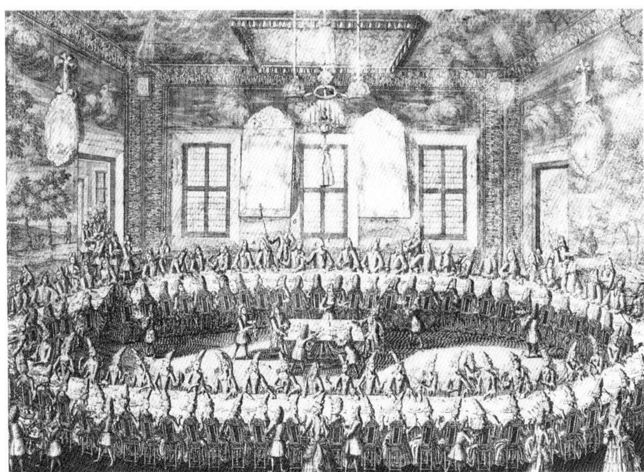

WEDDING OF PETER THE GREAT

by the 18th century, bowls were manufactured in great quantities. The biggest centre of Russian gold and silver work in the 18th century was Moscow, where master jewellers produced an almost limitless variety of precious objects including dishes, icon frames, book covers, liturgical items and ornaments.

Despite the modest, practical and business-like new way of life, Peter I could not entirely prohibit the silver tableware required for ceremonial dinner parties. On 3 September 1711 the Moscow Armoury Chamber was ordered to manufacture a 24-place silver dinner service. The order was: "three dozen plates, two dozen knives, forks and spoons, two dozen serving dishes, four salt-cellars, two trays, a mustard-pot, a vinegar-cruet, two braziers, a wash-tub and a wash-stand." Characteristically, all these items were ordered plain, with no decoration, carving or gilding. Unfortunately, this, the first dinner set commissioned by Peter I, has been lost, as have most silver articles of the first quarter of the 18th century. The new style of dinner service found widespread use, however, and became part of Russian life. Over time, shapes and ornament changed according to stylistic trends in Russian art and fashion.

Along with the traditional chasing and carving, precious objects of the first quarter of the 18th century were decorated with carved symbols and emblems. On a silver tray included in this exhibition (cat. no. 110) there are nine cartouches with carved images on the theme of Love and Death, subjects borrowed by silversmiths from a well-known book, *Symbols and Emblems,* first published in Amsterdam in 1705.

An event unprecedented in Russian history occurred in 1721. Under the Nischstadt Treaty at the end of the lengthy Northern War (1700–21), Russia was proclaimed an Empire and Peter I was given the title of Emperor by the Senate. Petersburg became the capital of the young Empire. Thus dawned a new period in the history of Russian politics and culture.

The second half of the 18th century saw the discovery and exploitation of the country's own deposits of silver and gold, with large-scale mining established at Nerchinsk in the Urals and near Ecaterinburg and Kolyvano-Voznesensk. Domestic mining of raw materials fostered an increase in the output of articles made of precious metals.

In the 1730s and 1740s, the growing popularity of tea and coffee led to the creation of many new types of silver utensils: teapots, coffee-pots, milk jugs, sugar bowls and tongs, tea-caddies, trays and slop-basins. The first samovars (vessels with pipes for boiling water) appeared. These were generally made of copper and were similar in shape to a pot. Later, their shape underwent changes reflecting the evolution of 18th-century rococo and classical styles. In the second half of the 18th century samovars were made of Russian silver. Included in this exhibition is the earliest silver samovar, produced in 1785 (cat. no. 116).

Typical of the decoration of silver objects dating from the first half of the 18th century is the fine chased decoration of smooth interlaced strips, with netting and shells on the protruding bolster surfaces, seen in this exhibition on the sugar bowl and salt cellar made in Moscow in 1740 (cat. nos 111 and 112). By the mid 18th century, rococo curls, palmettes, shells, cornucopias, flowers, leaves and the occasional bird had replaced delicate chasing. Rococo style, which became a determining mode in Russian art from the mid 18th century, was distinguished by an absence of angles, asymmetry of magnificent chased floral ornament, and thick gold background. The shell-shaped sugar bowl of 1762 and tea-caddy of 1775 (cat. nos 113 and 114) are important examples of rococo style.

The affluence of the Russian nobility in the mid 18th century promoted the development of the jeweller's art and helped it keep pace with new styles and fashions. New forms of tableware emerged: for example, spoons for extracting marrow from bones were very popular. These were small, usually silver, with a thin, straight grooved handle (cat. no. 122). Cruet-sets consisting of a stand with flask-shaped vessels for oil, pepper, sugar and mustard, generally with a loop attached to the stand serving as a handle, were widely used at the time. A shell-shaped ladle decorated with flowers and rococo curls, used for mulled wine, was an integral part of aristocratic life (cat. no. 121).

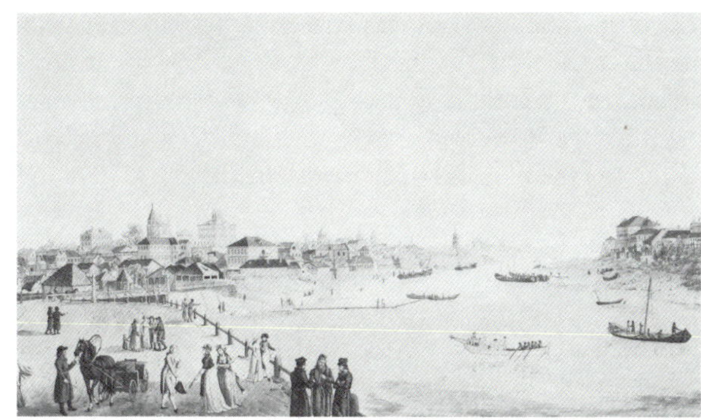

VIEW OF MOSCOW FROM THE LUSKY BRIDGE

A general increase in artistic activity in the second half of the 18th century affected gold and silver work. There was an improvement in the decorative quality of the jewellery produced and a considerable broadening

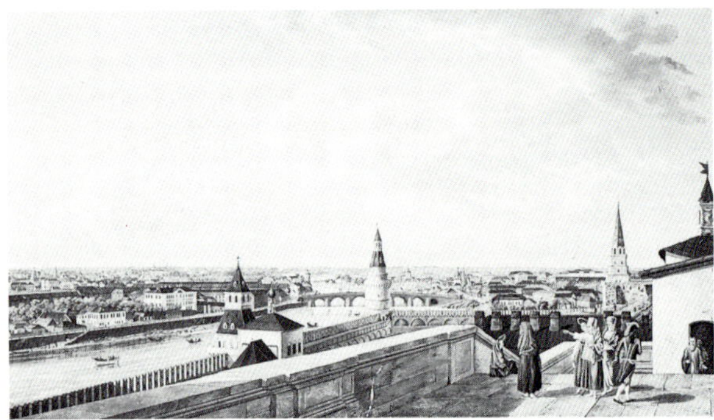

VIEW OF THE KREMLIN FROM THE STONE BRIDGE

of the range of articles manufactured. In the first half of the 18th century, the main users of valuable articles were the royal court and aristocracy. During the later period of prosperity, gold and silver articles were also ordered by merchants and members of the lower gentry. Regional workshops were set up from 1722 with the aim of raising the general level of skill among craftsmen. A great number of provincial artisans were therefore servicing a broad cross-section of the population through the two leading Russian jewellery distributors of the 18th century, in Moscow and Petersburg. Various soup bowls, dishes and salt-cellars of the 1760s to 1780s were decorated with rich chased ornamentation of coquettish curls, leaves, palmettes and rococo shells.

In the second half of the 17th century, during the rule of Tsar Aleksei Mikhailovich, emblems had begun to appear on gold and silver articles. These were not only of decorative value but also of personal significance for the owner; silver dishes were frequently decorated with emblems. The 1764 soup bowl made by the Petersburg master Charles Martin Dubulon (cat. no. 120) continues this tradition and vividly demonstrates the characteristics of the rococo style; an oval bowl is decorated with curls, shells and cartouches with asymmetrical handles and placement of ornament. The emblems of three royal families are also represented. The bowl originally belonged to the Moscow Commander-in-Chief, Prince Mikhail Nikitich Volkonsky, then to his brother-in-law, Field-Marshall Prince Aleksander Aleksandrovich Prozorovsky, and finally to his great-nephew, Master of the Hunt, Prince Feodor Sergeevich Golitsyn. The bowl was therefore a family heirloom, passing down generations, the memory of each bequeather preserved in the heraldic emblems.

The items displayed in the exhibition illustrate the development of Russian jewellery from the heavily ornamented examples of the middle and second half of the 18th century to the simplicity, harmony and elegance of classicism and the Empire style of the turn of the century. As early as the 1770s, along with the decoration of articles in rococo style, Russian gold and silver work showed the restrained line of classicism which recalled ancient Russian patterns, although a smooth surface edged with thin rims of bunches and beads was favoured over total starkness. Three of the articles exhibited, probably belonging to the one tea-set—a teapot, milk jug and sweet container—are decorated with a strip of cast beads along the edges and a flower laid on a leaf, a rococo motif comparatively rare in art objects of the last quarter of the 18th century (cat. nos 127, 129 and 130).

The late 18th-century Moscow tray (cat. no. 128) exemplifies a marriage of classical and early rococo styles. It is decorated with nielloed compositions depicting mythological scenes on a background of architectural landscapes and decorated with palmettes, curls, garlands, laurel leaves and wreaths. Nielloed images and ornaments are placed loosely, leaving greater space for the carved, gilded background on which elegant dark silhouettes parade. This exhibit is a good example of both Moscow nielloing and Russian jewellery in general in the late 18th century, when traditional subjects were incorporated into the contemporary aesthetic.

The most important motifs in Russian classicist ornament were slender garlands and wreaths, vases, bowls, urns, buildings, gods, goddesses, draped historical figures and baskets of flowers. Items made in this style have unconnected ornaments, thus leaving plenty of space for polished surface. The features of classicism are vividly represented in the decorous lines of the 1785 samovar (cat. no. 116). The samovar's smooth silhouette is decorated with delicate flowers and large leaves along the upper edge, thus determining its style and distinguishing it from other articles of the period.

In the first half of the 19th century, Russian classicism completed its development. Geometric forms became typical in jewellery of the period. Ornamentation of articles in the Empire style is found only in individual low reliefs on a smooth polished surface. The most perfect example of the Empire style on display is the spherical spirit lamp kettle of 1808 (cat. no. 131). In the 18th and 19th centuries boilers were widely used alongside samovars. The flame of the spirit lamp made it possible to maintain the required water temperature. In the 19th century boilers were a component of silver

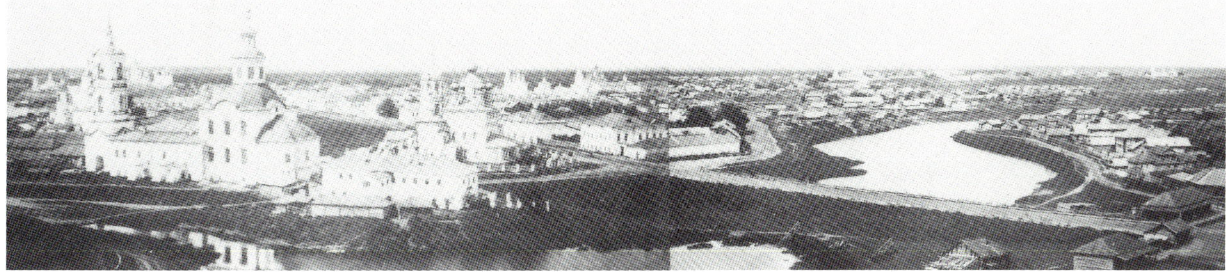

VIEW OF VELIKY (GREAT) USTYUG

tea sets, and were generally favoured over samovars by the aristocracy.

A cold fruit punch vessel (hock cup) of 1825–28 made in the new style (cat. no. 132) consists of a cylindrical vessel on a smooth stand. Decorated with the emblems of Count Aleksander Khristoforovich Benkendorff, the hock cup commemorates his commission as Commander of the Emperor's General Headquarters and Chief of the Third Section of His Majesty's Office.

Many of the works in the exhibition were made by foreign masters. Throughout the 18th century the Tsar's court housed many gold and silver masters of various nationalities, including Swedes, Finns, Germans and Frenchmen. Most operated in the workshop founded especially for foreigners in 1714. They had their own apprentices and mainly filled orders placed by the court and other members of the elite.

Of particular interest are the various nielloed silver articles in the exhibition. The art of niello undoubtedly reached its peak in Veliky Ustyug in the 18th and early 19th centuries. Works by the best masters of the period such as Mikhail Klimshin, Aleksei Moshnin and the brothers A. and S. Popov are masterpieces of the art of jewellery. New techniques were employed: lowered kantharos background, shaded background, gold and silver structures, clouds and birds. Elaborate nielloed articles were called for; the shapes of the scent bottles, snuffboxes and other articles made by the Veliky Ustyug masters were refined and various. The subjects of the neilloed pictures were borrowed from fashionable foreign book illustrations and prints. The high level of professionalism and artistry of the Veliky Ustyug masters of niello was recognized in 1745 when, within a framework of measures taken by the State to raise the standard of art production in Moscow, an order stated: "The best are mainly the masters of niello from Veliky Ustyug – Mikhail Matveev, son of Klimshin, Fenifite from Soli Vyshegod and Yakov Grigoriev, the son of Popov—to call them to Moscow to train the Moscow merchants in this respect".

Eighteenth-century articles from Veliky Ustyug differ from others in the variety of their niello engraving. As a rule, silver masters made pictures by shading or hatching in parallel lines. A nielloed composition, however, is always coupled with a gilt, slightly lower kantharos background. Romantic pastoral and hunting scenes, rural landscapes and architecture were the principal decorative motifs. The birth of Russian genre painting influenced the ornamentation of gold and silver articles made in the late 18th century.

The best nielloed works of the 18th-century Veliky Ustyug masters are included in the exhibition: a 1779 tray showing a feast set against a gilt background of radiating lines (cat. no. 143) and a 1780 casket with nielloed rural landscapes on a similar gilded background (cat. no. 142). Of particular appeal are the snuffboxes of various shapes and sizes; one of the most interesting is in the shape of a book with a nielloed inscription on the binding: "Olfactory book" (cat. no. 141). It is decorated with genre scenes; the inner lid shows a room containing a round table at which a man sits dressed in a robe and turban. A tobacco pouch and open book lie on the table, bearing the inscription "Amuses and enjoys". To the left, in the cartouche, reads "Cereals for the service of a man". Two dandies in cocked hats and French clothes are portrayed at the bottom. They are enticing the man in Russian dress to take snuff from the open box, thus reflecting the spread of the fashion for snuff in Russia in the mid 18th century. The scenes of Veliky Ustyug along the edge of the book represent a new subject in nielled objects from that region in the 1770s. This snuffbox of 1764 shows in its decoration the entire variety and perfection of the technique of Mikhail Klimshin.

In the late 18th and early 19th centuries the Veliky Ustyug masters were using maps and geographic representations of Veliky Ustyug, Vologda and Petersburg as decorative themes. The snuff box of 1796 (cat. no. 139) is decorated with a nielloed map of Petersburg, the capital of the Russian Empire. The fine bottle with a nielloed scene of ladies and cavaliers (cat. no. 144) lends colour to the group of works from Veliky Ustyug. This piece was made by the brothers Afanasy and Stefan Popov at the first Veliky Ustyug factory, which operated from 1761 to 1776.

From 1840 the niello industry of Veliky Ustyug gradually declined. During the 1830s and 1840s, however, the craft was taken up by another northern town, Vologda. Among the best Vologda masters of the first half of the 19th century were Ivan Zuev and Sakerdon Scripitsin. Both were highly professional engravers who made first-class examples of niello against a smooth silver background. Included in this exhibition are a tray of 1837 by Ivan Zuev (cat. no. 146) and a drinking vessel of 1841 by Sakerdon Skripitsin (cat. no. 145). In the second half of the 19th century Vologda experienced a decline in the niello trade as jewellery production diminished throughout provincial Russia.

The main achievements of the gold and silver masters of the 18th century relate to their elegance and high level of proficiency in the production of jewellery. The reforms made by Peter I at the beginning of the 18th century affected almost every aspect of Russian life, including dress and personal adornment. Attendance at assemblies became obligatory for both women and men, thereby destroying the traditionally stringent seclusion of women. In 1700 new, western European styles of clothing were introduced to the cities, presenting new opportunities for Russian jewellers. The nature of ornaments changed accordingly. Brooches of various shapes, hairpins, bracelets, earrings, necklaces and other items gradually replaced the older cassock ornaments.

The growth of the jeweller's art in Russia in the 18th century was stimulated by the establishment of national lapidary works, which led to the widespread use of precious stones in gold and silver jewellery. In 1725, by decree of Peter I, the first lapidary factory was built in Peterhof, near Petersburg, for processing, cutting and polishing gems and diamonds. In 1774 a second factory for processing coloured stones was built in Ecaterinburg in the Urals. Finally, in 1786, a polishing factory was built in Kolyvansk in Altai. Pieces such as brooches in the form of a spray of flowers, richly decorated with diamonds and semi-precious stones, were very popular at the time. Gems

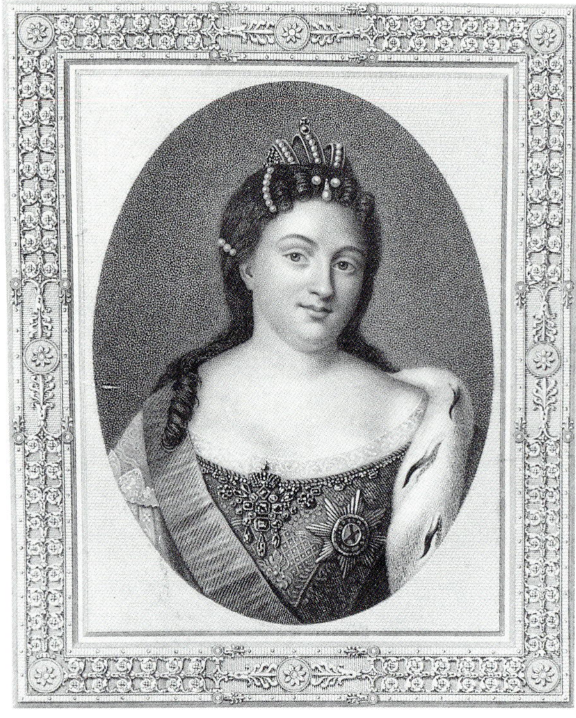

EMPRESS CATHERINE I, 1817

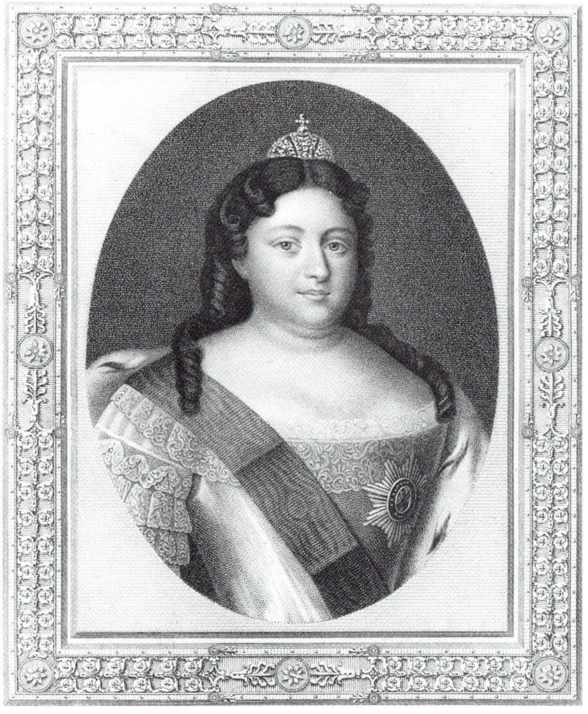

EMPRESS ANNA IVANOVNA, 1817

were hand-picked for their shape, colour and degree of light refraction and were assembled in as naturalistic a way as possible. Such decorative brooches often also served some practical purpose, such as gathering the pleats of a dress or fastening a collar.

Coloured stones enhanced the effect of these pieces, but from the second half of the 18th century the leading place went to the diamond in all its shapes and cuttings. Pearls also played an important role at this time. An attractive example is a pair of earrings made with snow-white pearls juxtaposed with rubies, almandites and other red stones (cat. no. 265).

A passion for antiquity and a tendency for women to dress in the draped style of classical statues led to a paucity of decorative jewellery in the early 19th century. At that time, the fashion was for bracelets of various widths, long pear-shaped earrings and others in the shape of a sickle with ears of wheat, and hair ornaments made of diamonds, rubies, pearls, enamel and semi-precious stones such as agate and topaz. Women's shoulders and necks were left bare. Large tortoise-shell, gold and silver combs, used to support highly-teased hairstyles, were decorated with precious stones, cameos and mosaic. Another feature of the period was a passion, common to many European countries at the time, for carved stones and gems which had thrilled Russia and the west upon their discovery by Napoleon during his Egyptian expedition (1789–1801). Gem-cutting became an applied art in itself. Cameos made by the best Moscow jewellers and those brought from abroad were well-received and were used to supplement diadems, combs, pins, belt buckles and brooches. The horn comb made by Ion Bergstrem (cat. no. 271) is a successful combination of artistic taste and the jeweller's skill.

River pearls held an important place in Russian jewellery art. In ancient times the clothes of the wealthy and distinguished, as well as secular and ecclesiastical articles, were decorated with pearls. As a rule, during the 18th century and the beginning of the 19th century, Russian masters used pearls gathered in abundance from the northern rivers. They used valuable imported pearls only in small quantities. In Novgorod, Arkhangelsk, the Vologda provinces, the Lake of Orega and Lake of Ladoga regions, Ilymen and the White Sea basin, the collection of pearls was carried out in an unsupervised, unsystematic and sometimes barbarian fashion. Premature opening of the shells sometimes killed the pearls before they had ripened, causing great losses.

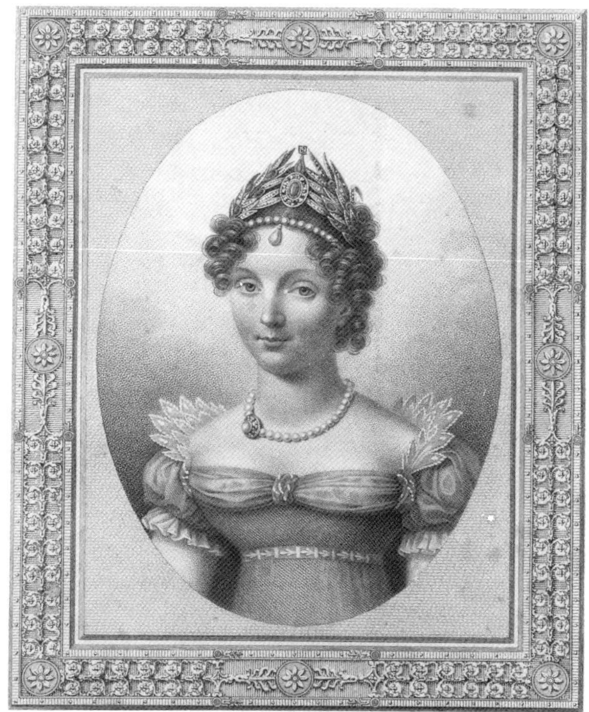

EMPRESS ELIZABETH ALEKSEEVNA, 1817

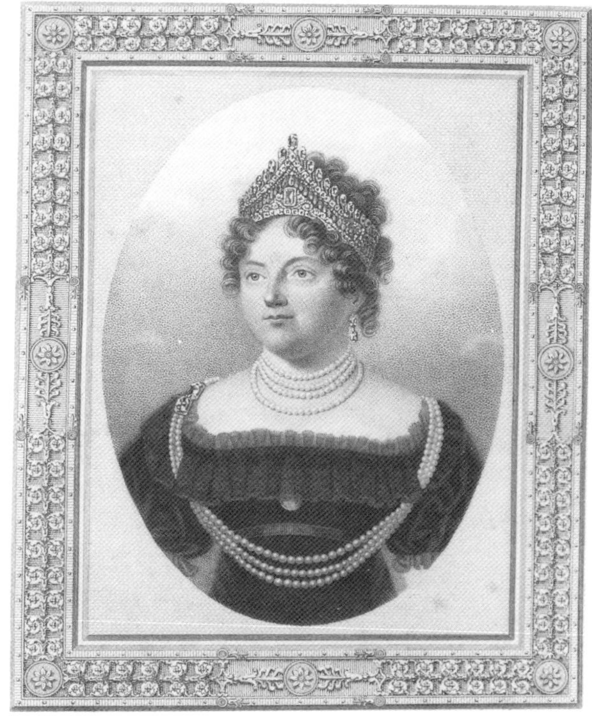

EMPRESS MARIA FEODOROVNA, 1817

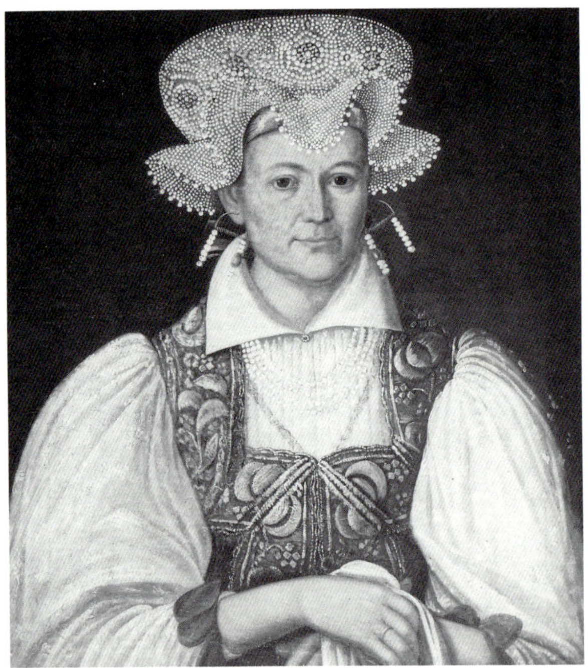

NOVGOROD PEASANT WOMAN, c. 1830–39

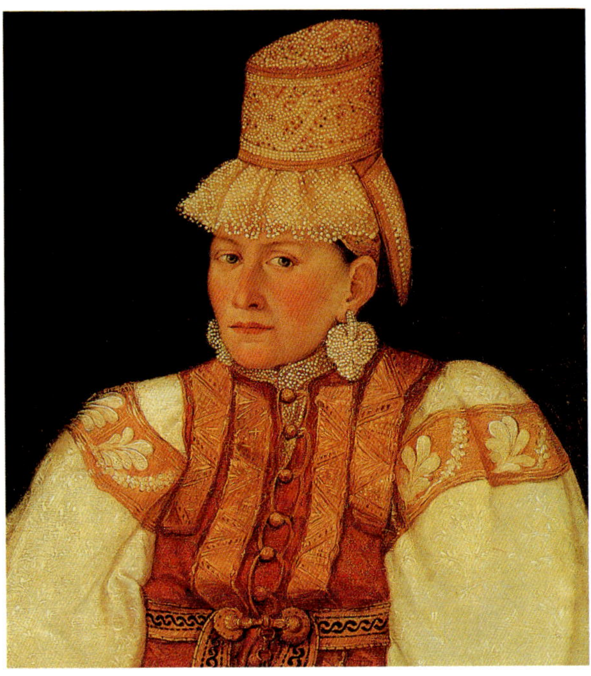

TVER PEASANT WOMAN, c. 1830–39

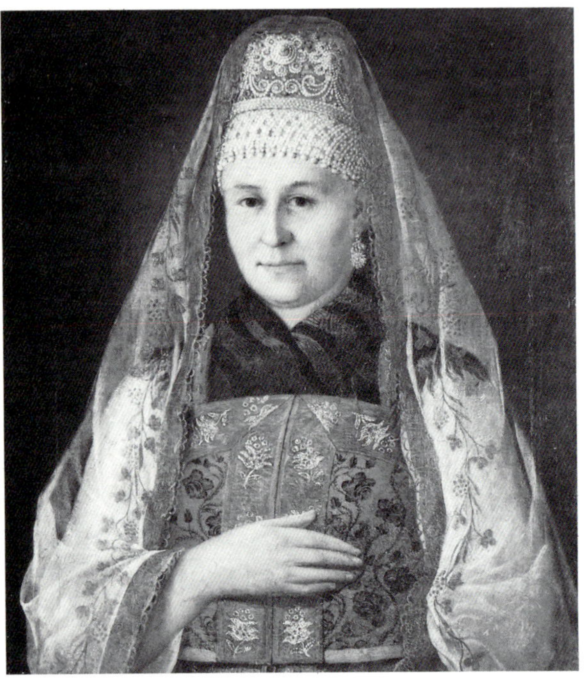

PEASANT WOMAN, c. 1840–49

Right up to the 18th century, however, this part of Russia's economic life was ignored by the government. Only during the reign of Peter the Great were the first decrees on pearl-fishing issued. In 1721 the first decree was adopted by the Bergboard, which had enacted regulations on fishing for pearls. But these protective State measures were ineffective. In 1731, during the reign of Anna Ivanovna, some leniency was exercised in the supervision of pearl-fishers. The Senate permitted general pearl-fishing, although large pearls had to be registered with the Board of Commerce. The pearl diver was promised an award and given permission to use and sell seed-pearls for personal gain. A decree of 1764 confirmed permission for mass pearl-fishing.

This trade was very popular among peasants. They gathered the pearl-shells, extracted and processed the seed-pearls and sewed them on their festive clothes, headdresses and necklaces. It is not known how pearl-fishing ranked against other peasant trades. Judging by the quantity of surviving pearl articles, it seems a small group of pearl dealers appeared among the peasant class, some assuming the role of professional artisans. The pearl industry and the arts of pearl embroidery and stringing grew most quickly during the late 18th and early 19th centuries. Of some artistic interest are light and attractive earrings of the period made from river seed-pearls of various shapes. Included in the exhibition are earrings in the shape of long open-work ribbons folded in two and woven with threads of seed-pearls. Most fashionable were earrings with fine pear-shaped copper pendants covered with a mesh of pearls. The open-work pearl bow gives an effect of lightness and elegance. Such earrings served as additional decoration for peasants' festive costume as well as for the everyday dress of the urban middle class.

104. Goblet
Russia, second half of 18th century
silver gilt
3.0 x 6.3 x 4.3 cm
843 OK 1364

105. Goblet
Moscow, 1790
silver gilt, niello
4.8 x 8.8 x 5.9 cm
51287 OK 134

106. Wine vessel
Moscow, 18th century
silver gilt, niello
11.9 x 5.8 cm
50218 OK 99

107. Drinking vessel
Moscow, 1792
silver gilt, niello
height: 8.0 cm; diameter: 7.0 cm
50209 OK 67

108. Cup
Russia, second half of 18th century
silver gilt, coconut shell
height: 25.5 cm; diameter: 7.0 cm
53031 OK 3812

Wine cup, of typical form, the body resembling a loving cup (bratina or brother cup) in the shape of a pumpkin or bunch of grapes; the stand usually in the shape of a vase, tree trunk or cast human body and base. Such cups usually had a separate lid topped with a spray of flowers or a cast eagle. The 18th century saw an increasing variety in the form and decoration of these types of vessels. There exist examples of humourous, conjugal and double cups made of precious metals, either alone or in combination with other materials. Cups dating from the late 17th and 18th centuries are distinguished by the use of coconut shell with silver and gilt. These developments were due to the general economic and cultural reforms of the country initiated by Peter I.

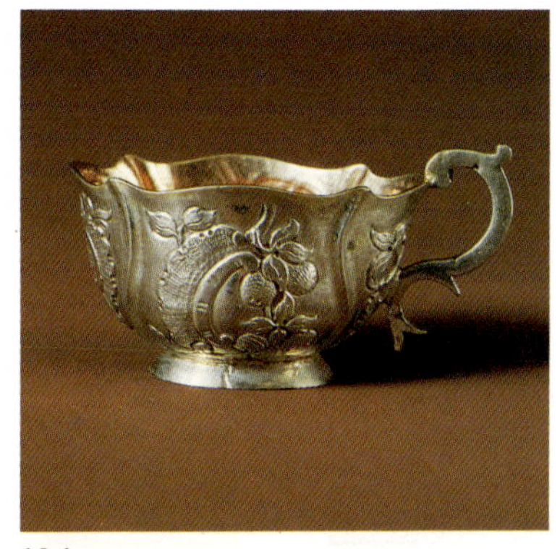
104

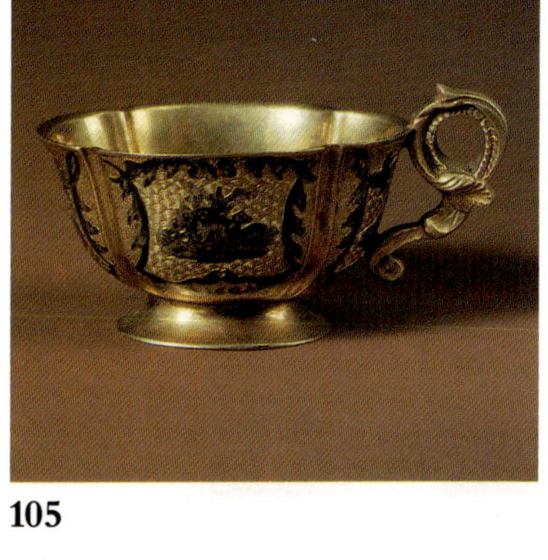
105

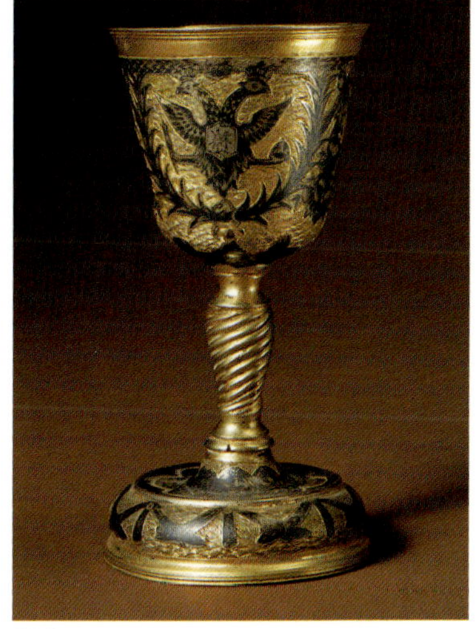
106

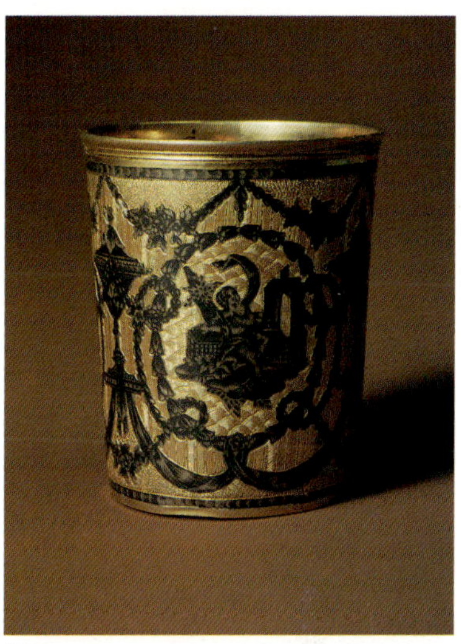
107

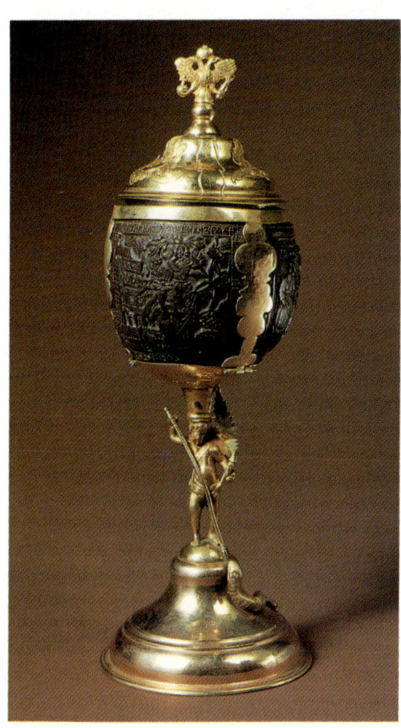
108

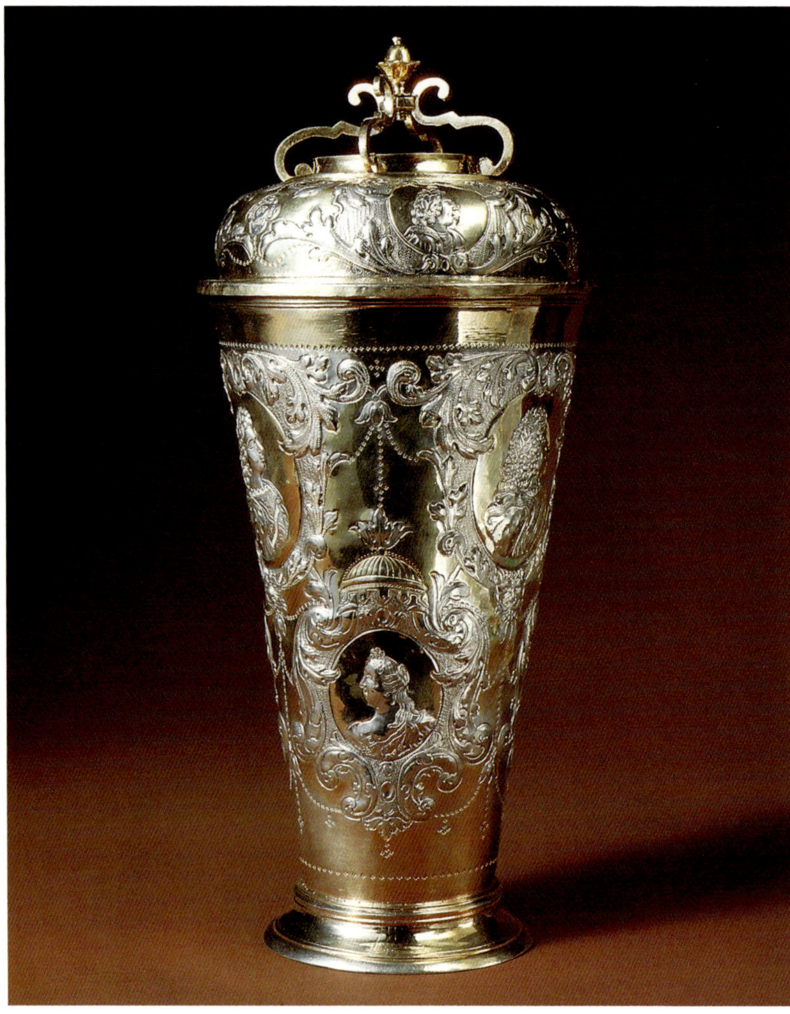

109

109. Wine vessel with cover
Timofeev Nikifor,
Moscow, 1735
silver gilt
height: 32.0 cm;
diameter: 14.7 cm
96368 OK 15192

Medallion commemorating the coronation of Anna Ivanovna as Empress of Russia in 1730 soldered to the centre of the cover. Anna Ivanovna (1693– 1740), the second daughter of Tsar Ivan Alekseevich and Praskoviya Feodorovna (née Saltykova), was the niece of Peter the Great. In 1710 she married Friedrich Wielhelm, the Duke of Kurland.

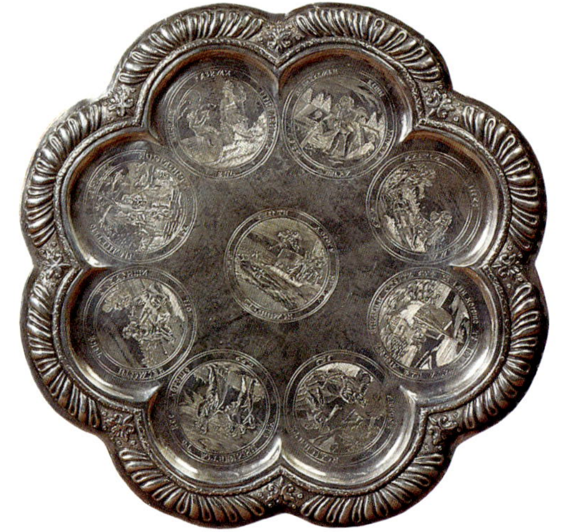

110

110. Tray
Moscow, first quarter of 18th century
silver
diameter: 27.4 cm
4600 OK 4377

Eight-section tray decorated with engraved images from the book *Symbols and Emblems,* arranged in nine circles with the following inscriptions: "796. Nobody will avoid death"; "326. Watered herbs grow better"; "653. To repent in a wrong time"; "654. The best swimmers are those who stick to proper love"; "656. Love is on the alert"; "662. That which is done with love is done well"; "710. Your friend unto death"; "751. Death cannot extinguish love"; "755. The mind is not enriched by wine".

The first edition of the book *Symbols and Emblems* was published in Amsterdam in 1705 and was reprinted in Russia in 1788 and 1811.

111. Sugar bowl
Moscow, 1740
silver
7.3 x 10.9 x 8.5 cm
98716 OK 15778

This is one of the earliest surviving examples of a Russian sugar bowl. Sugar bowls were first manufactured in Russia in the 1730s, co-inciding with the growing popularity of tea-and coffee-drinking. Containers for granulated sugar, which was particularly expensive, were in the form of a rectangular box with a hinged lid and internal lock to enable the mistress of the house to lock away this costly commodity.

112. Salt cellar
Moscow, 1740
silver gilt
13.0 x 14.0 x 14.0 cm
1044 OK 4752

Silver salt cellars were introduced to Russia in the 18th century. In the first half of the 18th century a dish for salt was placed on a high cylindrical stand with a round tray on ball feet.

113. Sugar bowl
Andrei Gerasimov,
Moscow, 1762
silver
9.5 x 17.5 x 11.3 cm
388 OK 5349

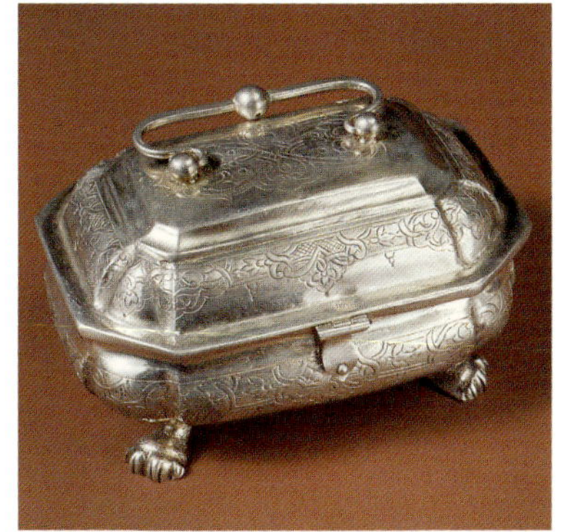

111

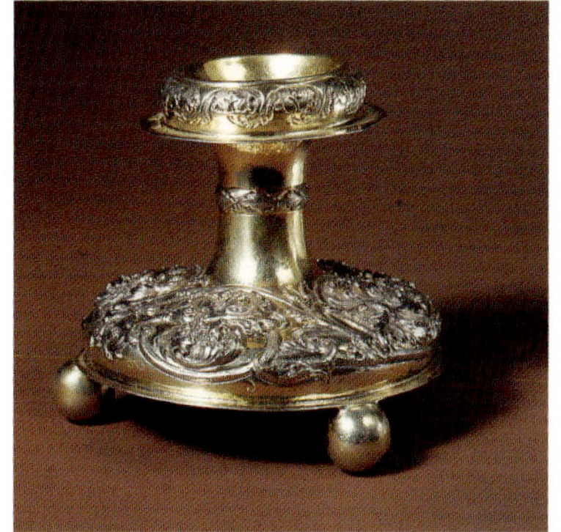

112

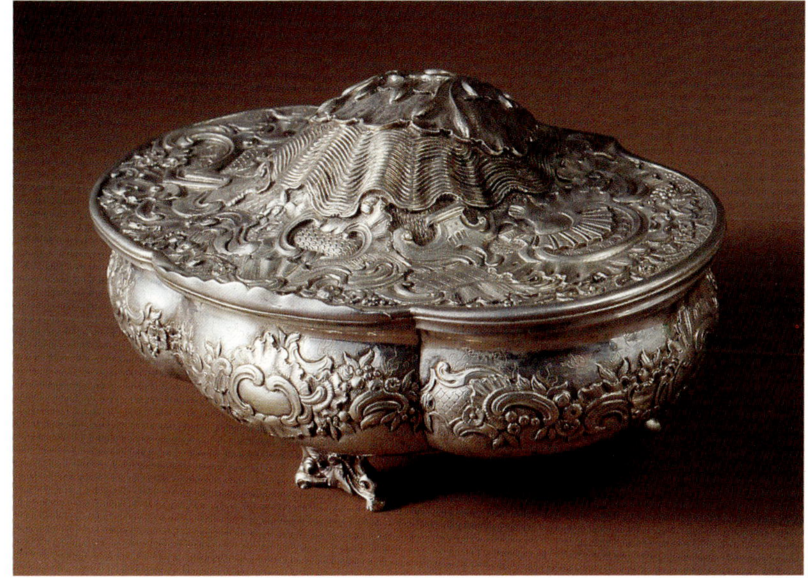

113

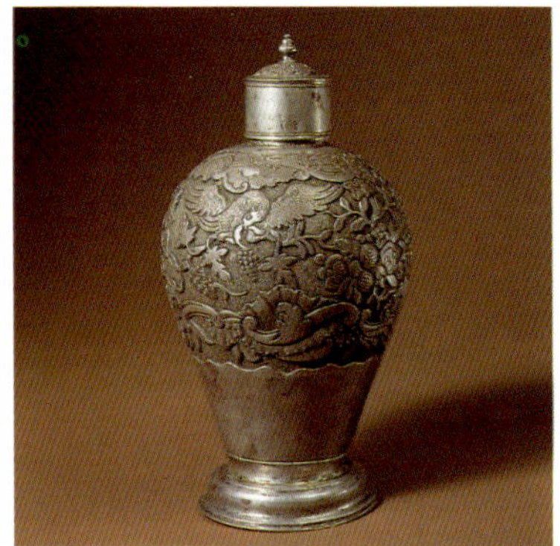
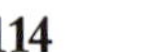

114

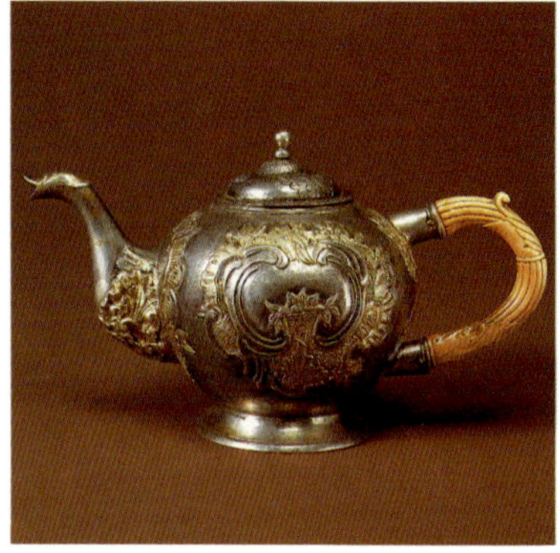

115

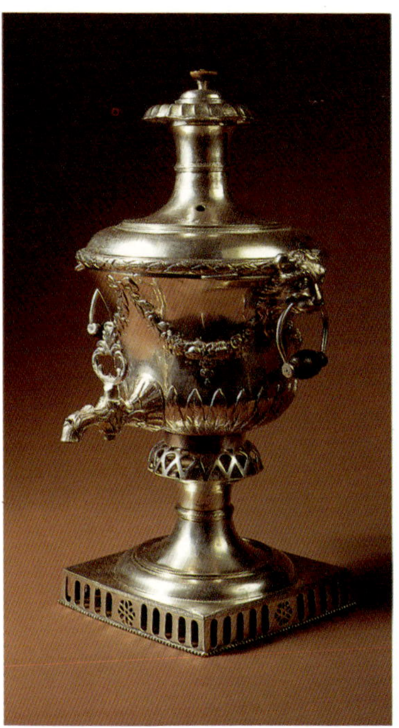

116

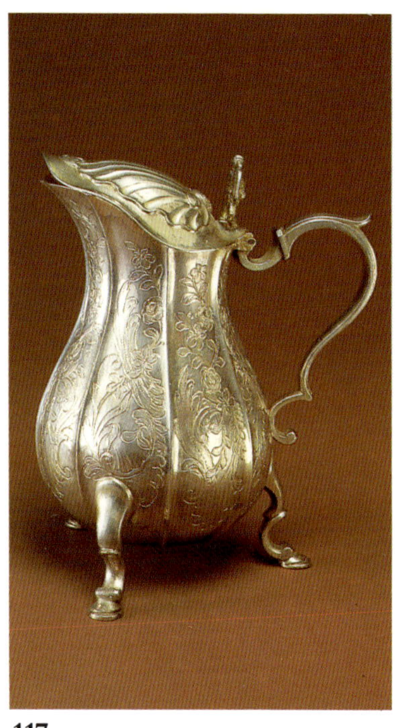

117

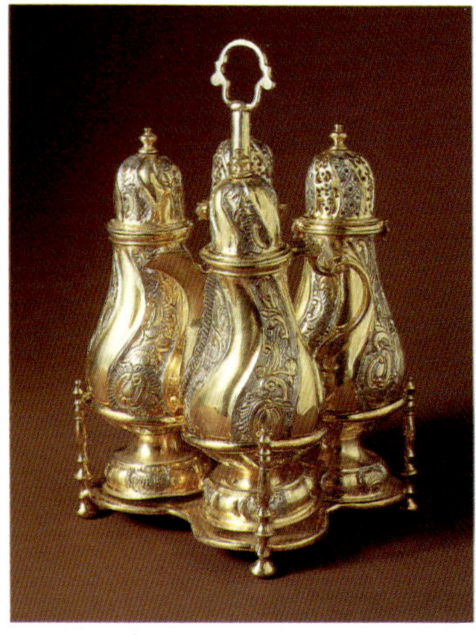

118

114. Tea-caddy
Grigory Andreev Plotov, Moscow, 1775
silver
height: 21.0 cm
265 OK 5298

115. Teapot
Andrei Ivanov, Moscow, 1762
silver gilt, bone
12.8 x 22.0 x 11.0 cm
104985 OK 22825

In the 17th century tea had been used solely as a medicine in cases of consumption and other pulmonary ailments. Teapots became common in Russian domestic life in the second quarter of the 18th century, as tea became a fashionable beverage.

116. Samovar
Moscow, 1785
silver, wood
height: 44.5 cm
53030 OK 3957

117. Milk jug
Ivan Peter Robers, Moscow, 1760s
silver
height: 15.9 cm
51373 OK 4999

118. Cruet set
Aleksander Bogdanov Gilderbrandt, Moscow, 1762
silver gilt
26.5 x 15.0 x 15.0 cm
53054 OK 4959

119. Platter
Ivan Mikhailov Nazarov, Moscow, 1770s
silver gilt
diameter: 32.7 cm
51326 OK 4342

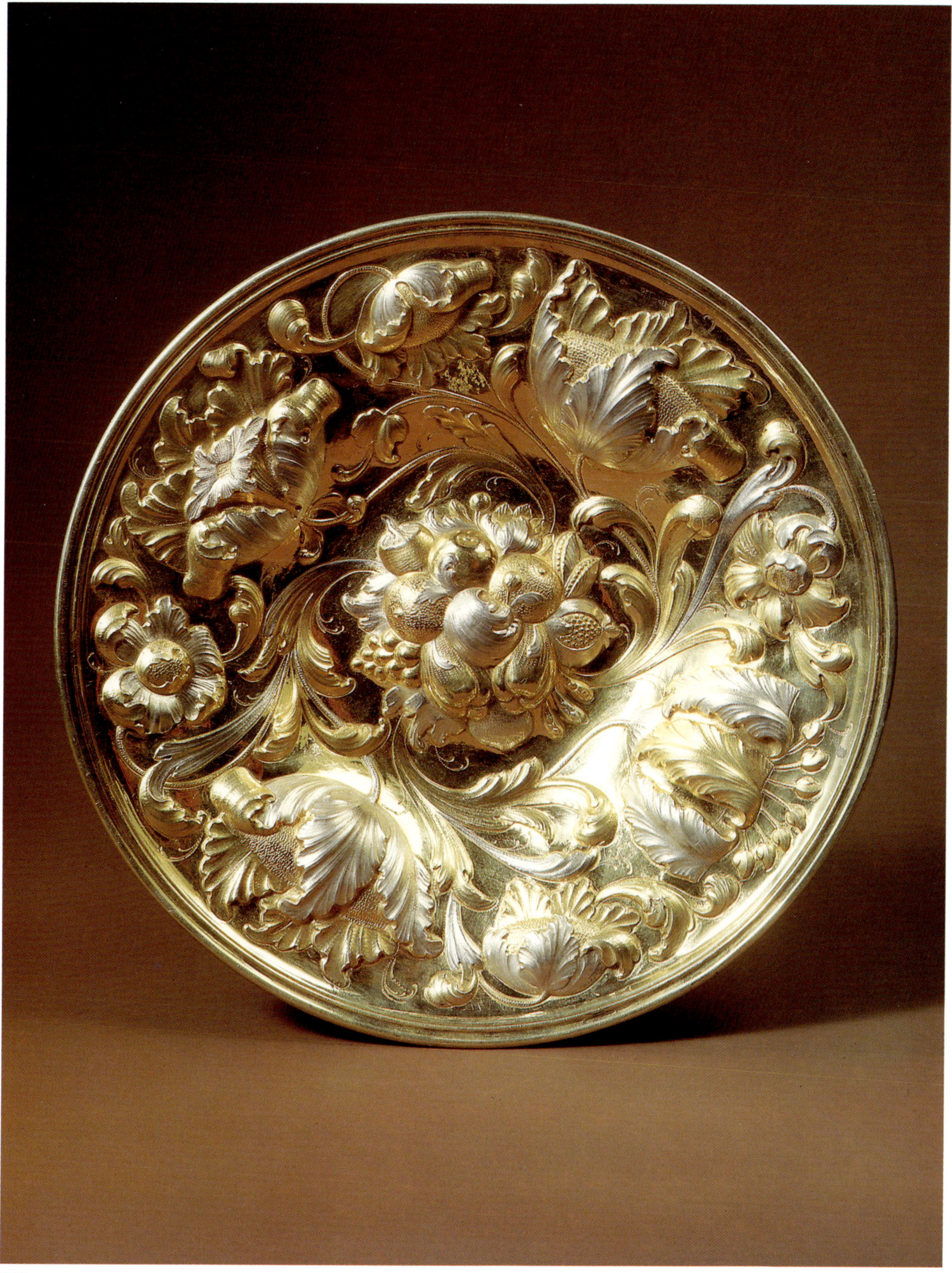

119

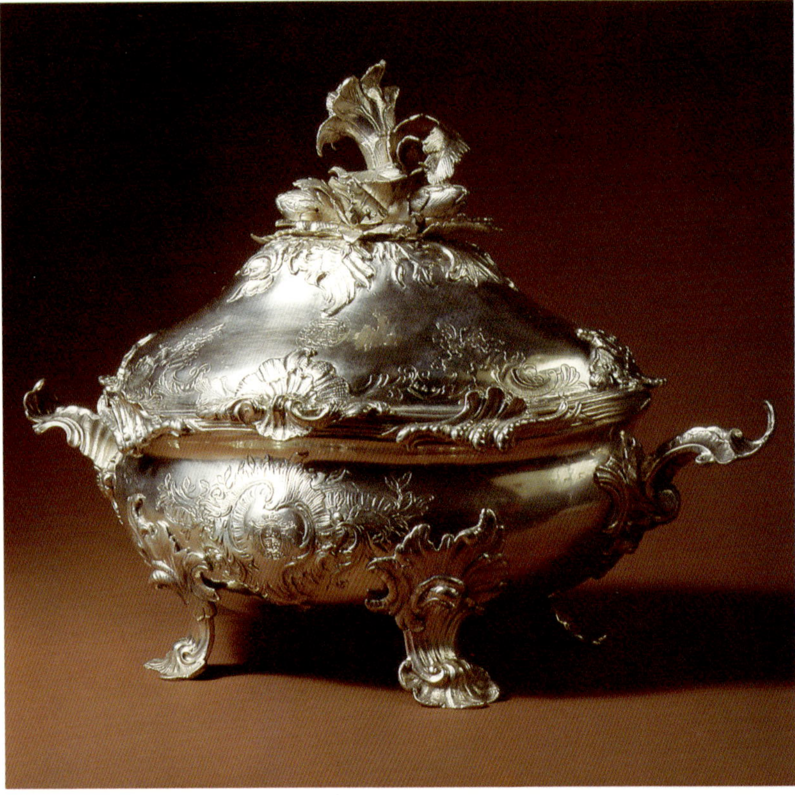

120

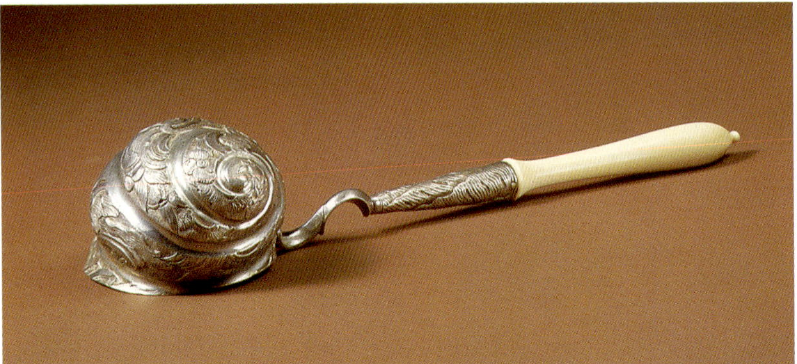

121

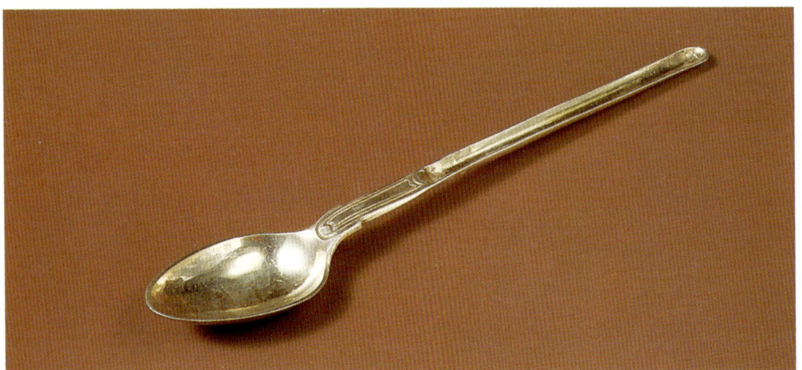

122

120. Soup tureen
Charles Martin Dubulon, Petersburg, 1764
silver gilt
34.5 x 7.0 x 23.5 cm
53030 OK 5455

The body of the tureen is decorated with cast circles and palmettes, figured chased cartouches made up of circles, leaves and rococo flowers and the chased coats of arms of Princes Golitsyn and Prosozovsky. The bowl probably belonged to Prince Mikhail Nikitich Volkonsky (1712–89), who was Commander-in-Chief in Moscow during the reign of Catherine II, as well as ambassador to Poland and the initiator of plans for the division of Poland. His daughter, Helena Mikhailovna (1747–1824) was married to Field-Marshall Prince Aleksander Aleksandrovich Prozorovsky (1732–1809). Their daughter Anna Aleksandrovna married the Master of the Hunt, Prince Feodor Sergeevich Golitsyn.

121. Wine ladle
Russia, 18th century
silver gilt, bone
length: 26.0 cm
53050 OK 3389

122. Spoon for bone marrow
Russia, second half of 18th century
silver gilt
length: 17.0 cm
55133 OK 3469

Spoons such as this, with a narrow, straight, grooved handle, used for extracting the marrow from the bones of boiled meat, were in daily use in the 18th century.

123. Soup tureen
Moscow, 1780s
silver gilt
28.0 x 26.0 x 26.0 cm
51338 OK 5446

124. Soup tureen
Designed by Karl Ivan Tammelin, Petersburg, 1758
silver gilt
14.0 x 24.5 x 13.0 cm
61038 OK 6031

125. Platter
Moscow, last quarter of 18th century
silver gilt
51.7 x 39.0 cm
51329 OK 4346

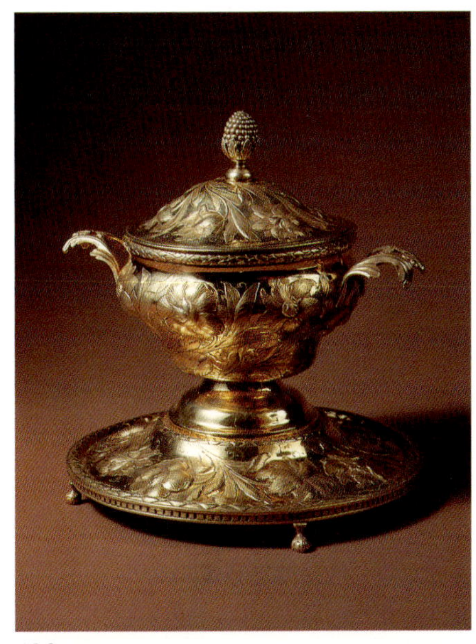

123

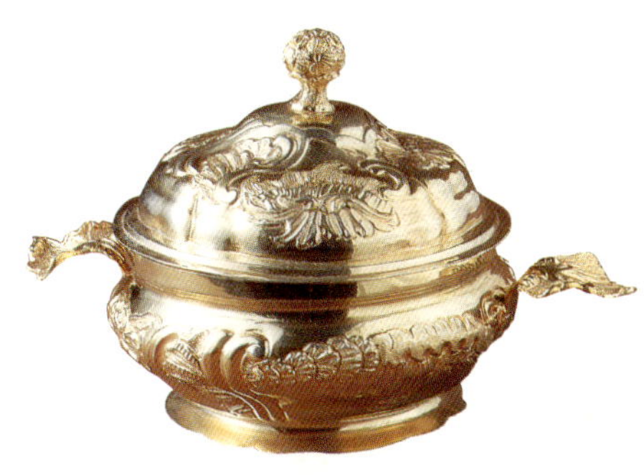

124

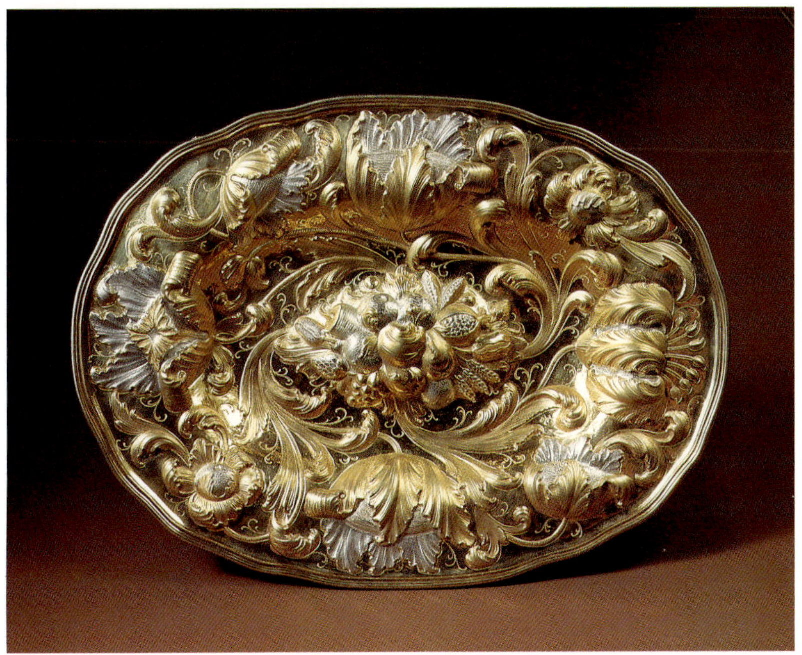

125

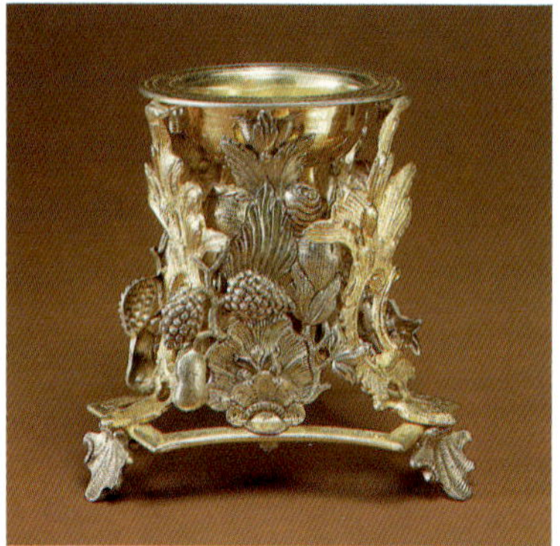

126

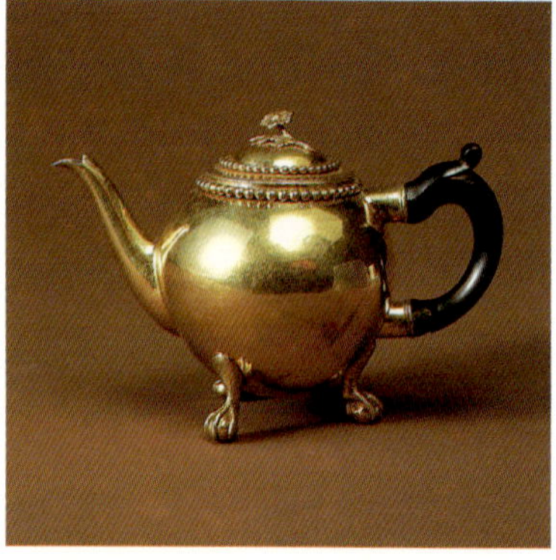

127

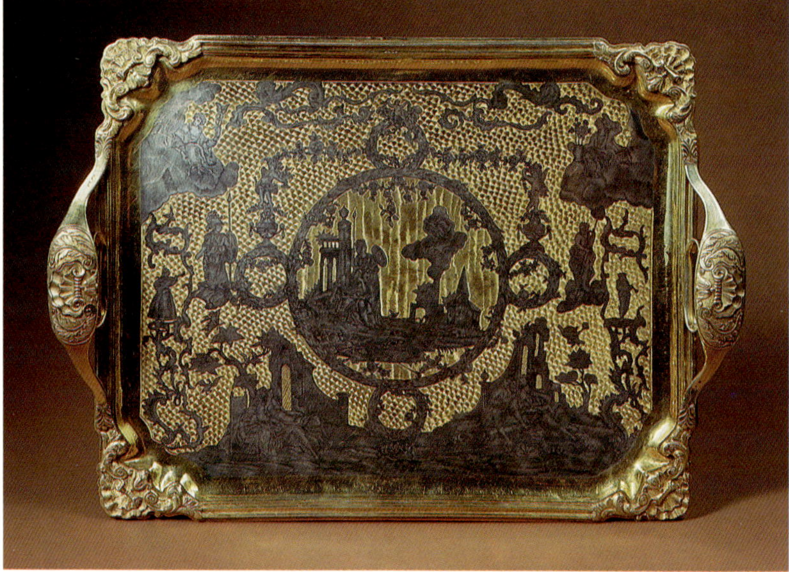

128

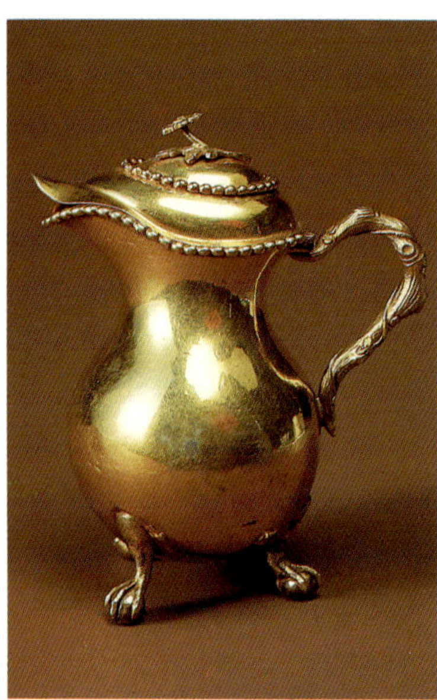

129

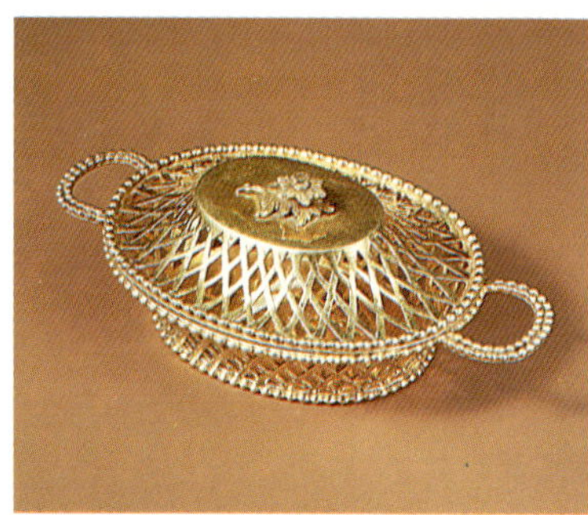

130

126. Salt cellar
Petersburg, 1767
silver gilt
12.1 x 8.0 x 8.0 cm
60080 OK 6924

127. Teapot
Petersburg, last quarter of 18th century
silver gilt, wood
height: 12.7 cm
7091 OK 5158

128. Tray
Moscow, late 18th century
silver gilt, niello
54.0 x 38.7 cm
51315 OK 586

Trays, which had been in daily use in Russia since the 18th century, varied in shape according to their purpose and date of manufacture. They were put on the table under a samovar or kettle, while two-handled trays were used to serve food or drink.

129. Milk jug
Petersburg, last quarter of 18th century
silver gilt
height: 14.5 cm
7091 OK 5157

130. Sweet container
Petersburg, 1780
silver gilt
5.4 x 15.8 x 8.8 cm
7091 OK 5073

131. Kettle
Moscow, 1808
silver gilt
height: 45.0 cm
51413 OK 3938

Kettles were used in Russia from the 18th century as part of a tea set and were generally preferred to samovars by the nobility and aristocracy. They comprise a kettle for boiling water on a stand over an alcohol lamp and come in various shapes: pear, sphere, flattened sphere, bell or truncated cone. The stand resembles a small trivet on figured legs joined at the top by a ring on which the kettle is placed.

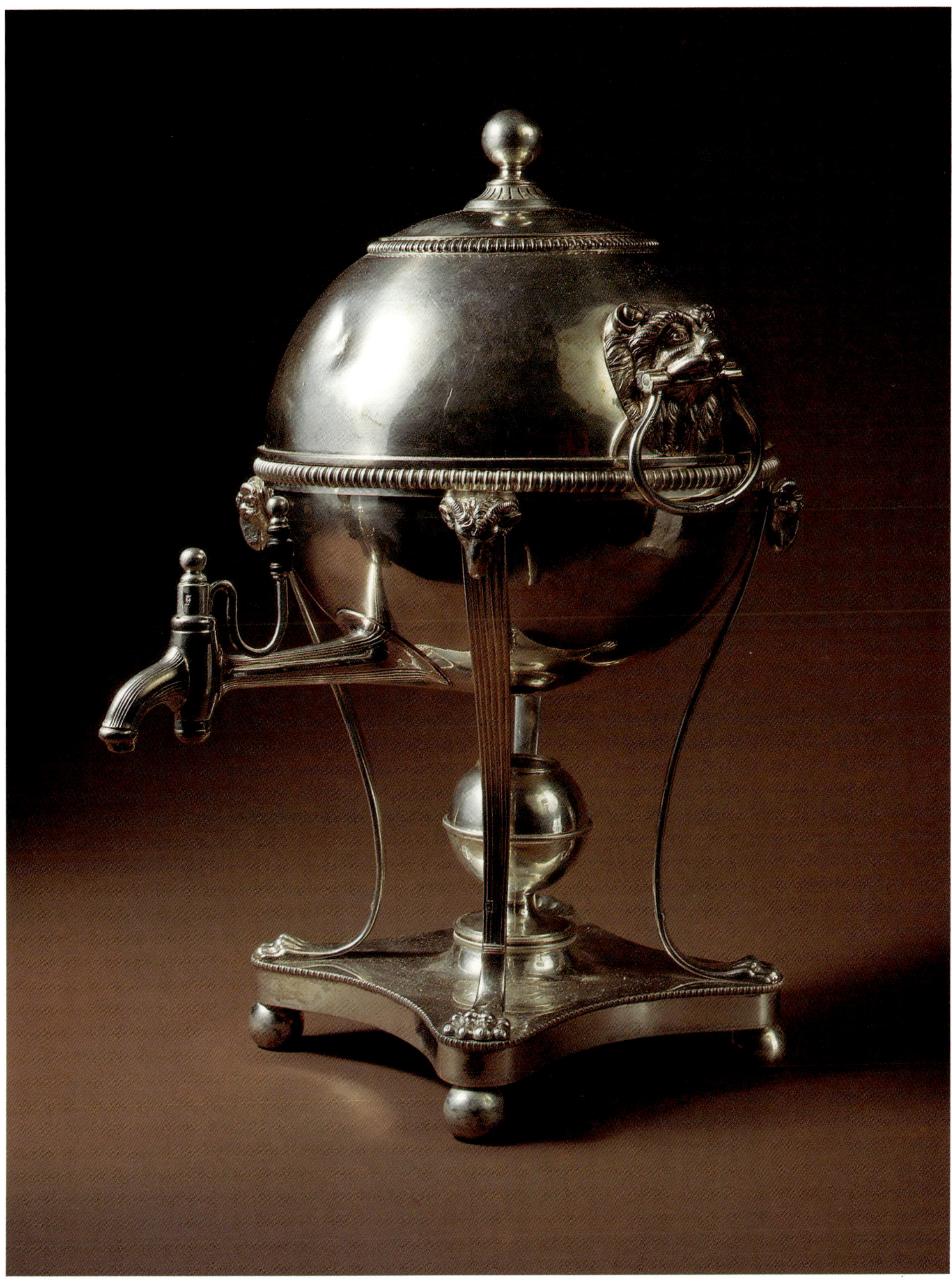

131

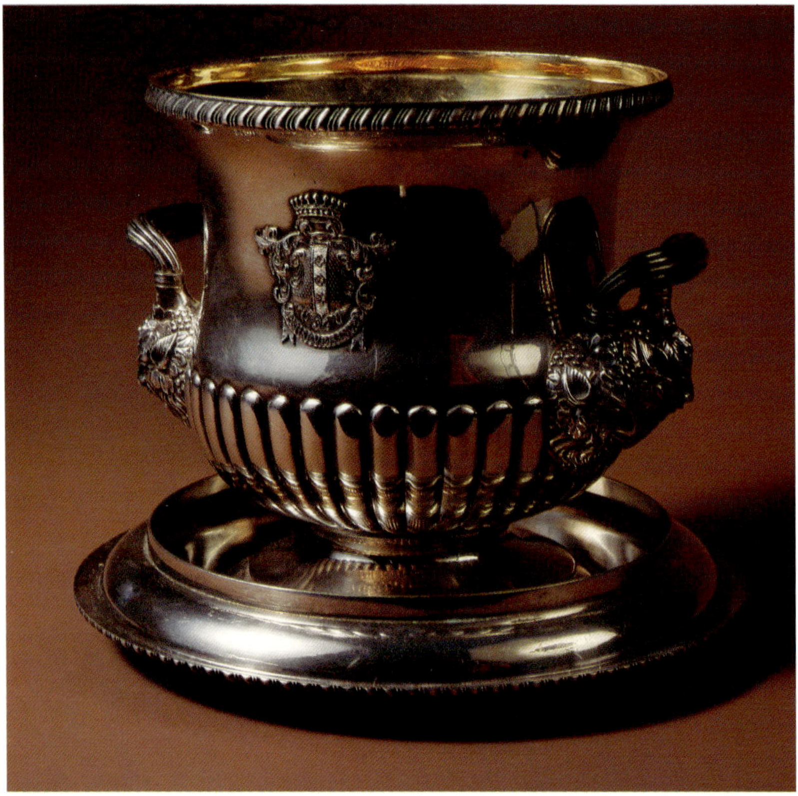

132

132. Hock cup on stand
Khristian Andrei Yantsen, Petersburg, 1825–28
silver gilt
24.0 x 19.5 x 19.5 cm; diameter of stand: 26.0 cm
106580 OK 23071

On each side of the cylindrical, vase-shaped hock cup is the coat of arms and Latin motto "Constancy" of Count Aleksander Khristoforovich Benkendorff (1783–1844). In 1798 Benkendorff was promoted to the position of Ensign of the Life Guards of the Semenov Regiment and was appointed aide-de-camp to Emperor Paul, who reigned from 1796 to 1801. In 1826 Emperor Nikolai I, who reigned from 1825 to 1855, appointed Benkendorff Commander of the Emperor's General Headquarters and Chief of the Third Section of His Majesty's Office. In 1828 he was appointed General of the Cavalry.

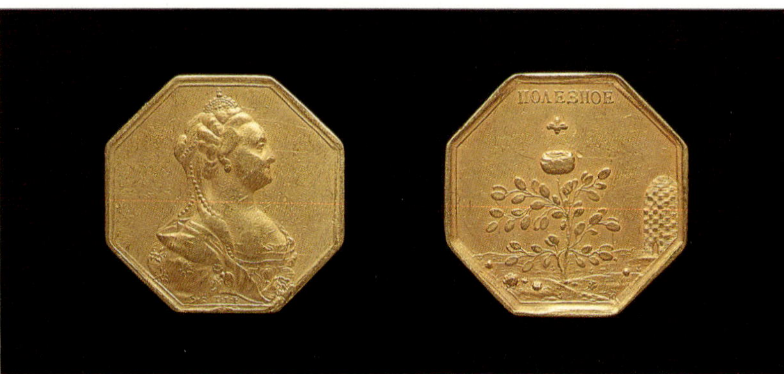

133

133. Counters for card games
Petersburg, last quarter of 18th century
gold
3.4 x 3.4 cm
81552 OK 13715

The obverse of each octagonal counter bears a bust-length profile of Catherine II, turned to the right; the reverse is decorated with Catherine's insignia, a flower, bee and beehive, and the motto "Useful".

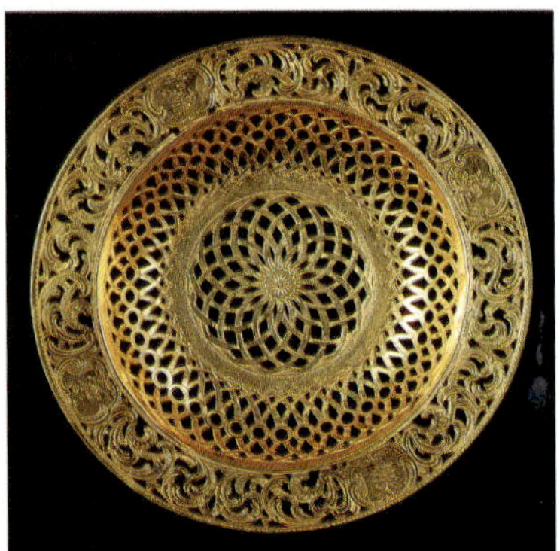

134

134. Plate
Petersburg, last quarter of 18th century
gold
19.6 x 19.6 cm
81518 OK 13551

Small pierced plate decorated with impresssed figures, carved botanical designs and the insignia of Empress Catherine II: flowers, bees and a beehive.

Catherine Alekseevna II (1729–96, née Princess Sofia Frederik August Anglalt-Tserbsk) married Peter III and was Empress of Russia from 1762.

135. Counters for card games
Petersburg, last quarter of 18th century
gold
diameter: 2.5 cm
81551 OK 13714

Each pierced counter bears a medallion with the lightly engraved flower, bee and beehive emblem of its owner, Catherine II.

The counters were used to tally up tricks during card games and were exchanged for money at the end of the game. They varied in form: circular, rectangular, oval or octagonal, according to their value. One side of the counter bore the suit of the cards, the other the coat of arms, motto, emblem or monogram of the owner. Counters from the 18th and 19th centuries have been preserved.

136. Counters for card games
Petersburg, last quarter of 18th century
gold
5.4 x 1.0 cm
81550 OK 13713

The flat, rectangular, open-work counters are decorated with the flower, bee and beehive emblem of their owner, Catherine II.

137. Snuffbox
Paris, 1744–45; setting: Veliky Ustyug, second half of 18th century
silver, niello, mother-of-pearl
4.2 x 7.8 x 6.0 cm
467 OK 335

138. Snuffbox
Veliky Ustyug, second half of 18th century
Silver gilt, niello
5.2 x 10.8 x 5.8 cm
456 OK 344

139. Snuffbox
Ivan Ostrovskikh, Veliky Ustyug, 1796
silver gilt, niello
diameter: 8.3 cm
3548 OK 277

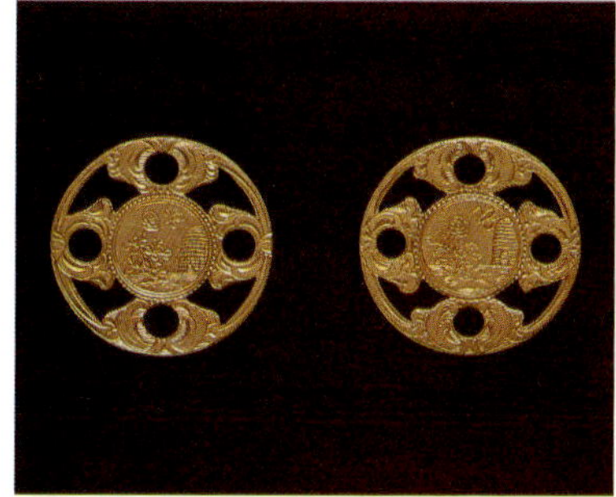

135

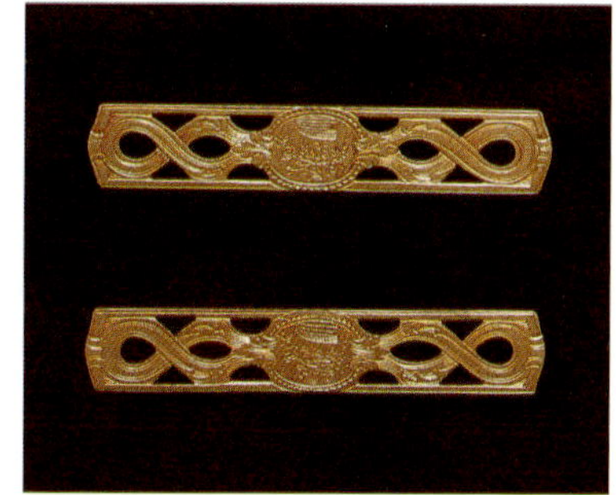

136

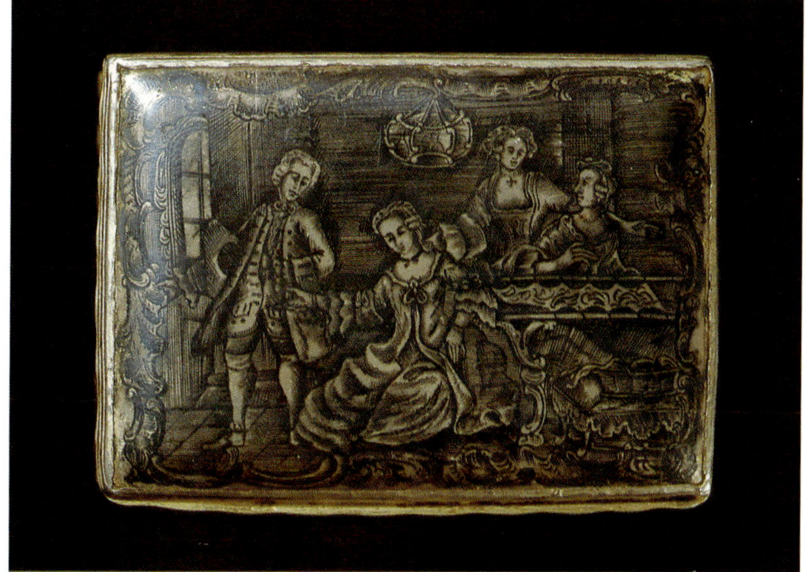

137

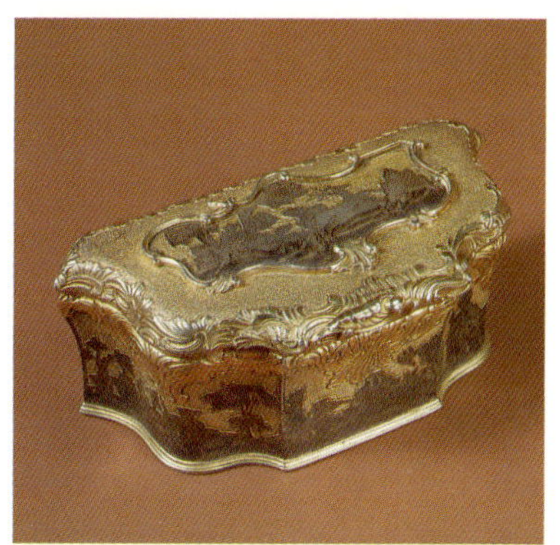

138

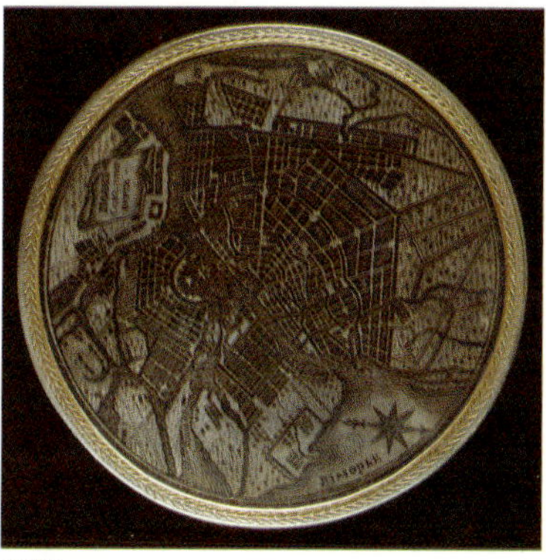

139

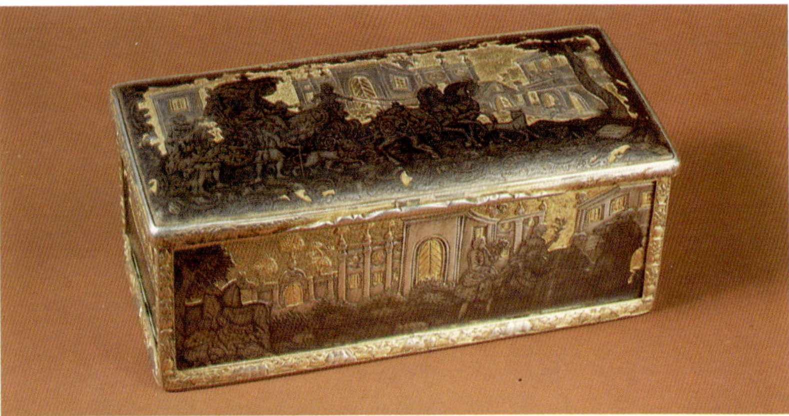

140

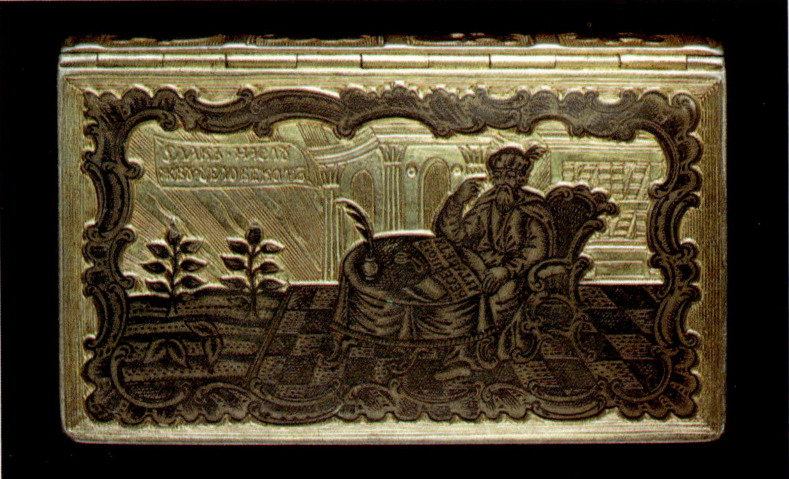

141

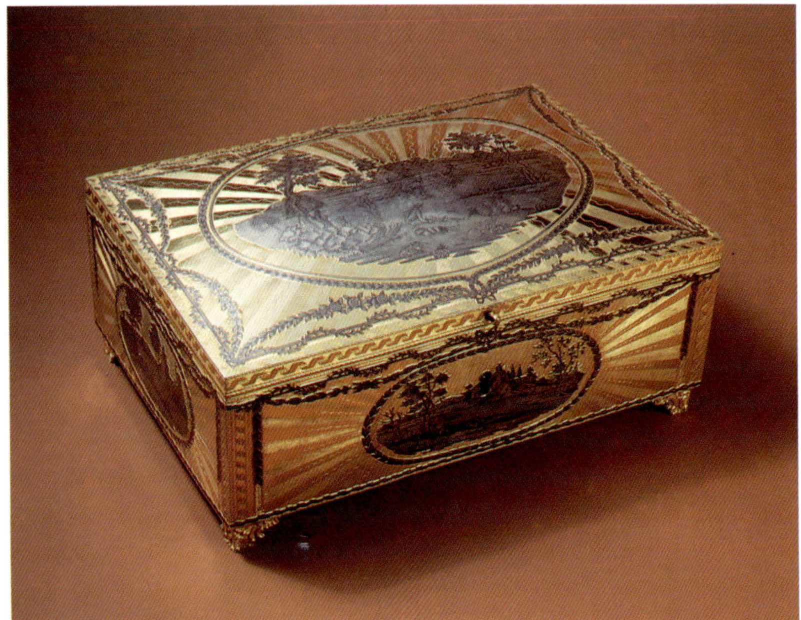

142

140. Snuffbox
Aleksei Moshnin, Veliky Ustyug, 1779
silver gilt, niello
2.5 x 9.4 x 5.7 cm
50628 OK 324

141. Snuffbox
Mikhail Matveev Klimshin, Veliky Ustyug, 1764
silver gilt, niello
4.7 x 12.0 x 6.0 cm
50621 OK 333

142. Casket
Veliky Ustyug, 1780
silver gilt, niello
16.8 x 36.8 x 25.0 cm
51408 OK 430

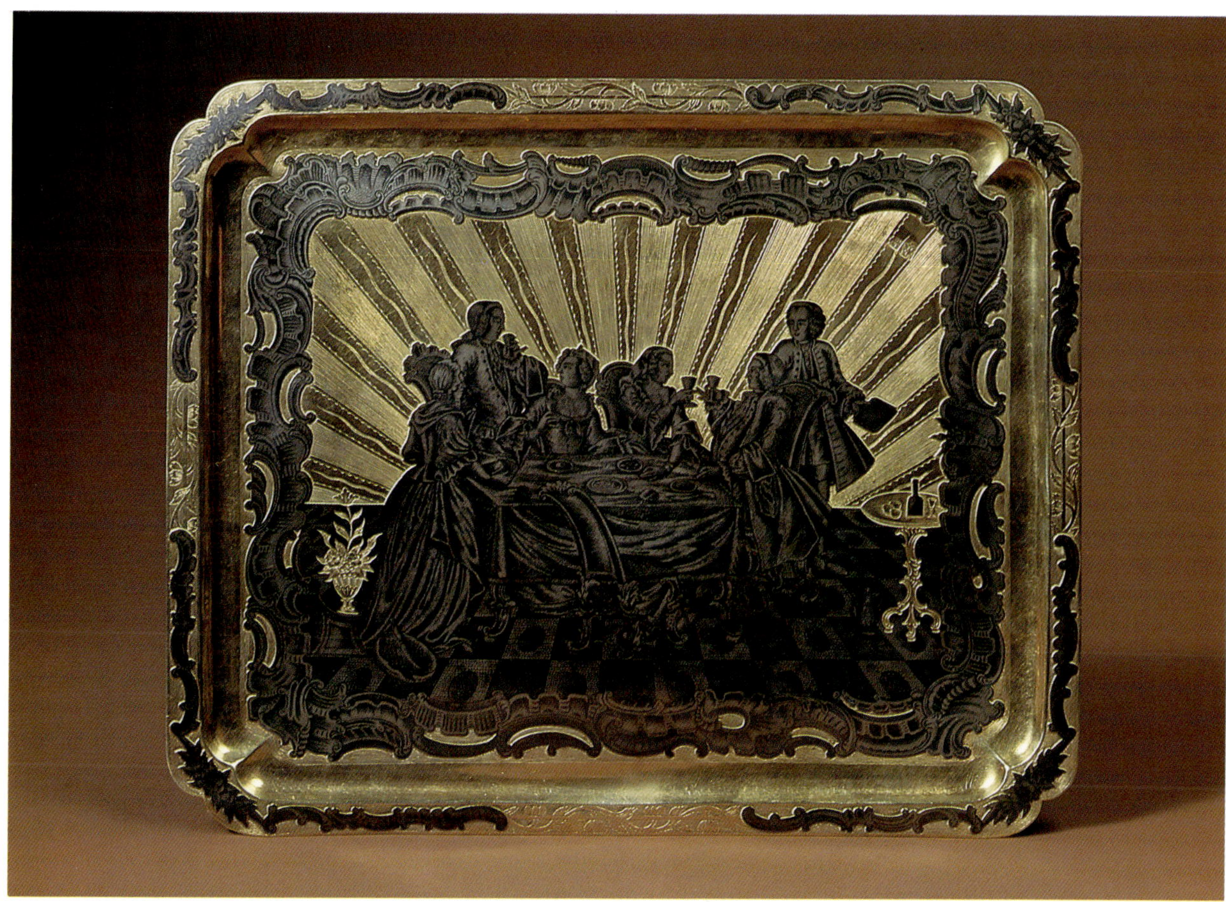

143

143. Tray
Aleksei Moshnin, Veliky
Ustyug, 1779
silver gilt, niello
28.4 x 34.0 cm
14170 OK 587

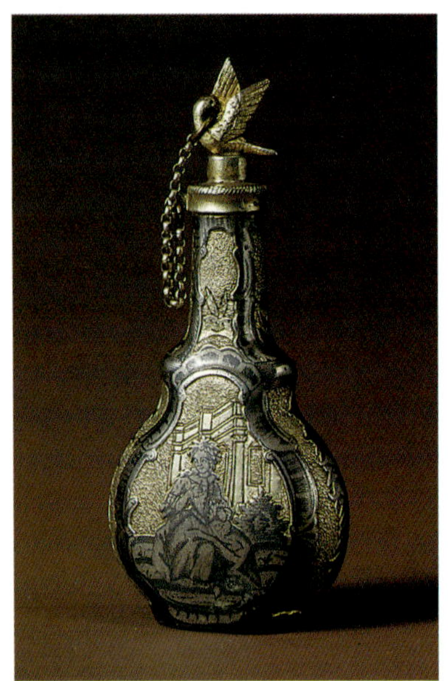
144

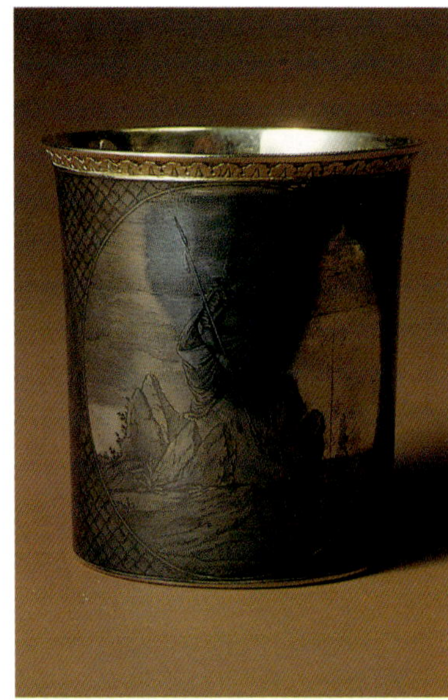
145

144. Bottle
factory of Afanasy and Stefan Popov, Veliky Ustyug, second half of 18th century
silver gilt, niello
8.3 x 3.6 cm
3746 OK 213

145. Drinking vessel
Sakerdon Skripitsin, Vologda, 1841
silver gilt, niello
7.7 x 7.1 x 7.1 cm
59965 OK 5473

146. Tray
Ivan Zuev, Vologda, 1837
silver gilt, niello
32.5 x 25.0 cm
53030 OK 186

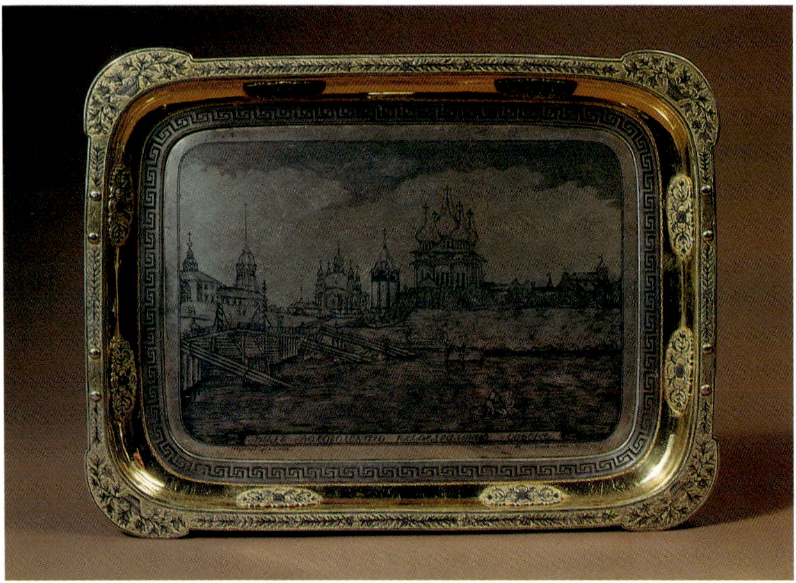
146

V

REWARDS

Decorations and Honours

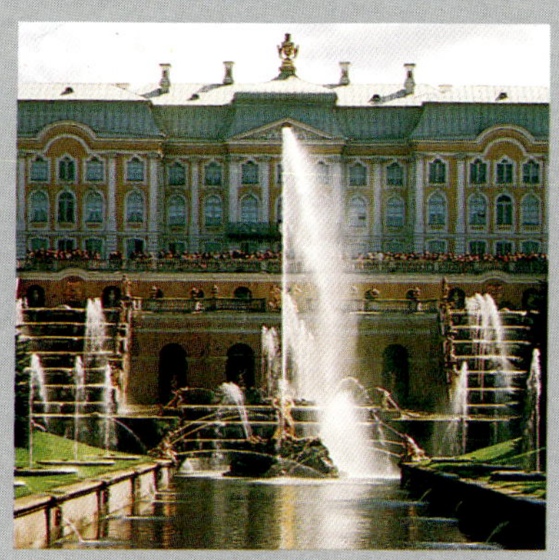

Decorative art came into its own in the silver and gold work of 17th and 18th century Russia.

Before merit orders were introduced in Russia, rewards for services to the Tsar and the Motherland took the form of money or valuable items such as fur coats, horses and silverware.

Initially, silverware for presentation was not made to order but simply taken from the store in the Tsar's treasury. However, by the 17th century the silver ladle had come to represent honourable distinction in diplomacy, military service, tax collection, trade and the arts. The Silver Chamber in the Kremlin began producing presentation ladles decorated with engraved insignia and inscriptions relating to the Tsar and the recipient's merits.

There were two main groups of decorative silver ladles: those given for tax collection and to Cossacks for unfailing loyalty.

During the 17th century the main sources of revenue for the troubled Russian treasury were customs and public-house duties. Each tavern had a fixed rate of annual payment that was determined by the previous year's duties. The Tsarist government appointed "people wealthy and prosperous" and "of the best kind" as tax collectors. For duties collected above the standard amount, tax collectors received a reward and for particularly large returns, ladles were awarded, the size and weight of the ladle reflecting the amount of revenue raised.

In the early 18th century the Tsar replaced elected tax collectors with "tax contractors": merchants whom it was not necessary to reward, except in outstanding cases, so production of silver ladles diminished. At the same time, ladles were used less frequently as drinking vessels and became engraved vases.

Included in the exhibition is a massive silver ladle (cat. no. 148) granted to Moscow merchant Mikhail Gusyatnikov for his initiative in proposing to the Senate that he establish public houses in Moscow and St Petersburg "thus encouraging others to participate in the trade". The ladle is in the form of a boat with high sides and wavy edges; large cast eagles adorn both sides, holding a garland and a twig in their beaks. However, it is considered a ladle by custom only, as it in no way resembles the old Russian boat-shaped prototype.

Many silver ladles granted to the Cossacks of Don, Volga and Yaik "for faithful service" have survived. The hardy Cossack troops had long been used by the Tsarist government for the defence of Russia's south-eastern frontiers against nomadic tribes and to help expand the state's territory. From the mid 18th century the most distinguished Cossacks were awarded, among other privileges, silver ladles engraved with the double-headed eagle and bearing an inscription with the Tsar's title, the name of the recipient and his virtues. An excellent example in this exhibition is a silver, gilded ladle bestowed in 1761 by the Empress Elizabeth Petrovna to the Chief of the Yaik regiment, Feodor Andreev Borodin, "for his faithful service" (cat. no. 149). The most interesting exhibit is a silver ladle bestowed in 1682 by the Tsar Feodor Alekseevich to the architect of the Armoury Chamber, Ivan Ievlevich Saltanov, "for churches, mansions and many other fine buildings" (cat. no. 147). The ladle, decorated with the double-headed eagle at the bottom, a pecking bird on the handle and inscription on the side, is of great artistic and historical value as it is considered to be a rare encouragement of achievement in the field of art.

Another type of award is the Tsarist gold medal for military service: a coin which varied in weight and size according to the rank of the recipient. In the 17th century, they were as widespread as ladles.

In the late 17th century Tsar Aleksei Mikhailovich, in consultation with foreign heralds, designed a new coat of arms for the Russian State. From then on medals were decorated with engraved double-headed eagles below three crowns, a unicorn on one side and St George the Victorious on the reverse. Chased gold medals surrounded by precious stones and pearls became distinguished awards for military service; the higher the military rank of the recipient, the larger and heavier the medallion. Among the first recipients of these were participants in the civil war for the Reunification of the Ukraine and Russia (1648–54), see cat. no. 150.

At the end of the 17th century the first Russian Order, "St Andrew Protokletos", was established by Peter I. Displayed in this exhibition are examples of the Order, which is in the shape of St Andrew's cross in blue enamel with a picture of the crucified saint (cat. no. 151). It was granted rarely; throughout the reign of Peter I, which was rich in outstanding military and historical events, the holders of the Order of St Andrew Protokletos numbered less than 40. Peter the Great himself was the seventh recipient of the Order, presented in 1703 for commanding the operation

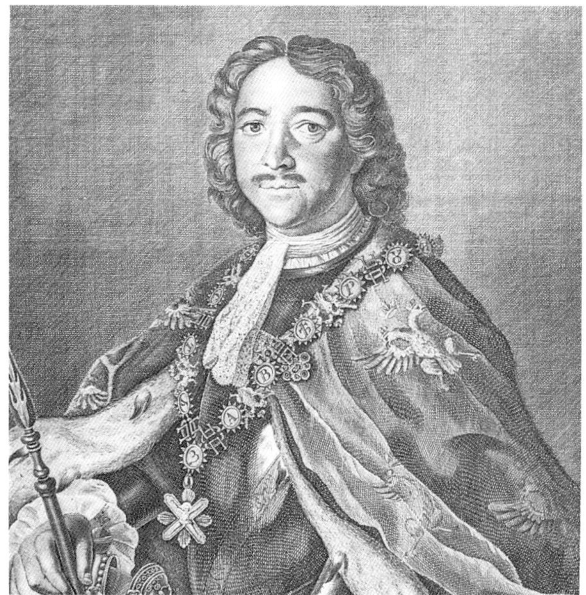

PETER THE GREAT, 1723

which resulted in the capture of two Swedish warships which had entered the mouth of the Neva River during the Northern War (1700–21).

In 1711 the first lady's Order appeared. According to legend, during the unsuccessful Prut Campaign, Catherine I donated all her jewellery as a bribe for the Turkish Commander-in-Chief. The new Order, initially named The Order of Liberation, was established to commemorate that event. During Peter I's lifetime only Catherine was awarded the Order.

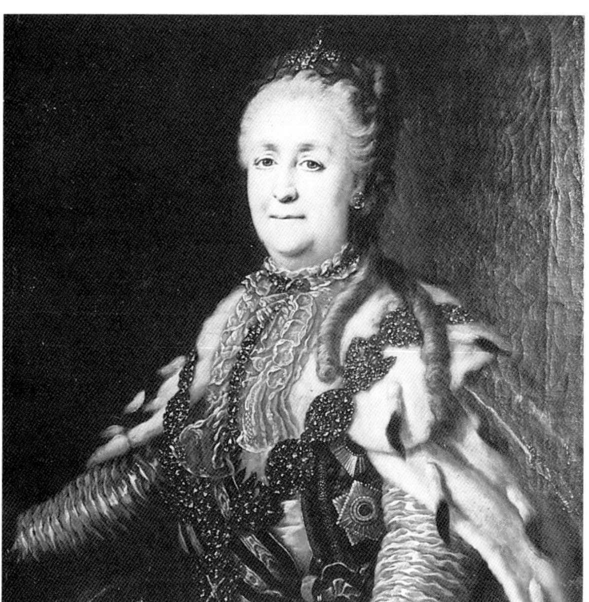

EMPRESS CATHERINE ALEKSEEVNA II, 19th CENTURY

Later, the Order was renamed "St Catherine" and granted to ladies of the inner sanctum of the Imperial Court (cat. no. 153). Another prestigious award was "Servant of the Tsar", an enamel miniature of Peter I framed in gold and diamonds (cat. no. 152). The development of miniature art in Russia occurred when Peter I, while on a trip to England in 1698, was introduced to the art of the British miniaturists and met Charles Boute, whom he asked to make some portraits of him after a painting by G. Kneller. The miniature displayed in this exhibition was painted to the order of Peter I, probably in England, and set into a gold open-worked frame with diamonds and enamel in Russia. The piece is a true masterpiece of the fine and applied arts of the early 19th century.

The Tsar's miniatures were produced in large quantities as Peter I was fond of presenting them, not only to the military commanders for victories in the battlefield, but also to men of society and even to ladies-in-waiting. The tradition of presenting the Tsar's enamel portraits was preserved for a long time.

In the second half of the 18th century, the ancient classics became closely connected with Russian attitudes and influenced Russian education. The proliferation of articles in the classical style indicated the prevailing outlook and were considered valuable gifts.

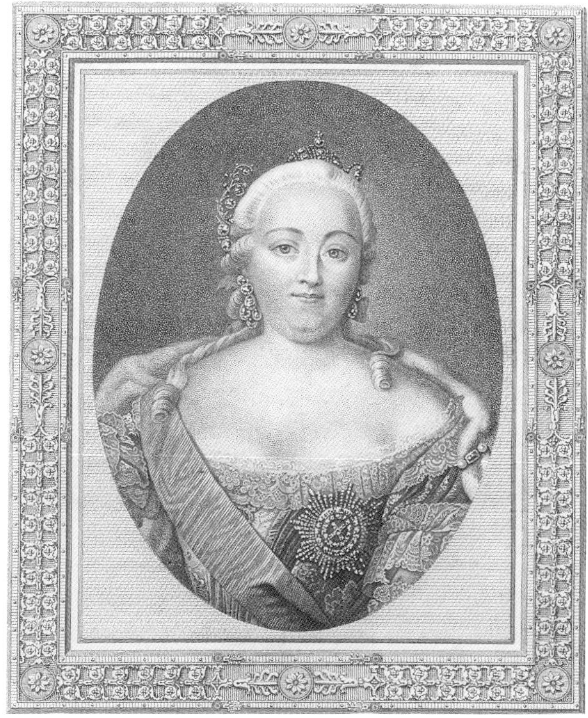

EMPRESS ELIZABETH PETROVNA, 1817

In 1769 in Petersburg, in accordance with a special order of Empress Catherine II, a large silver tankard was made by the court silver-master George Kuntsendorff as a present for the Nizhny Novgorod merchant Mikhail Andreev Kostromin. Along with the tankard he received 1000 roubles for assisting the brilliant self-taught inventor Ivan Petrov while the latter was designing an egg-shaped clock for the Empress. The tankard was made in the classicist style, in the shape of a column on a round base, decorated with garlands intertwined with ribbons. Wreaths of laurel leaves adorn the lid.

The use of enamel miniatures had been extended by 1750 to the decoration of snuffboxes, medallions and other objects. Included in the exhibition is a gold snuffbox with a charming enamel portrait of M.I. Kutuzov, made by St Petersburg master Iohann Velheim Keibel (cat. no. 156).

Of historical interest are gold snuffboxes of the 18th and early 19th centuries, decorated with engraved memorial medals celebrating the coming to the throne of Empress Catherine II in 1762. These medals were made by the Petersburg Court Master Jeweller Jean-Pierre Adour and medallist Iohann George Vechter (cat. no. 155). The low relief portrait of Emperor Aleksander I was made by the Petersburg master Iohann Vilheim Keibel and medallist Ivan Alekseevich Shilov (cat. no. 157).

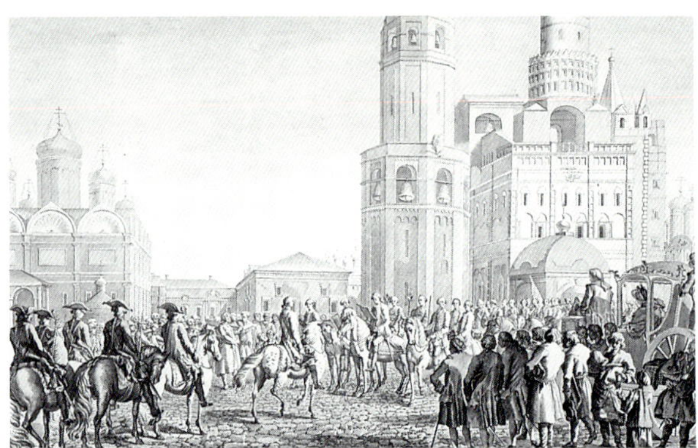

CORONATION OF TSARINA CATHERINE ALEKSEEVNA IN SEPTEMBER 1762

These snuffboxes, as well as those commemorating the Russian-Turkish War (1806–12) and the Patriotic War of 1812, embodied the best creative talent of the time. The decoration of the snuff-boxes relates to their designation as awards for military merit and to innermost members of the Court.

National growth resulting from the Patriotic War of 1812 was reflected in the gold and silver trade.

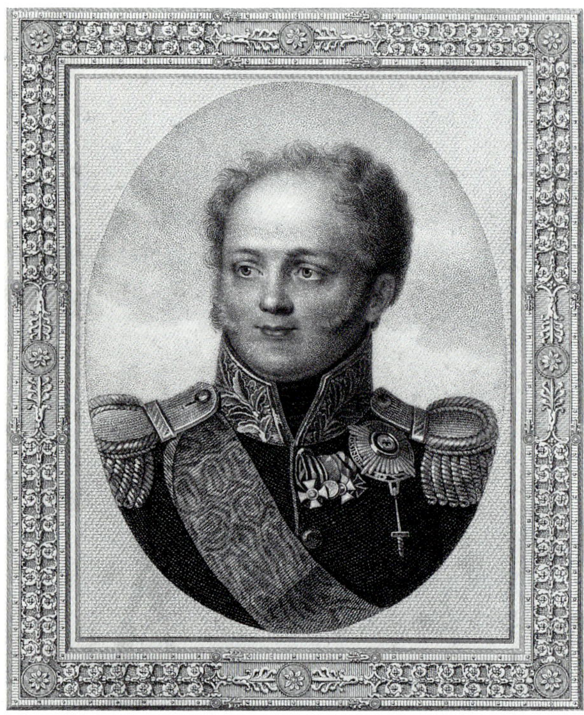

EMPEROR ALEKSANDER I, 1817

Displayed in the exhibition is the casket (cat. no. 158) for keeping the deed of Emperor Aleksander I, intended for presentation to the Moscow aristocracy for their contribution to the Patriotic War of 1812 and the victory over Napoleon. The casket was made by the Moscow master Mikhail Pivert by order of the Moscow gentry. It was intended that all further Imperial deeds would be kept in the casket, which would be located at the House of Lords, after which the casket was modelled; it is in the shape of a building with a high roof crowned with the double-headed eagle. Around the roof is a strip of soldered ovals under the Lord's Arms, and two sections showing military equipment. In the central oval on the front of the casket is the crest of Moscow and Moscow Province — St George the Victorious — and around it are the crests of ancient Moscow cities such as Klin, Bronnitsa, Volokolamsk, Kolomna, Serpukhov, Ruza, Bogorodsk, Vereya, Podolsk, Zvenigorod, Dmitrov and Mozhaisk. The sides of the casket are decorated with allegorical scenes in Imperial style, with the inclusion of gods and heroes as well as depictions of Kremlin Cathedrals and Ivan the Great's spire.

147. Ladle
Moscow, 1682
silver
13.9 x 34.5 x 23.3 cm
42069 OK 898

The inscription intertwined with circles and ribbons on the side of the ladle reads: "With the kindness of God, the Great Tsar and Grand Prince Feodor Alekseevich, the Autocrat of all Great, Small and White Russia, presented this ladle to Ivan Ievlevich Saltanov in the summer of 7190, March 6, in recognition of his construction of churches, mansions and many other important buildings".

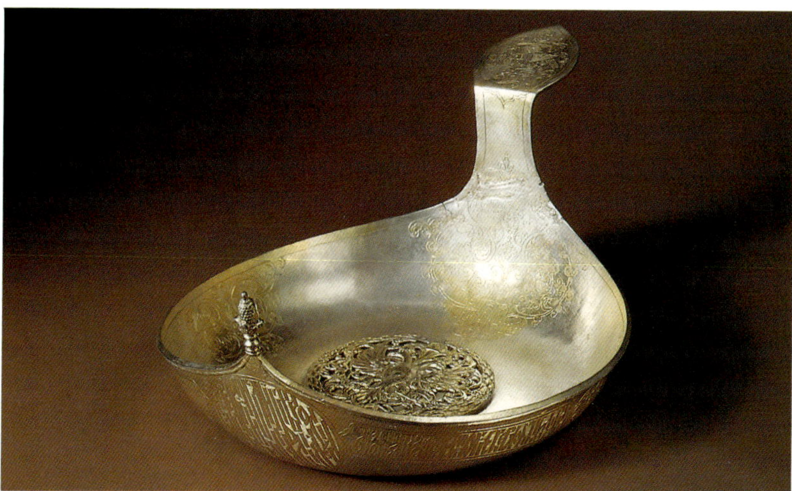
147

148. Ladle
Ilya Grigoriev Kuchkin,
Moscow, 1755
silver gilt
24.5 x 43.5 x 20.5 cm
57355 OK 3796

Engraved among chased cartouches of leaves, flowers, palmettes, cornucopia and bunches of grapes on the outer sides of the ladle is the inscription: "This ladle, from the Treasury of His Majesty the Emperor, was granted to the Moscow merchant of the first order, Mikhail Gusyatnikov, for his zeal in increasing State income in 1754".

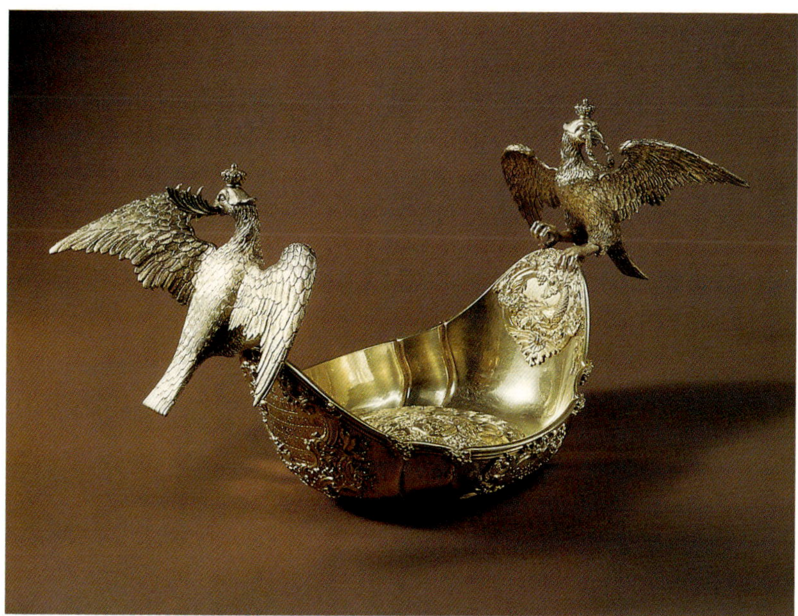
148

149. Ladle
Gavrila Gavrilov Zon,
Moscow, 1761
silver gilt
12.5 x 30.0 x 15.7 cm
31 OK 3788

The inscription on the elongated medallions, alongside the bust-length portrait of Empress Elizabeth Petrovna, reads: "With the Kindness of God, We, Elizabeth I, the Empress of All Russia, Autocrat, ... granted this ladle to the Ataman of Yaik, Feodor Andreev Stanitsa, son of Borodin, for his faithful service to Saint Petersburg, in the month of March, 1761."

Elizabeth Petrovna I (1709–61), daughter of Peter the Great, was Empress of Russia from 1741.

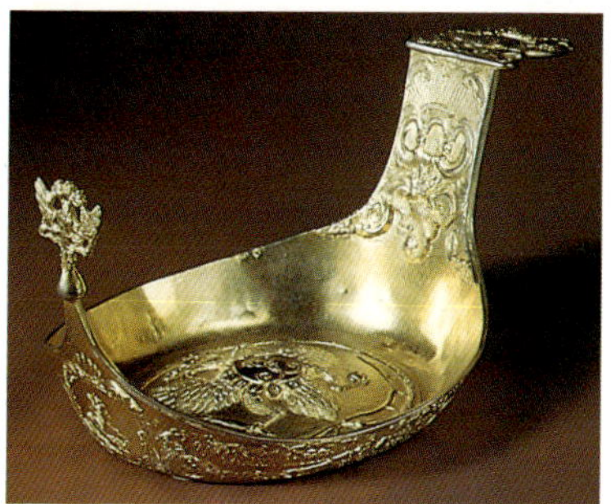
149

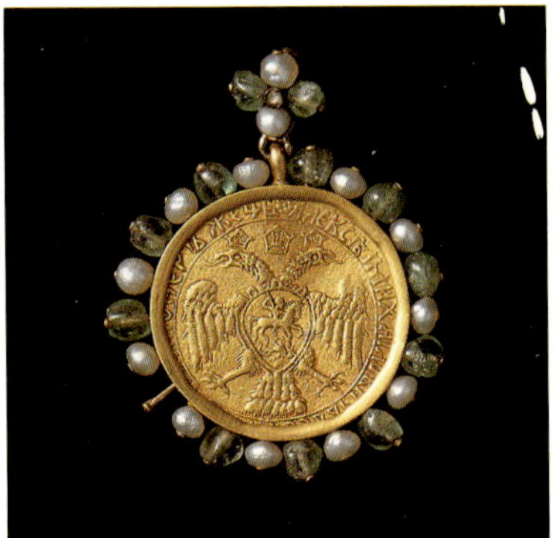

150

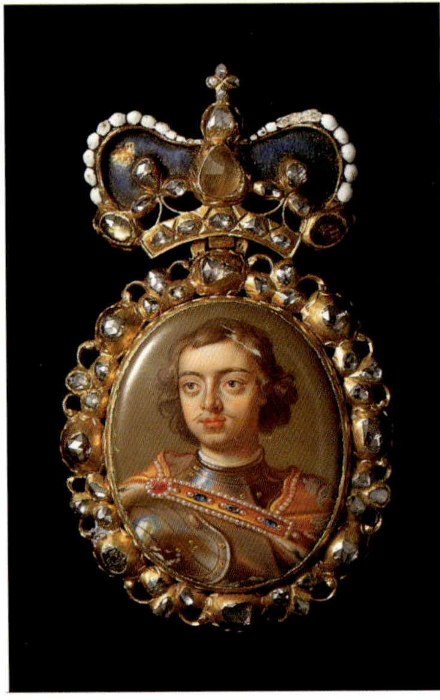

152

152. Medal of the Order of the Servant of the Tsar
setting: Russia, first quarter of 18th century; miniature: western Europe, early 18th century
gold, diamonds, enamel
8.3 x 4.8 cm
53032 OK 13921

The decoration of the Order of the Servant of the Tsar features an enamelled miniature of Peter I in an open-worked gold and diamond setting. On the reverse is a carved double-headed eagle with sceptre and orb and the inscription "For Valour".

Peter Alekseevich I (b. Moscow, 30 May 1672, d. Petersburg, 28 January 1725, buried Petropavlovsky Cathedral, Petropavlovsk Fortress), Tsar of Russia from 27 April 1682 and Emperor of Russia from 21 October 1721, was a statesman, military leader and diplomat. Early in the 18th century a new award, the Order of the Servant of the Tsar, bearing the portrait of Peter I, was introduced. As the highest honour during his reign, the Order was granted to military personnel and civilians in recognition of significant service to the state. The first recipients were the officers and heroes of the Battle of Poltava. During the reigns of Peter's successors, however, the Order came to be granted with less discrimination.

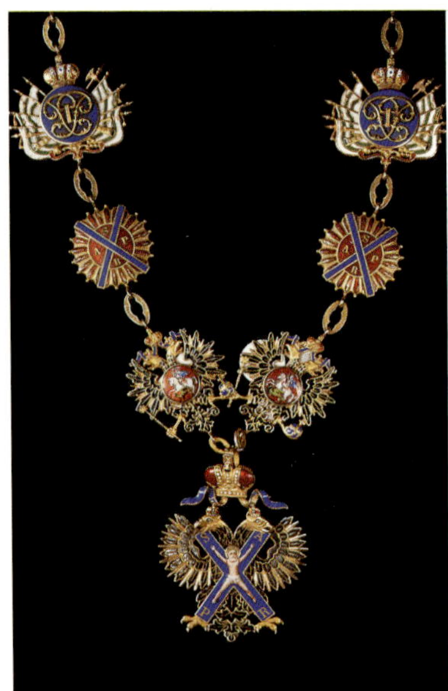

151

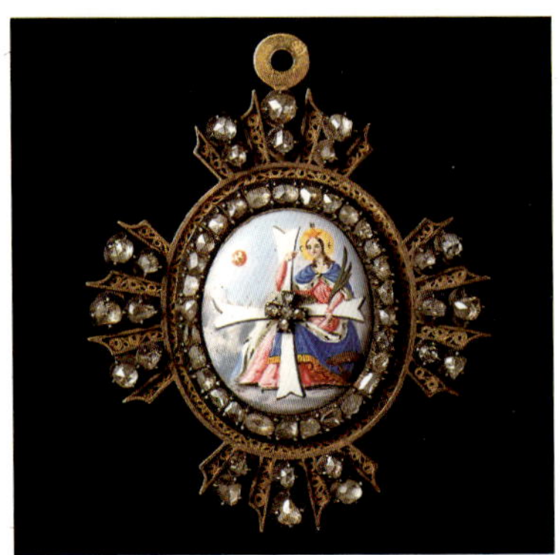

153

150. Medal of the Order of Tsar Aleksei Mikhailovich
Russia, second half of 17th century
gold, emeralds, pearls, diamond, diameter: 5.1 cm
OK 7036

On each side of the medal is chased a double-headed eagle under a triple crown. On one side a unicorn is depicted on the eagle's chest, on the other, an equestrian image of George the Victorious. The inscription reads "With the Kindness of God, We the Great Tsar Majesty and Grand Prince Aleksei Mikhailovich, Autocrat of All Russia".

Aleksei Mikhailovich (9 March 1629–9 February 1676), Tsar of Russia from 1645, was the son of Tsar Mikhail Feodorovich Romanov, who reigned from 1613 to 1645. Among the first to be awarded this medal were those who fought in the war for the reunification of the Ukraine and Russia (1648–1654).

151. Medal of the Order of St Andrew Protokletos
Iohann Vilheim Keibel, Petersburg,
last quarter of 19th century
gold, enamel
medal: 6.0 x 7.8 cm;
length of chain: 103.5 cm
73842 OK 6943

The symbol of the order is a double-headed eagle, on its chest a blue enamel cross with an image of St Andrew Protokletos crucified. On the reverse the motto "For Faith and Loyalty" appears against a white background.

153. Medal of the Order of St Catherine
Petersburg, 1841
gold, silver, enamel, diamonds
6.9 x 5.5 cm
16249 OK 11409

Oval medallion bearing an enamelled portrait of St Catherine in an ermine mantle, bearing a palm branch and a white Maltese cross. Around the head of the saint are the letters "CBE" (Great Martyr Saint Catherine).

154. Tankard
George Kuntsendorff,
Petersburg, 1769
silver
29.0 x 13.0 cm
384 OK 3736

The inscription engraved in the broad band along the top edge of the tankard reads: "Catherine II, Empress and Autocrat of All Russia, grants this tankard to Mikhail Andreev, son of Kostromin, for the virtue rendered to the mechanic Ivan Petrov, son of Kulibin, on 1 April 1769".

On 12 May 1769, the supplement to edition no. 38 of the Moscow Gazette published the following article:

"Today, 1 April, a self-educated mechanic, Ivan Kulibin, was introduced to Her Majesty the Empress by Duke Vladimir Grigorievich Orlov, a Gentleman of the Bedchamber of Her Majesty's Court and Director of the Academy of Sciences. The mechanic presented to Her Majesty the Empress a clock and other instruments, made by himself without supervision. The merchant Mikhail Kostromin, who had been funding this work without reimbursement for over four years, was also introduced. After inspecting the instruments, Her Majesty allowed the two men to kiss Her hand and granted them a thousand roubles each. She also granted the merchant Kostromin a silver tankard in recognition of his excellent virtue and ordered the instruments to be sent to the Cabinet of Curiosities."

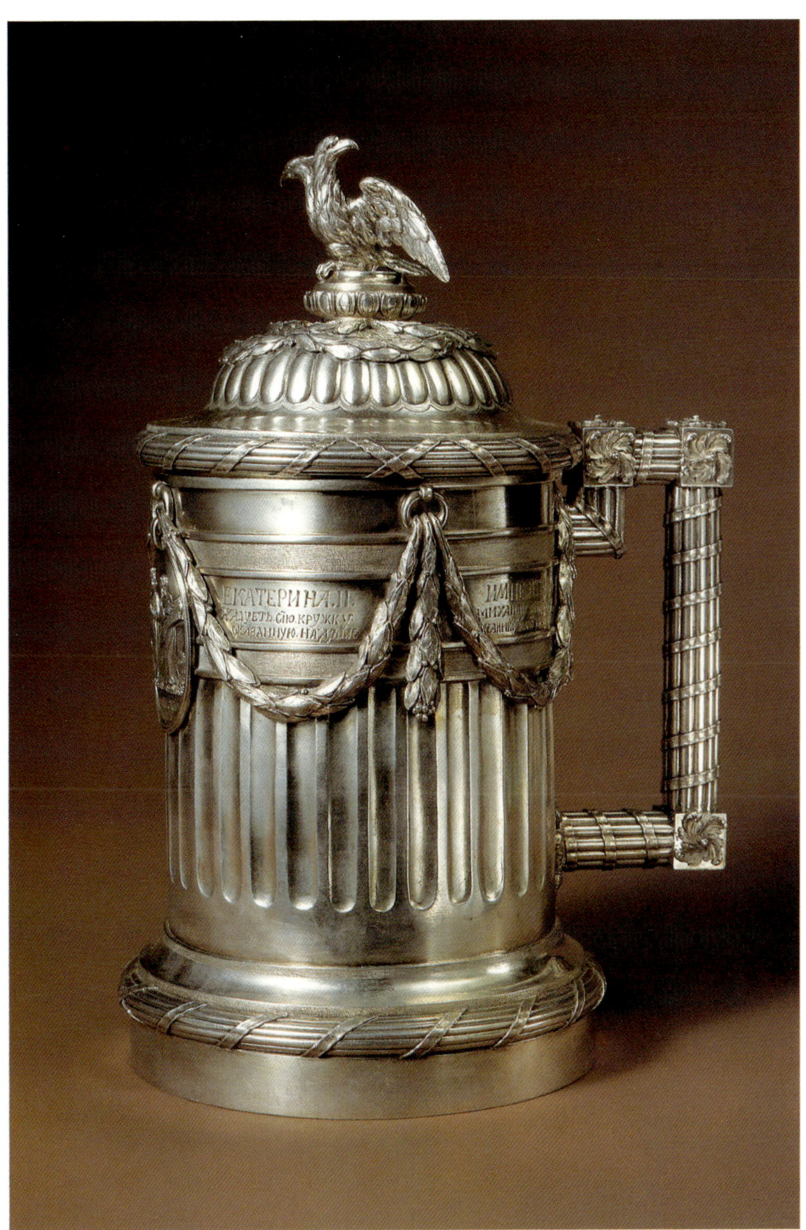

154

155. Snuffbox
Jean Pierre Adour; medallion:
Iohann George Vehter,
Petersburg, 1774
gold
3.8 x 8.4 x 8.4 cm
81483 OK 13518

The lid of the snuffbox is decorated with a chased medallion depicting the coronation of Catherine II; beneath the profile portrait is the inscription "B.M. Empress Catherine II, Autocrat of All Russia". The reverse of the medal depicts the entrusting of the symbols of power to Catherine II, with the inscription "This is Your Salvation. 28 June 1762."

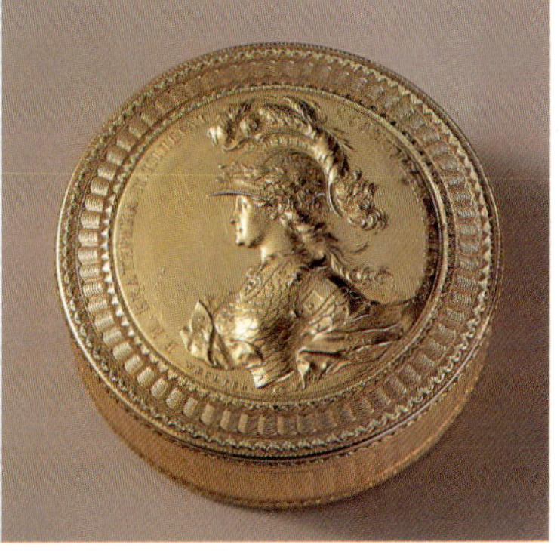

155

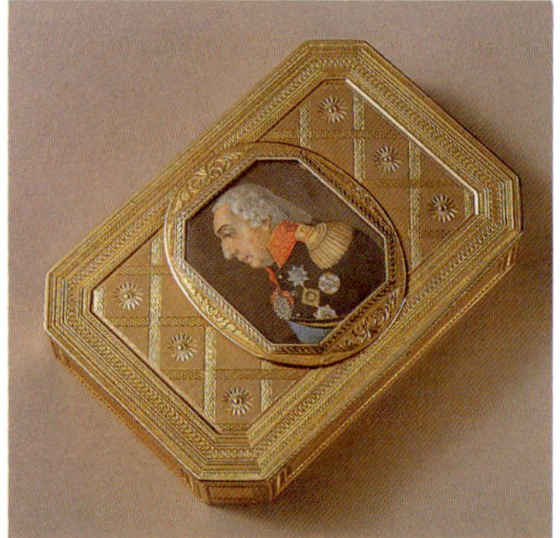

156

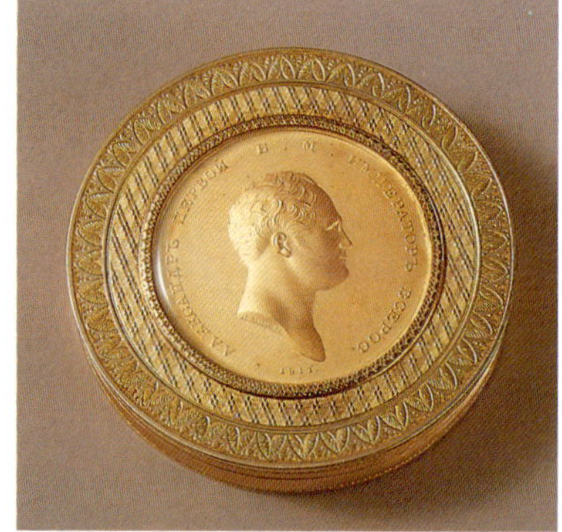

157

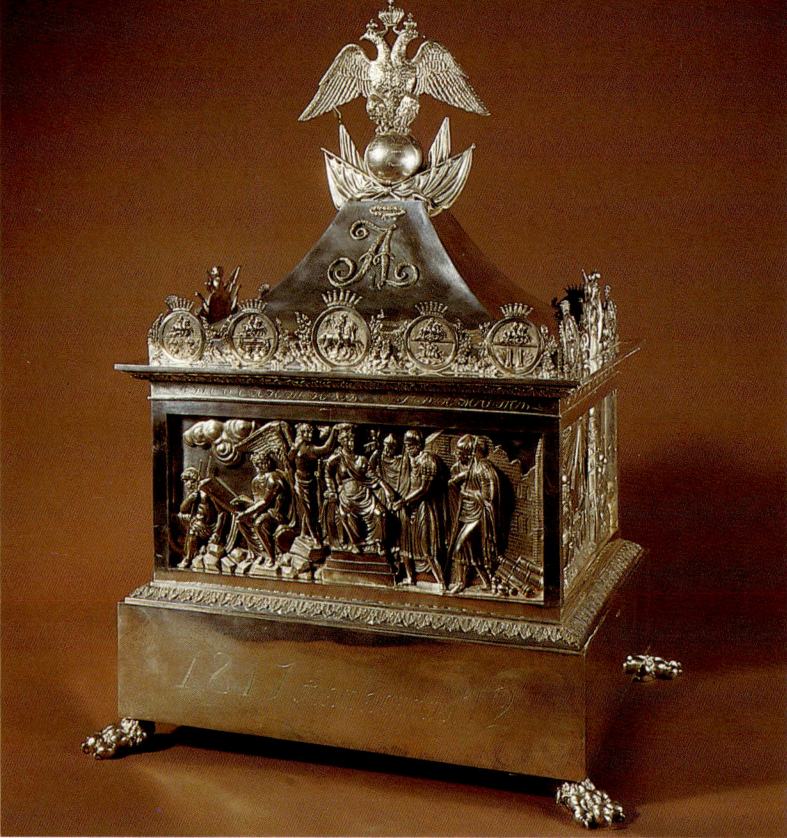

158

156. Snuffbox
Iohann Vilheim Keibel, Petersburg, 1810s
gold, enamel
2.3 x 10.0 x 6.8 cm
51134 OK 3043

In a carved oval frame on the lid of the snuffbox is a miniature portrait of Mikhail Illarionovich Kutuzov after the 1810 engraving by S. Cardelli.

Mikhail Illarionovich Kutuzov (Golinischev-Kutuzov, 15 September 1745–16 April 1813), Russian military leader, was appointed General-Field-Marshall on 31 August 1812. In August 1805 he was appointed Commander-in-Chief of the Russian Army sent to Austria. On 7 March 1811 he was appointed Commander-in-Chief of the Moldavian Army and on 29 October 1811 was granted the title of Duke as reward for the victory of Slobodzeya (Valahiya). In July 1812 he achieved the signing of the Bucharest peace treaty, in recognition of which he was granted the title of Highest Prince. At the beginning of the Patriotic War (1812) he was appointed Chief of the Petersburg and Moscow Home Guards and on 8 August 1812 became Commander-in-Chief of the Russian Army. On December 6 1812 he was granted the title of Prince of Smolensk and was awarded the highest of all military honours, the Order of George of the First Degree. He died in the German city of Buntslau and is buried in Kazansky Cathedral in Petersburg.

157. Snuffbox
Iohann Vilheim Keibel; medallion: Ivan Shilov, Petersburg, 1811
gold
2.1 x 7.8 x 7.8 cm
6537 OK 3055

Under glass on the lid of the box is a medallion bearing a low-relief profile portrait of Aleksander I with the inscription "Aleksander I B.H. Emperor of All Russia, 1811".

Alexander Pavlovich I (1777–1825), the son of Emperor Pavel Petrovich and Empress Maria Feodorovna, was Emperor of Russia from 1801 to 1825.

158. Casket
Mikhail Pivert, Moscow, 1817
silver, wood
86.0 x 53.0 x 41.0 cm
57084 OK 1833

Casket commissioned by the Moscow nobility to store the charter granted by Tsar Aleksander I.

VI

CHURCH ART

The Synodic Period

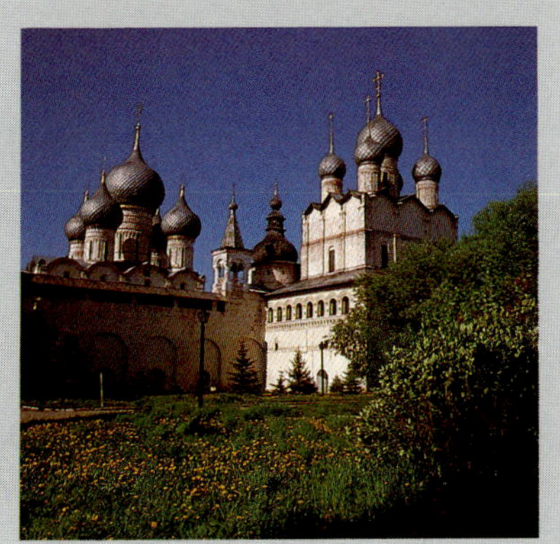

The general reconstruction of Russian life initiated by Peter the Great at the beginning of the 18th century was accompanied by reforms in the church. Following the demise of the Patriarchy of Adrian, Peter established a Collegiate Board, preventing the election of a new Patriarchy. In 1721 a new ecclesiastical administration, the Most Holy Governing Synod, was set up. It remained until 1917, when the Patriarchy was restored. This chapter in the life of the Russian Orthodox Church was subsequently named the Synodic Period.

During this period the Russian Orthodox Church grew tenfold; by 1917 it had increased from 20 to 64 eparchies, from 20 to 100 episcopates and to 50,000 churches and about 1000 monasteries. Between the 18th and 20th centuries the processes of spiritual enlightenment and missionary activity were considerably intensified. Up to 100 ecclesiastical schools and 55 seminaries were established in many towns. Ecclesiastical academies in Kiev, Moscow, Petersburg and Kazan continued their activities as the centres of Christian culture. Monographs covering all facets of thoeology began to be published and numerous periodicals such as scientific magazines and popular weekly almanacs appeared.

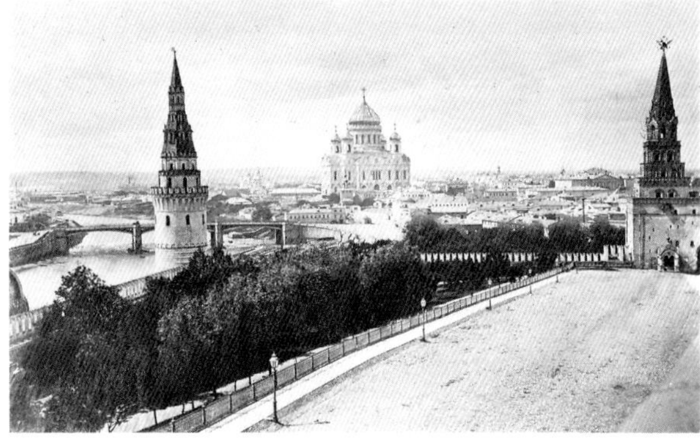
VIEW OF THE CHURCH OF CHRIST THE SAVIOUR

This increase in church activity was associated with a unique phenomenon which became a specific feature of Russian culture: the participation of laymen in theology. Nowhere in the world were there as many theologians as in Russia. Slavophil Khomyakov, the Aksakov brothers, "Zapadnik" Solovyov and the Synthetic School of the Trubetskoy Brothers all contributed to this highly important aspect of Russian study. Their achievements were followed by the flourishing of church art in the fields of music, architecture, icon painting, decorative art and, in particular, gold and silver work.

The most remarkable feature of a Russian Orthodox church is the great number of icons making up its principal decoration. Russian icons are one of the most extraordinary manifestations of Russian art. Stemming from the Byzantine tradition, Russian icon painting developed independently over many centuries and reflected the spiritual experience of the Russian people. For this reason some researchers call it "contemplation in colour". Silver and gold oklads (icon frames) appeared early. One of the most ancient oklads, made for a Novgorod icon in the 11th century, depicted Peter and Paul. Ancient oklads covered only the background and edges of the icon, but from the 16th century they began to conceal all but the face and hands of the subject. From the 18th century until the beginning of the 20th century, oklads became very diverse, reflecting all the artistic styles of the period: baroque, rococo, classical, imperial, historic and traditional. Silver oklads were often completed with rizas (chasubles) embroidered with river pearls, glass or filigree.

Icons with oklads made in Moscow in 1752 and 1779 have been included in the exhibition (cat. nos 160 and 159). They are richly engraved in the baroque manner. Engraving superseded enamelling as the prevailing decorative technique in the 18th century. Gone was enamel over relief, carving and champlevé; it was rare at that time to see blue, green or blue-green enamel in filigree ornaments, such as the oklad of the icon Worthy Pafnuty of Borovsk (cat. no. 161). Nevertheless, enamelling was a significant industry as in the late 18th century the two main centres of production, Moscow and St Petersburg, were joined by a third at Rostrov Yaroslavsky. They produced miniatures for oklads, icons, crosses and tabernacles. Later this manufacture increased due to the demand for small enamelled icons from the many pilgrims visiting Rostov. Images were copied from book illustrations, coloured engravings, and the icons and frescoes in Rostov churches. Enamel painters, such as the monk Amphilokhy, often painted frescoes as well as icons. Included in the exhibition is the Rostov icon of 1805; the silver gilt oklad is composed of 18 enamelled panels showing images of Dmitri Rostovsky, selected saints and others. This oklad, edged with a narrow ornamental strip and decorated with fine, slightly raised cartouches, is characteristic of its time (cat. no. 162).

In the first half of the 19th century, filigree oklads became very popular. They were made with silver wire and sometimes sometimes scattered with tiny silver balls. The richness and diversity of the silver lace are notable. There are two icons with such oklads in the exhibition (cat. nos 163 and 164).

From the mid 19th century, enamelled oklads began to reappear. By this time ecclesiastical objects were manufactured by almost every factory and workshop in the country, whereas previously they had been the business of individual masters. The most famous jewellery factories producing church objects were those of Olovyanishnikov, Nemyrov-Kolodkyn, Postnikov, Ovchinnikov, Khlebnikov and Mishukov. The exhibition includes works by one of the oldest firms, Ovchinnikov, which was well known from 1766 and had been granted the title of supplier to the court. In the early 20th century this firm largely followed the drawings and models of the painter S. Vashkov, a significant contributor to the renaissance and affirmation of national artforms; his originality characterises objects made by the firm. Vashkov succeeded in uniting the traditions of archaic art, purifying it, conventionalising the symbols of early Christianity and adapting the motifs characteristic of Russian art of the Kiev and Vladimir-Suzdal periods and the art schools of Moscow, Novgorod and Pscov to modern forms.

The Olovyanishnikov company revived the cloisonné technique of enamelling, lost during the period of the Tartar Yoke. Religious images combining cloisonné and painted enamel decorate the mitre (cat. no. 174), embroidered with mother-of-pearl beads, precious stones from the Urals, pearls, filigree and zern. The images are marked by a high degree of skill in execution, an ancient style of subtle graphic stylisation and a refined palette.

At the same time we can see pearl rizas on icons depicting the Virgin. The talent of Russian women for embroidering tiny pearl-balls had been famous since early times. An icon of the Virgin of Kazan with an enamelled silver oklad and pearl riza is included in the exhibition (cat. no. 166).

The Ovchinnikov company, represented by a small folding triptych (cat. no. 168), was awarded silver and gold medals at several Russian industrial exhibitions, which were important in Russian cultural life. The throne produced for the Church of Christ the Saviour in Moscow was considered by contemporaries the best ornament in the temple. The folding triptych is interesting as an example of a domestic icon, kept in the "red corner"– the part of the house where all family members gathered for prayer.

Of particular interest is the icon composed of enamelled panels (cat. no. 165) because of its association with the struggle against Napoleon in the Patriotic War of 1812. This war of liberation was important for Russia as for all European countries and became a catalyst for Russia's spiritual renaissance. The icon commemorates Russian soldiers who died for the freedom and glory of their Motherland.

The fundamental ritual of the Orthodox Church is that of the Eucharist, hence the Eucharistic cup, or chalice, is one of the church's most important symbols. The chalice is made up of three parts and is generally decorated with images of Christ, the Crucifix and the words of the Saviour at the Last Supper. From the early 17th century the base came to be decorated with images of the Passion. Themes changed according to trends in artistic style. Numerous chalices bear inscriptions describing important historical events or personages. The chalice of 1704 (cat. no. 172) relates to Tsar Aleksei Mikhailovich's daughter's taking of the veil in the famous convent of Novodvichy. The other chalice, dated 1823 (cat. no. 173), with its expressive classical female figures, symbolises a new period in the Russian State and its art: the Russian Empire.

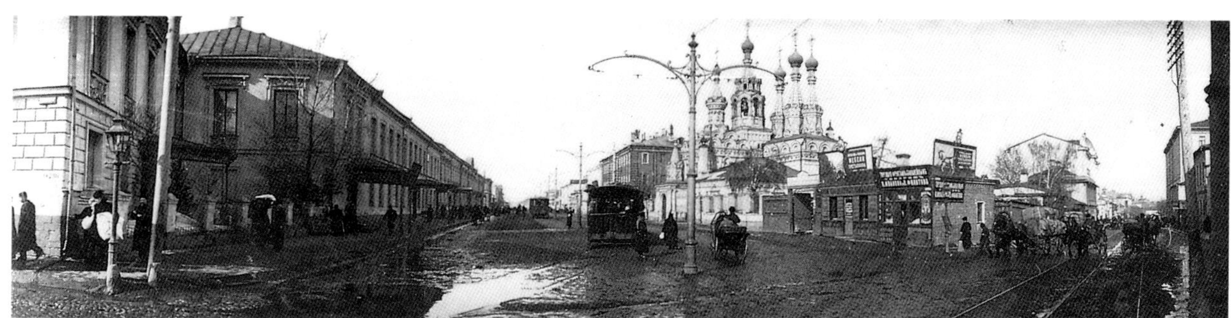

VIEW OF THE CHURCH OF THE BIRTH OF CHRIST IN PUTINKAH, MOSCOW

The Cross, symbol of Christian victory, is fundamental to religious art. As with other church objects, crosses were often decorated with an engraved, carved, nielloed or enamelled crucifix in the centre, the Saviour above and prayers on each side, employing a range of ornamental techniques, often completed with stones or pearls.

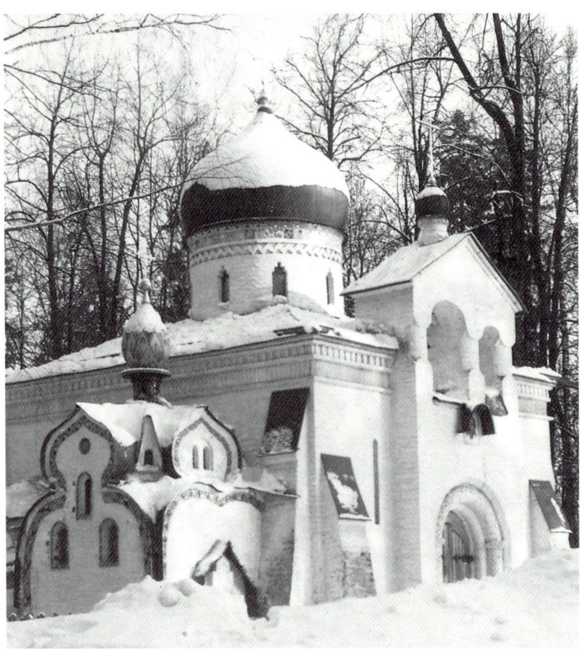

ABRAMZEVO CHURCH

The insignia of the clerical elite were also decorated with images of the Trinity, selected saints, the Crucifix, the Virgin and others, such as the silver panagia (cat. no. 176) made by Michael, A. Lopov's son. Lopov was a student of G. Mussikiisky, the first Russian court miniaturist, who gave us the portraits of Peter the Great and his family. The panagia shows three saints in a landscape. Another panagia, dated 1899 (cat. no. 178), was produced by the gold and silver works of Nemyrov-Kolodkyn, founded in 1872. This firm revived ancient methods of gem-cutting; the panagia is decorated by a large golden topaz with an image of the Virgin framed by grapes and stones.

The design of icon lamps varied enormously; they were made of metal, porcelain, glass or silver and decorated with ornaments and angels. Two examples are included in the exhibition; one is completely filigreed; the other is decorated with multi-coloured enamel (cat. nos 179 and 180). The principal festival of the Russian Orthodox Church is Easter, when it is customary to give a fresh egg dyed red, or a wooden, porcelain, stone, silver or golden egg. The examples in the exhibition (cat. nos 181 and 182) show the uniquely Russian nature of these important religious artefacts, and, together with the other liturgical vessels, ornaments and icons included in the exhibition, demonstrate the important role held by the Church in Russia.

159. Icon: Nine Martyrs and Worthy Mamant
Moscow, 1779
tempera on wood panel, silver gilt, rubies, diamonds
43.0 x 36.0 cm
dated, hallmarked
99475 OK 14901

160. Icon: The Virgin of Vatoped
frame: Andrei Gerasimov, Moscow, 1752
tempera on wood panel, silver gilt
51.5 x 39.5 cm
dated, hallmarked
77361 OK 10628

At the bottom of the frame is the inscription "The miracle-working image of the Holy Mother of God of Vatoped". The inscription on the reverse reads "Donated by Count Aleksei Evgrafovich and Countess Adelaida Albertovna Kamerovsky in memory of their beloved son Count Ippolit Alekseevich, who died according to the will of Our Lord at the age of 25 years on the 11th day of January 1875. The Icon had been in the possession of Countess Sofia Borisovna Volkhovskaya, Mother Superior of the Cathedral of the Holy Mother of God of Kazan".

The Cathedral of the Holy Mother of God of Kazan was founded in 1579. Sofia Volkhovskaya was the Mother Superior from 1801 to 1807.

161. Icon: Worthy Pafnuty of Borovsk
frame: Feodor Andreianov, Moscow, 1780
tempera on wood panel, silver gilt, enamel
dated, hallmarked
58383 OK 8130

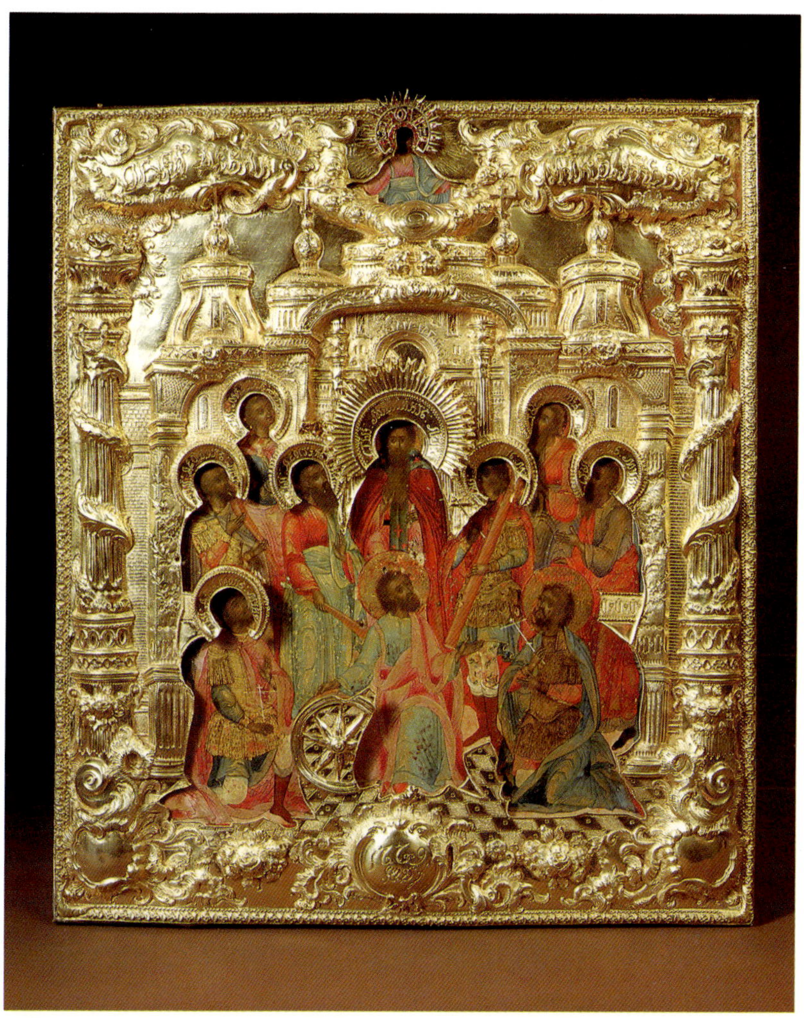

159

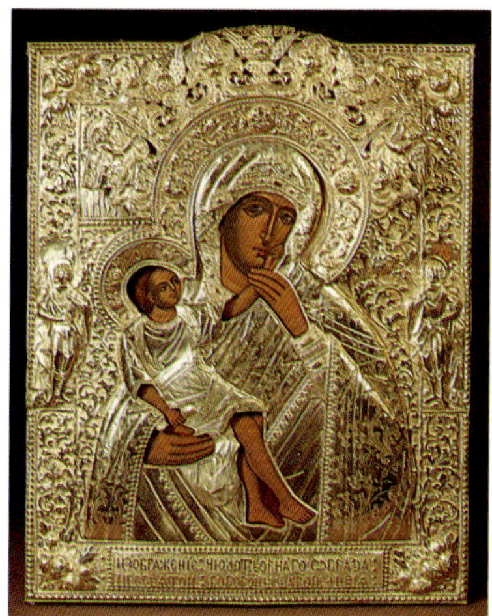

160

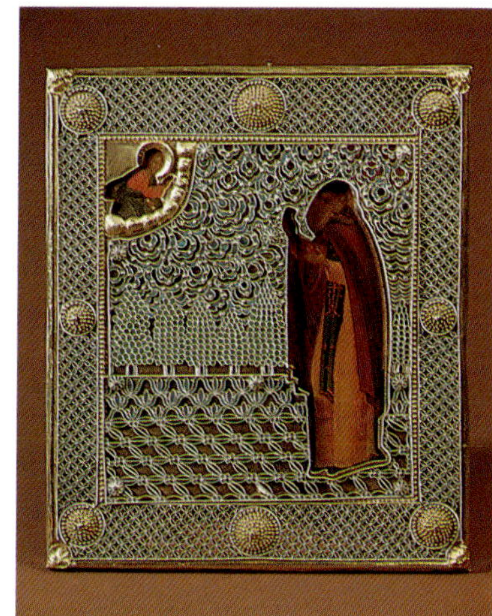

161

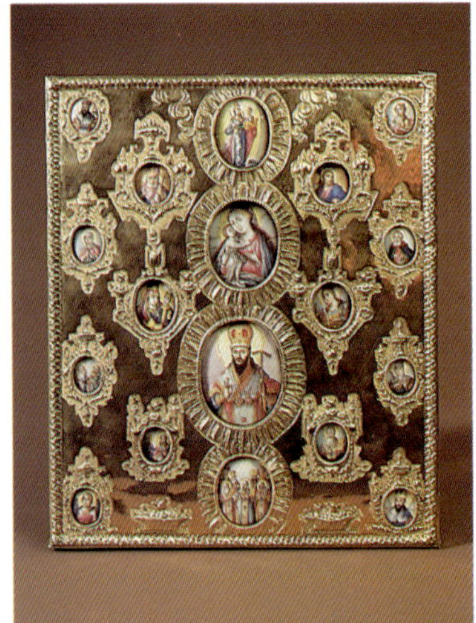

162

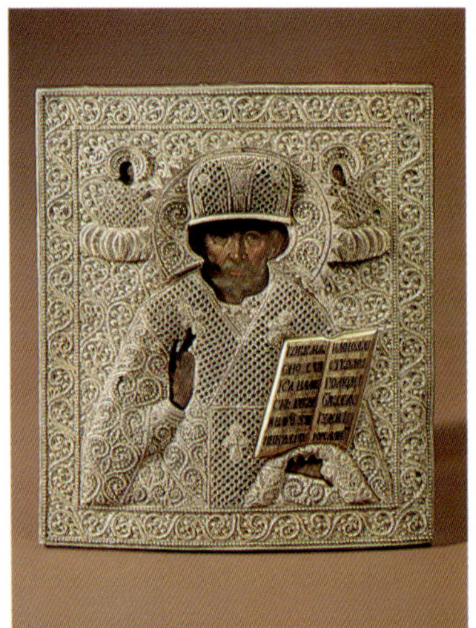

163

162. Icon
frame: Moscow, 1805; enamel: Rostov-the-Great, early 19th century
silver gilt, enamel, copper, wood
32.0 x 26.3 cm
77364 OK 10630

163. Icon: St Nicholas Thaumaturgus
Moscow, 1807
tempera on wood panel, silver gilt
30.3 x 26.1 cm
77356 OK 10048

164. Icon: Our Lady of the Intercession of the Perished
frame: Matvei Kostrov, Moscow, 1805
tempera on wood panel, silver, niello;
13.0 x 9.5 cm
dated, hallmarked
80091 OK 11833

Inscribed in niello on a silver band at the bottom of the frame is "The image of the Holy Mother of the Intercession of the Perished".

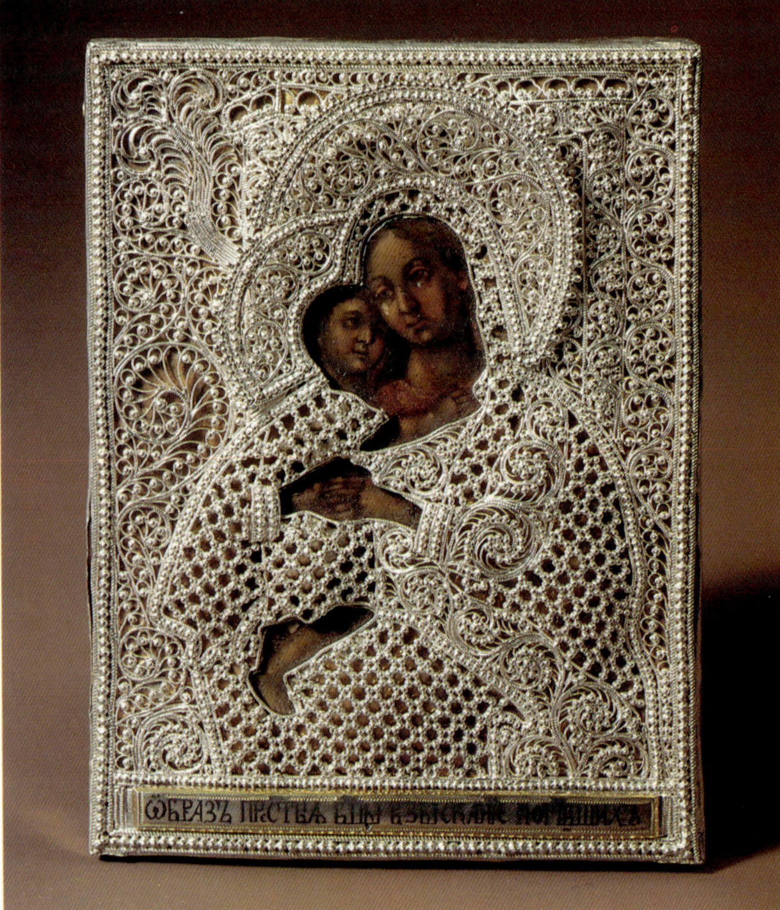

164

165. Icon
Moscow, 1812–31
silver, enamel, copper, wood
50.0 x 50.0 cm
68257 OK 9502

The inscription enclosed in four enamel cartouches reads: "The Holy Image of the life-giving Trinity of the Infantry Regiment of Vyalytsk was made in the city of Moscow in 1812, when Colonel Kushnikov was the Chief of the Regiment. It was restored in October 1831 under the supervision of Colonel Zagorsky, the Commander of the same Regiment, in memory of those killed in the years 1812, 1828 and 1829".

Surrounding the image of the Holy Trinity are depictions of the Nativity of the Virgin, the Nativity of Christ, the Annunciation, the Dormition, the Descent of the Holy Spirit, the Persuasion of Doubting Thomas, the Entrance of the Lord into Jerusalem, the Transfiguration, the Epiphany, the Ascension, the Resurrection and the Day of the Holy Cross.

166. Icon: The Virgin of Kazan
frame: Aleksander M. Makhalova, Moscow, 1896
tempera on wood panel, silver gilt, enamel, pearls, gold, textile
31.3 x 26.8 cm
dated, marked AAM, hallmarked 105074 OK 22865

167. Icon: The Virgin of Tikhvin, Russia, late 18th–early 19th century
tempera on wood panel, silver gilt, glass
38.0 x 30.0 cm
54627 OK 9939

Around the perimeter of the icon are depictions of St Peter, the Metropolitan John the Gracious, the Metropolitan Aleksei, John the Theologian, Aleksei the Fool for Christ's Sake and St Paraskeva.

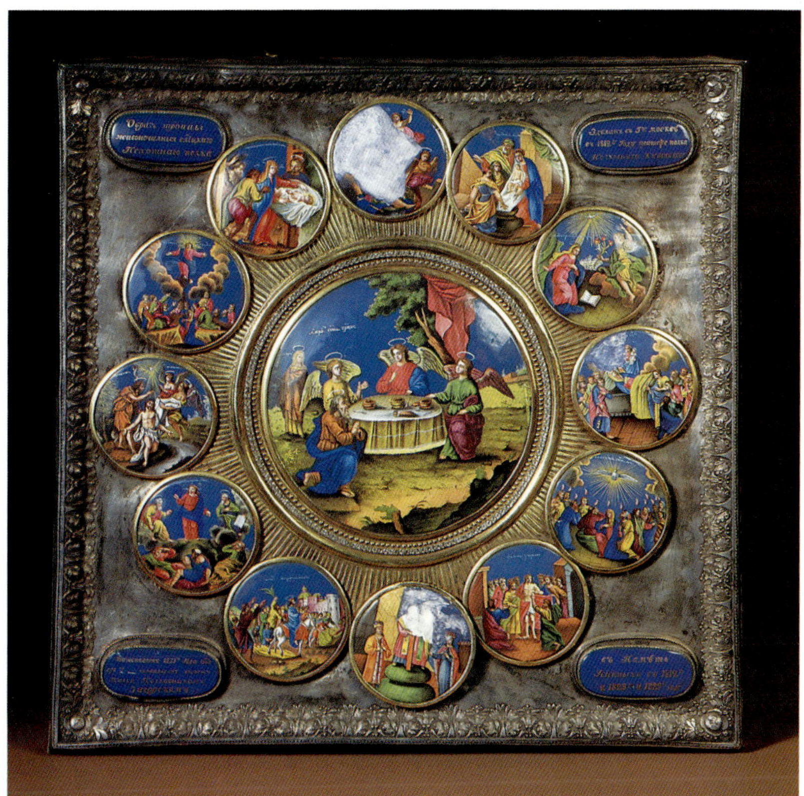

165

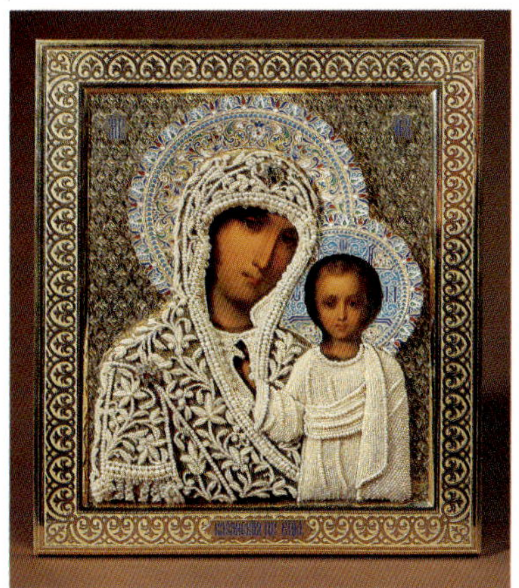

166

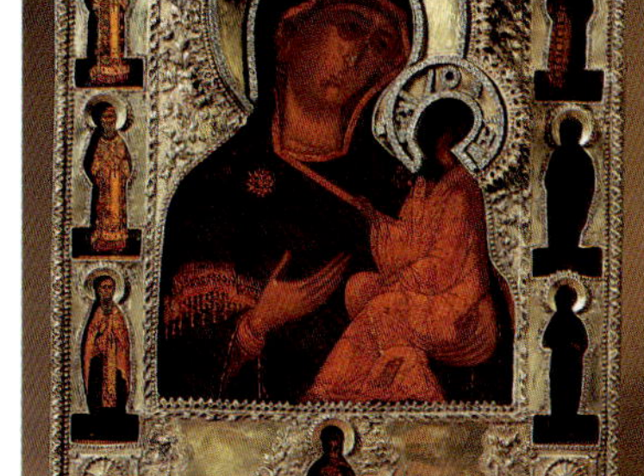

167

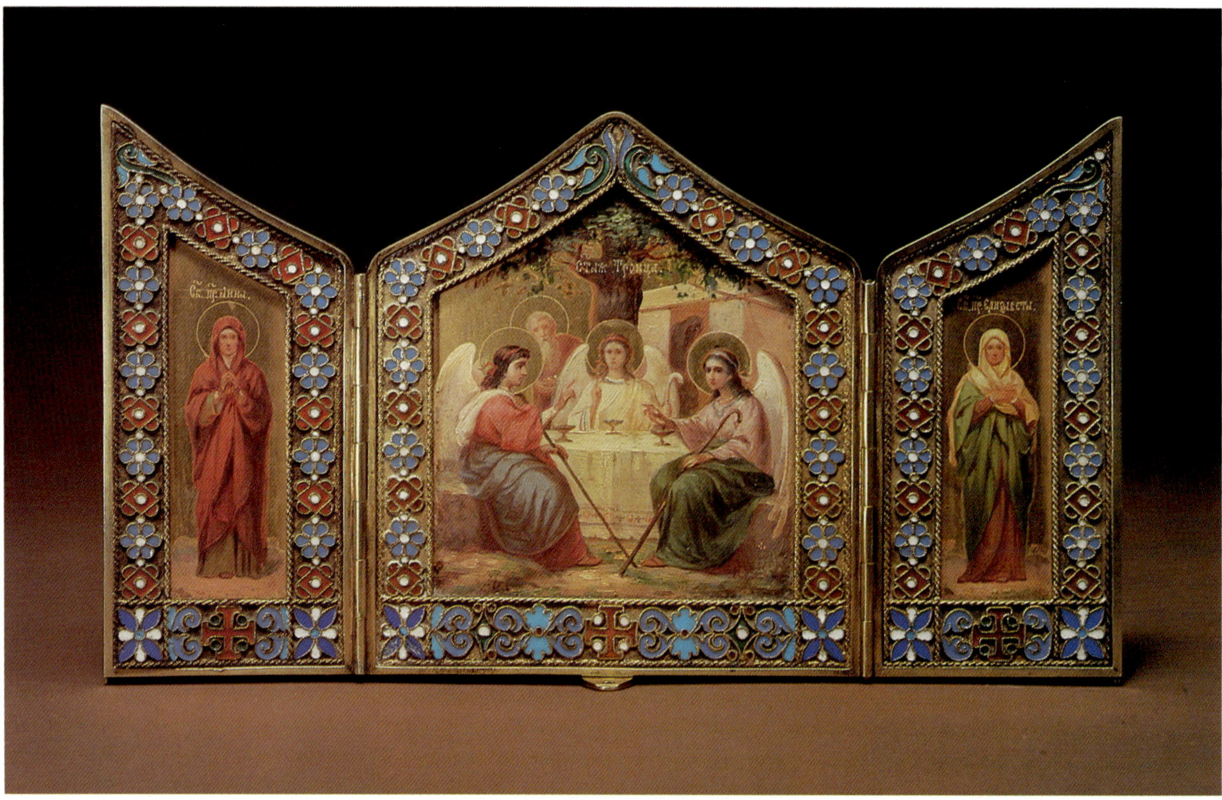

168 (i)

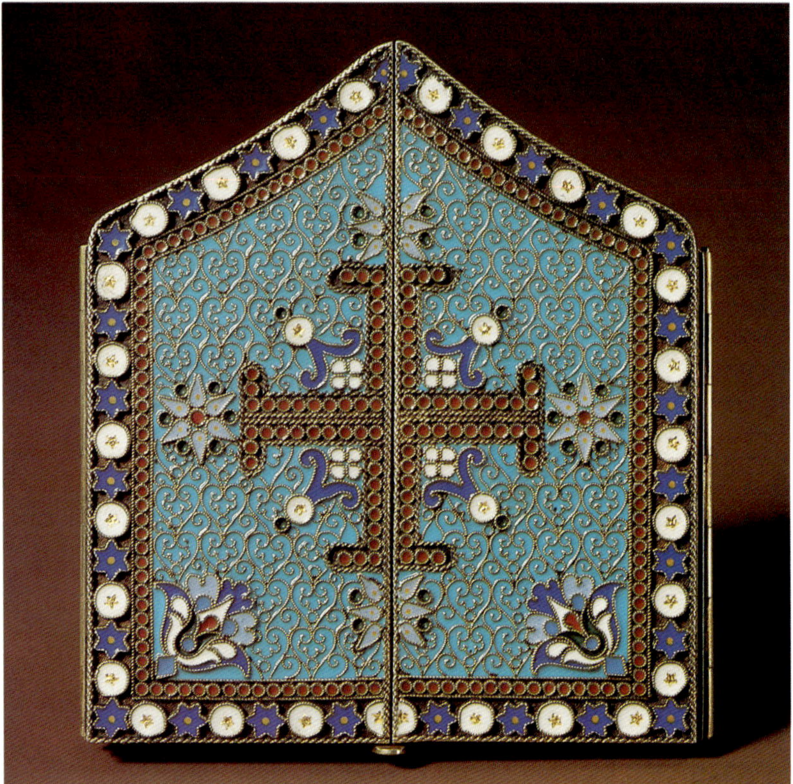

168 (ii)

168. Folding triptych
Moscow, firm of Ovchinnikov, 1911
silver gilt, enamel, oil
10.7 x 8.8 x 1.5 cm
dated, marked O. (Peter Ovchinnikov), hallmarked 89519 OK 14576

Triptych bearing the images of the Holy Trinity, St Anne and St Elizabeth. On the back of the chest is the inscription: "To the most deeply respected Anne Nikolaevna Unkovsky, with the blessings and heartfelt regards of her colleagues at the Moscow Elizabeth Institute. 6 September 1925, Moscow, 11 September 1925". Unkovsky was the head of the Moscow Elizabeth Institute, a college for young girls of the nobility, founded in 1823.

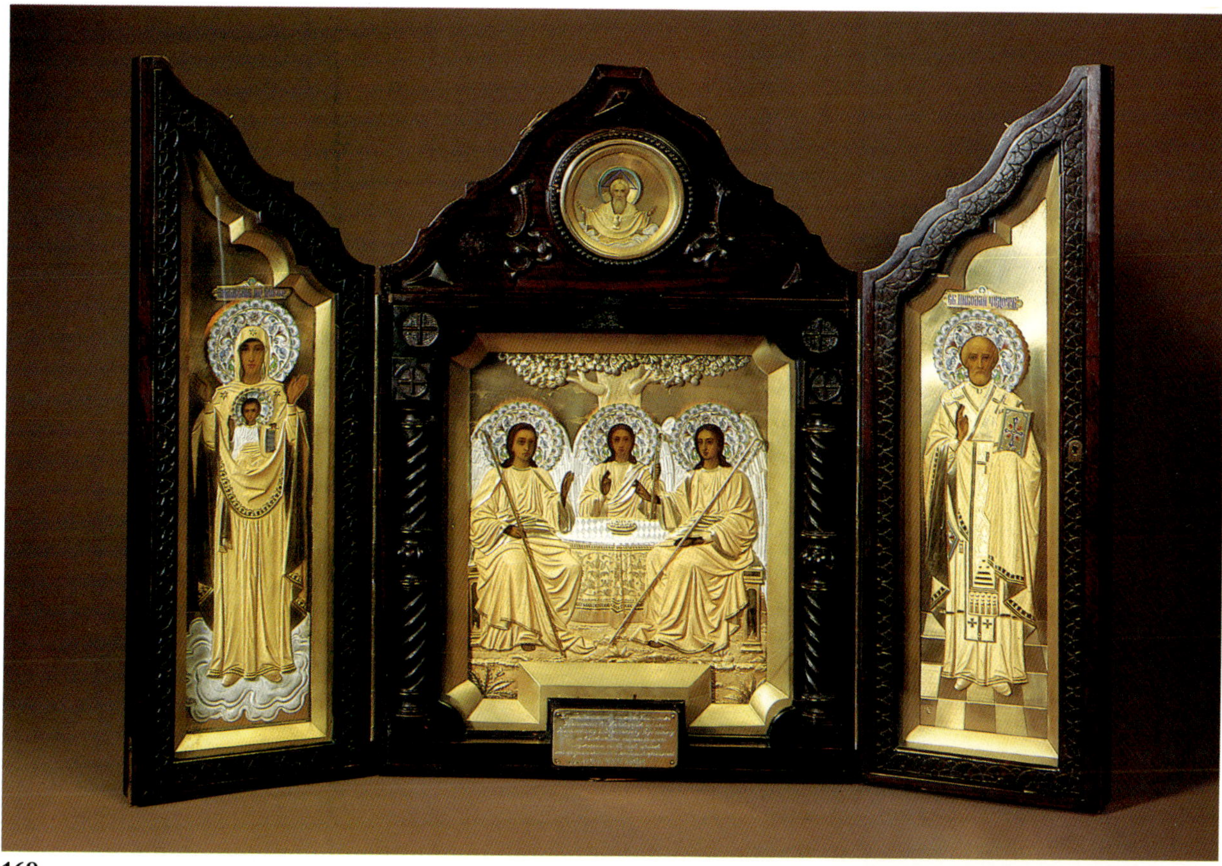

169

169. Folding triptych
first cartel of jewellers,
Moscow, 1915
oil on wood, silver gilt,
enamel, glass
78.5 x 59.0 cm
dated, hallmarked
103173 OK 21123

Triptych with images of the Holy Trinity, the Sign, St Nicholas and God of Sabaoth. The inscription on the copper plate fixed to the frame reads: "To the Very Reverend Father Superior of the Trinity Church in the village of Karacharovo, Father Aleksander Kuvakin, on the 25 years' jubilee of his pastoral service in this Church, from his grateful and loving parishioners. 27.XI.1890–XXV–27.XI.1915".

170. Altar cross
Moscow, 1752
silver gilt, niello, metal
21.8 x 35.8 cm
dated, city mark, hallmarked
57044 OK 7269

The front of the cross is decorated with niello images of the Crucifixion, the Prayers, God of Sabaoth and the Torments, while the cartouches on the reverse depict Christ carrying the Cross, the Apostles Peter and Paul, Mary Magdalene and the Holy Spirit as a dove.

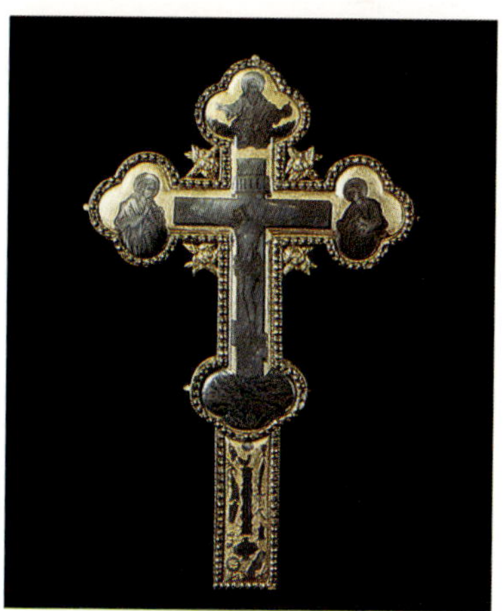

170

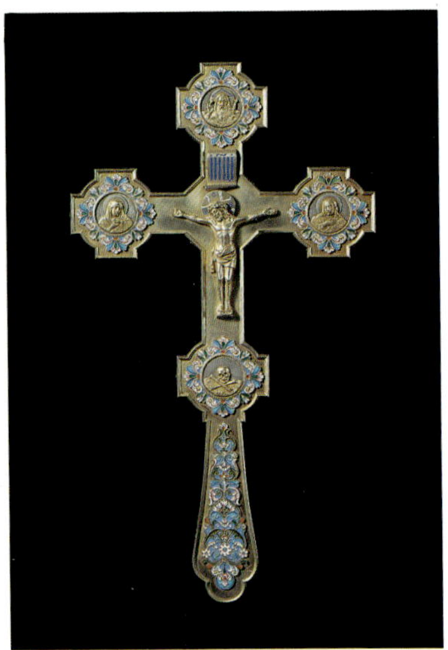

171

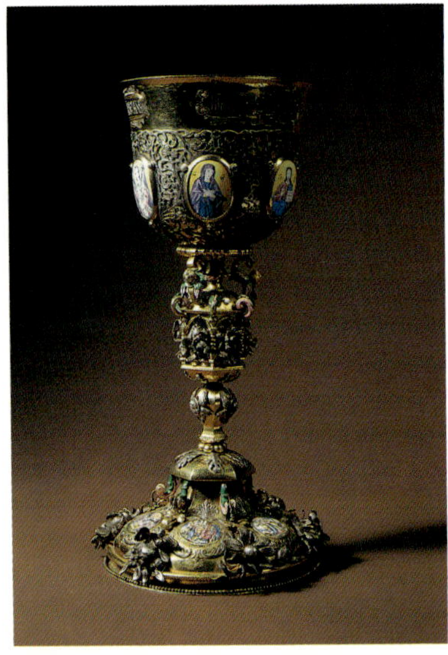

172

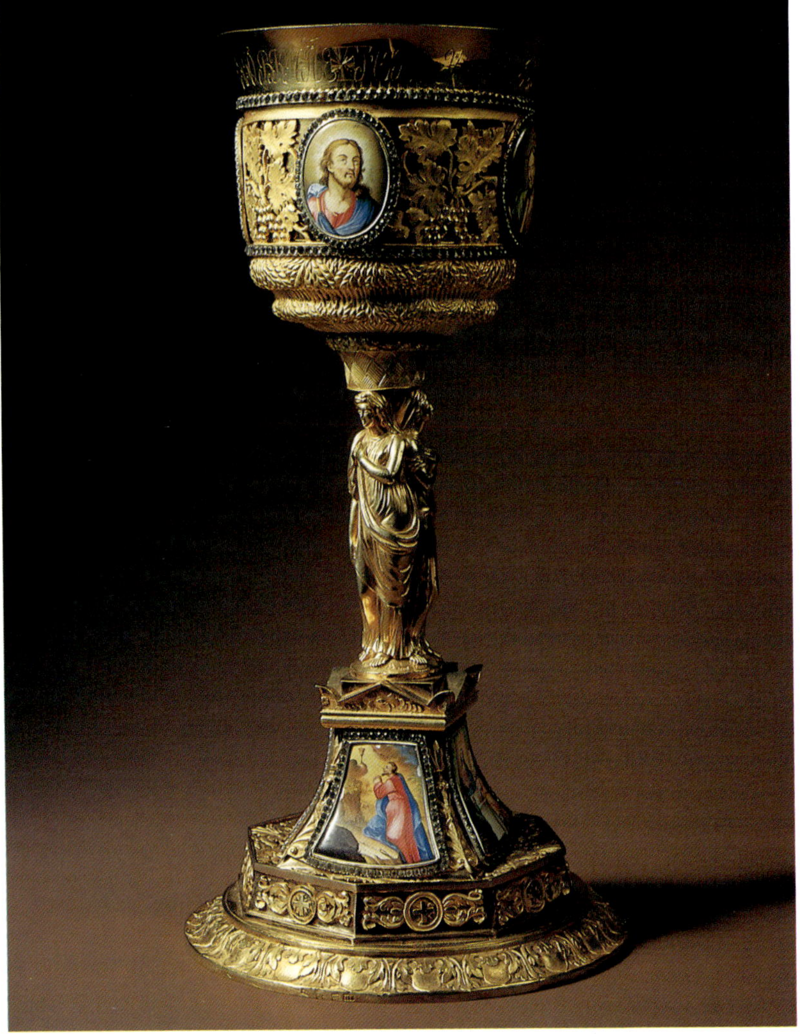

173

171. Altar cross
firm of Olovyanishnikov, Moscow, 1913
silver gilt, enamel
39.2 x 22.0 x 1.7 cm
Dated, marked, hallmarked
99095 OK 16057

Both sides of the cross bear the inscription "Donated by Faina Ivanovna Suvorov of the village Dubrovka to the Church of the Ascension, in the year 1913".

172. Chalice
Moscow, 1704
silver gilt, enamel
33.8 x 13.8 cm
77177 OK 9856

The bowl of the chalice is decorated with cloisonné images of the Deisus, the Crucifixion and Prayers. On the base are images of the Torments. Along the edge of the base runs the engraved inscription "On the 2nd of August in the year 1705, the Pious Great Sovereign, Princess Catherine (Ekaterina Alekseevna) bestowed these Holy Vessels on the Church of the Holy Mother of God Quick to Hearken, of Smolensk in Novodvichy Convent. Their weight is six pounds, their cost 170 roubles".

Princess Catherine (1658–1718), the daughter of Tsar Aleksei, was buried in the Novodvichy Convent in Smolensk, which was dedicated to the Mother of God of Smolensk and founded in 1524 by the Great Prince Vasily III, to commemorate the seizure of Smolensk. It was one of the most important fortresses in the ring of defences around Moscow, which included Donskoi, Danilov, Simonov and other monasteries.

In the 16th and 17th centuries ladies of the royal family and the noble boyards took the veil in the Novodvichy Convent. The chalice was donated by Princess Catherine as her dowry.

173. Chalice
Peter Grigoriev, Moscow, 1823
silver gilt, enamel, glass
38.1 x 14.6 x 14.6 cm
dated, marked PG, assay mark
77170/OK 9853

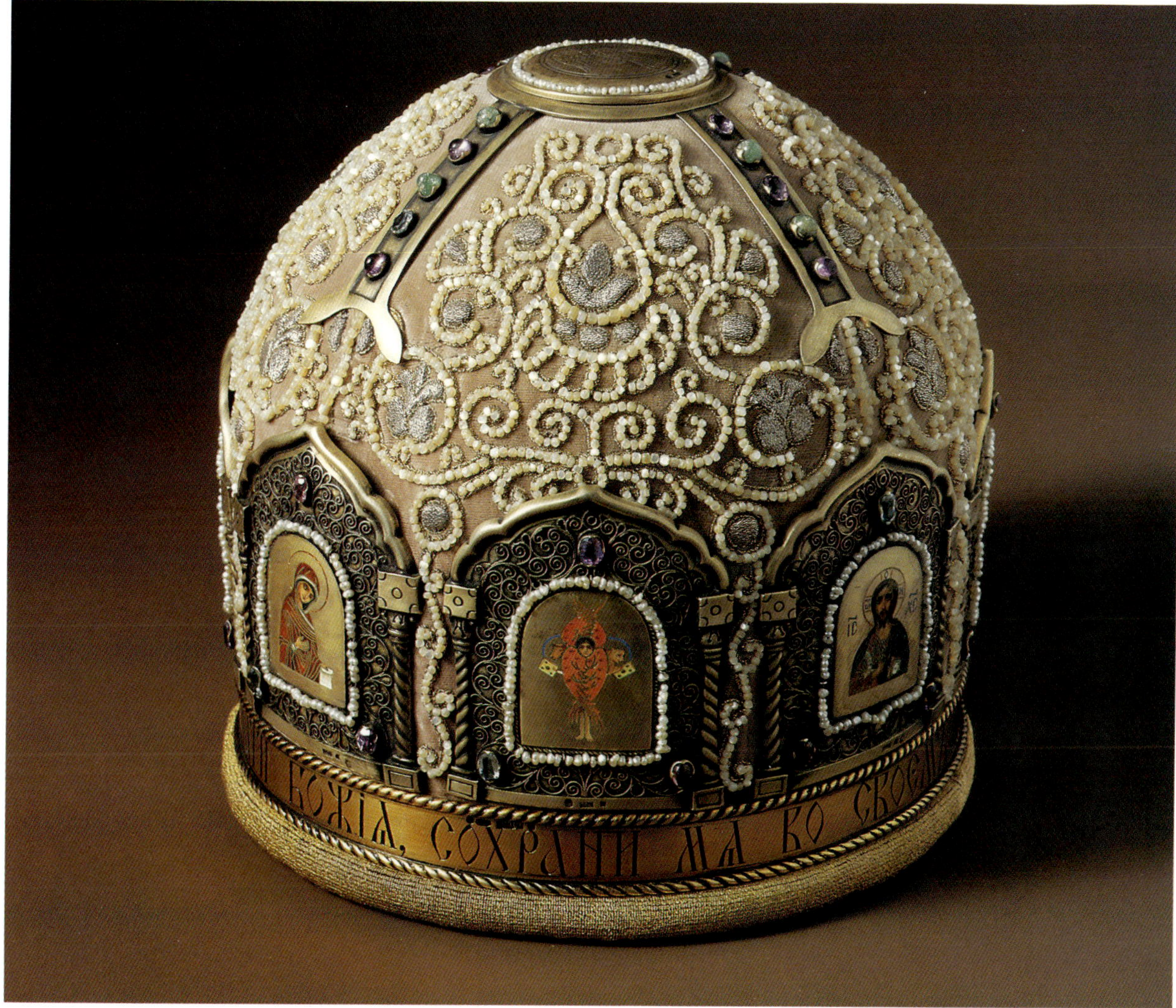

174

The smooth bowl of the chalice sits in an engraved shell, the lower part of which is decorated with ears of wheat, while the open-work upper section, bordered by a row of glass studs, is made up of vines, leaves and bunches of grapes as well as four enamelled plaques depicting the Crucifixion, the City of Jerusaleum, and the Deisus in which Christ, the Virgin and John the Baptist wear brightly coloured robes of blue, green-yellow and pale brown.

The stem of the chalice is made up of three female figures similar to caryatids. Contained in the shell which they support is the bowl of the chalice. The high base is in three levels, decorated with an engraved floral design and enamelled plaques with scenes of the Passion.

174. Mitre
firm of Olovyanishnikov, Moscow, 1908–17
silver gilt, enamel, pearls, semi-precious stones from the Urals, mother-of-pearl, velvet, textile
dated, marked, hallmarked
75692 OK 8787

The firm of Olovyanishnikov was under apppointment to the Court; from 1766 to 1917 it was well known in Moscow and Yaroslavl.

The mitre is adorned with cloisonné images of the Deisus, the Crucifixion and cherubim.

An inscription runs along the brim: "All my hope I vest in thee, Mother of God. Pray keep me safe under your protection".

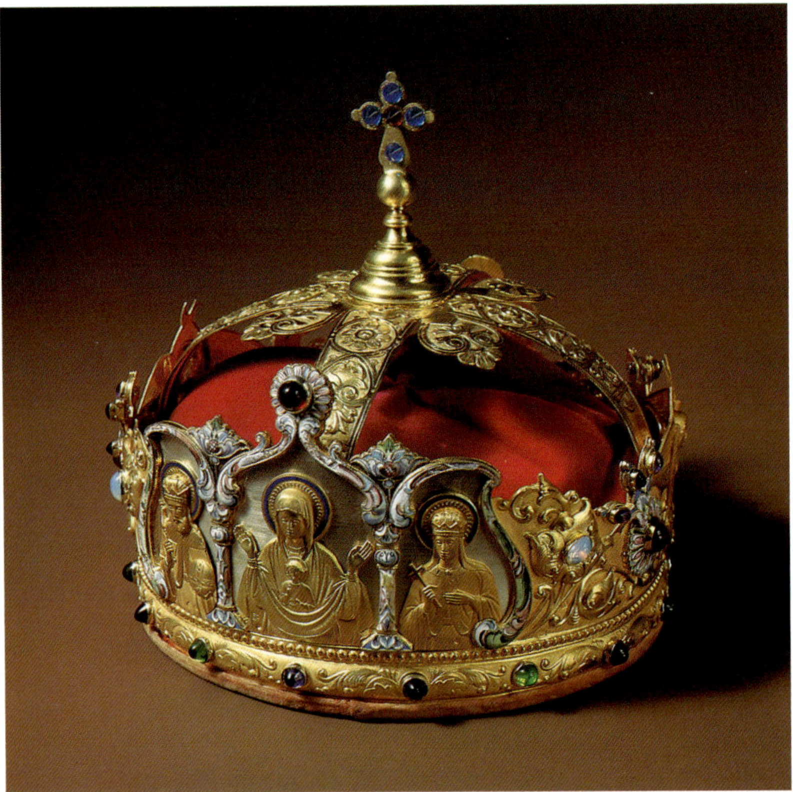

175

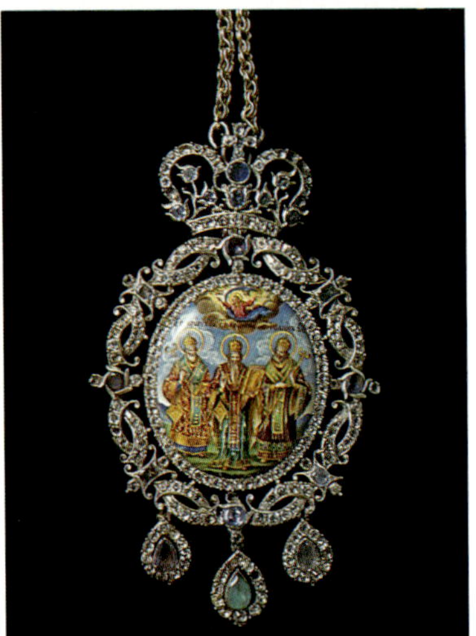

176

175. Wedding crown
V. Sikachov, Moscow,
1899–1908
silver gilt, enamel, glass
19.7 x 18.9 cm
dated, marked, hallmarked
80585 OK 13185

V. Sikachov became known as a silversmith from 1883 and from 1891 to 1917 was the owner of a silver workshop.

The wedding crown bears chased images of the Virgin, the Sign, St Konstantine, St Helen and the Archangel Michael.

176. Panagia (pectoral image)
Moscow, 1761;
cloisonné: Michael Lopov,
Petersburg, 1755
silver, enamel, sapphires, glass
12.0 x 7.4 cm;
length of chain: 102.0 cm
dated, hallmarked
77659 OK 9964

Michael Lopov, active between 1747 and 1774, was the son and pupil of A.P. Lopov, pupil of the first Russian miniaturist Gregory Musikiisky (active from 1709, d. 1737).

On the obverse are painted images of three saints: Vasily the Great, Gregory the Theologian and John Crysostom. The reverse bears an inscription on white cloisonné: "This image was painted by the master Michael Lopov on the 9th of February, 1775". A second inscription is engraved in silver: "This panagia was made by the jeweller of Varlaam Lashevsky, the Archimandrite of Don, on the 17th of August, 1761".

Varlaam Lashevsky (d. 1774), Rector of Zaikonospasskaya Academy, was transferred from the Mezhigorsky Monastery to the Donskoi Monastery in Kiev on 1 May 1753.

177. Censer
Moscow, 1702
silver gilt
height: 29.7cm
dated, city mark
44640 OK 9644

178. Panagia (pectoral image)
firm of N. Nemyrov-Kolodkyn, Moscow, 1899
gold, silver gilt, topaz, garnets, rubies
63990 OK 3659

The firm of N. Nemyrov-Kolodkyn was active from 1872 to 1916.

In the centre of the panagia is a large topaz engraved with an image of the Virgin of the Sign. On the reverse is the inscription "To His Excellency Tikhon, a member of Honour of the Nickolo-Vagankovsky Charity Committee, from the grateful members of the Committee. The 8th of September, 1899".

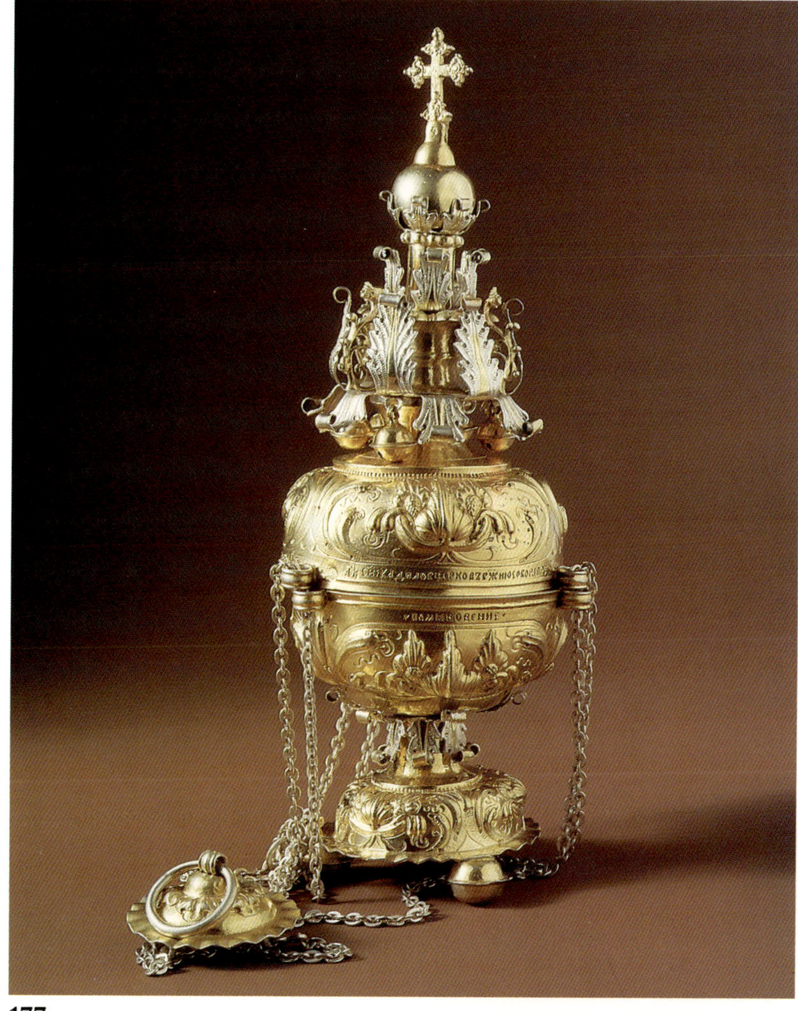

177

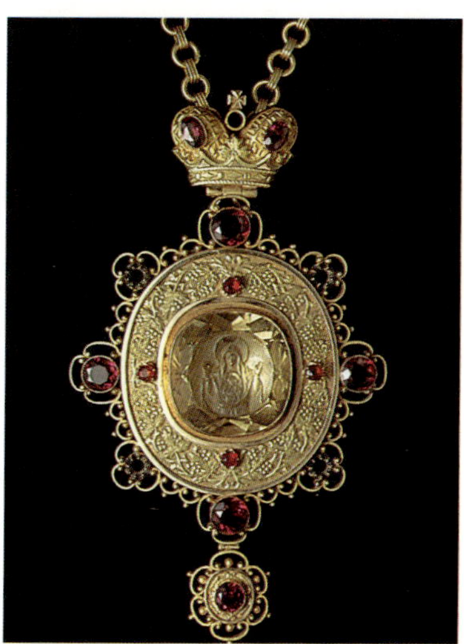

178

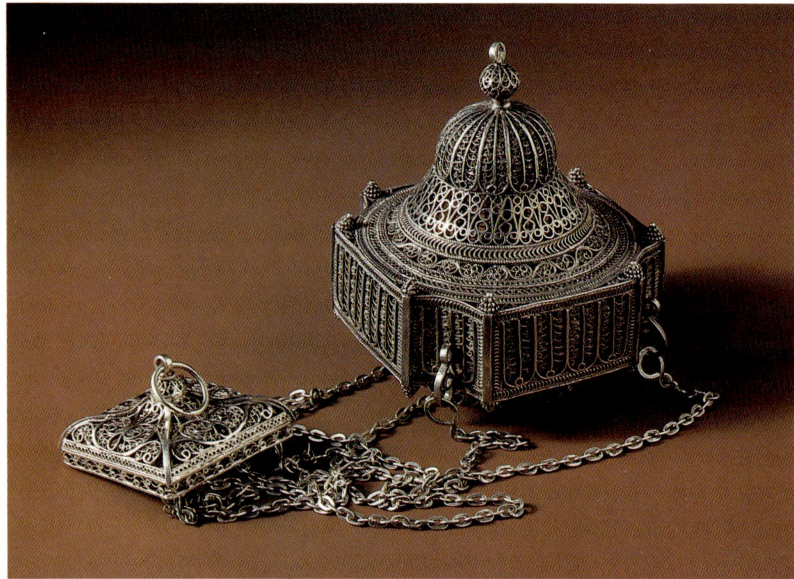

179

179. Icon lamp
Russia, 19th century
silver
Height: 12 cm
77214 OK 10600

180. Icon lamp
Ivan Alekseev, Moscow, 1895
silver gilt, enamel
9.2 x 15.3 x 15.3 cm
dated, marked, hallmarked
100425 OK 16652

Ivan Alekseev owned a gold and silverware factory from 1876 to 1917.

181. Easter egg
Moscow, 1899–1908
silver gilt, almandites, chrysoprase
6.1 x 4.6 x 4.6 cm
103173 OK 18358

182. Easter egg
Probably Moscow, 1880–90
silver gilt, enamel
6.8 x 4.7 x 4.7 cm
marked A.C.; other marks covered
103173 OK 18359

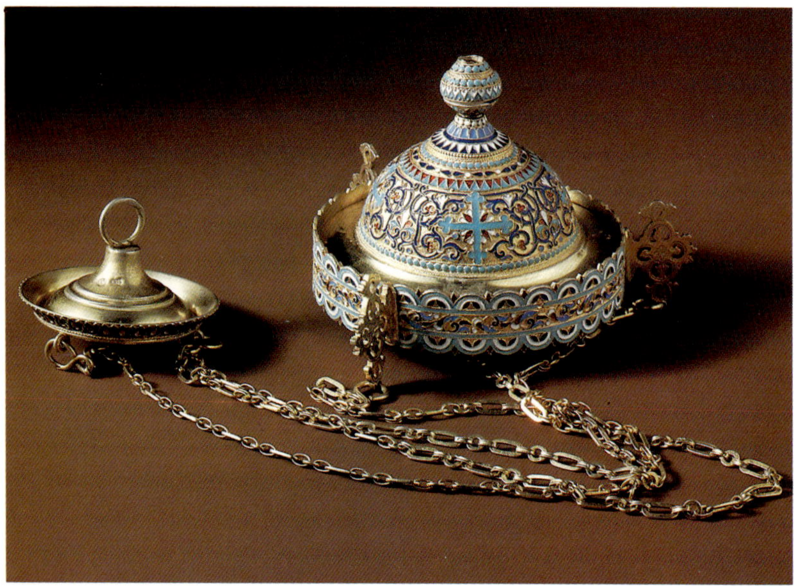

180

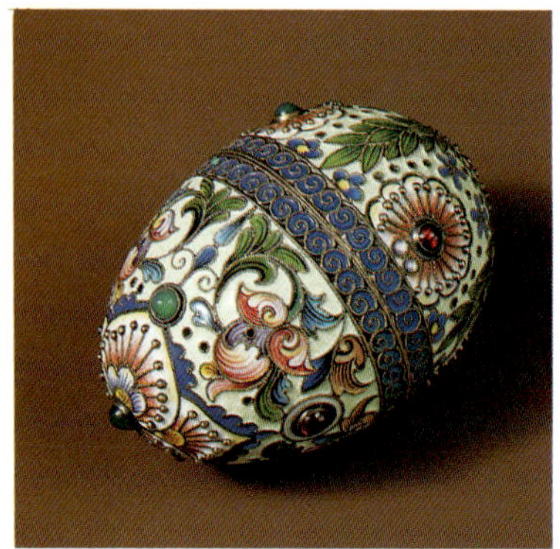

181

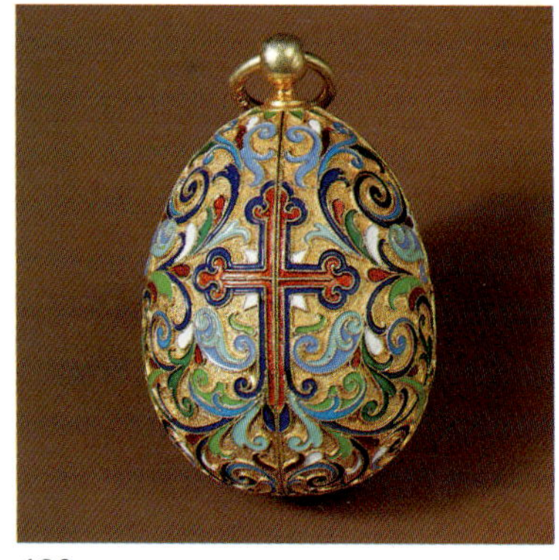

182

VII

SILVER CENTURY

Jewellery Art in Russia

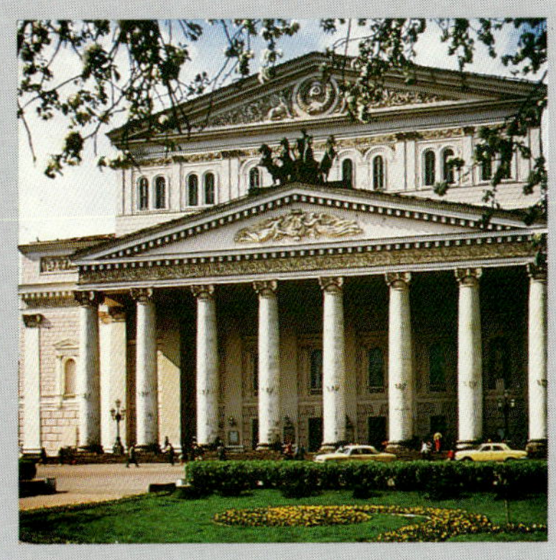

Russia in the late 19th and early 20th centuries was characterised by a flourishing of the arts. This remarkable period contributed to the world's artistic heritage such outstanding figures as the writers Dostoyevsky, Tolstoy and Chekhov, the philosophers Solovyev and Berdyaev, the composers Mussorgsky, Glinka, Tchaikovsky and Rachmaninov, the architects Shekhtel and Shervud, the painters Repin, Korovin, Serov and Vrubel and in the field of ballet, Pavlova and Diaghilev.

The greatest jewellers of the time, Fabergé, Ovchinnikov and Khlebnikov, symbolised the "silver century" of Russian applied arts. Of particular importance was the development of a national Russian style, starting in the mid 19th century with the blending of ancient Russian traditions and folk art with sculpture, architecture, painting, drawing and Art Nouveau. Jewellery-making drew upon its own thousand-year history, beginning with the cloisonné enamels of Kievan Rus, which underwent a popular revival. During this period Russian jewellers were constantly awarded at world fairs and exhibitions. Experts in Russia and abroad were unanimous in their opinion of Russian jewellery as technically and artistically superb.

In the mid 19th century jewellers endeavoured to meet the popular demand for items reflecting Russian national styles. They therefore made replicas of ethnographic pieces, copied traditional decorative techniques and depicted Russian cities and monuments and scenes from Russian history and folklore. Salt-cellars, ladles, spoons and bratinas based on wooden peasant prototypes and 17th-century models, often inscribed with folk sayings and proverbs, appeared. Silver was used to imitate folk materials such as linen, wood or birch bark. Ink-wells were made in the form of village wells, vases in the shape of peasant children reaping wheat and cups featured embossed scenes of hay-mowing. For the first time, jewellery, previously the domain of a wealthy elite, focused on the common people: their history, daily life and handicrafts.

In the mid 19th century the Moscow firm of Gubkin, established in 1841, came to prominence, receiving the Imperial Warrant in 1853. Included in the exhibition is a nielloed ladle featuring scenes of Moscow (cat. no. 185). The firm was famous for the creation of unusual surface finishes and textures; at the 1861 exhibition they displayed a small biscuit dish covered, as if carelessly, by an imitation linen napkin so realistic that an observer remarked, "one involuntarily wanted to touch it. The fly on the napkin completed the illusion". Similar dishes were later produced by the firms of Ovchinnikov and Khlebnikov, an example of which is included in the exhibition (cat. no. 202).

From the mid 19th century the art of enamelling underwent a revival, reflecting the striving after ancient Russian techniques. During the period 1860–70, enamel became the most popular decorative technique, resuming the important place it had held in metalwork in the 17th century. As in earlier times, enamel was combined with filigree, beating and embossing, in contrast to the 18th and early 19th centuries, when enamel was generally used alone in miniatures on steel plaques. Late 19th and early 20th century enamel work sparkled with a palette of up to 100 colours, and was distinguished by new techniques of blending with precious metals as well as innovative designs.

Along with 17th-century enamelling techniques such as the use of filigree, long-forgotten methods such as cloisonné, enamel over a guilloche ground and stained-glass effects reappeared. As well, new techniques such as enamel lacquer and matt enamel were developed. Leaders in this field were the firms of Ovchinnikov, Khlebnikov, Olovyanishnikov, Kurlyukov and Rükert in Moscow; and Fabergé, the Gracheyov Brothers, Tillander and Britzin in Petersburg.

Enamel was frequently combined with filigree, covering the surface against an embossed background. Enamel over a guilloche or incised ground was also common and lent itself to the representation of folk patterns reminiscent of embroidery and wood carving. Some of the most original pieces were metal salt-cellars with imitation wood or linen surfaces and inscribed proverbs, made by the Petersburg firm of K. Albrecht (cat. no. 187).

In the early 19th century Petersburg was the artistic centre of Russia. It set the fashions and artistic trends and was the home of all the leading craftsmen and artists of the day; its Academy of Fine Arts was renowned. By the mid 19th century, however, the revival of interest in history and traditional artforms had caused an abrupt shift to Moscow as the creative centre of the nation. Despite some common trends, the Moscow and Petersburg artistic styles differed markedly in all fields of endeavour, including gold and silver work.

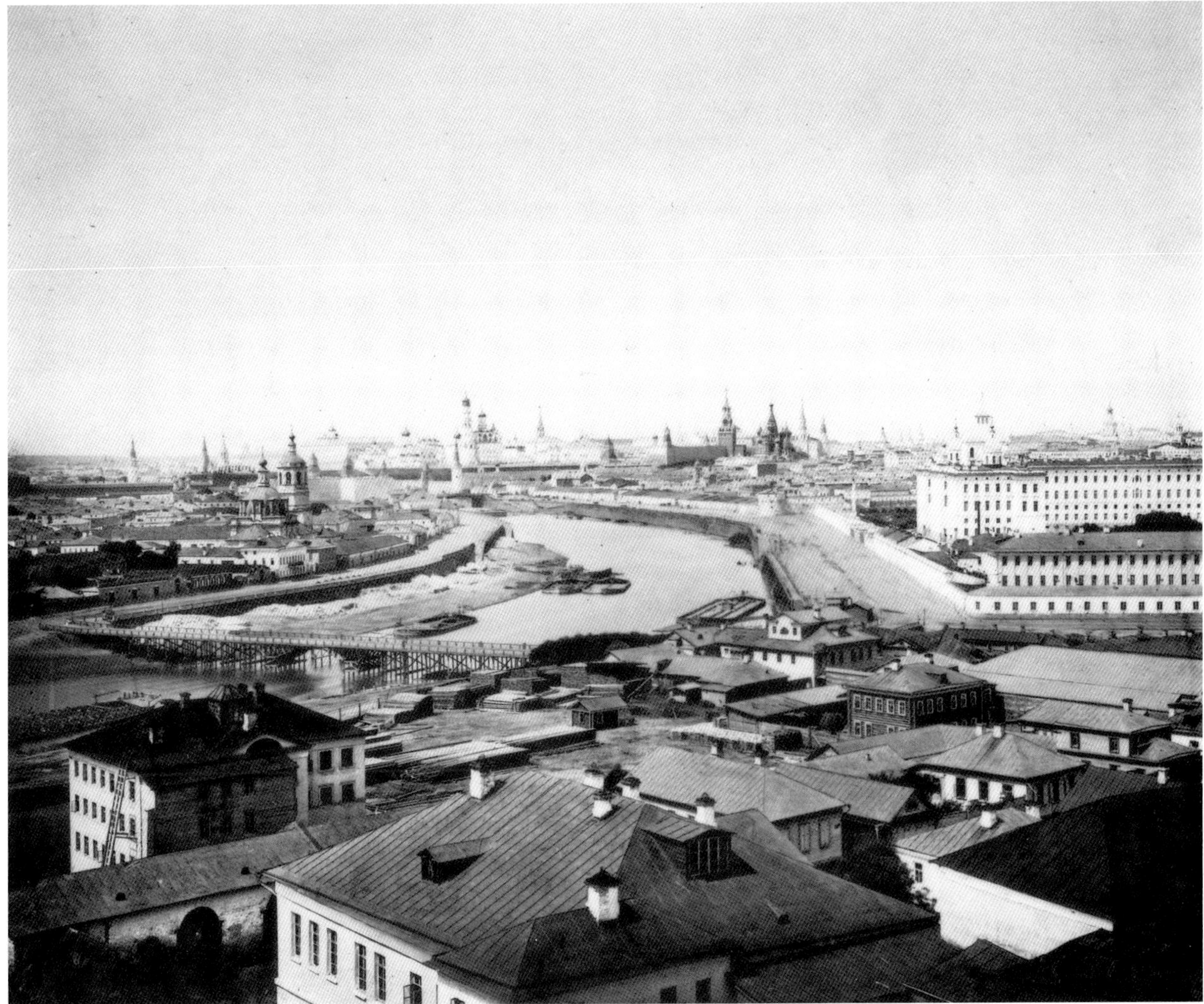

VIEW OF MOSCOW

The distinctive feature of Moscow life was the greater role played by the wealthy merchant class, dominated by families such as the Mamontovs, the Tretyakov brothers, the Schukins, the Naidenovs, the Ryabushinkskys and many others. In 1856, M. Pogodin said of these Moscow merchants, "They spare no effort in serving Russia, by donating money to charity, setting up fine art collections and supporting various initiatives.". Hence the development of the Russian style, with its attractive and approachable realism and depictions of everyday life, Moscow streetscapes and ancient monuments, met with an enthusiastic response among all levels of society, and in particular found many supporters among the art patrons of the wealthy merchant class.

The late 19th and early 20th century opened a new era in the history of Moscow. During this period of economic and cultural development, many schools, colleges and museums were founded and the city acquired an attractive appearance. In all spheres of creativity, artists such as Vasnetzov, Mamontov and Polenova were striving after natural beauty, not only reviving ancient Russian art but inspired by it to create completely new forms. The revival of Russian national styles began in Moscow in its School of Art, through the adoption of ancient Russian decorative principles.

The outstanding exponents of this trend in the area of silver and gold jewellery were the two best Moscow firms, P. Ovchinnikov and I. Khlebnikov. Deeply impressed by the splendour of ancient Russian art, which for almost two centuries had been forgotten and overshadowed by western European influences, these craftsmen revived the old forms in their work. The firm of P. Ovchinnikov, founded in 1853, received in 1865 the Imperial Warrant at the All-Russian Arts and Manufacting Exhibition in Moscow, where its works were hailed as "items of distinguished originality of design, superb workmanship and a developing national style". A report after the Exhibition stated: "The name of Mr Ovchinnikov is famous almost all over Russia. He has achieved this fame alone, through his vigour, hard work and skill. Beginning as a craftsman, Mr Ovchinnikov has, through his 20-year career, brought his craft to a higher degree of perfection". Ovchinnikov made an important contribution to the development of Russian themes in the decoration of silver pieces. Historic, genre and domestic scenes, which were cast, beaten or embossed, were very popular. Included in this exhibition are examples such as the tankard with an embossed scene of peasants returning from hay-mowing. The firm was also acclaimed for its use of polychrome enamels. The works from 1870 to 1890 reveal the splendour of Russian lace designs and a limitless range of decorative silver items. Designs based on the illuminations of hand-written books devoted to ancient Russian art were used to decorate gospel covers, icons, liturgical vessels, tableware, caskets, blotting pads, boxes and other items. These brilliant works were the result of scholarly study of ancient Russian art combined with the creative talent of the artist and manufacturer, Ovchinnikov.

The firm of I. Khlebnikov did much to revive and develop the Russian style. It produced items in all the major styles of the late 19th and early 20th centuries: historic Russian, neo-Russian, and Art Nouveau. Khlebnikov was the first firm under the Imperial Warrant to be mentioned at a World Fair when, in Vienna in 1873, he was said to have displayed a "well-composed, large collection of items in the Russian Style", which attracted "the keen interest of experts" and won two medals.

The techniques of embossing and casting flourished during this period. The oustanding Russian jeweller, I. Sazikov, was one of the first to create silver sculptures

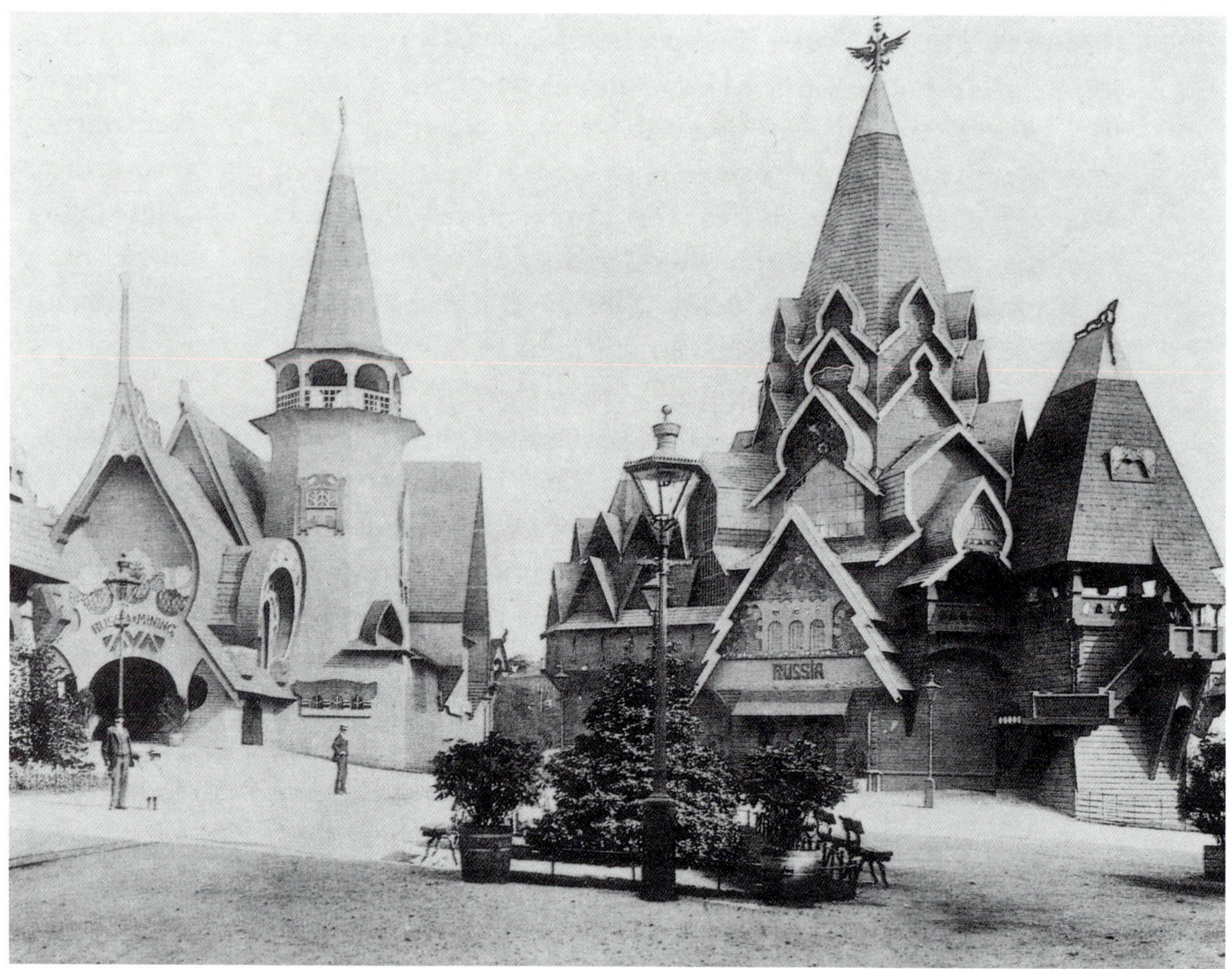

RUSSIAN PAVILION, GLASGOW INTERNATIONAL EXHIBITION, 1901

and embossed low-reliefs in the Russian style. The firms of Nicholls and Plincke, Ovchinnikov, Khlebnikov, the Gracheyov Brothers and Fabergé continued this trend. An excellent example is the tankard (cat. no. 198) made by Khlebnikov in 1872 to commemorate the bicentenary of the birth of Peter the Great. It is decorated with an embossed depiction of the founding of Petersburg; Peter the Great, standing on the uninhabited bank of the river Neva, is surrounded by clergymen and his confederates.

Great attention was always paid to the manufacture of decorative dishes, blotting-pads and albums, usually made to commemorate important events or people. The craftsmen, being allowed great freedom in their choice of decorative techniques, created some highly original pieces, exploiting in full a rich and diverse range of styles, artistic trends and ornamental methods. Included in the exhibition are two blotting-pads of contrasting style and technique. The first (cat. no. 200), dating from 1886, has a low-relief depiction of mounted knights; the second (cat. no. 204) features a high-relief image of boyars in the neo-Russian style.

The spirit of nationalism was particularly evident in Russian fine arts and manufactured items during the late 19th and early 20th centuries. The need to combine the efforts of experienced craftsmen and artists with historical knowledge, technical skill, creativity and imagination attracted such well-known artists as Vasnetzov, Vrubel, Rerikh, Polenov, Malyutin, Benua and Bilibin to design jewellery at the Abramtzev, Talashkin and Stroganov Art School workshops. They became known for their development of the Russian Style in the applied arts, which during that period underwent various stages of evolution, from the historical-archaeological to the romantic neo-Russian.

While Art Nouveau, which dominated Europe around the turn of the century, was a strong and specific style in itself, it had variants in each individual country under its influence. In Russia it was combined with an active search for national forms, resulting in a unique variant of Art Nouveau: the neo-Russian style, essentially characterised by old Russian forms enhanced by a freer use of proportion, rhythm and historical illustrative elements. This style was born in Moscow. The wine service, (cat. no. 216), tea-glass holder (cat. no. 219) and ladle (cat. no. 217) are examples of this style.

It was logical for the Petersburg firm of Fabergé to open a second branch, charged mainly with producing silver goods and tableware, in Moscow, historically the centre of Russian silversmithing. In Petersburg the firm, which was under the Imperial Warrant, produced works mainly for the Tsar and the nobility; in Moscow it made pieces for a wider cross-section of society, particularly the wealthy merchant class. The stylistic contrast between works produced by the Petersburg and Moscow branches is due mainly to this difference of clientele. Examples of each are included in the exhibition.

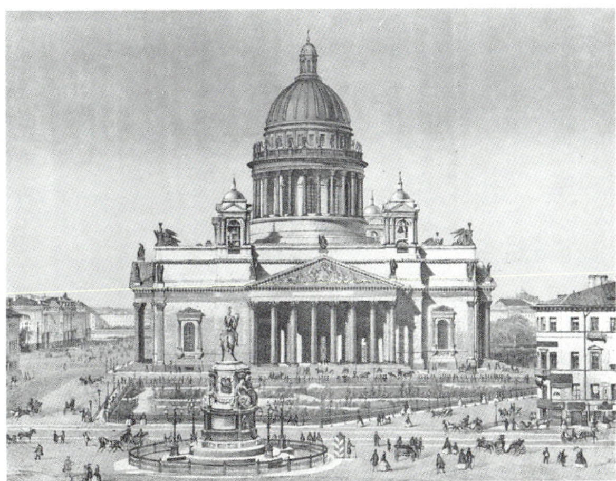

VIEW OF PETERSBURG

Petersburg's traditional orientation to western European culture and fashion continued into the late 19th and early 20th centuries. The city boasted Russia's richest collections of western art, in institutions such as the State Hermitage and the Academy of Fine Arts and private collections such as that of Baron Shtyglitz. The Mir Iskusstva (World of Art) movement, an attempt to make Russian culture more European, began in Petersburg. In gold and silver work, this movement had always been associated with the collaborative

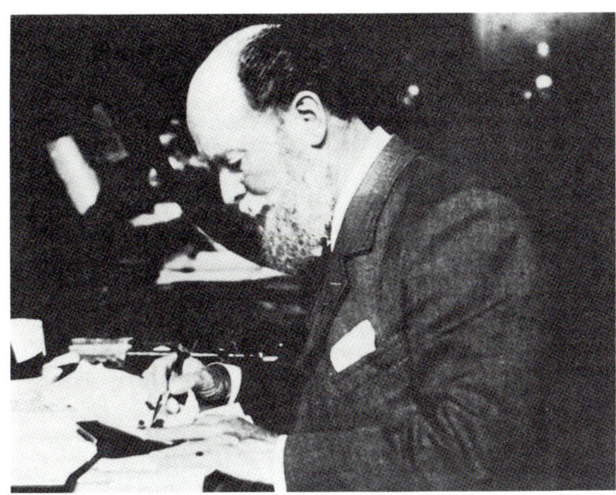

KARL FABERGÉ, 1915

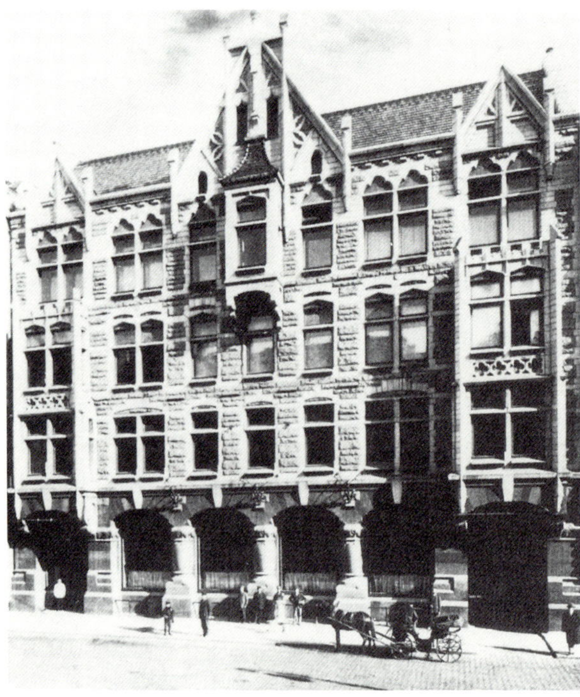

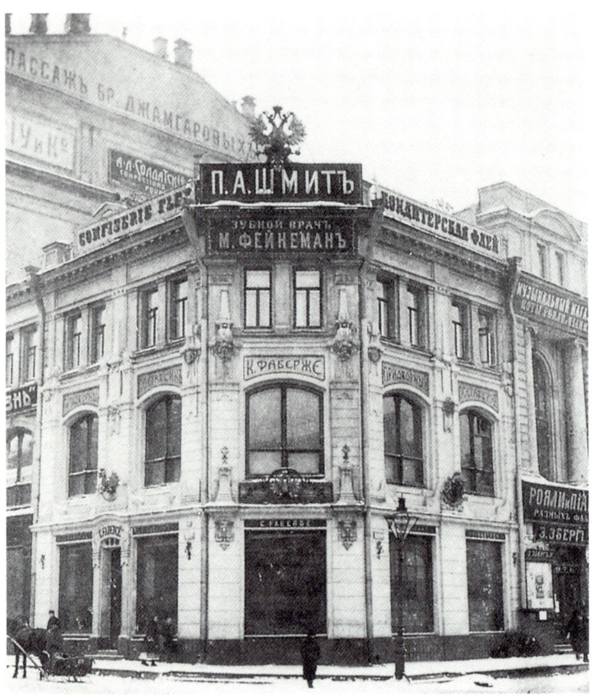

FABERGÉ SHOPS, PETERSBURG AND MOSCOW

efforts of Russian and foreign craftsmen, particularly in Petersburg during the reign of Peter the Great.

The leader of Petersburg gold and silver work was the world-renowned firm of Carl Fabergé, which produced a vast range of items, from ornaments, watches, frames, bouquets and sculpture to cutlery, tableware and boxes. Their valuable Easter eggs—elegant, beautiful and imaginative masterpieces decorated with precious stones and enamels—are considered the apotheosis of the jeweller's art and brought the firm lasting international acclaim. Fabergé's diversity of output, superb affinity for materials and decorative style ensured a high ranking for the firm, both in Russia and abroad. Included in the exhibition is an opal-enamelled clock by one of Fabergé's leading craftsmen, H. Vigstrom, as well as a frame, tea-glass holder, cigarette case, box made of rock-crystal and an obsidian hippopotamus (cat. nos 229–234).

The Imperial firm of the Gracheyov Brothers, also a major producer of silver and gold items, was awarded a gold medal at the Paris World Fair in 1890. The company produced cutlery sets, tea-services, liturgical items, tableware and sculpture, employing all styles and decorative techniques. Included in the exhibition are a samovar and tray executed in a strict classical style (cat. no. 236).

The wide range of silver and gold objects, including liturgical items, produced in Russia in the mid-to-late 19th century and the early 20th century, shows a mixture of artistic styles, decorative forms and ornamental designs. As with all of Russia's creative output at the time, their unique forms and decorative style resulted from the nation's search for artistic renewal.

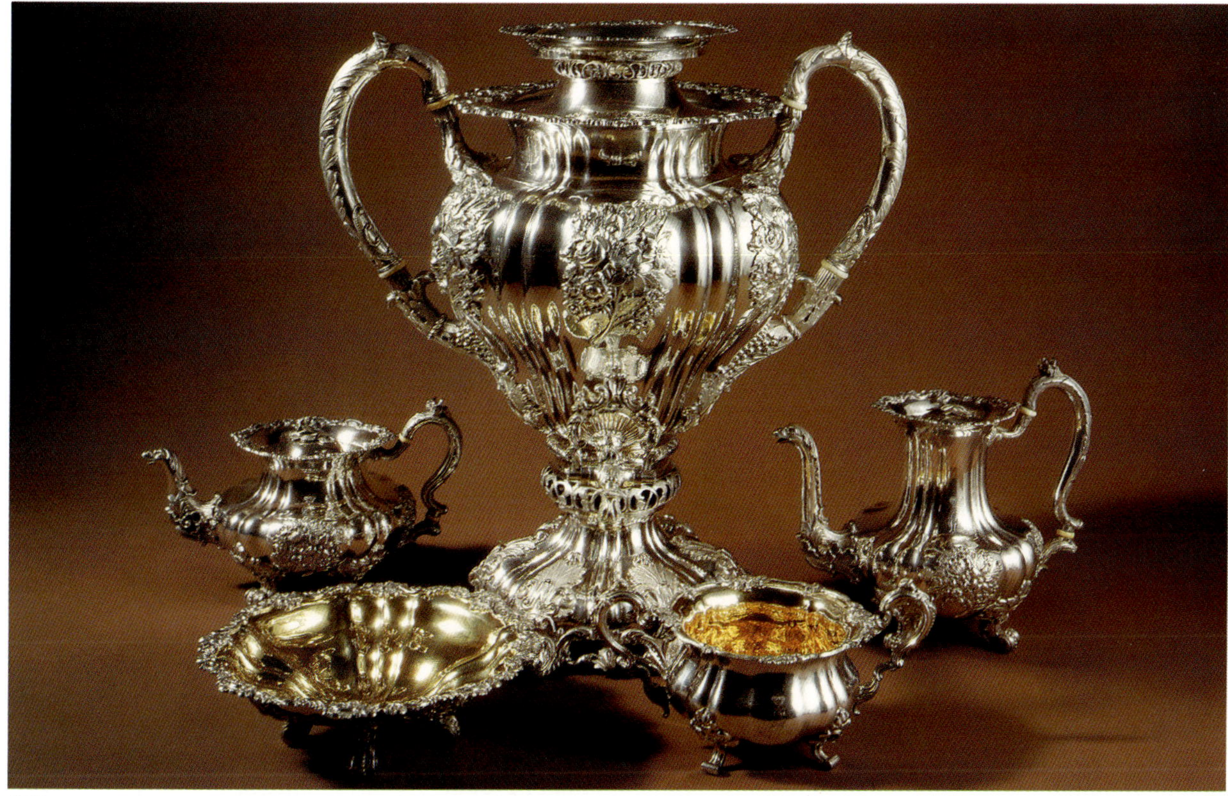

183

183. Travelling tea service
Karl Boyanovsky; tray: Ignaty Pavlovich Sazikov; sugar bowl: Karl Adolf Seipel, Petersburg, 1838–64
silver gilt, mother-of-pearl, bone
height of samovar: 52.0 cm; tray: 81.0 x 52.0 cm; tray: 39.3 x 21.9 cm; biscuit containers: 11.8 x 35.0 x 33.4 cm; teapot: 17.8 x 14.5 x 14.5 cm; slop-basin: 8.2 x 25.4 x 25.4 cm; sugar bowl: 13.0 x 16.0 x 16.0 cm; coffee pot: 24.2 x 12.5 x 12.0 cm
dated, mark: BOIANOWSKI, CAS (SAZIKOV), assay mark 68257 OK 8308-8318

This tea service belonged to the Great Prince Sergei Aleksandrovich Romanov (1857–1905), the fourth son of Tsar Aleksander II, who married the Grand Duchess Elizabeta Feodorovna (1864–1918), the sister of Empress Aleksandra Feodorovna. The Prince fought in the Russian-Turkish war of 1877–78, was Commander of the Preobrazhensky Regiment, Commander of the forces of the Moscow military district, Chief of the Second Battalion of the Household Infantry and the 38th Tobolsk Infantry Regiment and a member of the State Council. From 1891 he was Governor-General of Moscow and from 1881 Chairman of the Imperial Russian Historical Museum, Marshall of the Orthodox Palestinian Society, Most Honourable Protector of the Society of Historical Painters, the Imperial Society for Animal and Plant Acclimatization and the Committee for the Organization of the Emperor Aleksander III Fine Arts Museum, an honourable member of the Imperial Academy of Arts, the Imperial Archaeological Society, the Historical-Genealogical Society and the Elizabeth Charity Society and Most Honourable President of the Aleksandrovkaya Community of the Sisters of Charity.

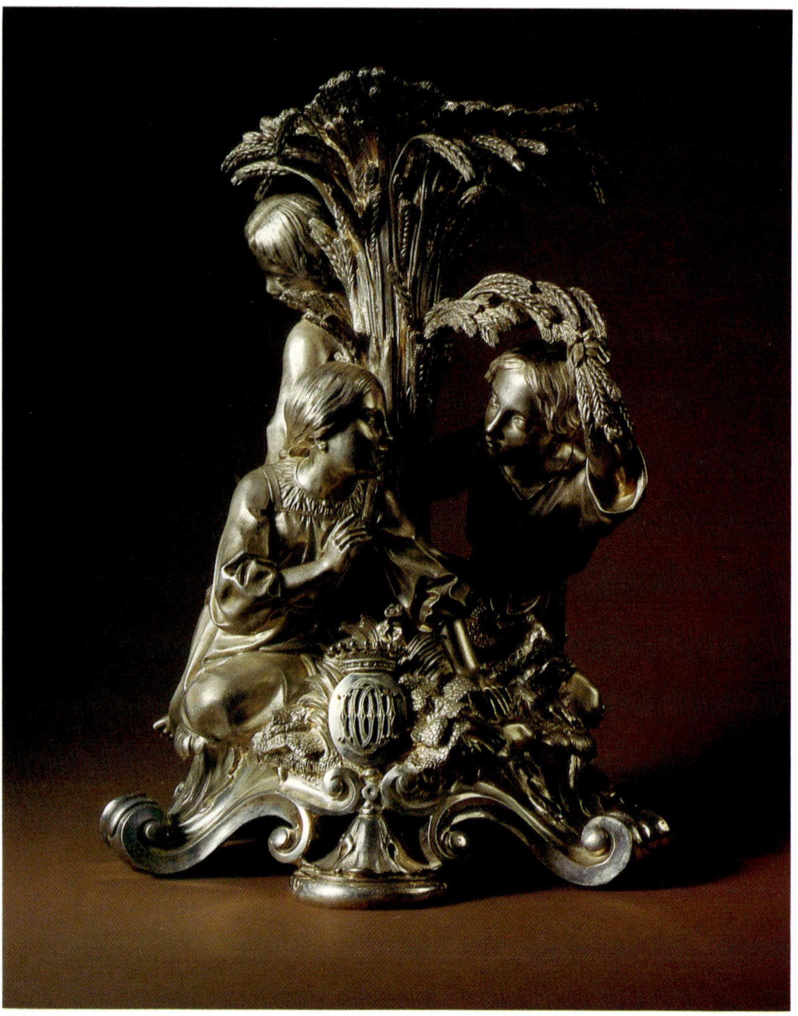

184

184. Vase
firm of Nickols and Plinke, Petersburg, 1867
silver
height: 38.5 cm
dated, marked NP, assay mark 53030 OK 5434

Nickols and Plinke owned a silver workshop known from 1815 to 1898.

185. Ladle
firm of I. Gubkin, Moscow, 1856
silver gilt, niello
6.1 x 22.2 x 15.1 cm
dated, marked GUBKIN, assay mark
53030 OK 169

I. Gubkin founded a silver workshop in 1841. His sons Ivan, Dmitri and Mikhail continued the work of their father. The firm was a supplier to the court from 1855 to 1880.

The Moscow Kremlin and Winter Palace are depicted in niello. At the bottom is the inscription "Ryazan 1857 Prize of the Society of four-year-old stallions".

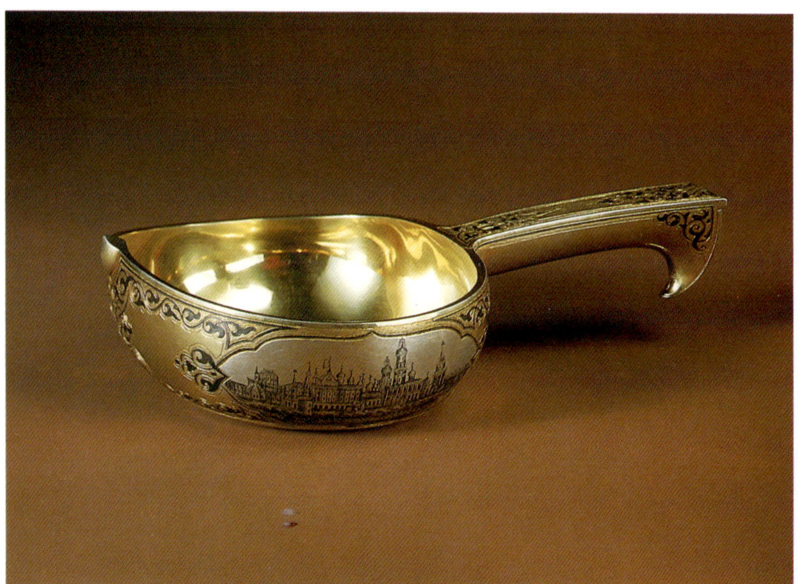

185

186. Salt cellar
Mitrofan Nikolaievich Ryndin, Moscow, 1889
silver gilt
13.1 x 10.7 x 10.5 cm
dated, marked m.p., assay mark
102423 OK 18500

Mitrofan Nikolaievich Ryndin owned a silver workshop known from 1883 to 1917.

187. Salt cellar
Kirill Feodorovich Albrecht, Petersburg, 1882
silver gilt, enamel
11.3 x 5.5 x 5.8 cm
dated, marked KA, assay mark
83589 OK 14143

On the back of the salt cellar reads the inscription "With a loaf of bread, a man can find paradise under a fir tree". Along the edge of the lid runs "There is no talk without pepper and salt" and "Honesty is the best policy".

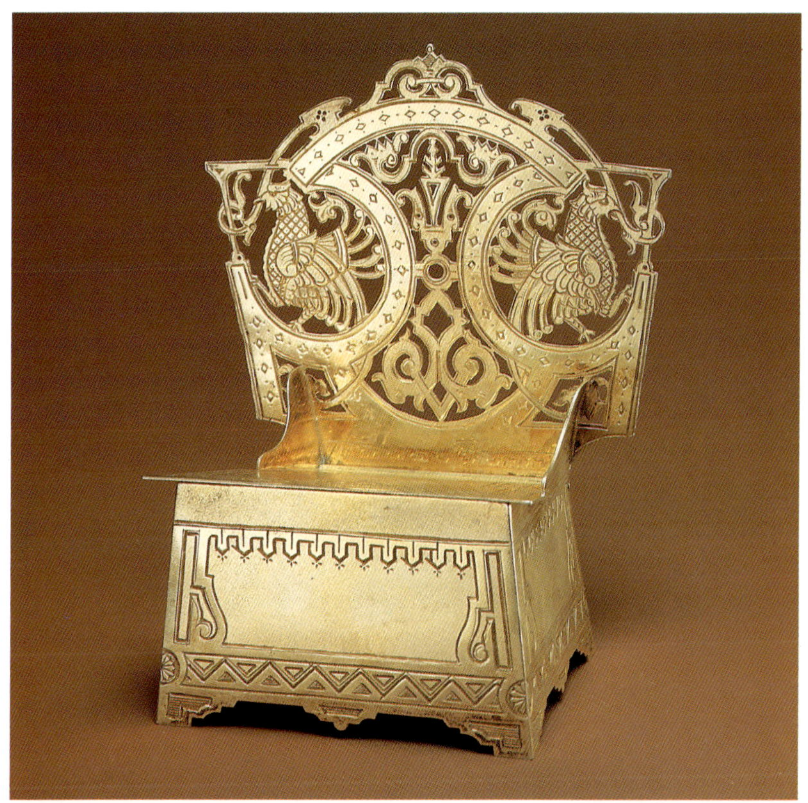

186

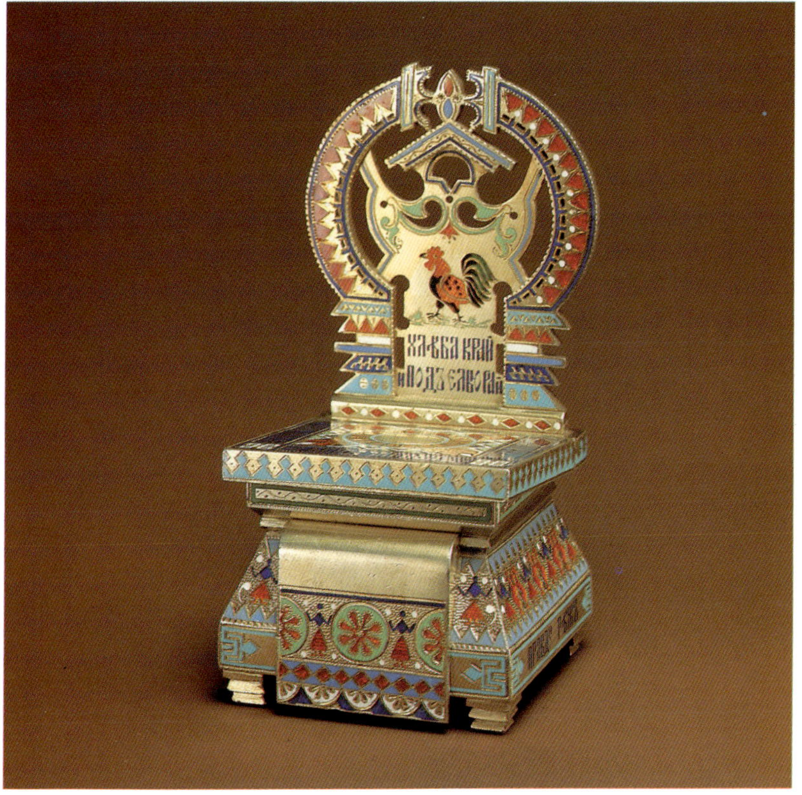

187

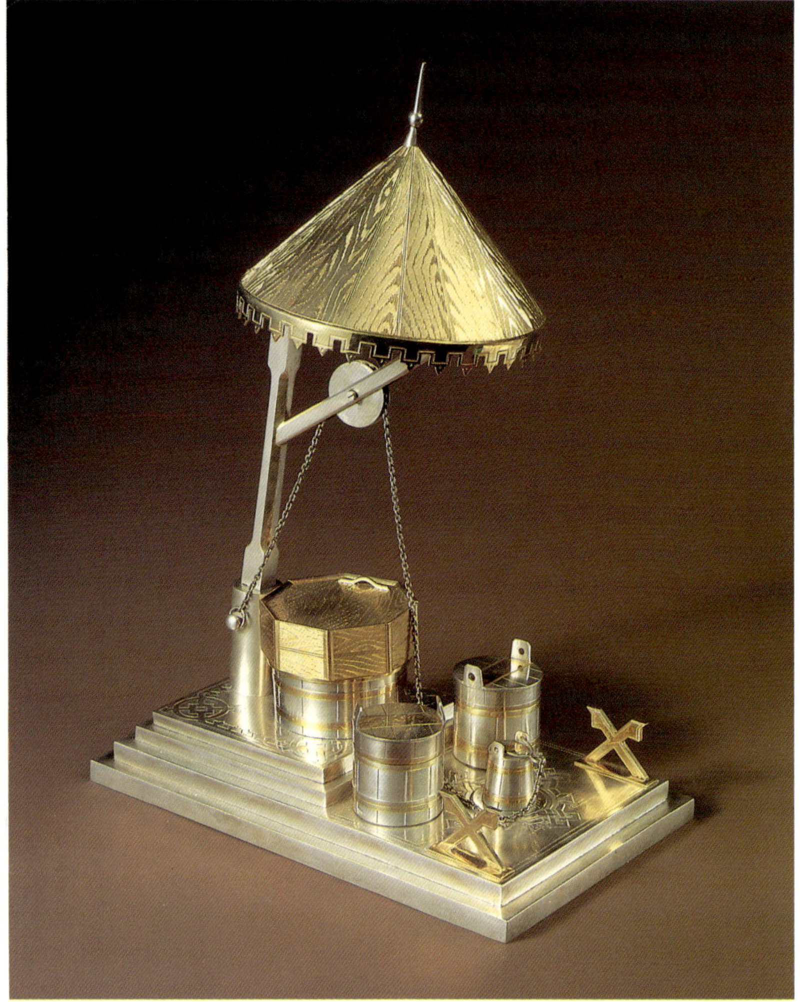

188

188. Writing set
Karl Werlin, Petersburg, 1876
silver gilt
24.5 x 19.0 x 11.5 cm
dated, marked KB, assay mark
OK 15602

Karl Werlin was active as a silversmith from 1871 to 1878.

189. Caviar dish
Astrakhan, 1884
silver gilt, niello
dated, assay mark
81631 OK 13663

An inscription in Armenian reads "To Petres Adamyan from Caucasian Armenian Fishermen. Astrakhan. 1884."

Petres Adamyan was a prominent Armenian actor in the second half of the 19th century. He was noted for performing Shakespeare in Russia.

190. Glass holder
Peter Loskutov, Moscow, 1885
silver gilt
8.0 x 10.5 x 7.1 cm
dated, assay mark
99111 OK 16071

Peter Loskutov was known as a silversmith between 1852 and 1885.

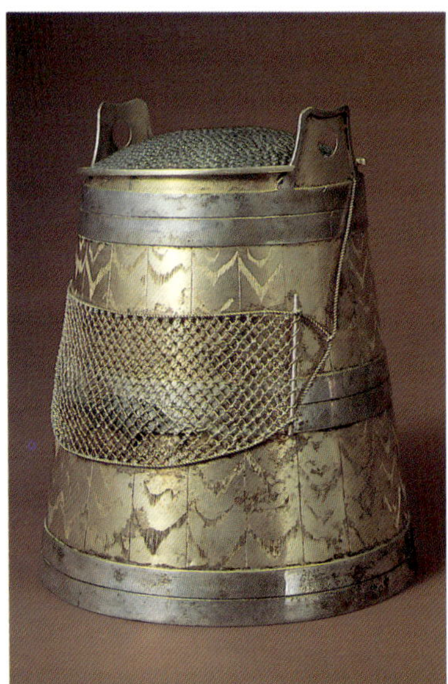

189

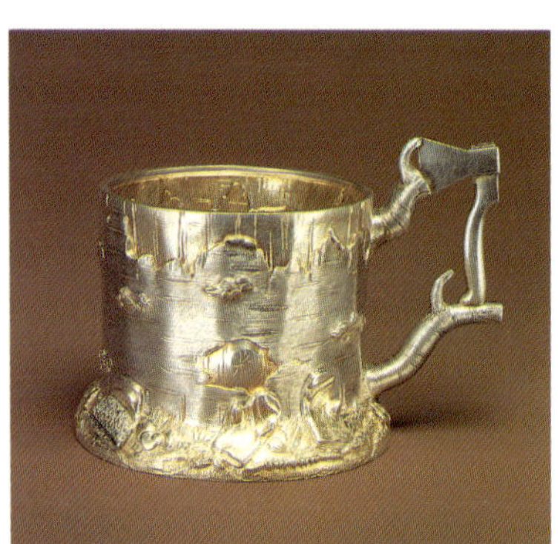

190

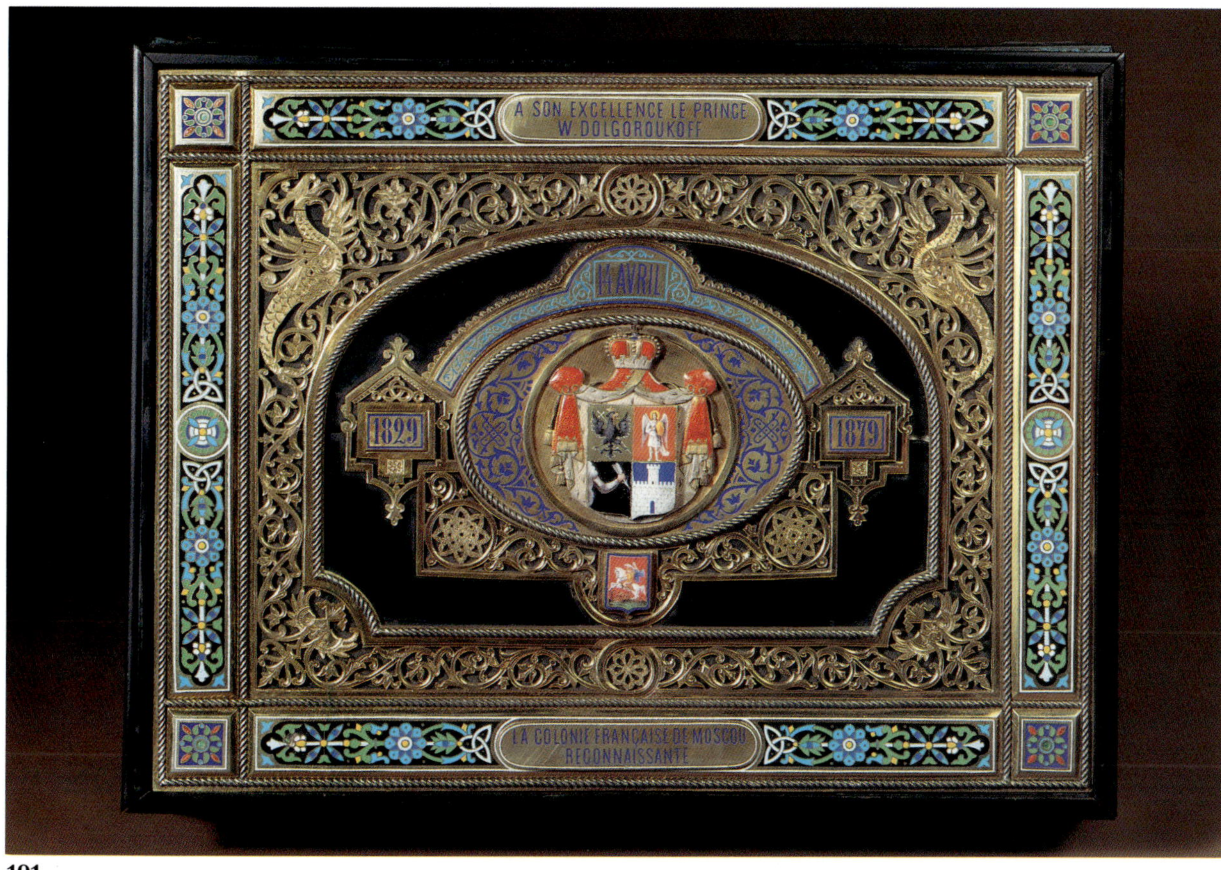

191

**191. Casket
firm of P. Ovchinnikov,
Moscow, 1879
silver gilt, enamel, wood,
textile
7.0 x 37.0 x 28.8 cm
dated, marked P.O., assay
mark
70156 OK 13925**

On the lid of the casket is the inscription "To Prince V.A. Dolgoruky from the French colony in Moscow, 1879".

After completing his studies at the Junior Ensigns School of Guards, Prince V.A. Dolgoruky (1810–91) served in the Household Mounted Regiment and the Polish Company and was later appointed General Provisions Master and a member of the Military Council. In 1865 he was appointed Governor-General of Moscow.

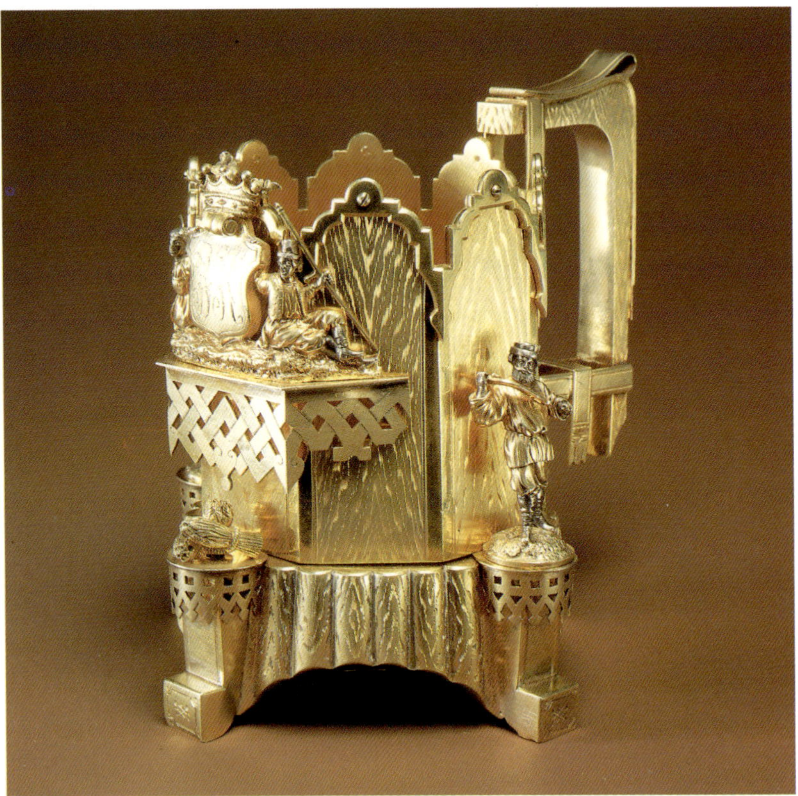

192

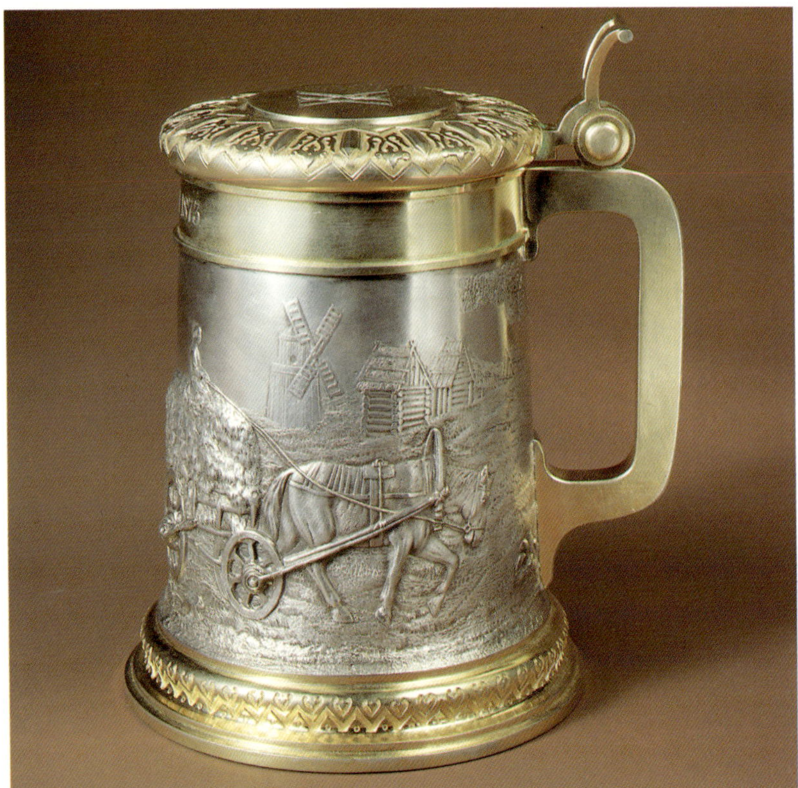

193

192. Glass holder
Aleksander Nikolaievich Sokolov, Petersburg, 1890
silver gilt
height: 13.5 cm
dated, marked AHC, assay mark
79085 OK 11200

Aleksander Nikolaievich Sokolov was the owner of a gold, silver and bronze workshop between 1858 and 1890.

193. Tankard
firm of P. Ovchinnikov, Moscow, 1873
silver gilt
height 18.5 cm
dated, marked P. OVCHINNIKOV, assay mark OK 22653

P. Ovchinnikov (1830–88) founded his firm in 1853. From 1865 it was a supplier to the court. His sons continued his work until the closure of the firm in 1917.

194. Table clock
firm of P. Ovchinnikov,
Moscow, 1904
silver, marble
57.0 x 25.0 x 21.0 cm
dated, marked P.
OVCHINNIKOV, assay mark
71203 OK 12451

195. Dish
firm of P. Ovchinnikov,
Moscow, 1889
silver gilt, enamel
diameter: 44.8 cm
dated, marked P.
OVCHINNIKOV, assay mark
102405 OK 17427

The inscription reads "To Peter Antonovich and Anna Frantsevna Mussi, from the Weaving Cartel". The Mussis were silk manufacturers.

196. Bratina (loving cup)
firm of P. Ovchinnikov,
Moscow, 1896
silver gilt, enamel
17.5 x 12.2 x 12.2 cm
dated, marked
OVCHINNIKOV, assay mark
78814 OK 11178

197. Cigarette case
firm of P. Ovchinnikov,
Moscow, 1883
silver gilt, enamel
2.5 x 10.0 x 7.0 cm
dated, marked P.
OVCHINNIKOV, assay mark
84832 OK 14310

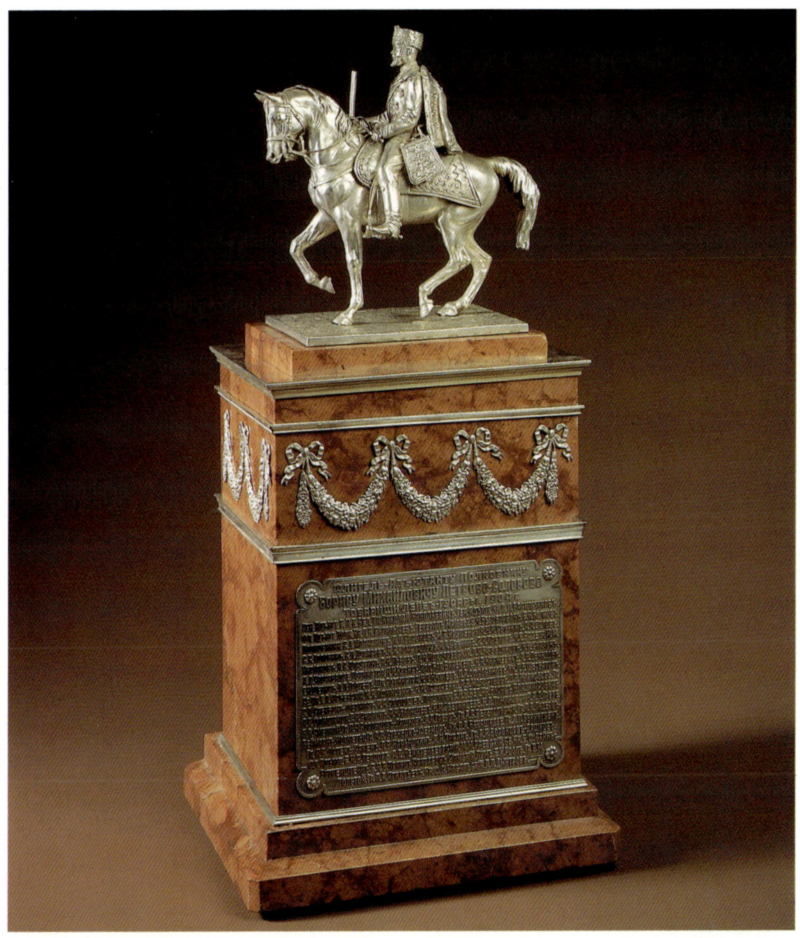

194

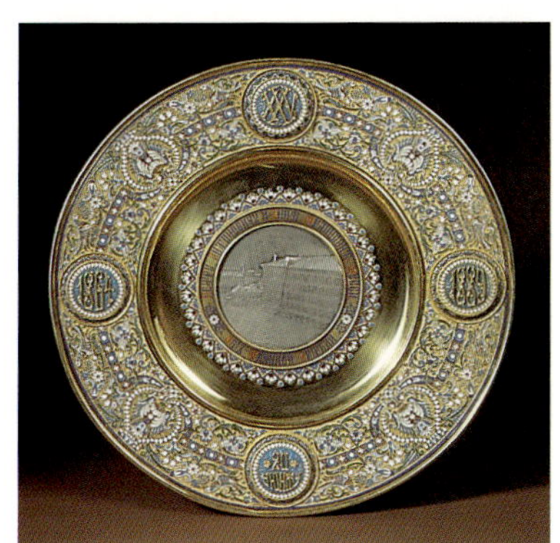

195

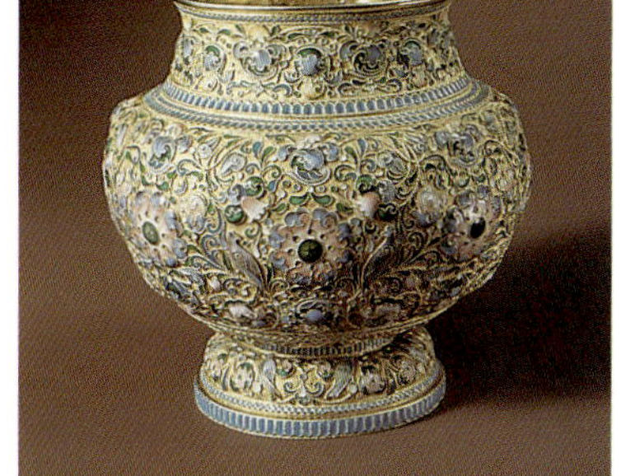

196

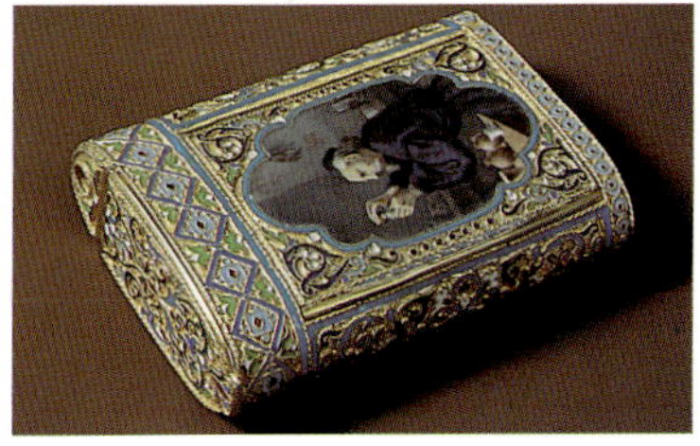

197

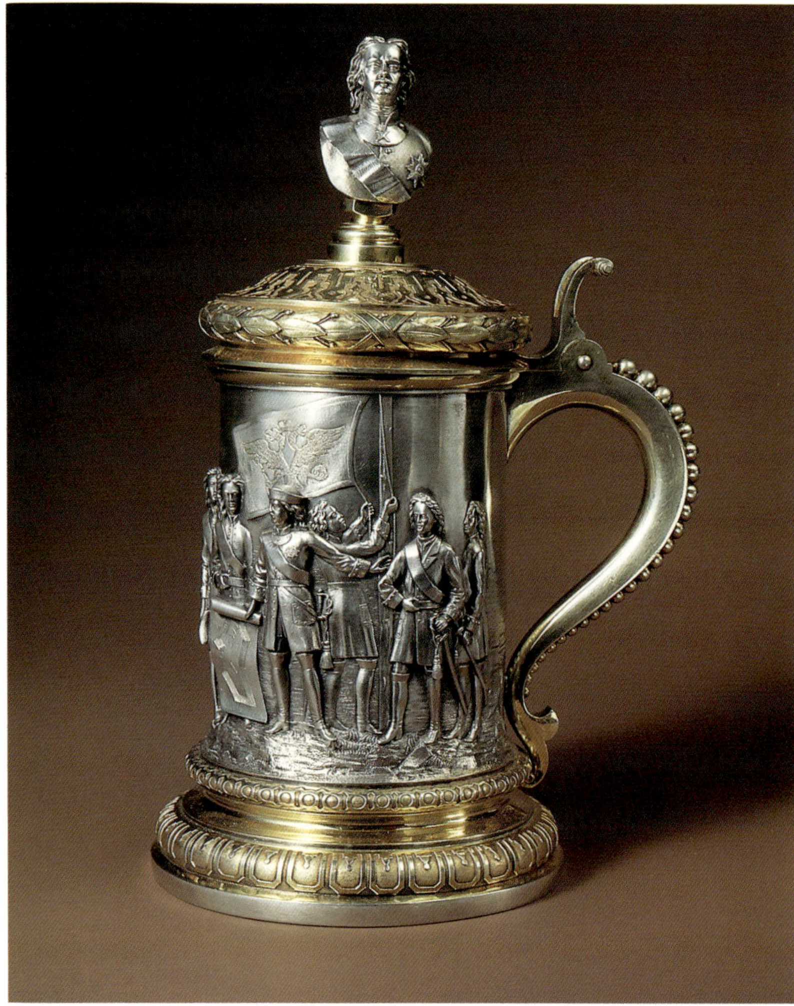

198

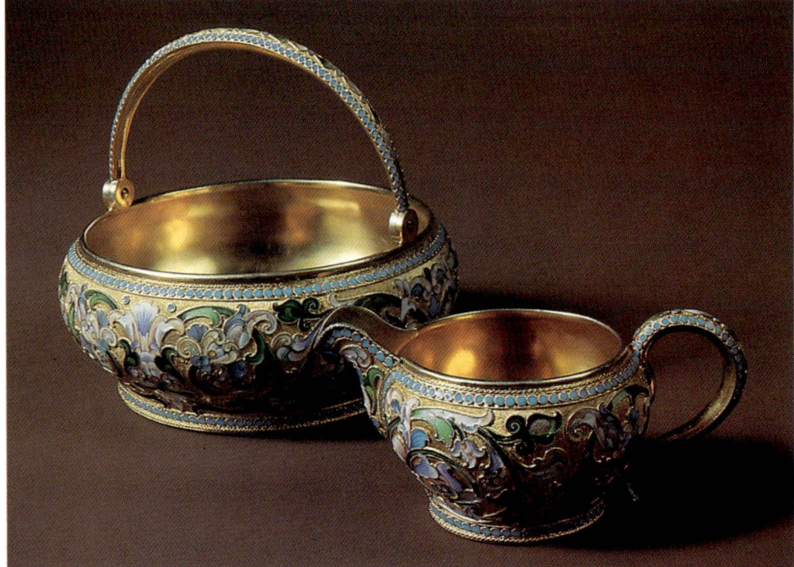

199

198. Tankard
firm of I. Khlebnikov,
Moscow, 1872
silver gilt
height: 29.2 cm
dated, marked
I. KHLEBNIKOV, assay mark
84294 OK 14249

The firm of I. Khlebnikov, founded in 1871, was a supplier to the court from 1873 to 1917.

199. Sugar bowl and milk jug
firm of P. Ovchinnikov,
Moscow, 1899–1908
silver gilt, enamel
sugar bowl: 6.5 x 11.5 x 11.5 cm;
milk jug: 7.8 x 11.5 x 6.1 cm
dated, marked
P. OVCHINNIKOV, assay mark
99087 OK 16050

200. Blotting pad
firm of I. Khlebnikov,
Moscow, 1886
silver, enamel, diamonds,
paper, textile
44.0 x 34.0 cm
dated, marked
KHLEBNIKOV, assay mark
70156 OK 13362

The inscription on the cover reads "To His Excellency Prince Vladimir Andreevich Dolgoruky, to commemorate the twentieth anniversary of his Presidency of the Imperial Moscow Racing Society, 1885, Dolgorukovsky Prize".

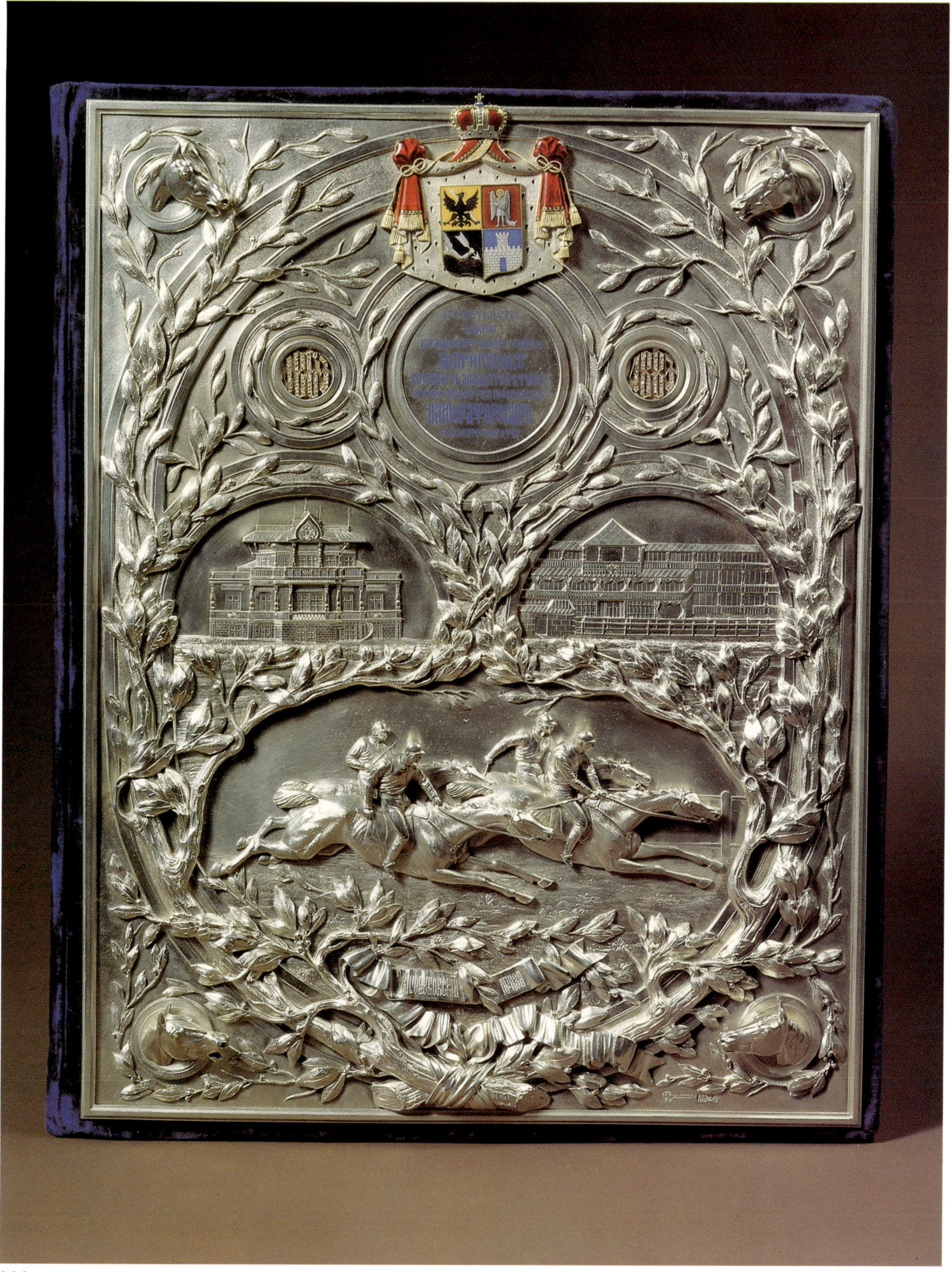

200

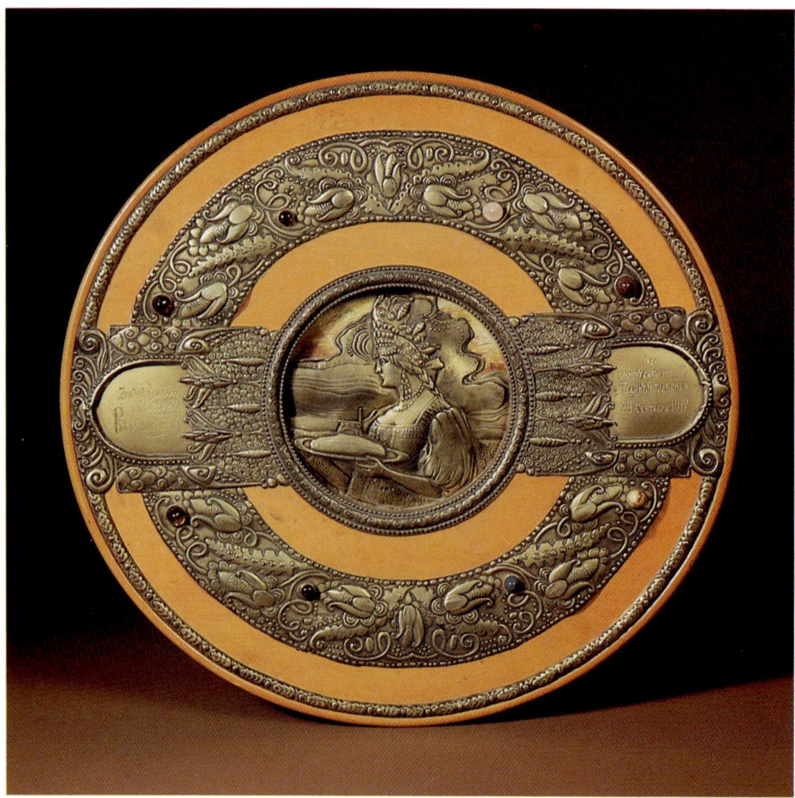
201

201. Dish
firm of I. Khlebnikov,
Moscow, 1912
silver, wood, semi-precious stones from the Urals
diameter: 41.5 cm
dated, marked
KHLEBNIKOV, assay mark 53030 OK 6968

The inscription on the dish reads "To dear Masters and Brothers Ryabushinsky, from the weaving mill workers, September 29, 1912". The Ryabushinsky family of merchants played an important role in the industrial and financial life of Russia in the second half of the 19th and early 20th centuries. They owned cotton, linen and paper industries.

202. Tray
firm of I. Khlebnikov,
Moscow, 1885
silver gilt
7.0 x 64.3 x 38.0 cm
dated, marked
KHLEBNIKOV, assay mark 83562 OK 14086

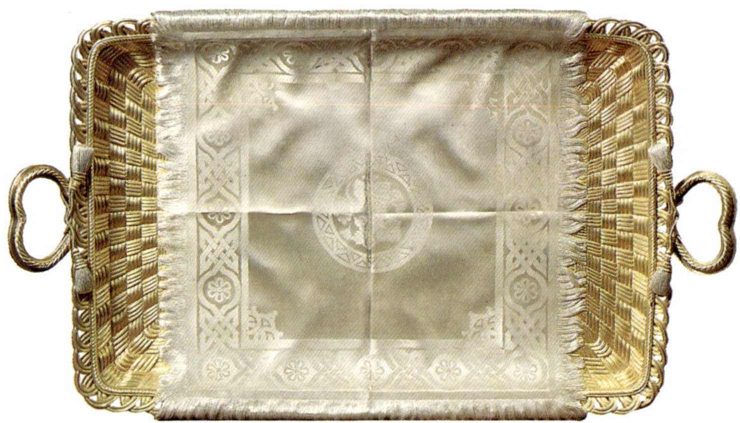
202

203. Ink blotter
firm of I. Khlebnikov, Moscow, 1880s
silver, wood, textile
17.0 x 21.0 x 8.3 cm
dated, marked KHLEBNIKOV, assay mark
83571 OK 14131

204. Blotting pad
firm of I. Khlebnikov, Moscow, 1916
silver gilt, leather, paper
49.0 x 36.0 cm
dated, marked KHLEBNIKOV, IKH, assay mark
95469 OK 14914

On the lower part of the board is the inscription "To dear Commander Junior Captain Ivan Abramovich Cherepanchenko, from his grateful students in the 2nd company of the 3rd platoon of the 3rd Moscow School for Officer Training, in the 1914–16 war".

During World War I six ensign schools were established in Moscow.

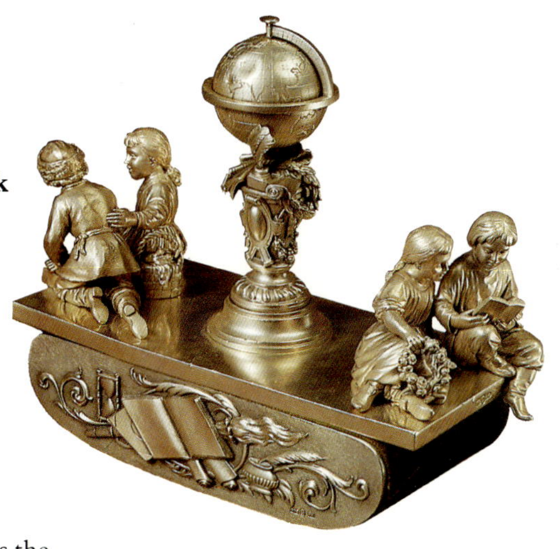

203

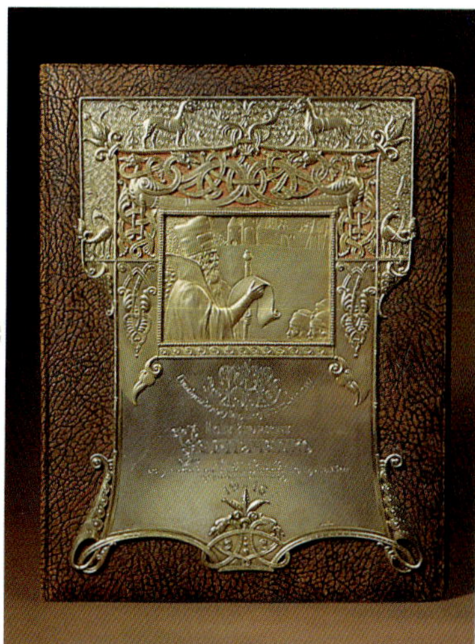

204

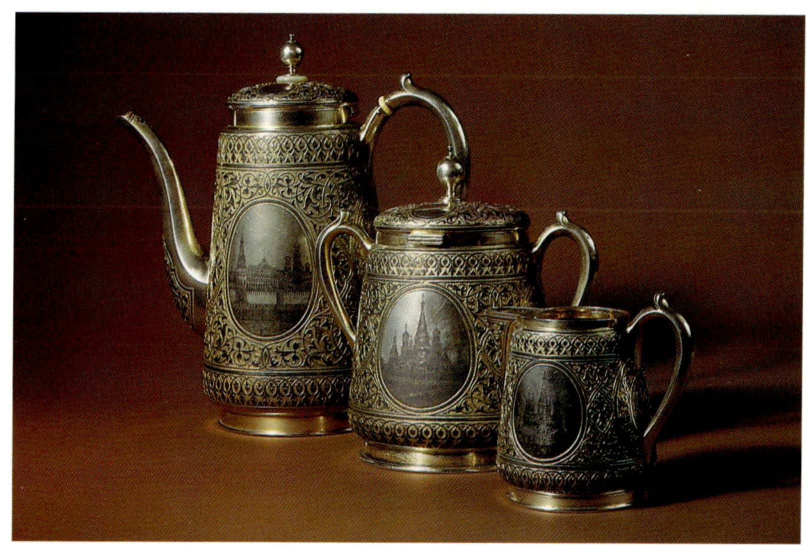

205 206 207

205. Coffee pot
firm of M. Sokolov, Moscow, 1893–94
silver gilt, niello
height: 24.5 cm
dated, marked MC, assay mark
100288 OK 16373

206. Sugar bowl
firm of M. Sokolov, Moscow, 1893–94
silver gilt, niello
height: 18.0 cm
dated, marked MC, assay mark
100288 OK 16374

207. Milk jug
firm of M. Sokolov, Moscow, 1893–94
silver gilt, niello
height: 11.8 cm
dated, marked MC, assay mark
100288 OK 16375

The coffee service comprising cat. nos 205, 206 and 207 is decorated with niello images of Moscow, the Great Kremlin Palace, St Basil's Cathedral, the Cathedral of Christ the Saviour and the wall of the Kremlin with the Redeemer Tower.

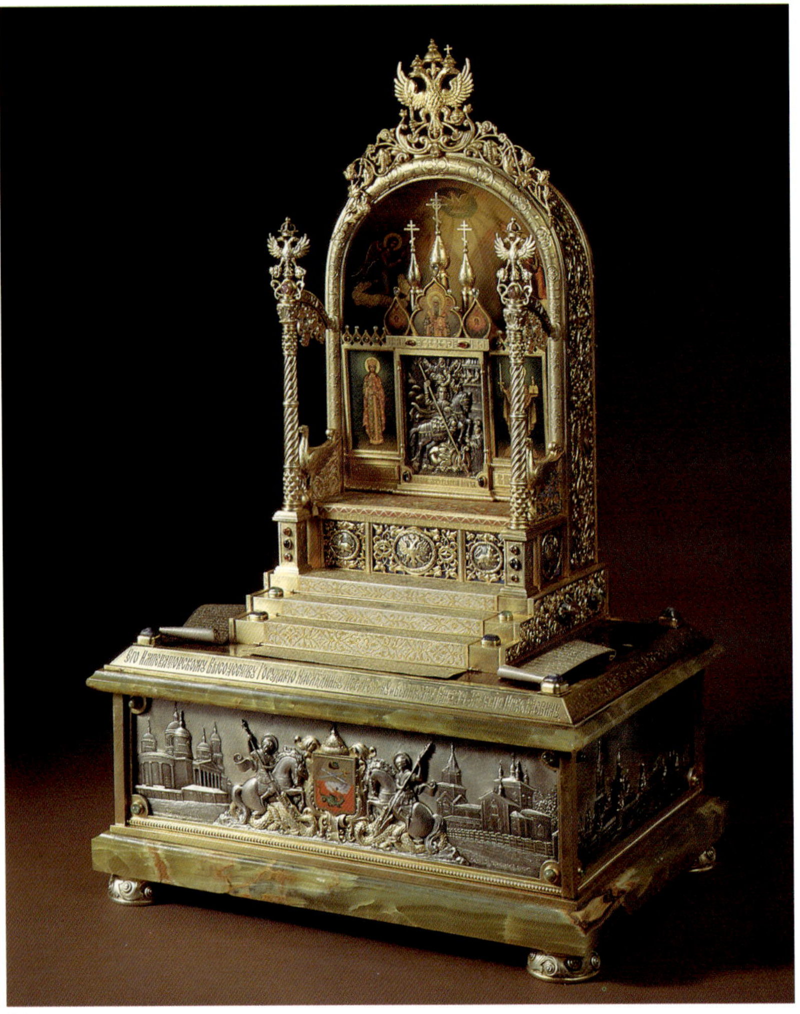

208

208. Casket
firm of I. Khlebnikov,
Moscow, 1913
silver gilt, emeralds, sapphires, rubies, pearls, lapis lazuli, marble, porphyry, enamel, wood
63.0 x 45.0 x 38.0 cm
dated, marked KHLEBNIKOV, assay mark 908888 OK 14592

Enamelled on the front of this rectangular casket with sliding drawer is the coat of arms of the town of Yegoryevsk between images of St George the Victorious, the White and Red cathedrals of Georgia, the Technical School and the Troitsky Monastery in Yegoryevsk. The lid is in the form of a stylized double throne of Tsars Ivan and Peter. The rear of the throne is decorated like an altar with angels, cherubs, the Metropolitan Aleksei, St Nicholas the Miracle Worker, the Great Martyr Aleksander and an embossed icon of St George.
On the back of the throne are the Romanov coat of arms, the Cap of Monomakh and the inscription: "From the Mechanical-Electro-Technical School of the town of Yegoryevsk, which is under the patronage of and named after His Imperial Majesty Tsar Heir Crown Prince and Great Prince Aleksei Nikolaievich in the year of 1913.
It is in this important year, the three-hundredth anniversary of the Romanovs' joyous reign, that the first students graduate from this school." Along the lower edge of the throne runs the inscription "To His Imperial Majesty Tsar Heir Crown Prince and Great Prince Aleksei Nikolaievich".

Near the steps of the throne are fixed two scrolls with the inscription "In accordance with the ancient legend and decayed inscription this carved image of the Great Martyr St George was donated to the village of Vysokoye, now the town of Yegoryevsk, in 1500, by Boyar and Voivode George Yuri Zakhariev, father of Roman Yurievich, grandfather of Nikita Romanovich and the Tsarina Anastasia Romanovna, grandfather of Patriarch Filaret Nikitich and great grandfather of Tsar Mikhail Feodorovich Romanov, after the seizure by George of the Lithuanian town of Dorogobush. The legend testifies to the fact that this image was with the forces of Prince Dmitri Mikhailovich Pozharsky at his first victory over the Poles in 1608–10, as it is noted in detail in the chronicle of the Patriarch Nikon. This inscription was carved on the 6th of December, 1847, during the happy reign of the Romanov descendant Tsar Emperor Nikolai Pavlovich, on the seven-hundredth anniversary of the historical existence of Moscow and the present town of Yegoryevsk".

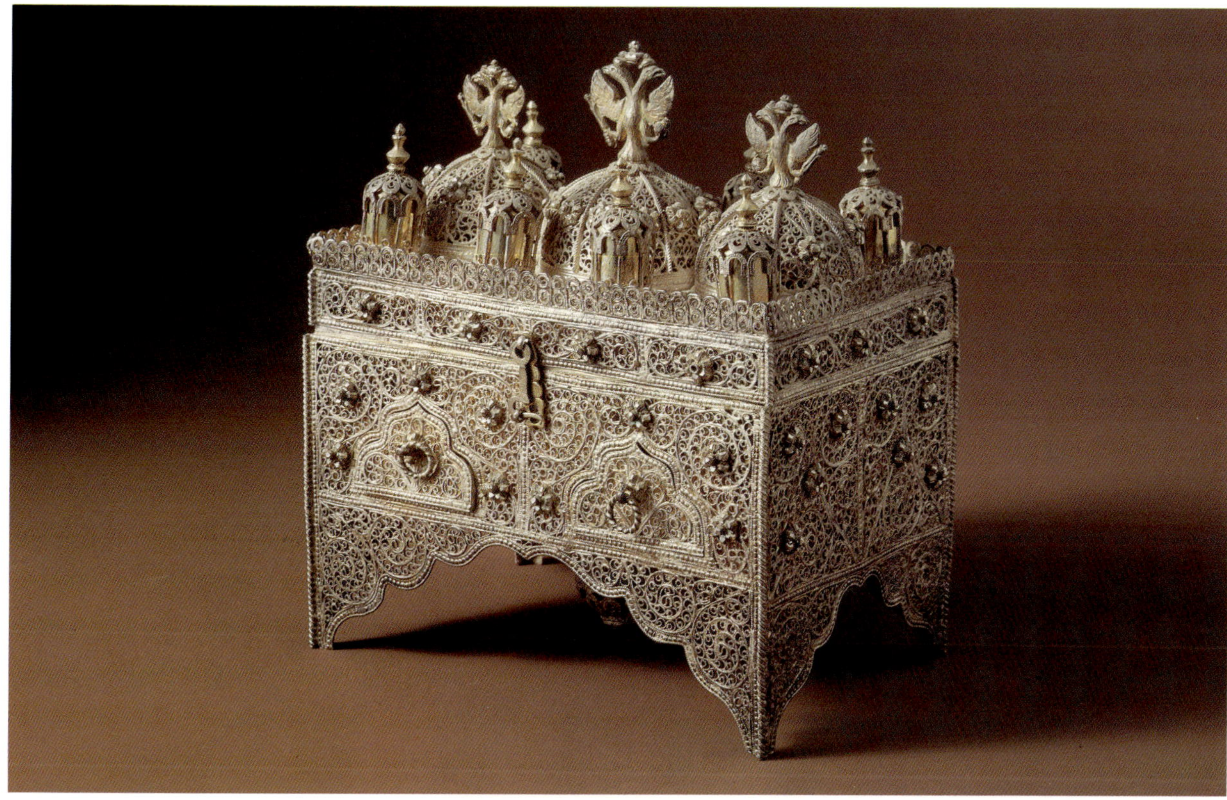

209

209. Casket
Russia, late 19th century
silver, pearls, silk
18.0 x 15.2 x 10.0 cm
51390 OK 4436

210. Bratina (loving cup)
firm of O.Kurlyukov, Moscow, 1894
silver gilt
height: 19.5 cm
dated, marked O. KURLYUKOV, assay mark
68257 OK 6843

The inscription along the crown reads “This bratina is like the sea of Solovetskoye; one drinks from it the health of fine fellows”. On the bottom is inscribed “To our cordial friends from the fellows of Izmailov, as a keepsake of the visit to Moscow in May 1896”.

O. Kurlyukov operated a gold and silver workshop from 1884 to 1917.

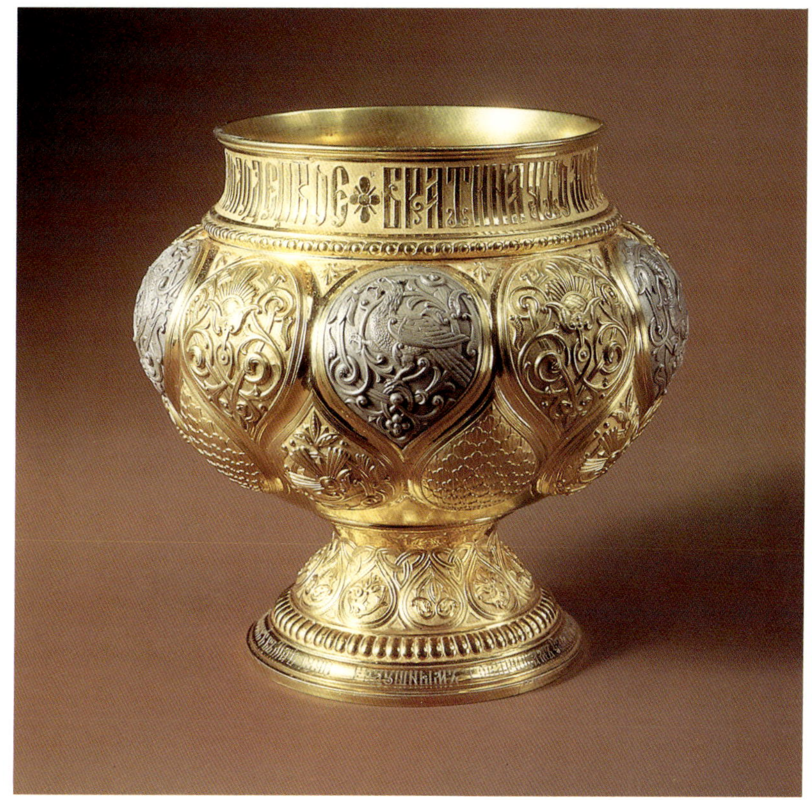

210

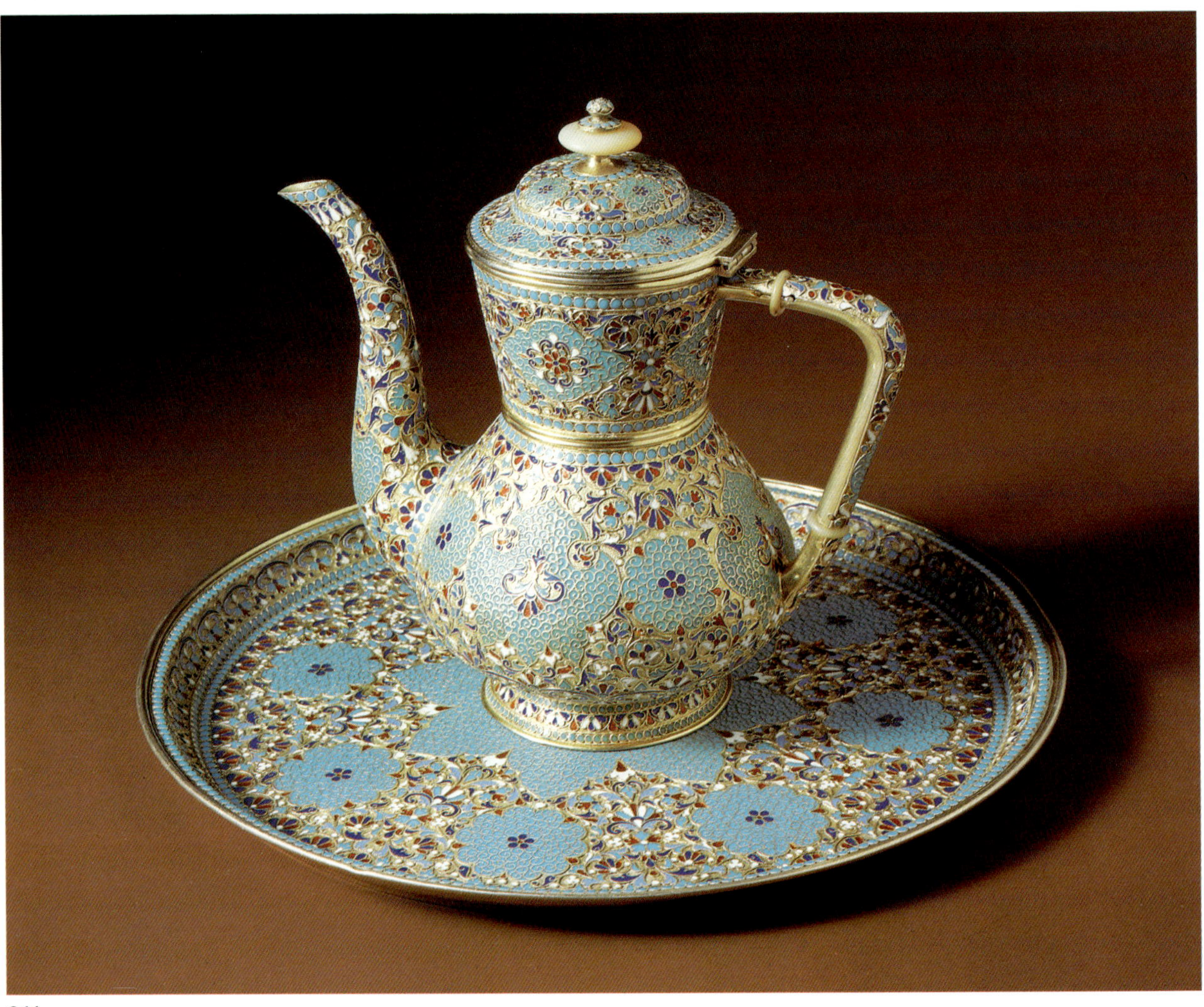

211

211. Jug and tray
firm of Gustav Gustavovich Klingert, Moscow, 1880-90
silver gilt, enamel
jug: 17.8 x 17.7 x 9.5 cm; diameter of tray: 26.3 cm
dated, marked GK, assay mark 103173 OK 18367

Gustav Gustavovich Klingert operated a gold and silver workshop from 1865 to 1917.

212. Vase
firm of Maria Vasilyevna Semyonova, Moscow, early 20th century
silver, enamel
5.2 x 4.9 x 4.9 cm
102493 OK 17518

Maria Vasilyevna Semyonova was, up to 1917, the owner of a silver workshop founded in 1852 by her father, S.M. Semyonovna.

213. Ladle
workshop of Feodor Ivanovich Rückert, Moscow, early 20th century
silver, enamel
5.0 x 9.2 x 5.8 cm
dated, marked FR, assay mark
104909 OK 22789

Feodor Ivanovich Rückert owned a silver and enamelling workshop known from 1880 to 1917.

214. Teapot
Vasily Semyonovich Agafonov, Moscow, 1899–1908
silver gilt, enamel
height: 13.0 cm
dated, marked BA, assay mark
78828 OK 11180

The silverware factory of Vasily Semyonovich Agafonov operated from 1895 to 1917.

215. Vase
Evgeny Andreevich Roshet, Moscow, 1899–1908
silver, enamel
5.3 x 6.0 x 5.3 cm
dated, marked EP, assay mark
107614 OK 23314

The gold and silver workshop of Evgeny Andreevich Roshet operated from 1899 to 1917.

216. Wine service
Moscow, 1908–17
silver gilt
height of pail: 22.0 cm;
length of ladle: 21.5 cm;
height of cups: 7.5 cm
dated, assay mark
104001 OK 22642-22649

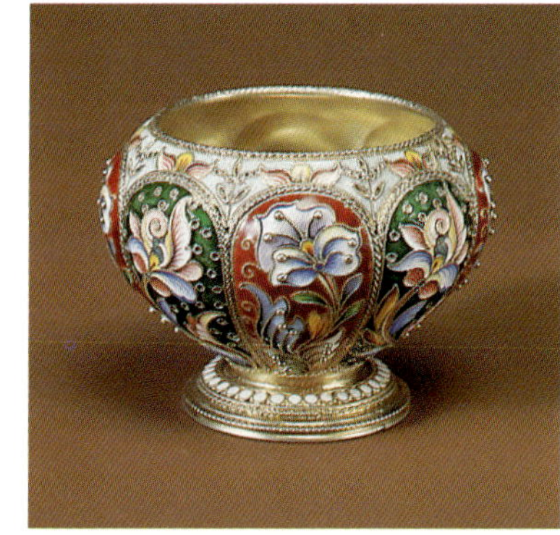

212

213

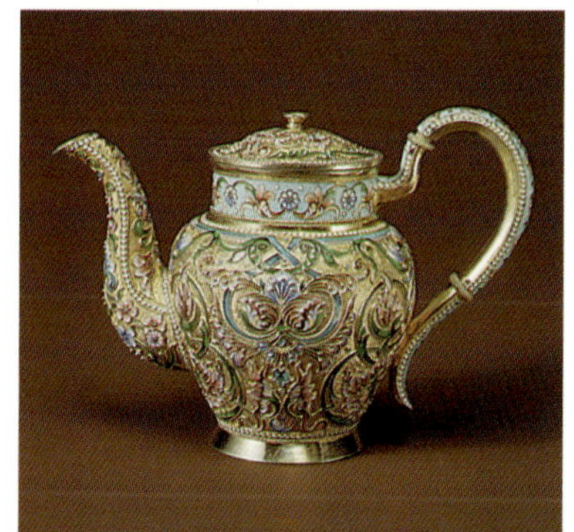

214

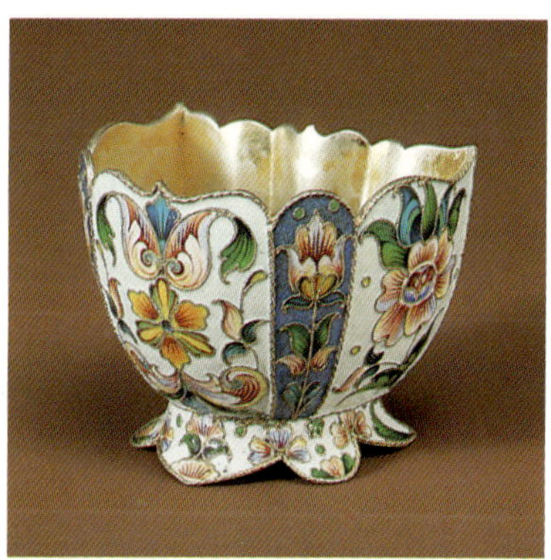

215

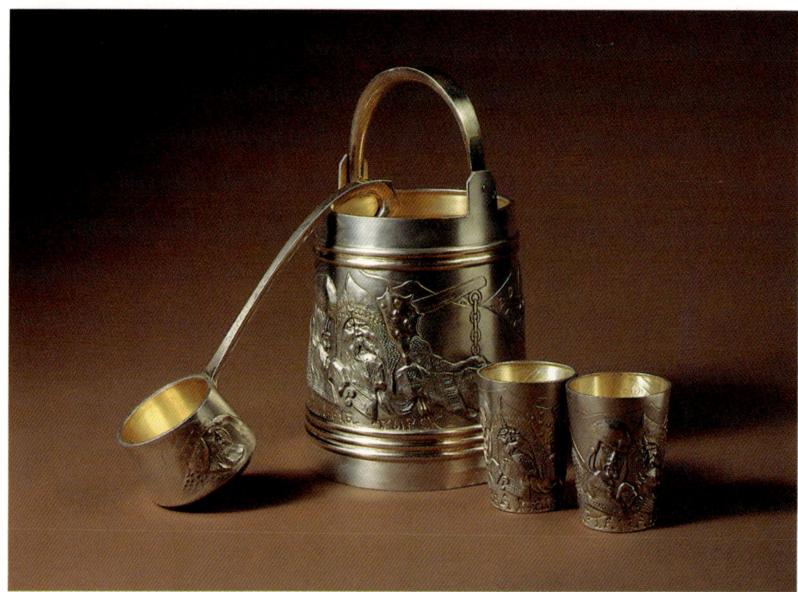

216

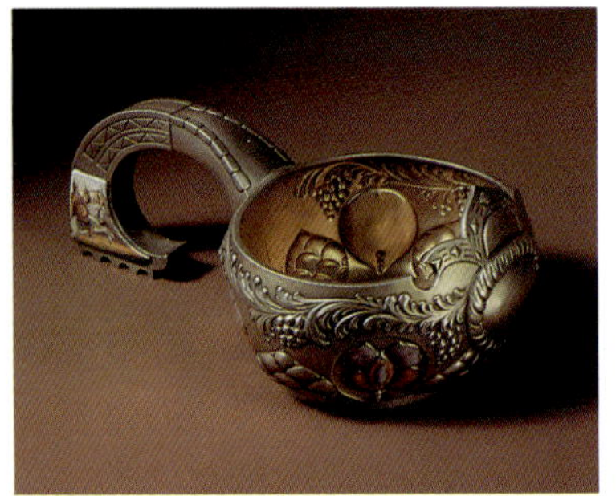
217

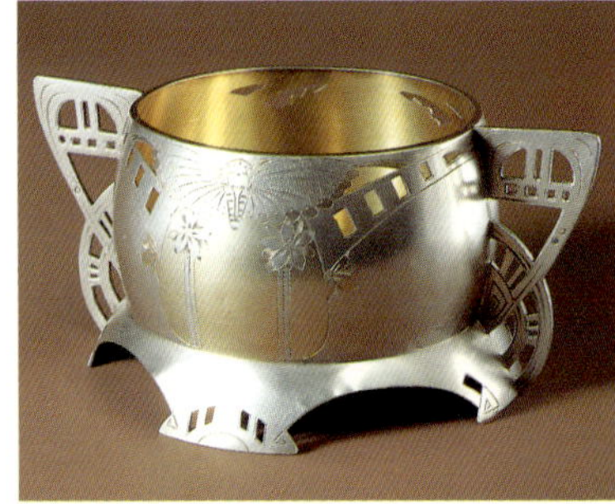
218

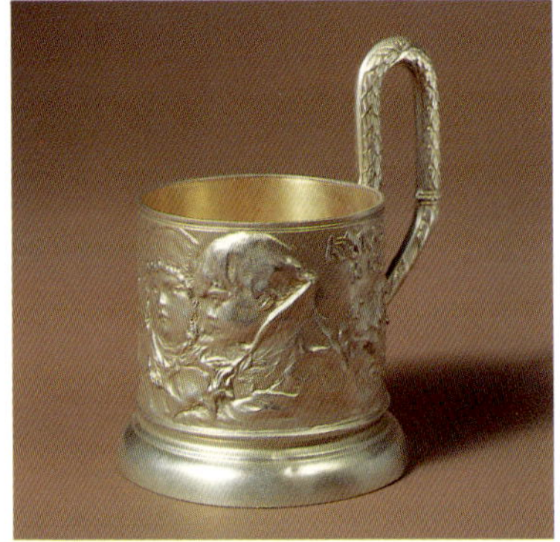
219

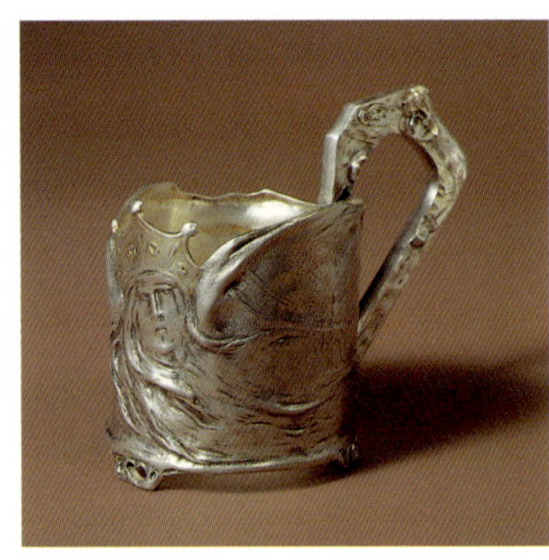
220

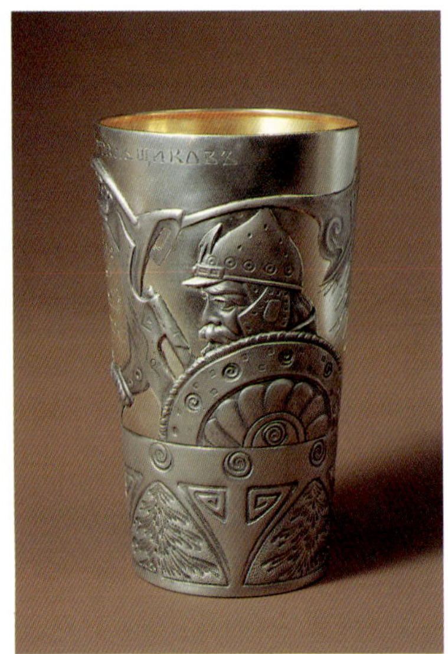
221

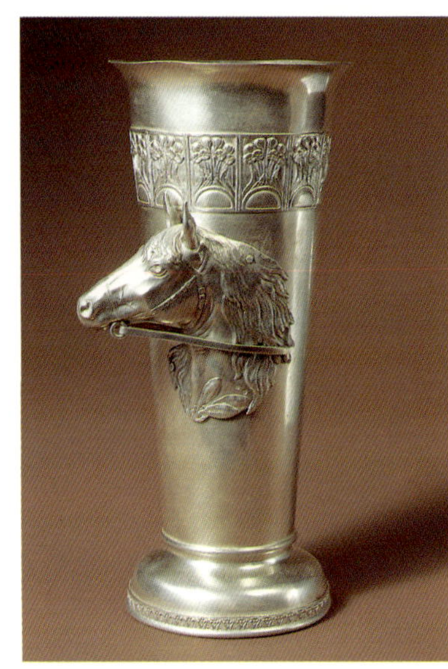
222

217. Ladle
Moscow, 1908–17
silver gilt, enamel
16.7 x 45.0 x 25.0 cm
dated, marked HIT, assay mark
83566 OK 14152

218. Sugar bowl
Pavel Dmitrievich Amerikantsev, Moscow, 1908–17
silver gilt
8.0 x 16.7 x 9.5 cm
dated, marked PA, assay mark
101276 OK 18868

219. Glass holder
Pavel Dmitrievich Amerikantsev, Moscow, 1908–17
silver 11.5 x 11.5 x 7.2 cm
dated, marked PA, assay mark
OK 19090

Pavel Dmitrievich Amerikantsev owned a gold and silver workshop in the early 20th century.

220. Glass holder
Moscow, 1899–1908
silver
10.2 x 13.5 x 7.0 cm
dated, assay mark
101833 OK 20595

221. Drinking vessel
Mikhail Goloshchapov, Moscow, 1912
silver gilt
13.6 x 8.1 x 8.1 cm
dated, marked MG, assay mark
53054 OK 4738

Mikhail Goloshchapov owned a handicraft workshop from 1883 to 1917.

An inscription on the vessel reads "1887–XXV–The 29th September, 1912. To the Commercial-Industrial Assocation of P.M. Ryabushinsky and Sons, from the Cartel personnel".

222. Drinking vessel
Aleksander Ivanovich Piskaryov, Moscow, 1908–17
silver
21.4 x 9.6 x 9.6 cm
dated, marked AIP, assay mark
101814 OK 17055

Aleksander Ivanovich Piskaryov owned a silver workshop in the early 20th century.

223. Vase
firm of Fabergé, Moscow, 1893
silver
dated, marked K. FABERGÉ, assay mark
107220 OK 23197

The firm of Fabergé was one of the most famous companies in Russia. Fabergé operated in Petersburg from 1842 to 1917, became a supplier to the court in 1882, and opened a Moscow branch in 1887.

224. Ash tray
firm of Fabergé, Moscow, 1887–90
silver gilt
8.0 x 11.0 x 6.5 cm
dated, marked K. FABERGÉ, assay mark
102867 OK 17760

225. Photograph frame
firm of Fabergé, Moscow, 1908
silver, enamel, wood, glass, paper, gold
64.0 x 67.5 cm
dated, marked K. FABERGÉ, assay mark
69620 OK 6474

The reverse bears the inscription "To the Vice-Regent of His Imperial Majesty in the Caucasus, General Aide-de-Camp Count I.I. Vorontsov-Dashkov, from his retinue on the 50th anniversary of his service as an officer. Aide-de-Camp Captain Prince A.Z. Chavchavadze and Officers. Tiflis, March 25, 1908".

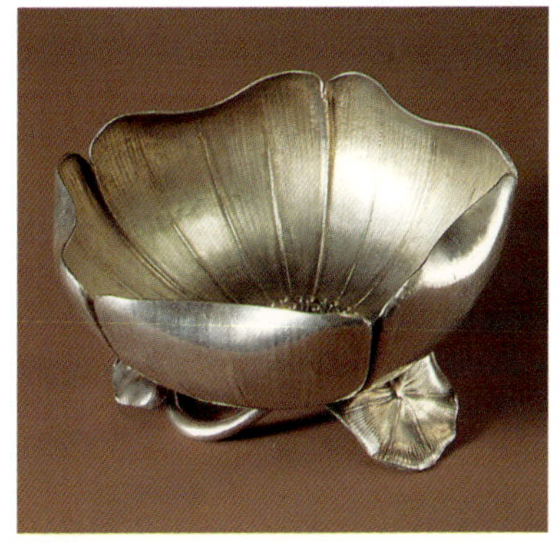

223

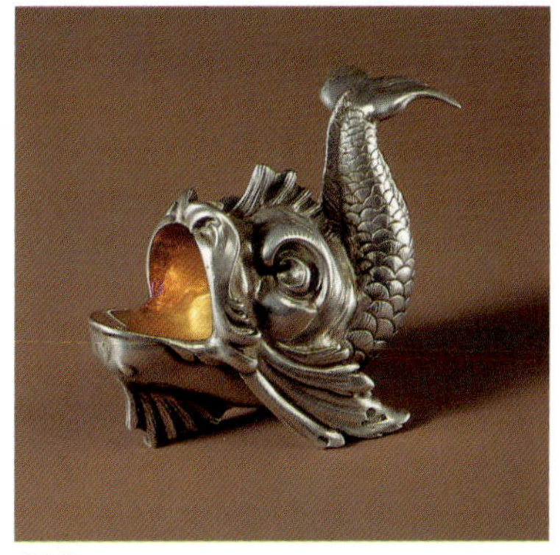

224

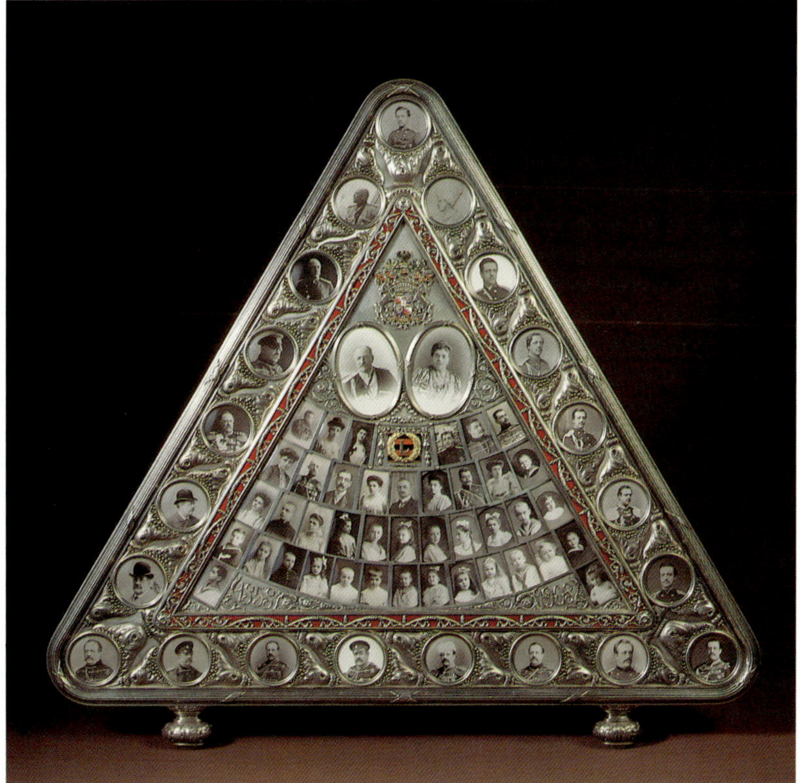

225

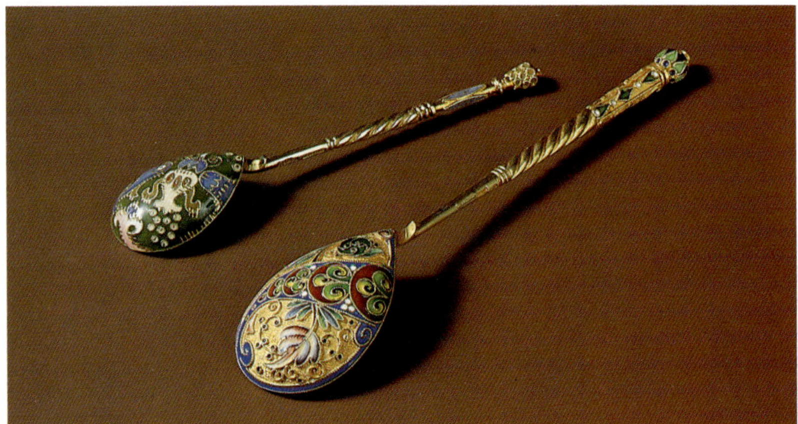

226 227

226. Coffee spoon
firm of Fabergé; workshop of F. Rückert, Moscow, 1908–17
silver gilt, enamel
length: 10.8 cm
dated, marked K. FABERGÉ FR, assay mark
101257 OK 18251

227. Teaspoon
firm of Fabergé, 11th cartel of jewellers, Moscow, 1908–17
silver gilt, enamel
length: 14.3 cm
dated, marked FABERGÉ, IIA, assay mark
102157 OK 18236

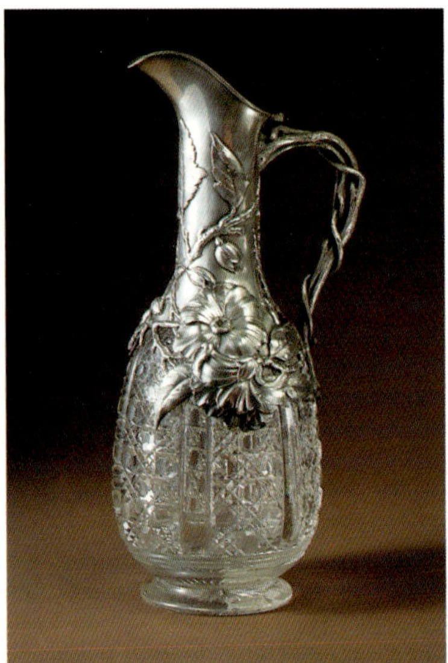

228

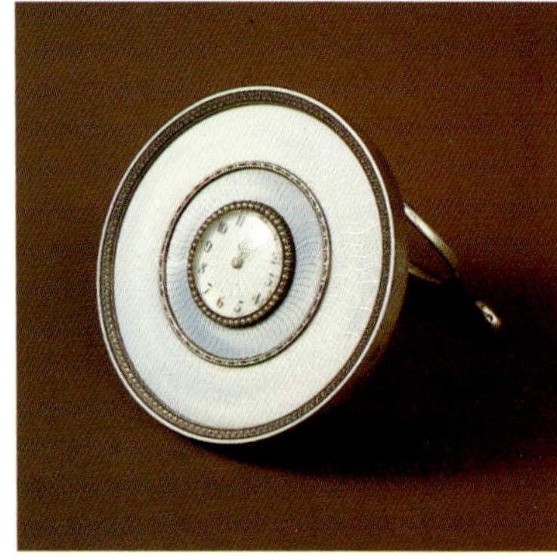

229

228. Jug
firm of Fabergé, Moscow, 1899–1908
silver, crystal
height: 30.0 cm
dated, marked K. FABERGÉ, assay mark
107694 OK 23326

229. Clock
firm of Fabergé, workshop of H. Vigstrom, Petersburg, 1899–1908
gold, silver, enamel, pearl, ivory, metal
diameter: 8.0 cm
dated, marked FABERGÉ, H.V., assay mark
98863 OK 15969

Heinrich Vigstrom (1862–1930?) was one of the greatest Fabergé masters, creator of the famous Fabergé Easter eggs and many stone articles and other pieces.

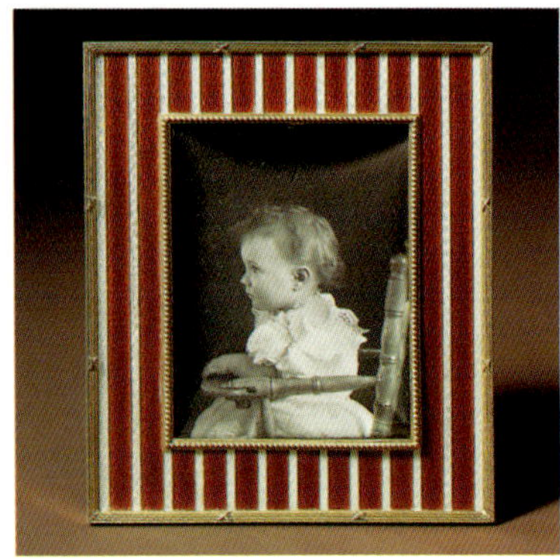

230

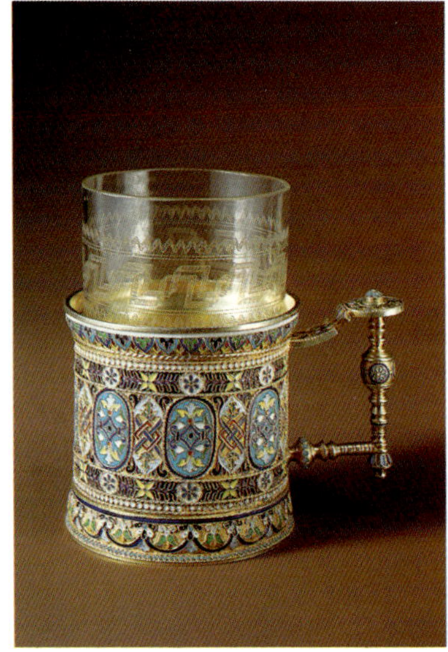

231

230. Frame
firm of Fabergé, workshop of H. Vigstrom, Petersburg, 1908–17
silver gilt, enamel, ivory, metal
9.4 x 11.3 cm
dated, marked FABERGÉ, H.V., assay mark
73832 OK 6935

231. Glass-holder
firm of Fabergé, workshop of H. Vigstrom, Petersburg, 1899–1908
silver gilt, enamel, glass
9.2 x 14.0 x 9.7 cm
dated, marked K. FABERGÉ, H.V., assay mark
102157 OK 17229

232. Cigarette-case
firm of Fabergé, workshop of H. Vigstrom, Petersburg, 1908–17
gold, diamonds
1.4 x 8.4 x 6.2 cm
dated, marked FABERGÉ, HV, assay mark
98908 OK 15862

233. Box
firm of Fabergé, Petersburg, 1908–17
gold, sapphire, rock crystal, mother-of-pearl, gouache
2.3 x 5.6 x 4.0 cm
marked K. FABERGÉ
107464 OK 23273

234. Hippopotamus
firm of Fabergé, Petersburg, early 20th century
obsidian, diamonds, rodonite, agate
6.2 x 9.0 x 5.5 cm
107464 OK 23274

235. Cup and saucer
firm of Fabergé, workshop of Julius Rappoport, Petersburg, 1908–16
nephrite, silver gilt
height: 6.5 cm;
diameter: 10.5 cm
dated, marked JR, K.F., assay mark
107694 OK 23328/1-2

Julius Rappoport (1864–1916) was a great master of the Fabergé firm, active in Petersburg from 1883 to 1916.

236. Samovar and tray
Mikhail and Simeon Grachyov, Petersburg, 1899–1908
silver gilt
height of samovar: 56.0 cm;
tray: 41.0 x 24.8 cm;
slop-basin: 7.0 x 17.8 x 17.8 cm
dated, marked
BR. GRACHYOVS, assay mark
83563 OK 14087

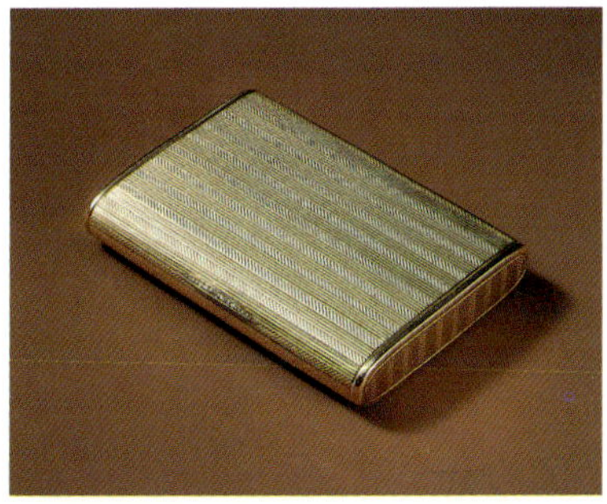

232

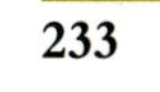

233

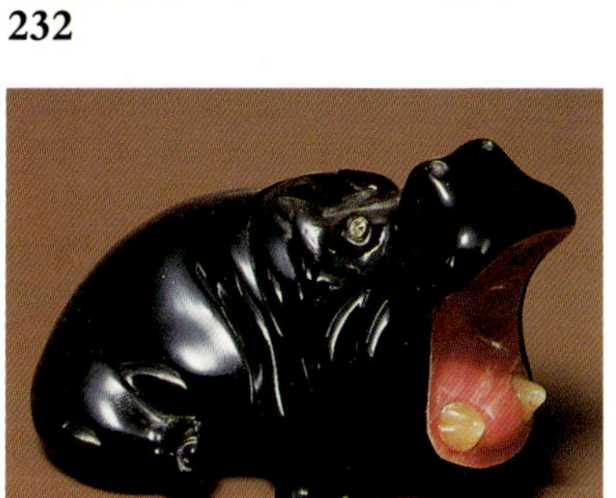

234

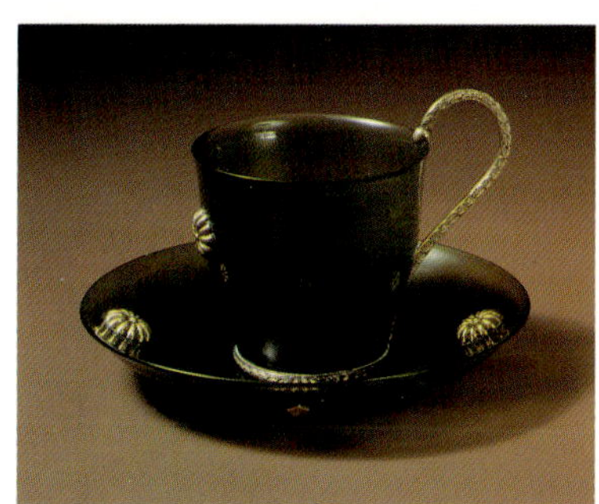

235

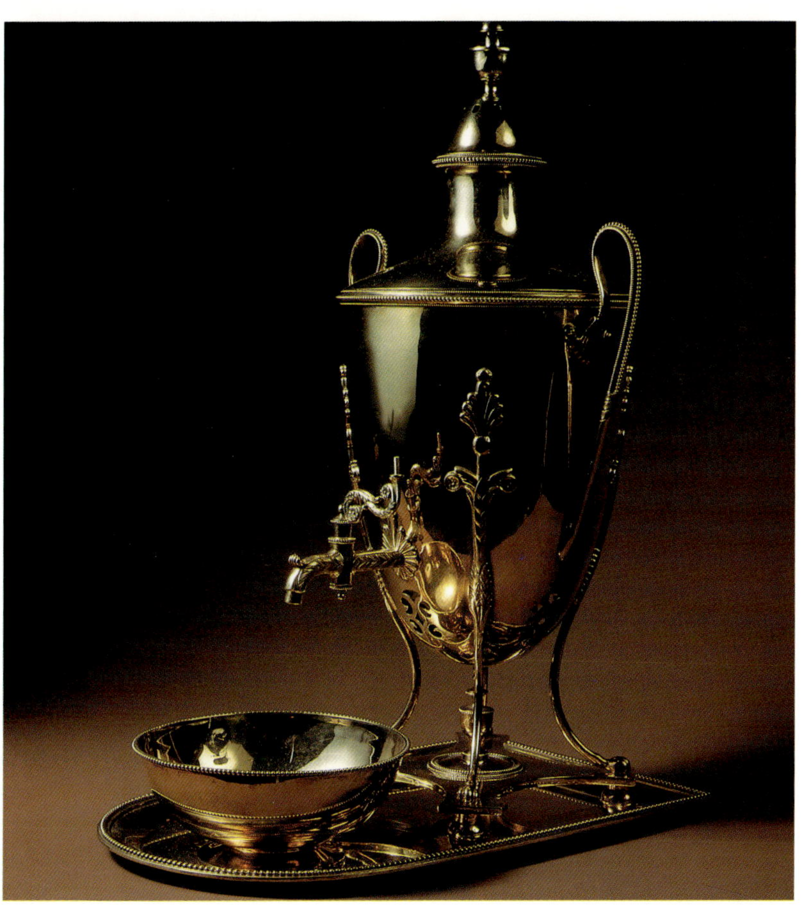

236

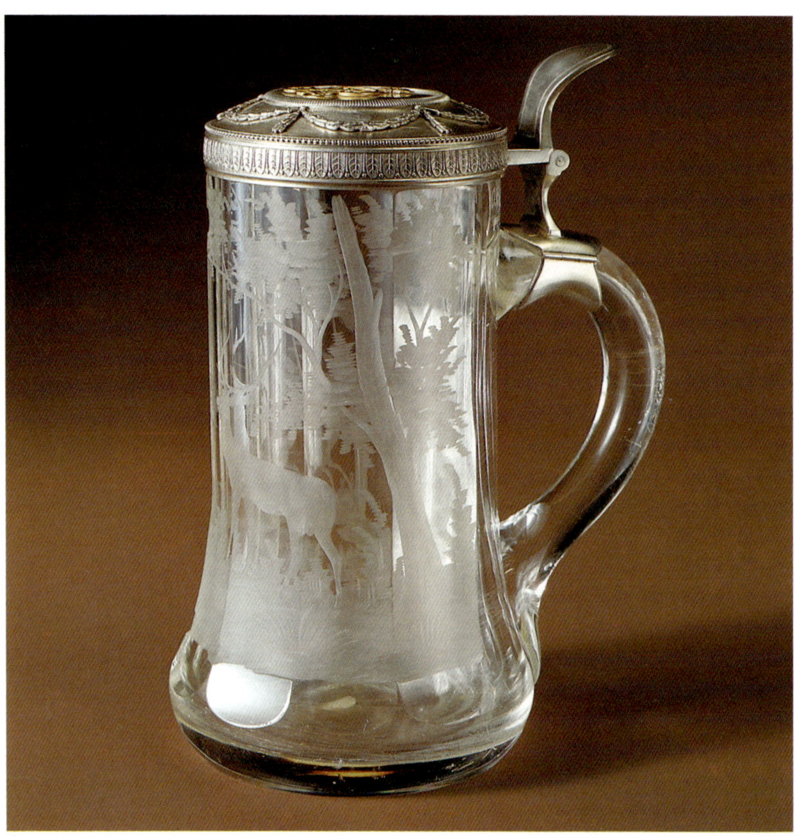

237

237. Tankard
Karl Ioganovich Bock,
Petersburg, early 20th century
silver, glass
18.6 x 7.5 x 7.5 cm
Marked BOCK
68257 OK 6861

Karl Ioganovich Bock owned a silver workshop from 1840 to 1917, and was a court supplier from 1901.

238. Set for fruit punch
Petersburg, 1904
silver gilt, enamel
height of trivet: 50.8 cm;
pail: 25.5 x 17.0 x 17.0 cm;
cups: 5.8 x 4.8 x 4.8 cm
dated, marked P.L., assay mark
68257 OK 6668-6681

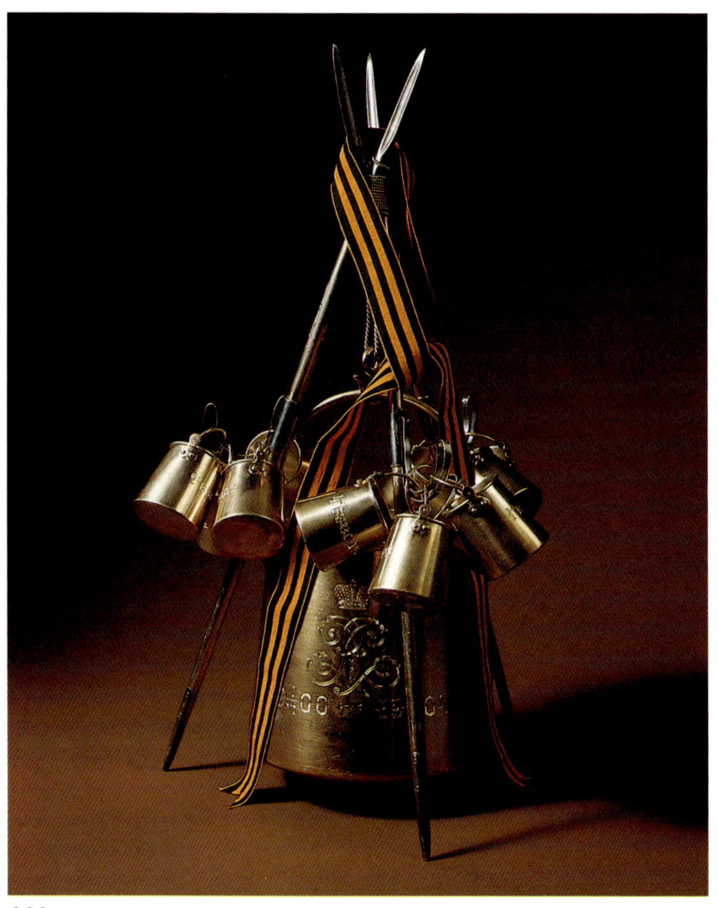

238

VIII

JEWELLERY

Ornaments of the 16th–20th Centuries

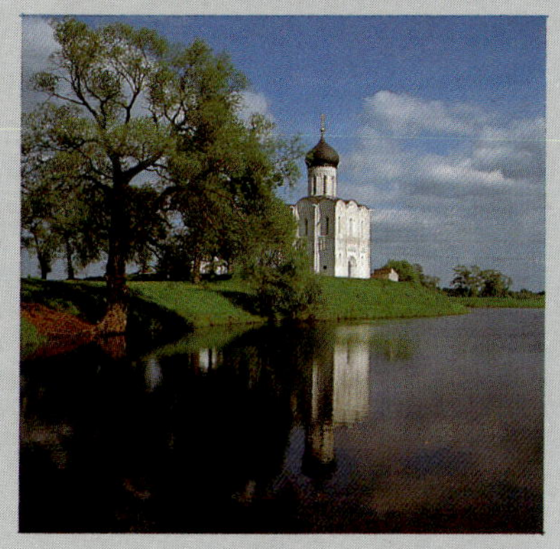

The gold and silver work of Russia embodies, as does the jewellery of any country in any epoch, mankind's eternal search for ways to make his appearance more appealing; to strike harmony between inner spirit and outer decoration. Jewellery can tell us about the aesthetic characteristics of the different strata of Russian society from the 16th to the early 20th century.

In the 16th and 17th centuries, Russian dress was not in any way determined by class. Rather, it was dictated by practicality and ancient custom. The numerous pictures found in illuminated manuscripts and on icons and frescoes illustrate the history of Russian dress. Russian jewellers made wide use of imported sea pearls and local freshwater pearls, as well as amber, semi-precious stones and glass. Accessories made of gold, silver and precious stones served to show the status of the owner. Festive dress of the 16th and 17th centuries differed from European counterparts in the simplicity of the cut and the complete draping of the figure, leaving no part uncovered. This is one of the reasons costume ornaments were so abundant; they fastened the clothes in various ways.

Portraits of tsars, noble boyars and prominent military leaders show that a form of decoration using metal lacework was one of the most popular accessories for fashionable people of the time. Lacework ornaments were made from delicate interconnected plates of different shapes; the base material was gold, decorated with precious stones and enamels. Lacework, stitched or fastened to collar, sleeves or hem, made dresses look luxurious and attractive. Lacework from Tsaregrad had been imported to Russia from Constantinople for some time. It was often made by Greek jewellers, who worked at the Emperor's court in Moscow and from whom Russian jewellers successfully learned the secrets of its production.

Lacework artistry peaked in the second half of the 17th century; during this period the pieces made by Moscow jewellers equalled those made by foreign masters. Russian jewellers turned national ornamental patterns into motifs for their laceworks and thus contributed to the distinctive style of their jewellery. There are two types of lacework in this exhibition; the first type, composed of rectangular plates with slits and painted with pale enamel, is decorated by a tulip with a flat emerald in the centre of the flower; the second is decorated by a three-petalled flower with diamonds. Lacework was also used to decorate ecclesiastical garments, book covers and other church accoutrements. Pendants, plaques and hoops—decorated with hammer work, enamel, niello and precious stones—were used for the same purpose.

Buttons were another important accessory of Russian dress in the 16th and 17th centuries. These practical and aesthetically valuable items were manufactured by the jewellers of the Gold and Silver Chambers in Moscow, as well as by the jeweller button-makers, who then sold their products in the Silver Row on Red Square, the only place in Moscow where silver jewellery could be bought. Buttons of gold or precious stones were mainly applied to festive dress; silver buttons were widely used for the everyday clothes of Tsars and nobility, affluent town-dwellers and peasants. These buttons are fascinating in their diversity of form, size, ornamentation and technique. The style and material of the clothes determined the number and form of the buttons, which were fastened to the dress with the help of a ring. The largest button exhibited (cat. no. 241), from a formal overcoat, is gilded with rich embossed floral ornament against a background of low relief. Often the buttons were decorated with precious stones and enamel. The pear-shaped buttons are of special beauty and complexity, with multi-coloured enamel against the filigree. The number of these ornaments on fur coats and caftans (a type of Russian coat) varied during the 16th century; sometimes there were 24, but more often 11. There were also smaller buttons of finer technique, applied to dresses, cups and chokers.

Earrings were of great importance and in wide demand. In the 16th and 17th centuries a separate group appeared among the silversmiths: earring jewellers. Moscow men wore one earring; women two. In the collections of the State History Museum are various earrings, made in different centres of Russian gold and silver work.

Earrings called "dvoichatki", which originated in the 15th century, are regarded as the most ancient type. They were a perfect complement to Russian national dress in the 16th and 17th centuries. These earrings were always a variation of the same principle: two pendants (hence the name dvoichatki or double earrings) in the form of rods fastened to a wide hoop. Different materials, techniques and mounting made each earring unique.

Their diversity is exemplified by the earrings in the exhibition, some of which have pearls, amber or golden beads threaded onto the rods. This type of earring was especially popular with mercantile and peasant communities up to the late 19th century, as they were in accord with the national aesthetic norms and ideals of the time.

The large earrings, "golubtsy", originating in the applied arts of Novgorod of the 16th and 17th centuries, are also distinctive. Their name was coined on the basis of the similarity of the earrings' shape to the stylised figure of the "golub" (pigeon), or of two birds back-to-back. This design is typical of Novgorod and the filigree and heart-shaped decorations help establish their origin.

The Moscow earring jewellers of the 17th century had a distinctive style, making articles of complex shape from openwork plates or pendants in the shape of a crescent, accentuating festive and decorative aspects. Precious stones, pearls, enamel and brightly coloured glass enriched such pieces.

In the late 17th and early 18th centuries, a new style of Russian earring emerged: square gold pendants set with precious stones, usually rubies. During the 18th century this style was further developed and enhanced through a wider use of semi-precious stones.

Although finger rings were one of the favourite pieces of jewellery for Russians, in the 16th and 17th centuries these lacked national character and were similar to those made in Europe and among Russia's oriental neighbours, largely because many jewellers who made rings were of foreign origin.

Gold and silver chains were also very popular with both men and women in medieval Russia. In the 16th and 17th centuries, chains of flat rings were sewn to fabric and worn over clothes. These were both decorative and practical, sometimes attaching a flask with wine or water or a cross.

Russian jewellery in the 16th and 17th centuries was largely determined by clothes and lifestyle. It was moulded and shaped by the national spirit. But later the style of these items underwent dramatic changes, retaining some Russian national traditions from the era of Peter the Great while at the same time starting to develop along the lines of European fashion. The reforms of Peter the Great affected all spheres of Russian life and also influenced the way people dressed. The austere life of an Old Russian family, with the virtual seclusion of women, was replaced by their obligatory presence at balls and feasts, where men and women could mix quite freely.

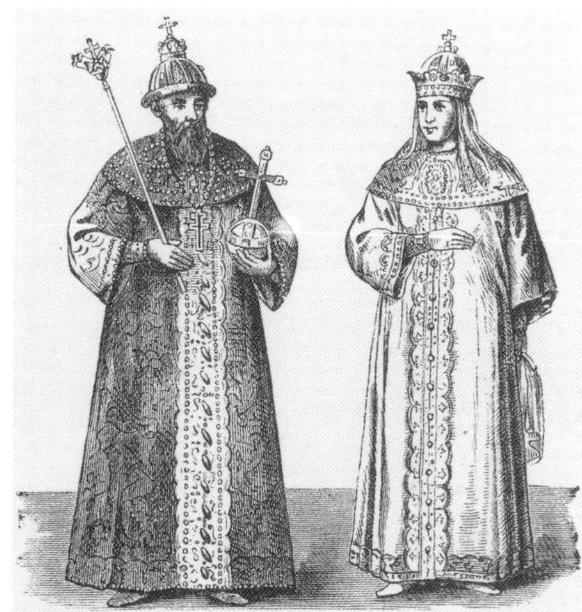

TSAR AND TSARINA IN GALA DRESS, 17th CENTURY

The introduction in 1700 of a new urban dress similar to that common in Europe set jewellers a new challenge. The style of ornaments changed in the first half of the 18th century. Monisto-necklaces, laces and ryasnos were replaced by brooches, hair-pins, bracelets, earrings and necklaces.

The peak of Russian jewellery-making in the 18th century occurred with the emergence of the first Russian lapidary works; in 1725, by order of Peter the Great, the works were constructed in Peterhof for polishing semi-precious stones and cutting diamonds; in 1774 another factory was founded in Ecaterinburg for processing precious stones; and in 1786 a grinding factory was constructed in the Altai region in Kolyvanskaia. This led to the widespread use of precious and semi-stones in gold and silver work of the time.

Brooches in the shape of bouquets with stems and petals studded with semi-precious stones, which pinned the folds of a dress or fastened collars, were popular at the time. The choice of precious stones and the sparkling of their facets created a naturally harmonious effect. The shape of the bouquets, their position and mounting enhanced this effect.

Although the diamond was favoured, the combination of pearls with rubies and other red stones was also popular. Included in the exhibition are 18th-century earrings using this combination.

Although a fascination with antiquity led to the restriction of the number of jewellery items worn in the early 19th century, a variety of ornaments were popular at the time: different types of bracelets, long earrings shaped like pearls or sickles with ears of wheat, and hair ornaments formed as sickles with diamonds, rubies, pearls, enamel, semi-precious stones, agates and topaz. Bare shoulders and necks were left unadorned. Combs of tortoise-shell, gold and silver, decorated with precious stones, mosaic and cameos and supporting high coiffures, became very fashionable.

After the Egyptian expedition of Napoleon (1798–1801), all Europe was captivated by the beauty of carved gems. In Russia gem-carving became a separate branch of the applied arts. Cameos made by the best Russian carvers as well as those brought from abroad were keenly sought as ornaments for diadems, combs, brooches, pins and bracelets. The horn comb exhibited here (cat. no. 271) is an example.

The special beauty and fineness of Russian jewellery reached its epitome in ornaments, which symbolised the very essence of the most refined genre of jewellery art. Brilliant examples are the ornaments of the late 19th century to early 20th century. They show the stylistic complexity of the period of the modern revival of traditional art, during which goldsmiths enjoyed great freedom of expression, culminating in the greatest era of the craft.

The jewellery firms of Bolin, Fabergé, Chichelev and Kehly were the most famous and at the first world exhibition in London in 1851 articles made by Bolin's jewellers ranked very highly.

At the exhibition in Petersburg in 1870, Bolin was awarded a gold medal and was granted the right to use the State Seal for "the perfect beauty of jewellery, exquisite selection of stones and refined ornaments". These were the highest awards in Russia. Bolin fulfilled numerous orders from the Tsar's family and the court. Included in the exhibition is a brooch in the shape of a beetle studded with diamonds and sapphires (cat. no. 281).

The modern style enriched the ornamentation of jewellery and raised the importance of the palette of precious stones. No epoch attached greater importance to items of jewellery, which acquired a language of their own. Ornaments acquired twisting lines, highly polished surfaces and changed their colour range; fashion now demanded green-gold chrysolites and coloured pearls.

Jewellers were carried away by the bizarre and charming world of insects and they made brooches and earrings in the shape of butterflies, dragonflies and beetles decorated with precious stones. The mysterious sheen of pearl, mother-of-pearl and opal and the sparkle of diamonds made these materials very fashionable, embodying the romantic spirit of the time.

In the early 20th century ornaments made at the jewellery firms of Nikolai Linden, Beilin and Son and Rimmer offered a great variety of unique diamond pieces. Included in the exhibition is a bracelet (cat. no. 290) from the jewellery workshop of N. Strulyov, decorated with delicate chrysolite. The pendant brooch in the shape of a stylised apple with diamonds, made by the prominent jeweller Shposhnikov, is also of great interest (cat. no. 285). Quite a few items were made by jewellers' workshops. It is likely that the necklace made out of two circles of sapphires and rubies surrounded by sprays of diamonds and diamond rosettes (cat. no. 288) was ordered as a wedding present and manufactured by the second cartel of jewellers.

239. Button
Russia, 15th–16th century
silver, filigree
3.0 x 2.0 x 1.9 cm
accessioned 1905;
formerly collection:
P.I. Schukin
116659 OK 20356

Openwork button made up of two hemispheres joined by a small filigree cordon. The surface is covered with minute granules and the end is adorned with a minuscule pyramid made up of four granules. A serrated ring is used to attach the button.

240. Button
Russia, 16th–17th century
silver, pearls, enamel, engraving
2.5 x 1.5 x 1.5 cm
75701 OK 8445

241. Button
Moscow, first half of 17th century
silver gilt, turquoise, chasing
7.4 x 4.6 x 4.6 cm
56115 OK 7412

242. Button
Moscow, second half of 17th century
silver, stone, enamel, filigree
6.0 x 3.8 x 3.8 cm
11490 OK 7418

243. Metal lacework
Moscow, second half of 17th century
gold, enamel, emeralds, engraving
2.5 x 2.6 cm
80868 OK 14306/1-5

The lacework consists of five openwork rectangular cuff-links, adorned with polychrome enamel. The centre of each cuff-link bears a gold tulip and flat emerald.

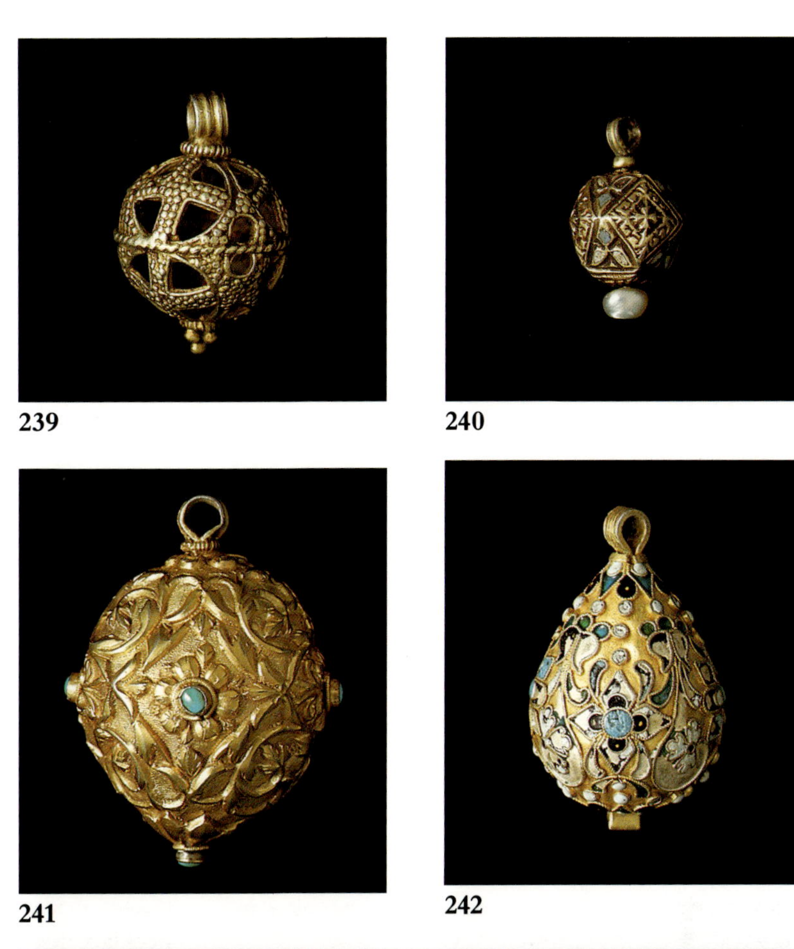

239 240

241 242

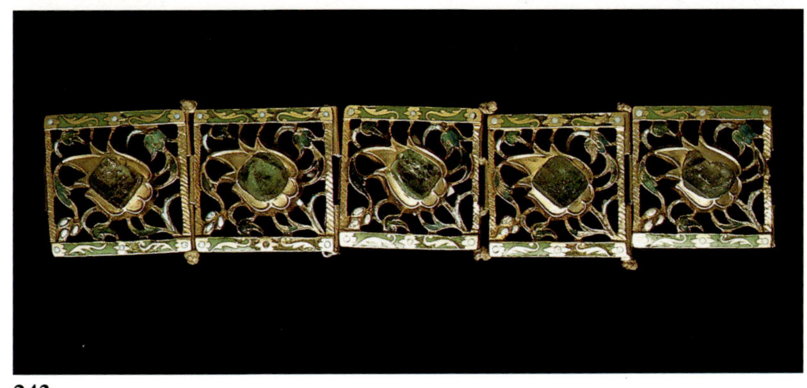

243

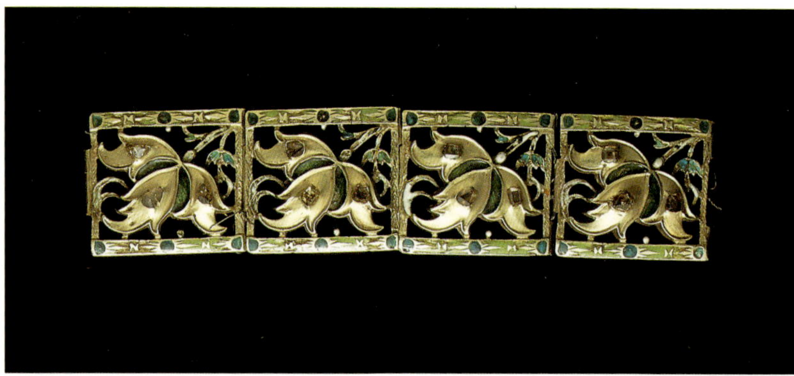

244

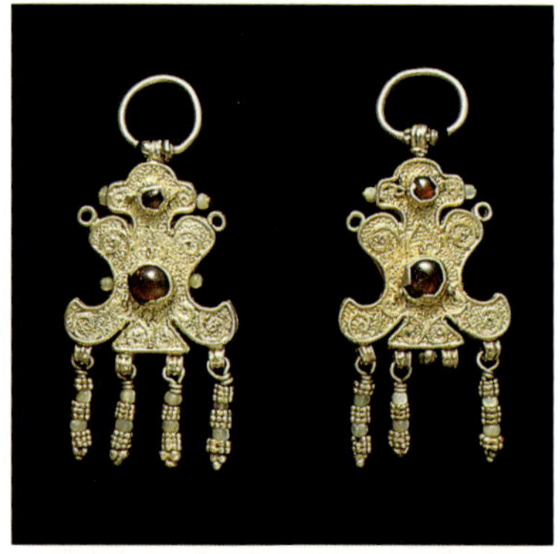

245

246

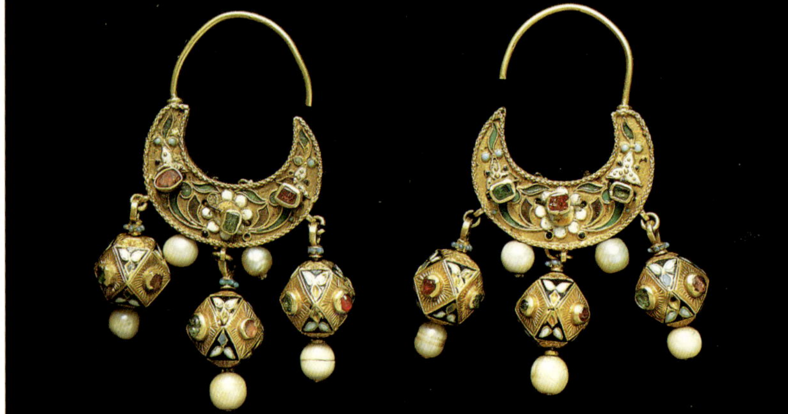

247

244. Metal lacework
Moscow, second half of
17th century
gold, diamonds, enamel,
engraving
2.4 x 2.6 cm
50164 OK 3507/1-4

245. Earrings, pigeon-shaped
Novgorod, 16th–17th century
silver gilt, stones, glass,
mother-of-pearl, filigree
8.0 x 3.5 cm
17045 OK 16245

246. Dvoichatki
(double earrings)
Russia, 17th century
silver, pearls, amber
length: 4.4 cm
67793 OK 7596

247. Earrings
Moscow, second half of
17th century
gold, emeralds, rubies, pearls,
enamel
7.6 x 4.5 cm
13092 OK 6519

248. Earrings
Russia, 17th century
silver gilt, filigree, semi-precious stones from the Urals, zern
length: 5.7 cm
80868 OK 14297

These earrings are decorated using "zern", a technique of forming patterns of metal grains.

249. Earrings
Moscow, second half of 17th century
silver, pearls, glass, enamel, engraving, filigree, zern
6.9 x 2.6 cm
54657 OK 14692

250. Earrings
Stroganovsky craftsmen, Solvychegodsk, late 17th century
silver, pearls, painted enamel, engraving
5.2 x 2.4 cm
12707 OK 14681

251. Earrings
Russia, last quarter of 17th century
silver, pearls, gilt, glass
5.0 x 2.5 cm
12691 OK 14849

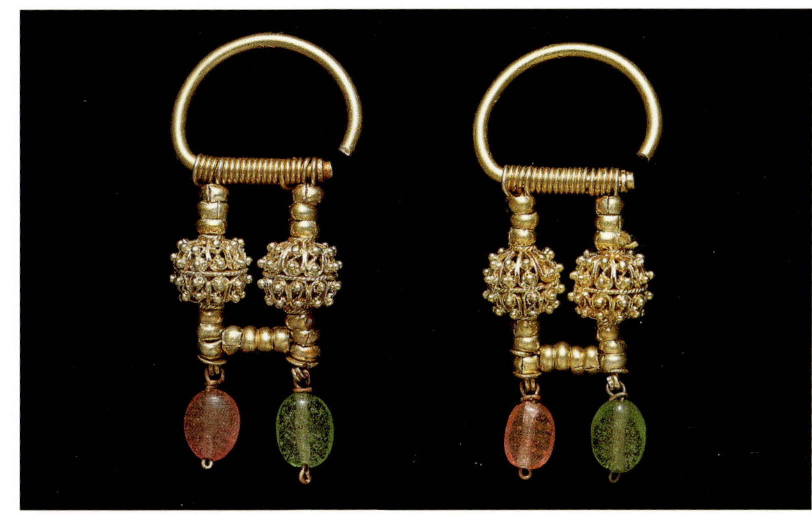

248

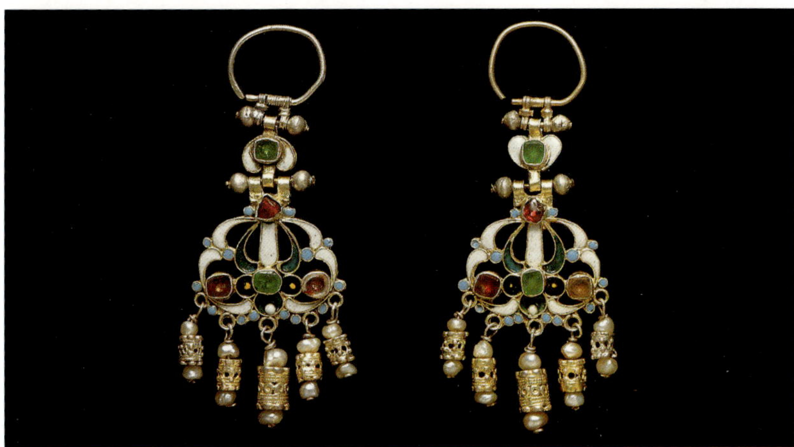

249

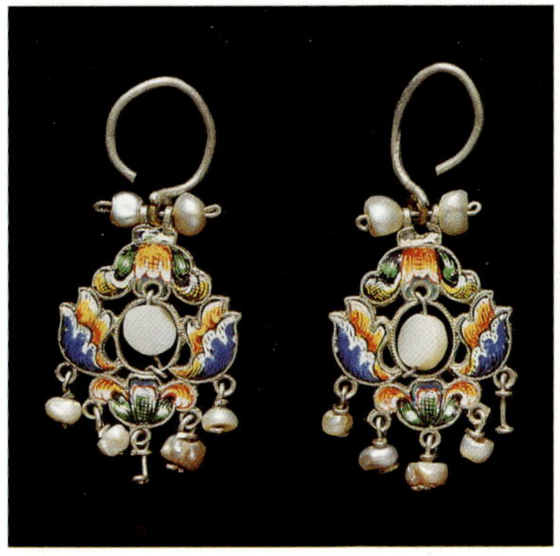

250

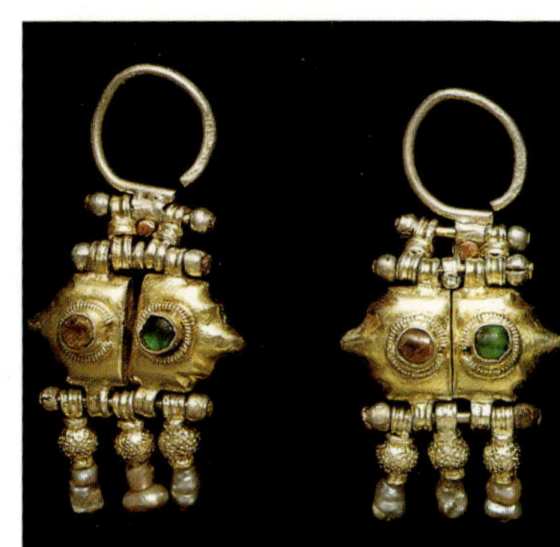

251

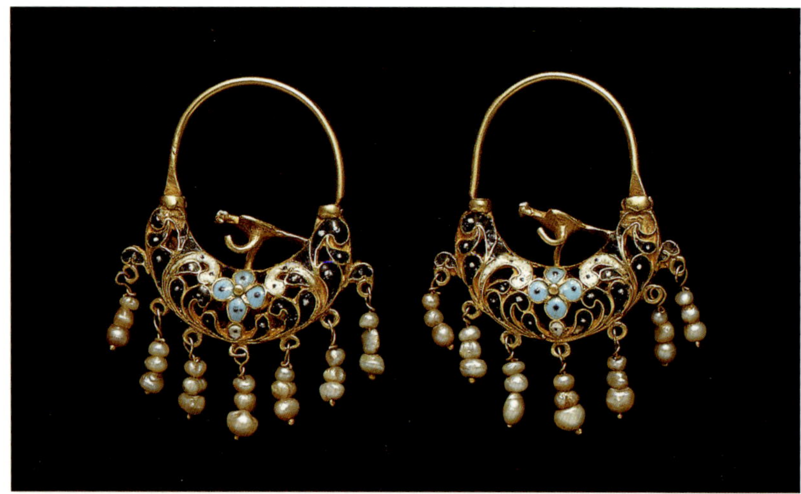

252

252. Earrings
Moscow, last quarter of 17th century
gold, enamel, pearls, engraving, casting
5.2 x 3.6 cm
61858 OK 14302

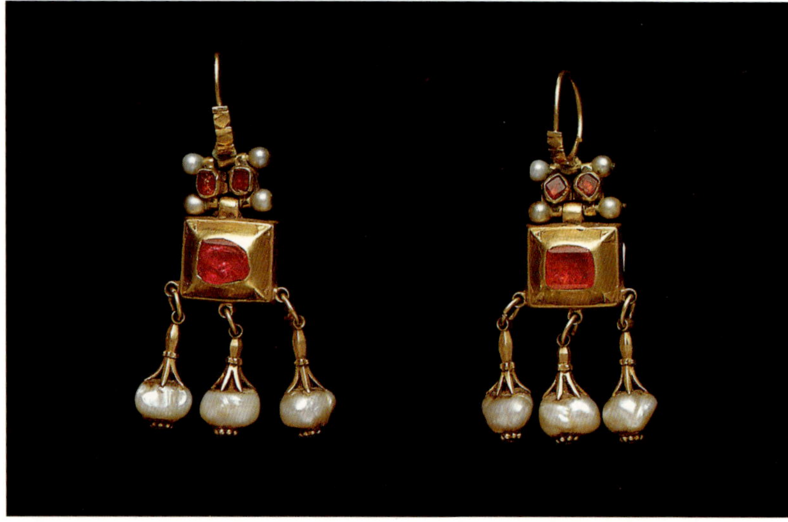

253

253. Earrings
Moscow, late 17th–early 18th century
gold, rubies, pearls, casting
length: 5.4 cm
17307 OK 6511

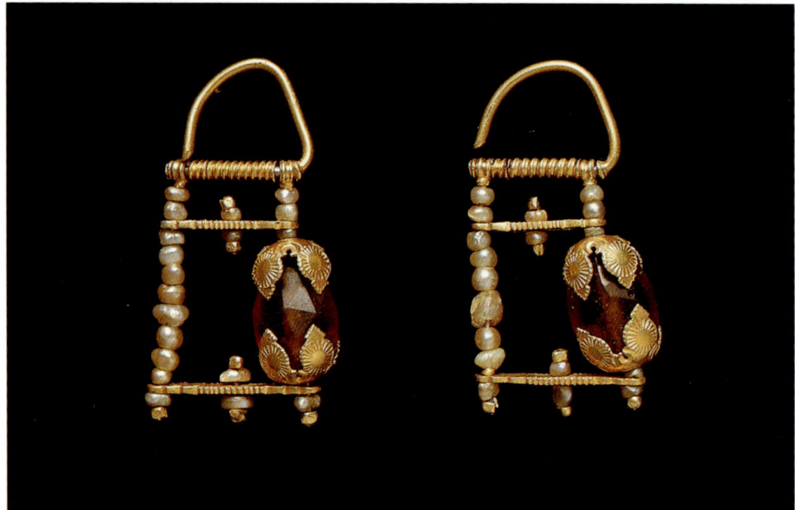

254

254. Earrings
Russia, 17th century
silver gilt, pearls, glass, engraving
5.0 x 2.5 cm
26287 OK 15016

255. Pendant, in the form of a two-headed eagle
Russia, late 17th–early 18th century
silver, almandites, emeralds, rubies, enamel, engraving, casting
6.6 x 3.3 cm
30831 OK 3533

256. Cross on chain
Novgorod, 17th century
silver, filigree
length: 84.0 cm
29474 OK 7946

257. Chain
Russia, 17th century
silver, enamel, chasing
length: 116.0 cm
76110 OK 17473

258. Chain
Russia, late 17th century
silver gilt, mother-of-pearl, filigree, casting
length: 105.0 cm
13426 OK 2533

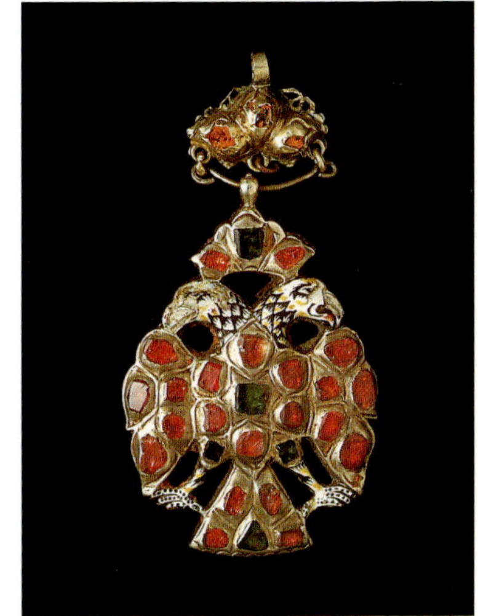

255

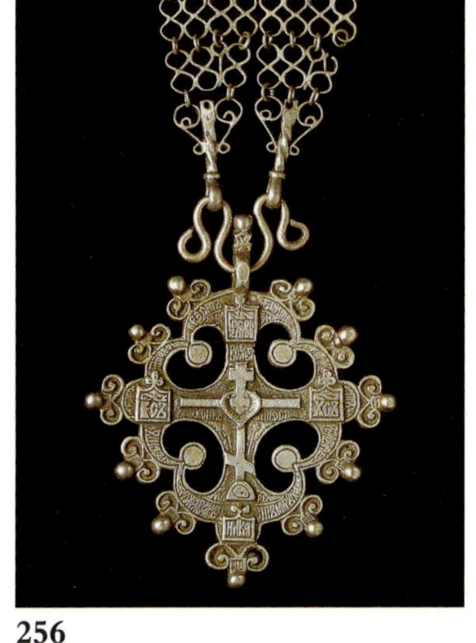

256

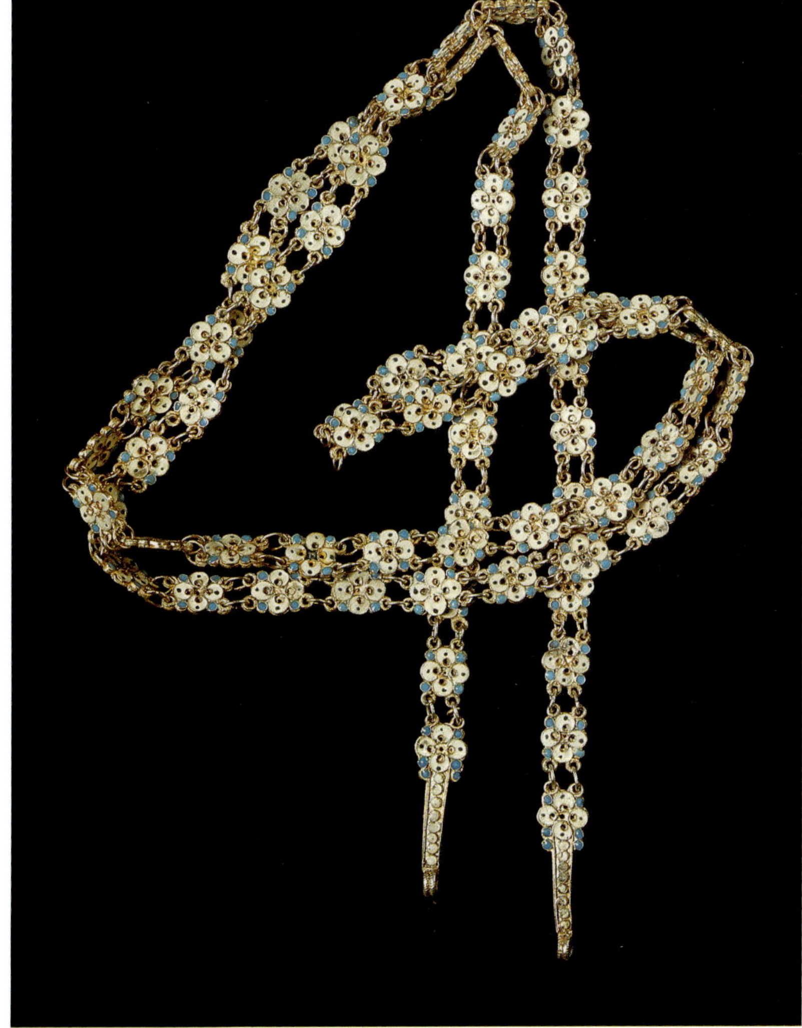

257

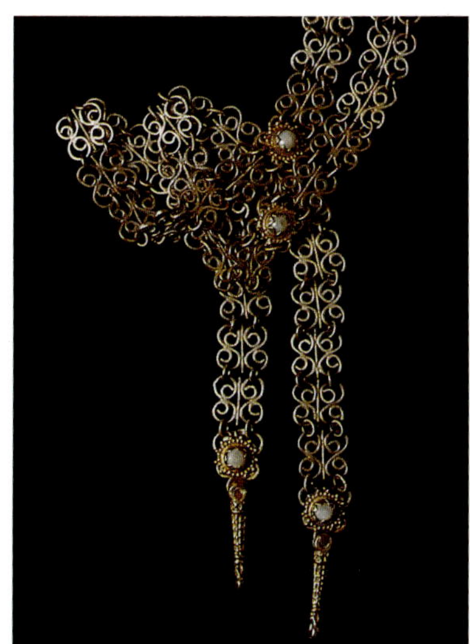

258

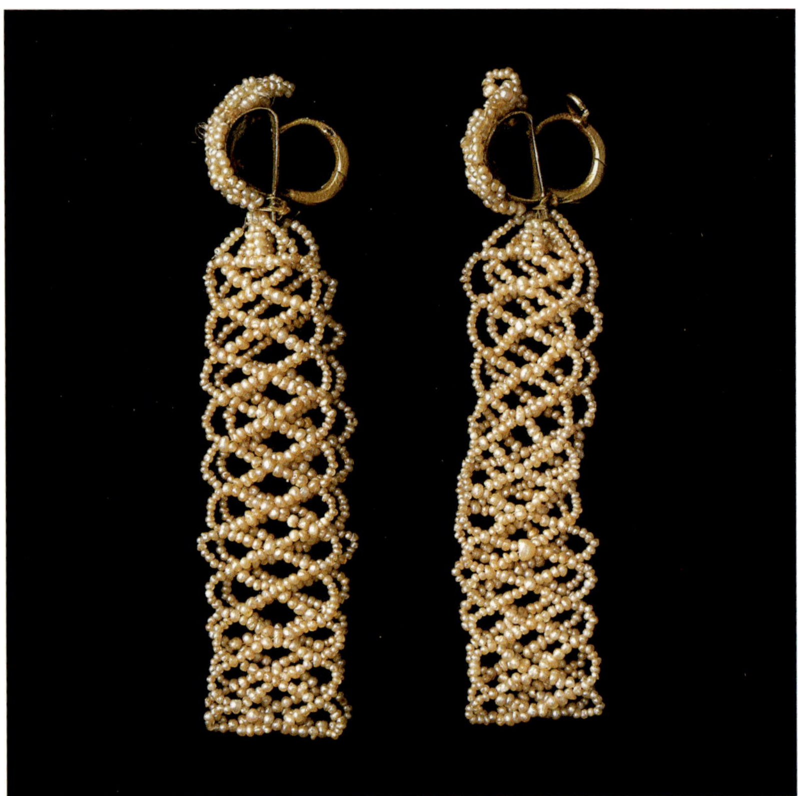

259

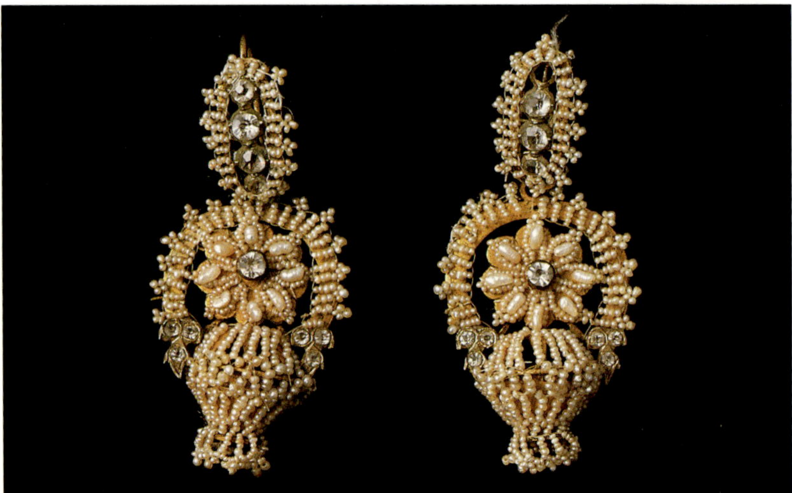

260

259. Earrings
Northern Russia, 17th century
silver, copper, pearls
length: 9.0 cm
17391 OK 15095

260. Earrings
Northern Russia, 18th century
silver, copper, pearls, glass
7.0 x 3.0 cm
17426 OK 15058

261. Earrings
Northern Russia, 17th century
silver, copper, pearls, glass
7.0 x 3.0 cm
17461 OK 15051

262. Earrings
Russia, first half of 19th century
gold, moss-agate, glass
5.8 x 1.7 cm
12710 OK 13057

263. Earrings
Petersburg, 1845
gold, enamel
7.8 x 2.3 cm
12789 OK 13251

264. Earrings
Russia, first quarter of 19th century
gold, silver, diamonds
4.6 x 2.6 cm
14565 OK 2101

265. Earrings
Russia, second half of 17th century
silver gilt, pearls, almandites, red stones
length: 3.7 cm
13159 OK 14824

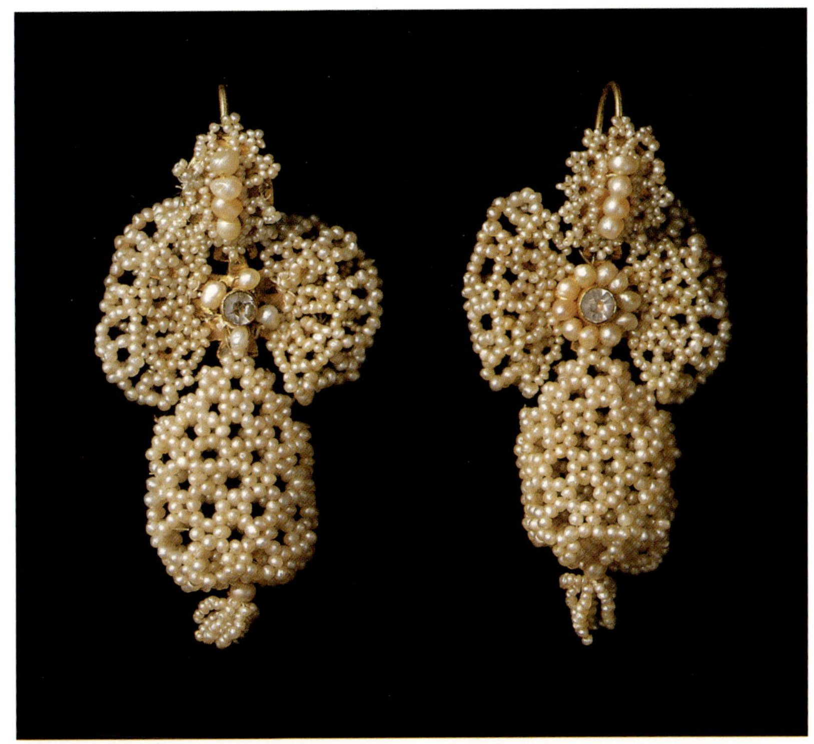

261

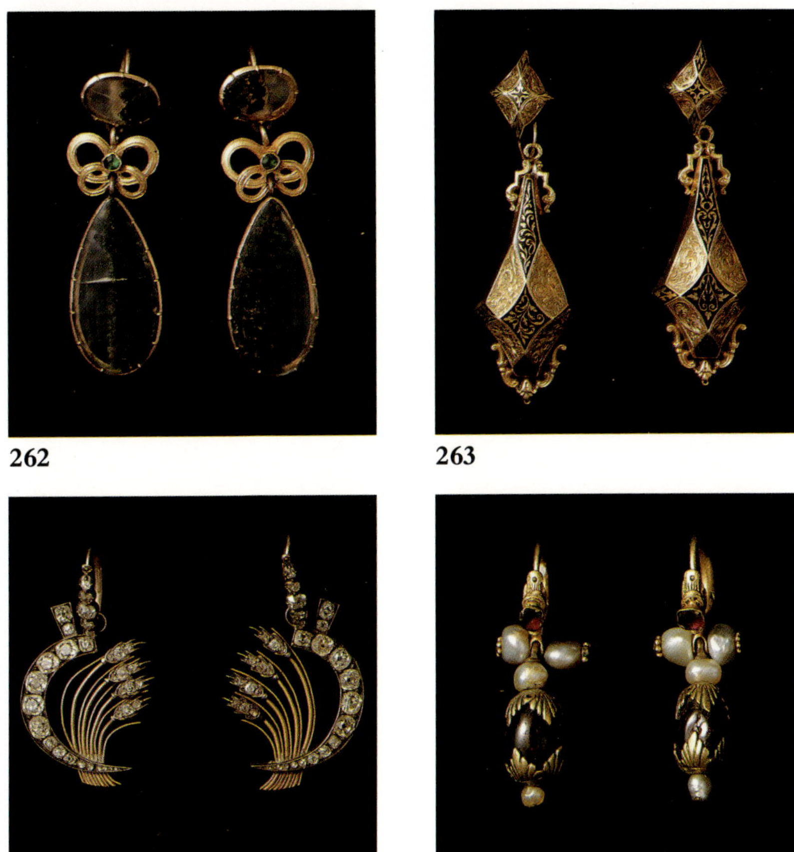

262

263

264

265

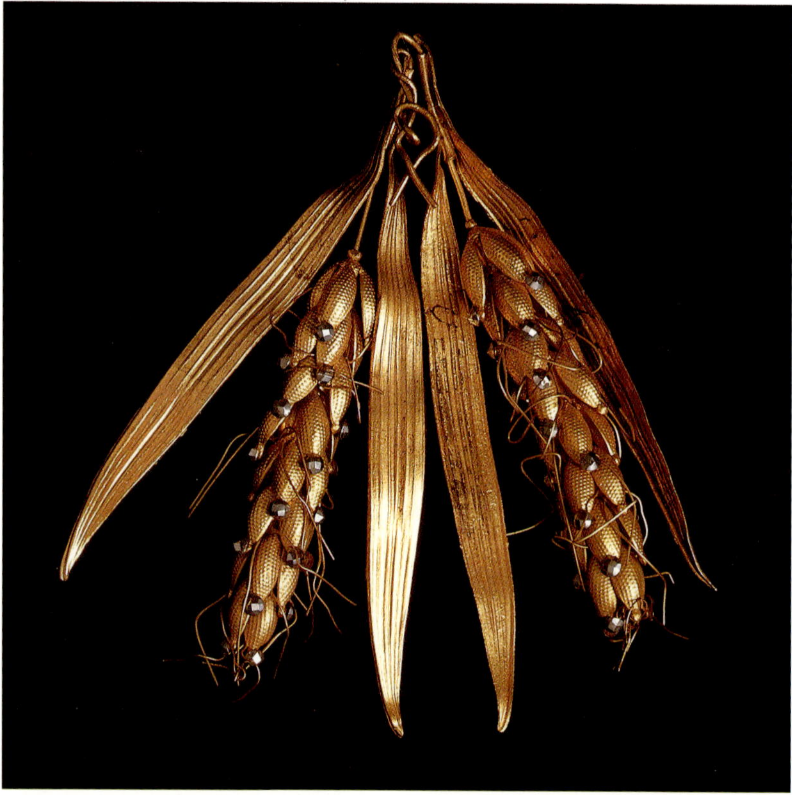
266

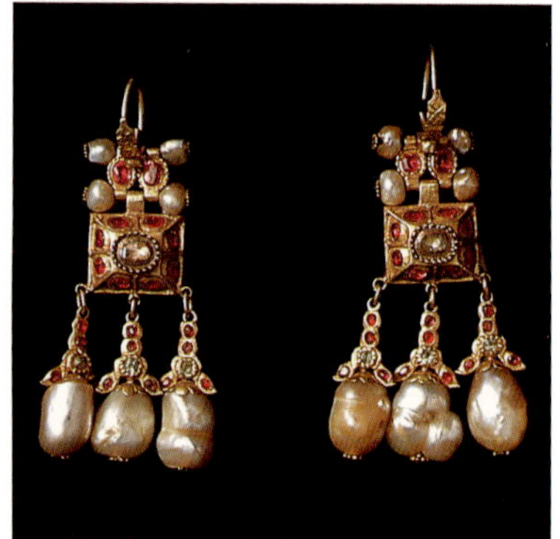
267

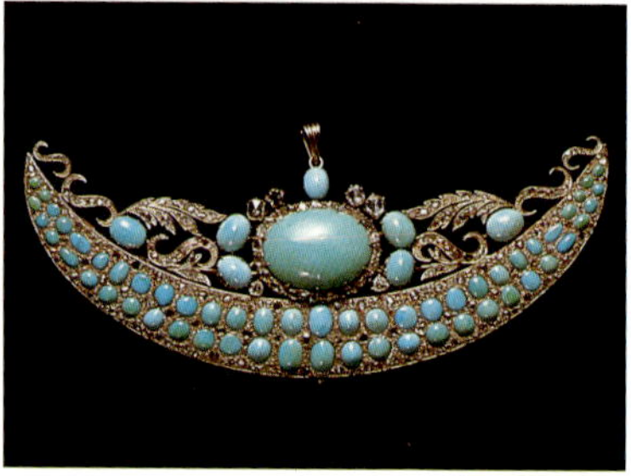
269

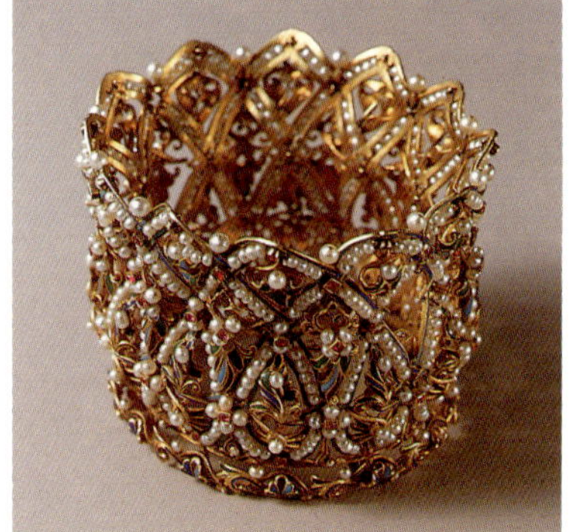
268

266. Hair ornament
Russia, first half of 19th century
gold, steel
length: 7.7 cm
73700 OK 7018

267. Earrings
Russia, early 18th century
gold, emeralds, rubies, diamonds, pearls
length: 6.0 cm
14593 OK 6508

268. Cuff bracelet
Russia, second quarter of 19th century
gold, rubies, pearls, enamel
5.6 x 7.4 x 6.8 cm
74142 OK 7140

Cuff bracelets, worn on each arm to fasten wide blouse sleeves, became fashionable in the second quarter of the 19th century.

269. Pendant brooch
Russia, first half of 19th century
gold, silver, diamonds, turquoise
6.5 x 16.5 cm
14376 OK 2015

270. Brooch
Russia, 18th century
gold, silver, brilliant- and rose-cut diamonds, emeralds, turquoise, glass
5.7 x 4.0 cm
14814 OK 1994

This bouquet-shaped brooch features a jewelled camomile with an oblong emerald studded with rose-cut diamonds, turquoise-studded forget-me-nots with centres of rose-cut diamonds, leaves studded with rose-cut diamonds and green glass, and buds of brilliants and diamonds.

271. Comb
Ion Bergstrem, Petersburg, 1795–1816
gold, horn, diamonds, agate, enamel
15.2 x 9.9 cm
6706 OK 15513

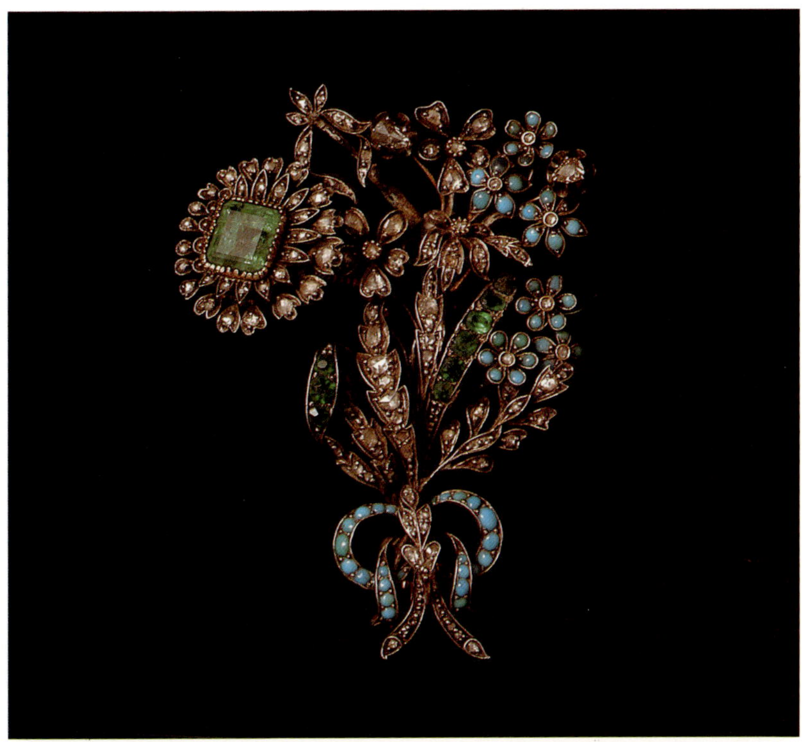

270

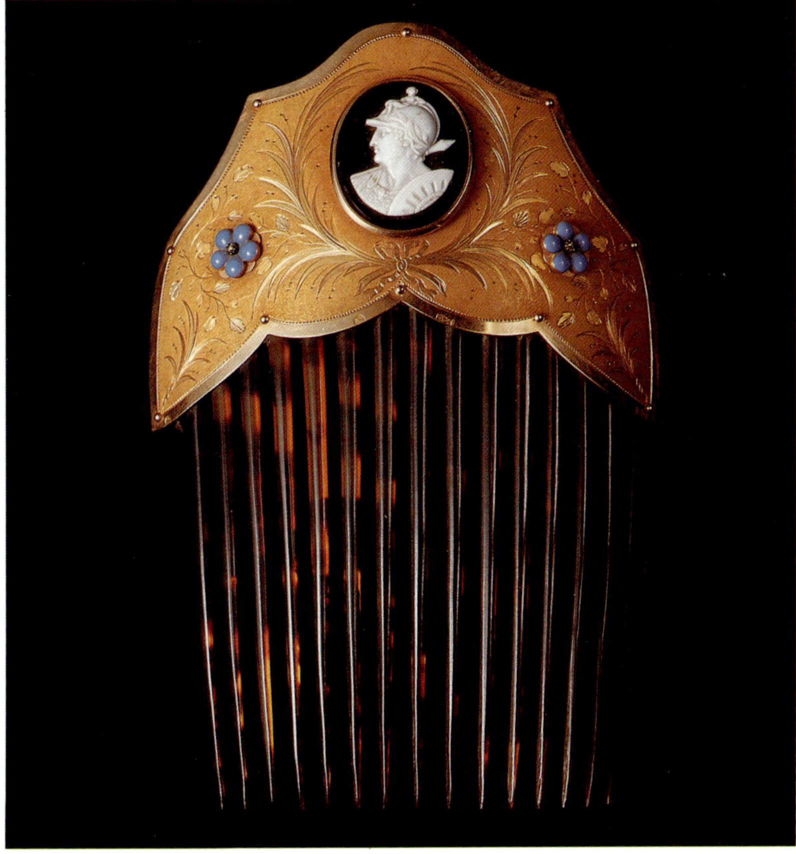

271

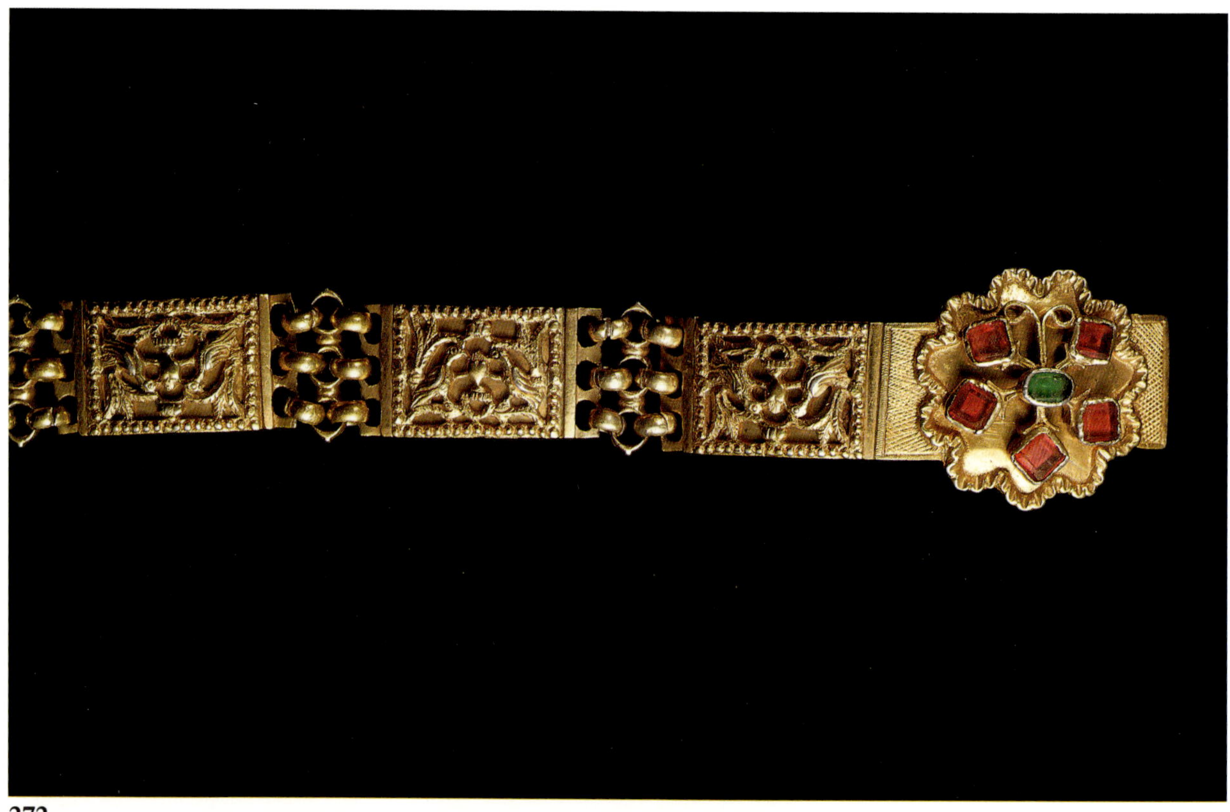

272

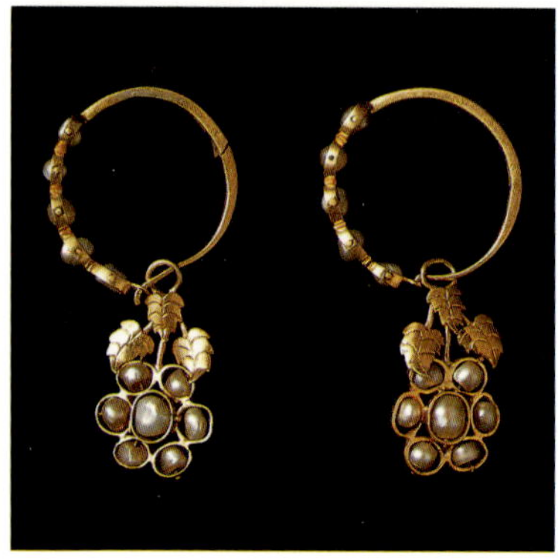

273

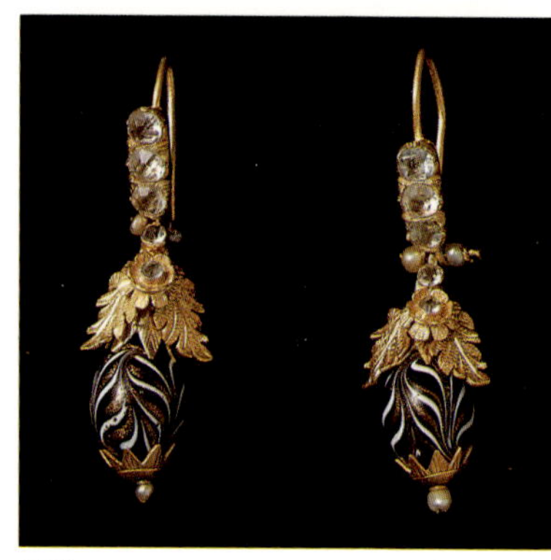

274

272. Belt and buckle
Russia, second half of 18th century
silver gilt, stones
2.0 x 80.0 cm
5045 OK 1228

273. Earrings
Russia, first half of 19th century
silver, pearls
5.5 x 1.5 cm
17324 OK 15075

274. Earrings
Russia, first half of 19th century
silver, pearls, glass beads
5.5 x 1.7 cm
54679 OK 14995

275. Earrings
Russia, first half of 19th century
silver, pearls, aventurine
7.2 x 2.6 x 1.4 cm
74215 OK 14777

276. Earrings
Russia, first half of 19th century
silver, pearls, amethyst, glass
7.8 x 1.3 cm
55008 OK 14848

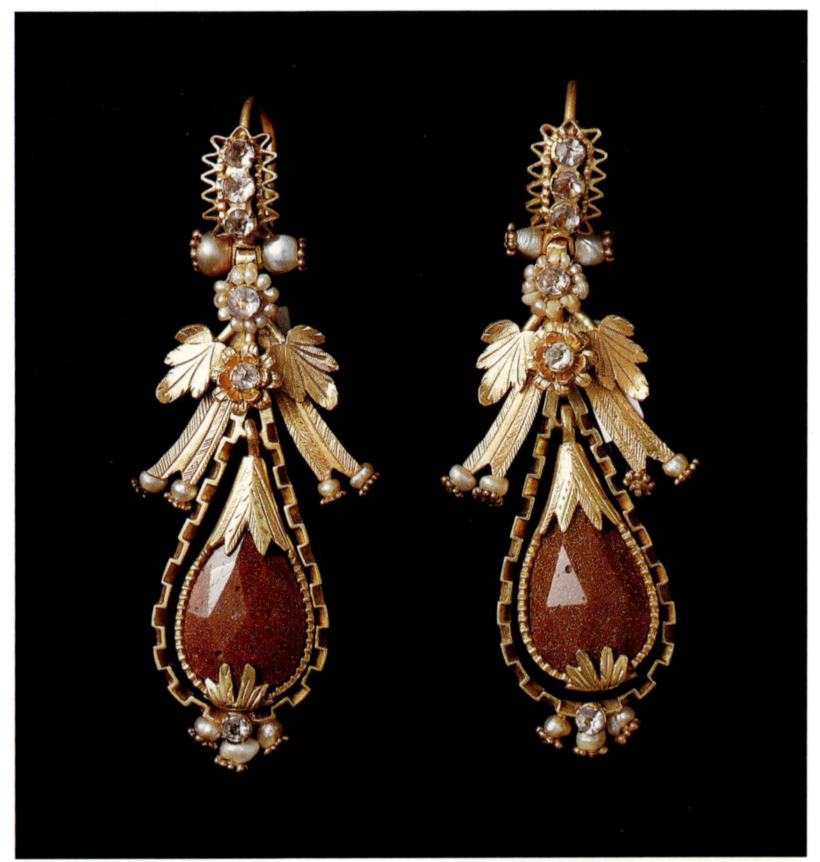

275

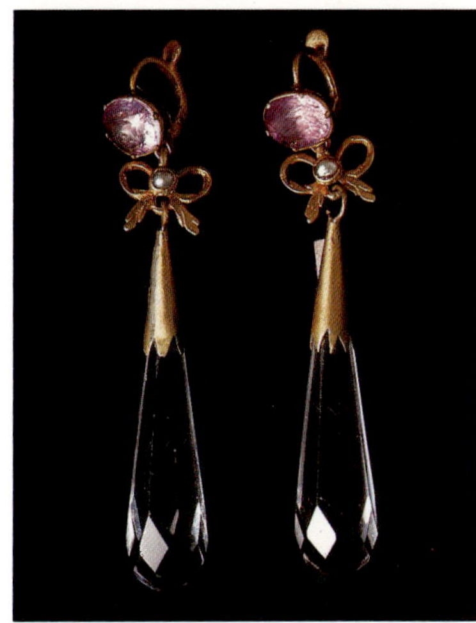

276

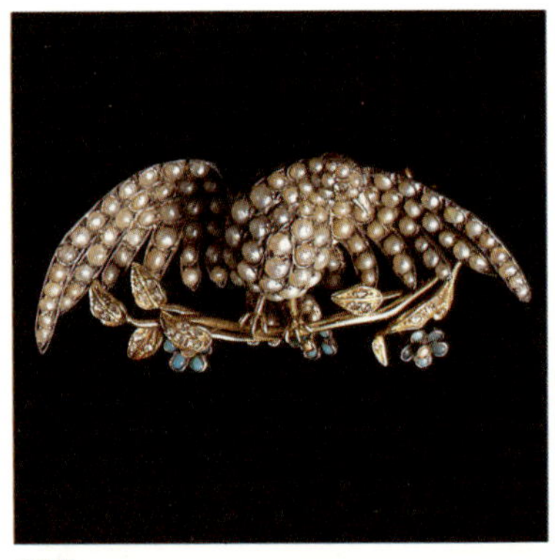
277

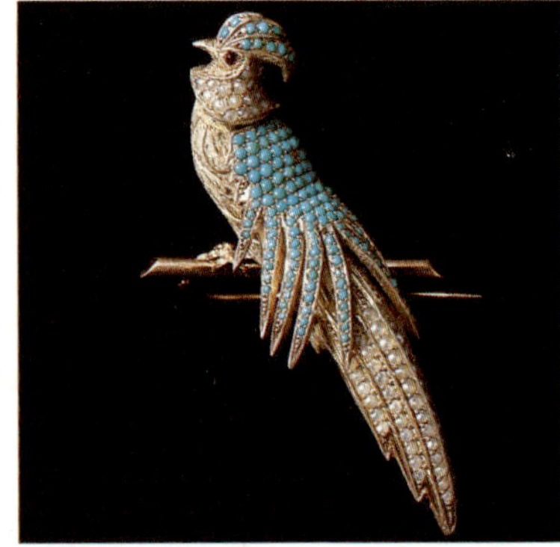
278

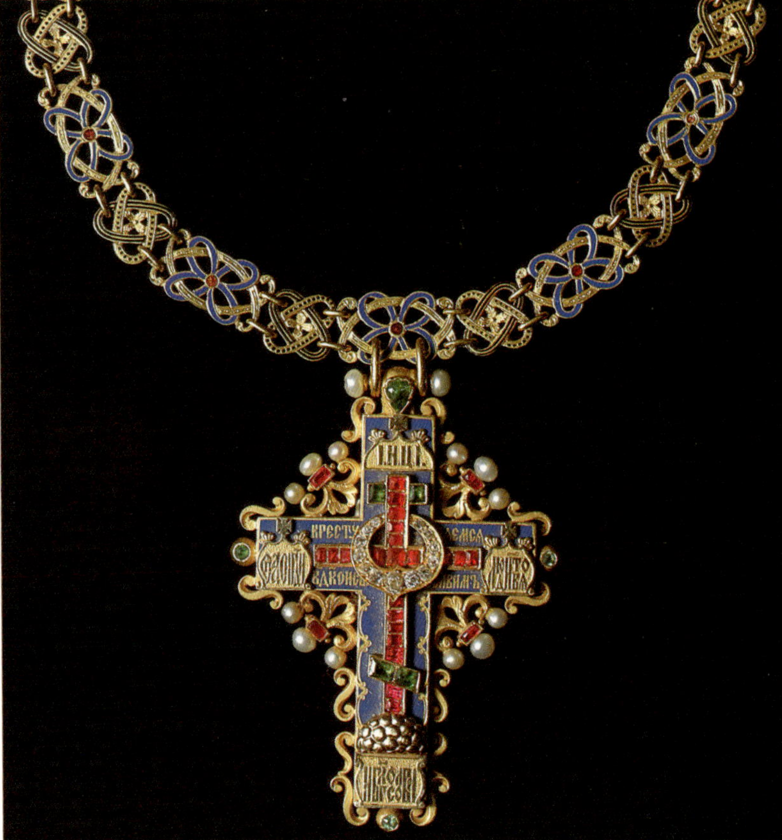
279

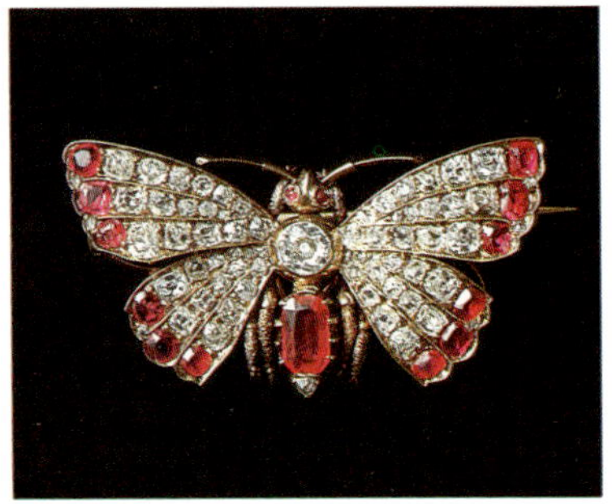
280

277. Gold brooch
Russia, second quarter of 19th century
gold, silver, pearls, turquoise, rosettes
3.0 x 5.5 cm
14808 OK 1986

278. Brooch
Moscow, first half of 19th century
silver gilt, turquoise, pearls
5.0 x 3.5 cm
53274 OK 1988

279. Necklace with cross
Moscow, 1867
gold, rubies, emeralds, diamonds, pearls
6.2 x 4.3 cm
dated, assay mark
16903 OK 2305

280. Brooch
Petersburg, late 19th–early 20th century
gold, diamonds, rubies
3.8 x 2.0 cm
dated, assay mark
106813 OK 23084

281. Brooch
Karl Edward Bolin,
Petersburg, 1880–90
gold, diamonds, sapphires, rubies
6.0 x 3.0 cm
dated, marked KI, assay mark
107001 OK 23092

Karl Edward Bolin founded a firm of court jewellers in 1831, which operated until 1917.

282. Earrings
Russia, first half of 19th century
silver gilt, pearls, glass
6.2 x 2.5 cm
53293 OK 1990

283. Brooch
Russia, second half of 19th century
gold, enamel, diamonds
4.5 x 4.0 cm
107080 OK 23167

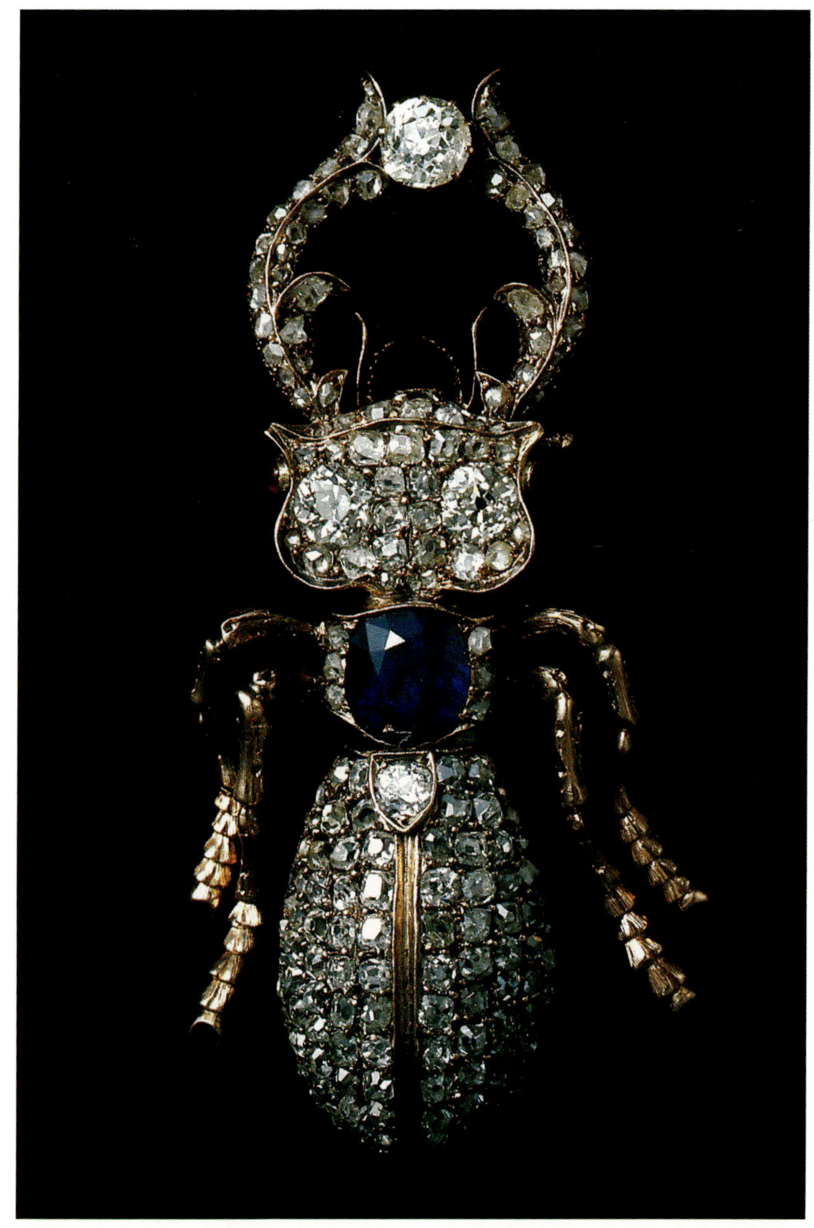

281

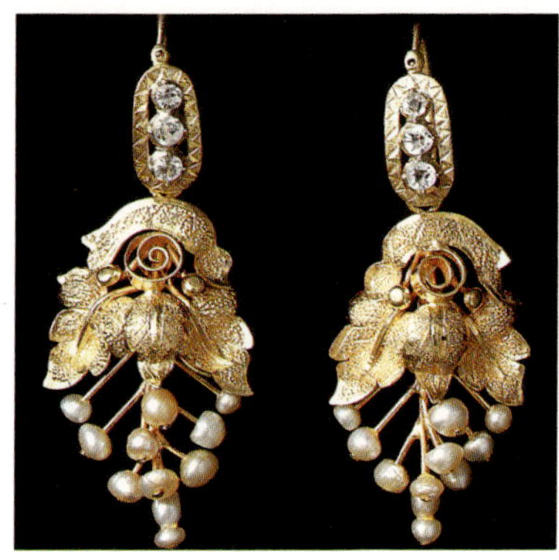

282

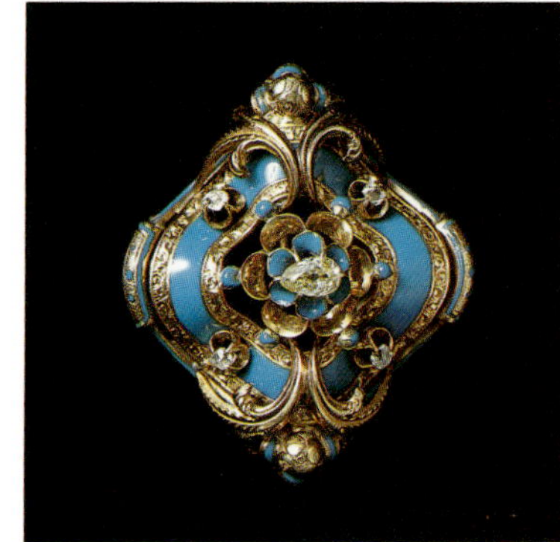

283

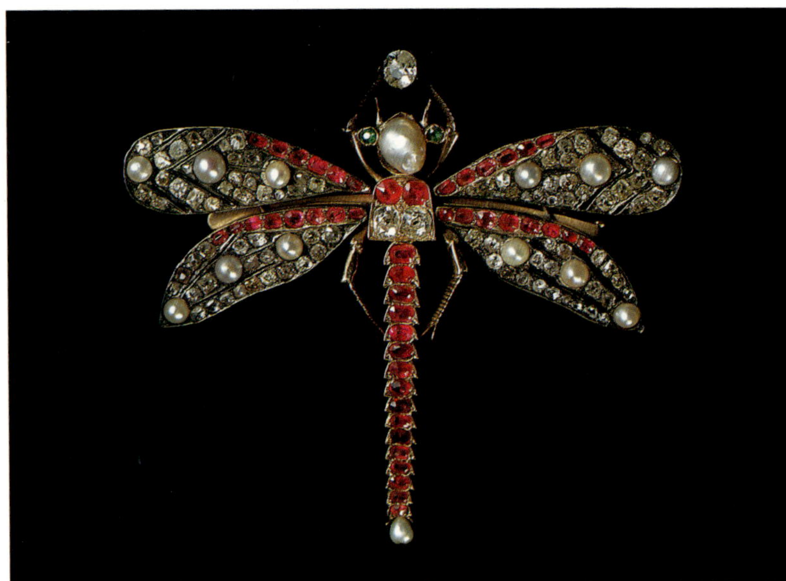

284

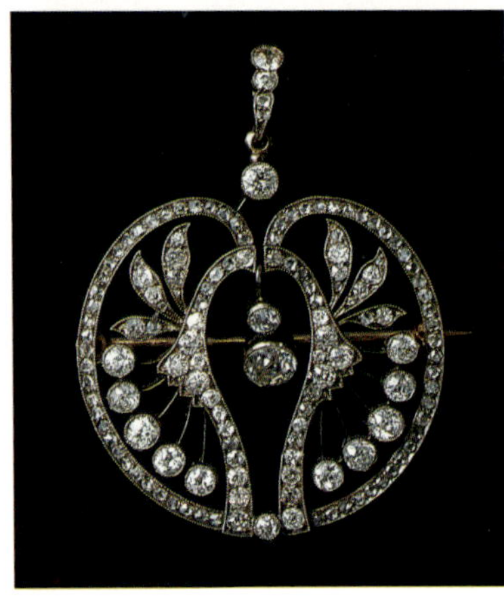

285

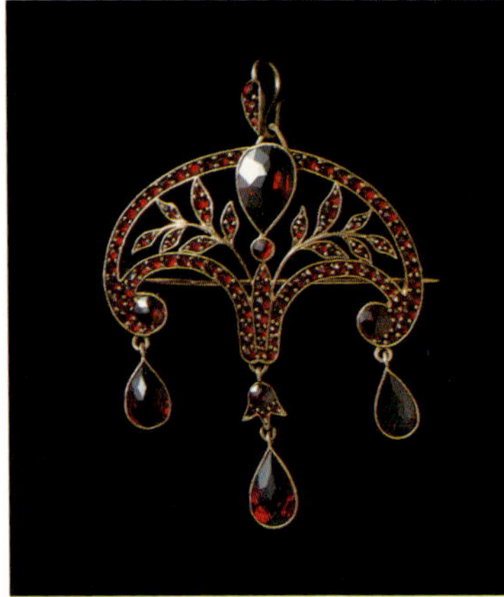

286

284. Brooch
Vasily Agafonov, Moscow, 1908–17
gold, rubies, uncut diamonds, pearls
6.2 x 7.0 cm
dated, marked BA, assay mark
106594 OK 23072

The silver workshop of Vasily Agafonov was known from 1895 to 1917.

285. Pendant brooch
Sergei Ivanovich Shposhnikov, Moscow, 1908–17
gold, cut and uncut diamonds
4.5 x 3.2 cm
dated, marked SSH, assay mark
106996 OK 23090

Sergei Ivanovich Shposhnikov was known as a silversmith and jewellery merchant from 1897 to 1908.

286. Pendant brooch
Petersburg, 1899–1908
gold, garnets
6.6 x 4.4 cm
dated, assay mark
104001 OK 22694

287. Brooch
Moscow, late 19th century
gold, enamel, semi-precious stones from the Urals
5.5 x 5.9 cm
assay mark
103173 OK 18306

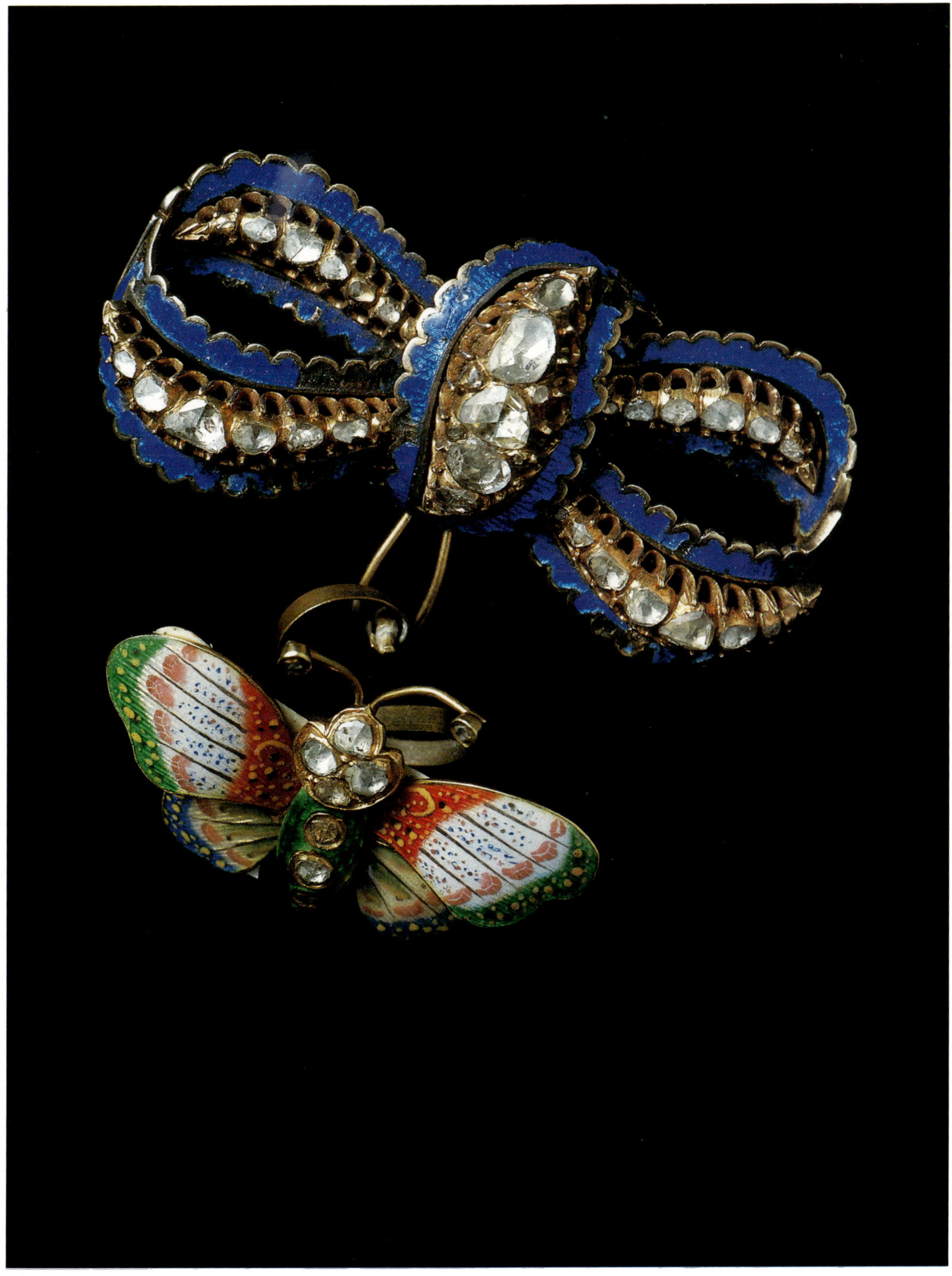

287

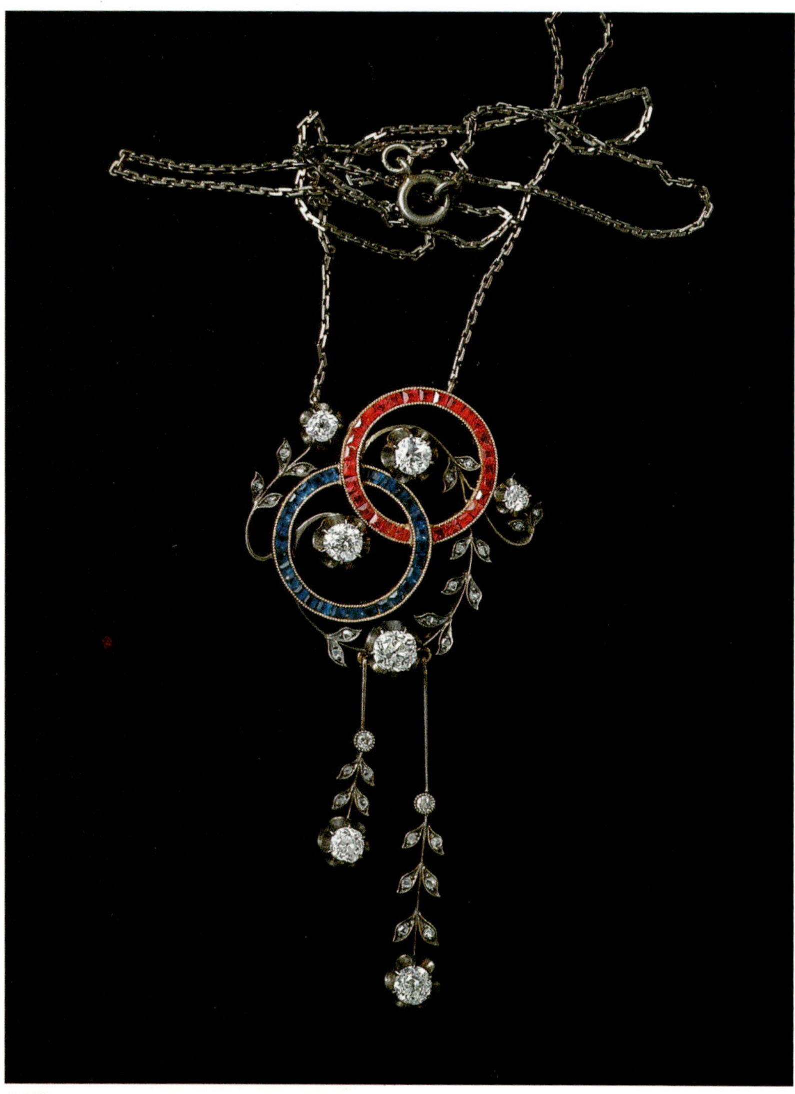

288

288. Necklace
second cartel of jewellers,
Moscow, 1908–17
gold, rubies, sapphires, uncut diamonds
6.5 x 3.0 cm;
length of chain: 48.0 cm
dated, marked 2AYU,
assay mark
107435 OK 23269

289. Brooch
Moscow, late 19th century
gold, pearls, diamonds
6.5 x 4.5 x 3.0 cm
marked, assay mark
107080 OK 23170

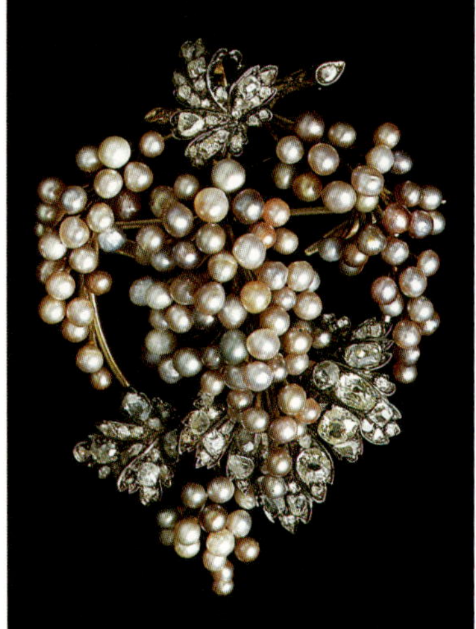

289

290. Bracelet
Nikolai Feodorovich Strulyov, Moscow, 1908–17
gold, chrysolite
7.0 x 6.2 cm
dated, marked HC, assay mark
1005708 OK 22988

Nikolai Feodorovich Strulyov owned a silver workshop known from 1883 to 1917.

291. Bracelet
Russia, late 19th–early 20th century
silver, gold, turquoise, pearl, uncut diamonds
4.0 x 7.6 x 7.3 cm
104001 OK 22695

292. Bracelet
Russia, mid 19th century
silver, garnets
16.5 x 4.5 cm
18067 OK 17482

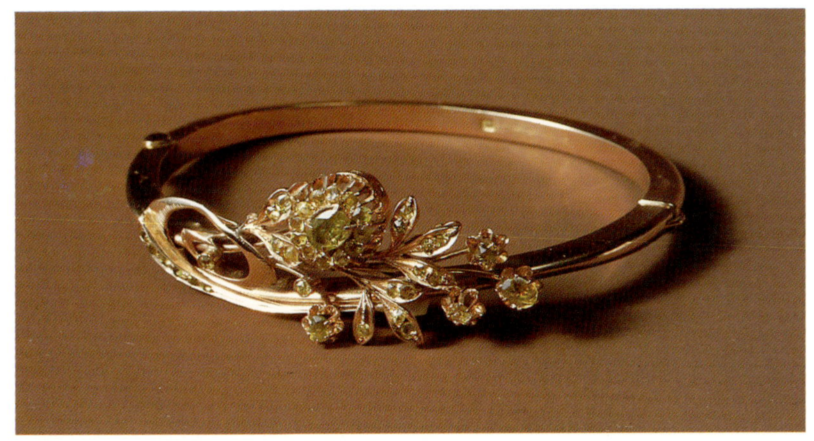

290

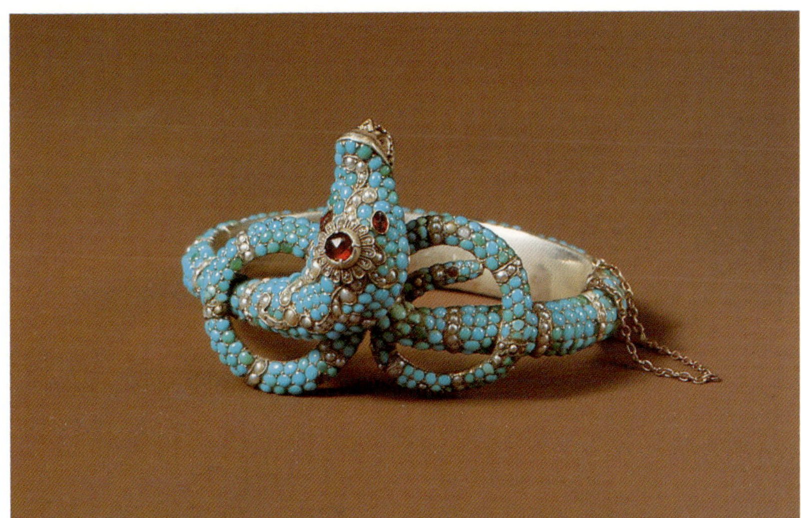

291

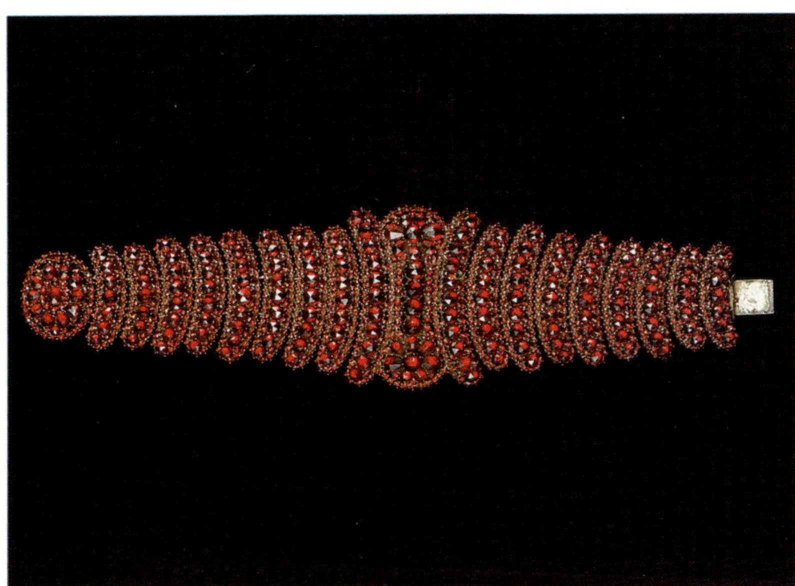

292

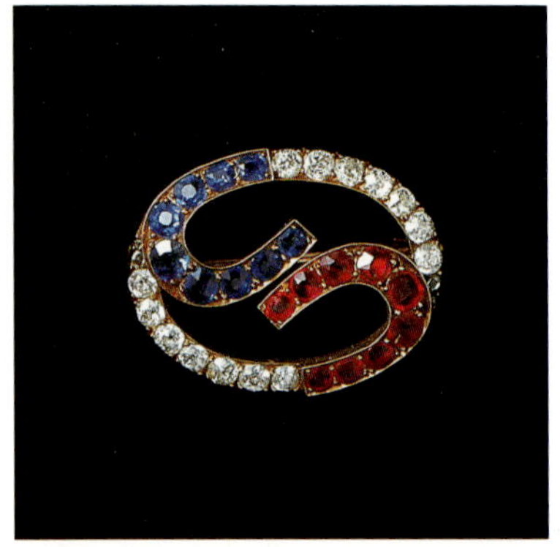

293

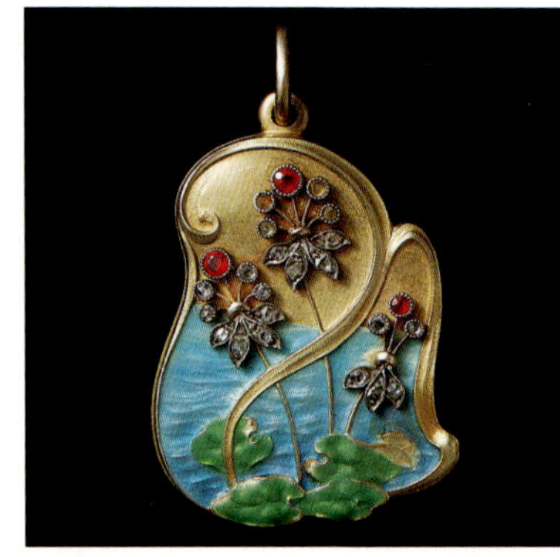

294

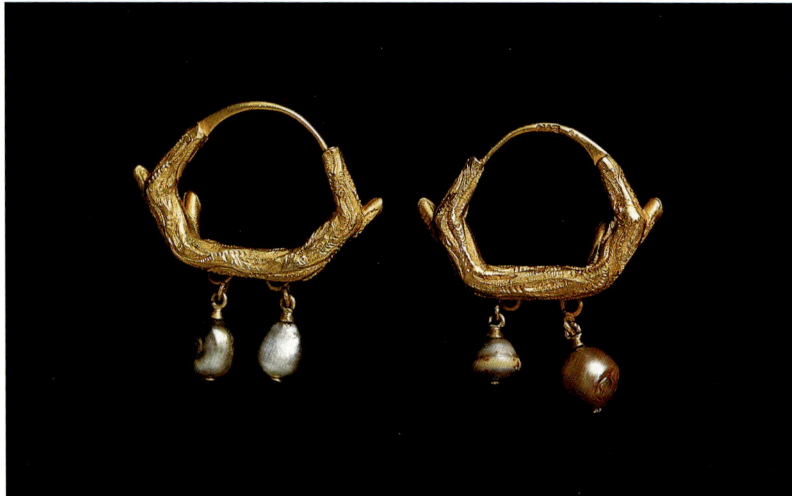

295

293. Brooch
Friedrich Khristian Kekhli, Petersburg, early 20th century
gold, sapphires, diamonds, rubies
2.8 x 2.2 cm
107651 OK 23286

Friedrich Khristian Kekhli owned a jewellery workshop known from 1874 to 1908.

294. Locket
first cartel of jewellers, Moscow, 1908–17
gold, enamel, uncut diamonds, rubies
6.0 x 4.0 cm
dated, marked IAJ, assay mark
107210 OK 23222

295. Earrings
Russia, mid 19th century
gold, pearls
3.7 x 3.5 cm
53294 OK 1877

IX

MODERN JEWELLERY ART

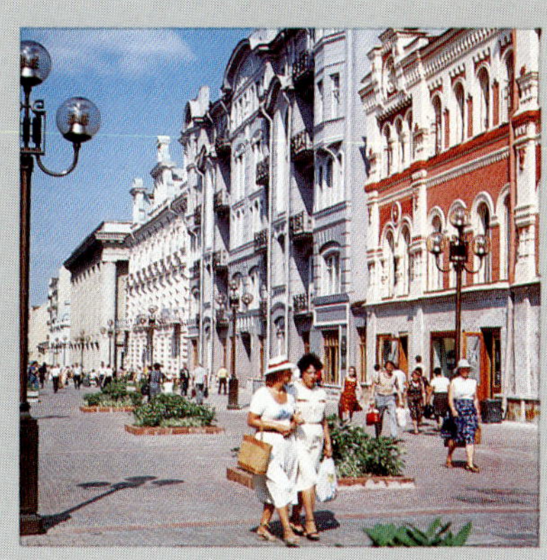

In the 1920s and 1930s, jewellery-making in Russia was concentrated in the hands of the cartels, co-operative associations of craftsmen in the traditional centres of gold and silver work: Veliky Ustyug (the Northern Niello Cartel), Bronnitzy and the ancient chain-making centre, the villages of the Kostroma region—Krasnoe on the Volga and Sidorovskoe—and Podolsk, a centre for the production of ornaments and charms since the 19th century.

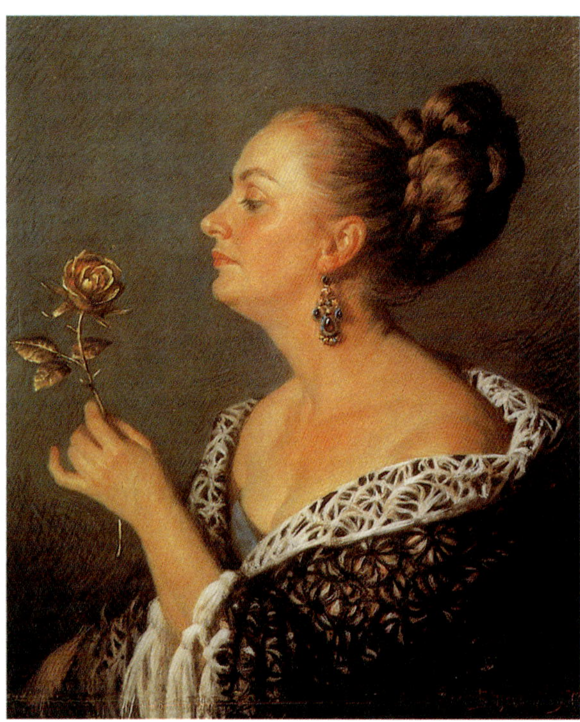

PORTRAIT TITLED *THE GOLDEN ROSE* BY BORIS SHCHERBAKOV

However, jewellery was not manufactured on an economic scale until the 1950s, when factories were established for the purpose. The post-war period saw a revival of jewellery-making as a branch of the decorative arts in its own right. As the great Russian tradition in this field of creativity had been broken, the major task in the 1960s was to study and revive traditional techniques. This requirement largely determined the future direction of the development of Russian jewellery. Over a short period of time, jewellers studied the entire Russian jewellery continuum; out of this study grew the modern Russian style of gold and silver work.

Included in this exhibition are two items made by the Moscow artist-jeweller Y. Sarykin, who revived the old technique of translucent, or stained-glass window enamel, previously produced by the best firms of the 19th and 20th centuries such as Ovchinnikov, Khlebnikov and the Grachyev Brothers. The beautiful bratina or loving cup (cat. no. 297) is decorated with a light openwork design filled with transparent enamel and studded with gold grains.

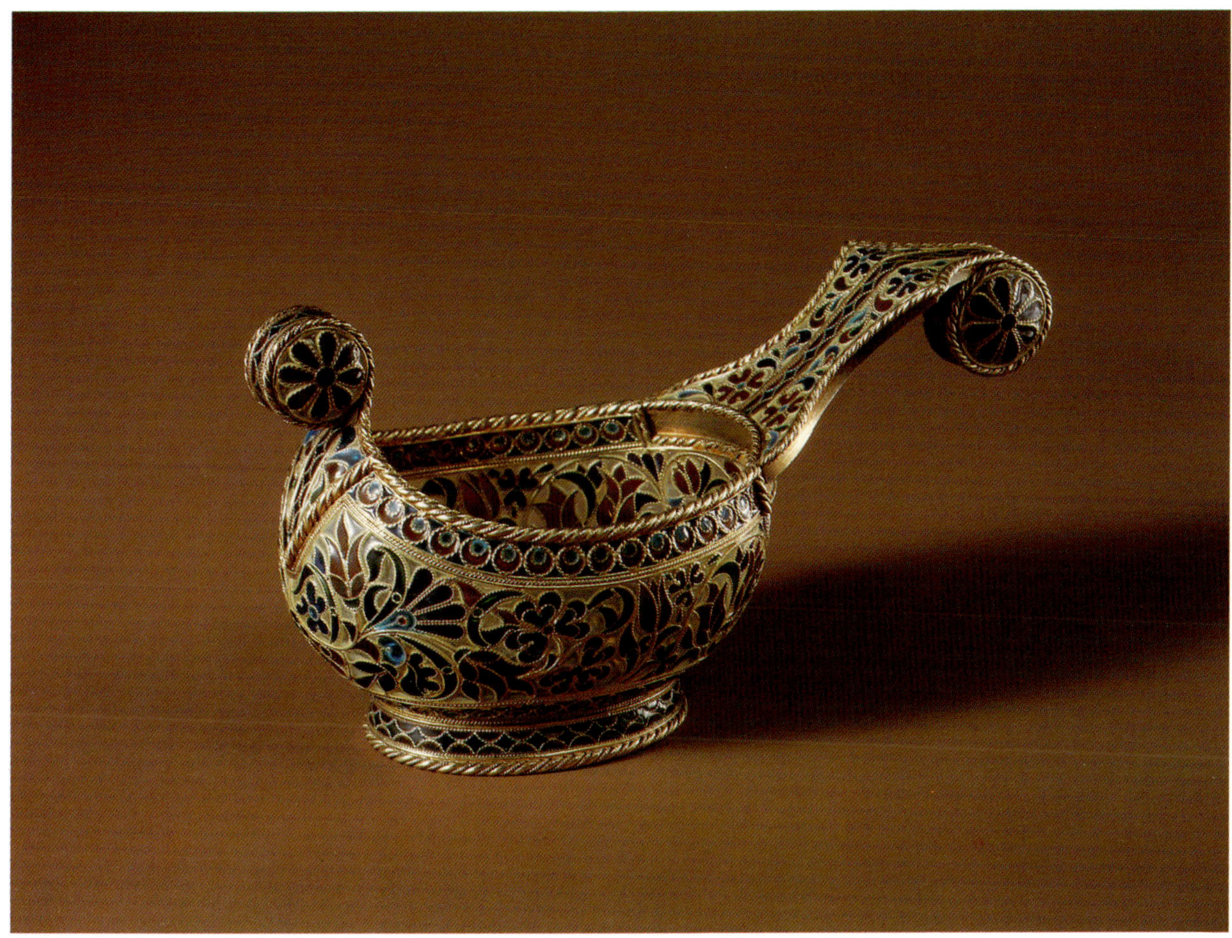

296

296. Ladle
Y. Sarykin, Moscow, 1982
silver gilt, cloisonné, filigree
5.0 x 16.0 x 7.0 cm
105881 OK 23080

The open-work filigree pattern is filled with transparent cloisonné.

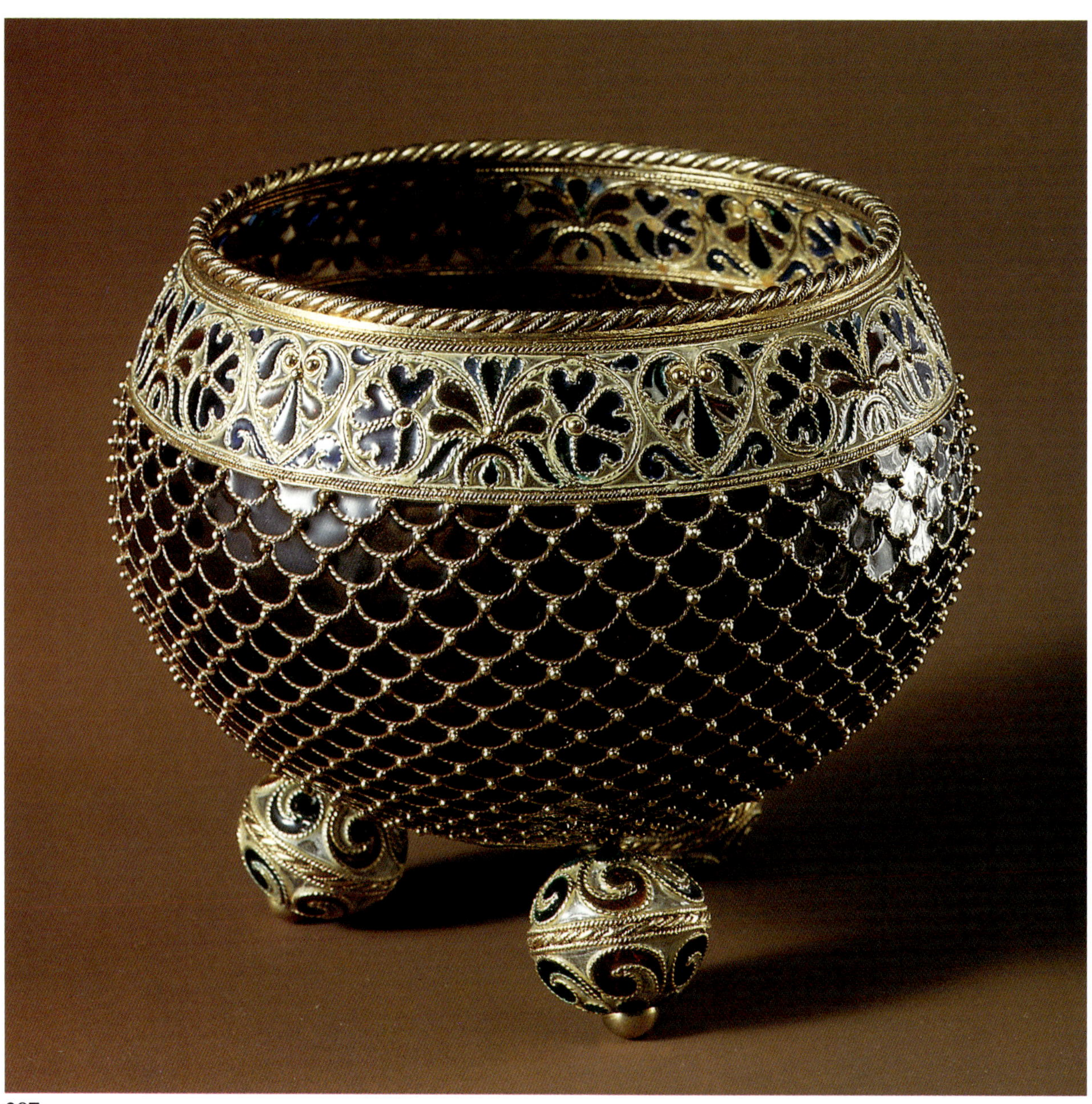

297

297. Bratina (loving cup)
Y. Sarykin, Moscow, 1982
silver, cloisonné
10.0 x 8.5 x 8.5 cm
105881 OK 23029

The open-work filigree pattern is filled with polychrome transparent cloisonné and decorated with zern beads.

SELECTED BIBLIOGRAPHY

BOCHAROV, G.N., *Metalwork in Old Russia of the 10th–Early 11th Centuries,* Nauka, Moscow, 1984

KORZUKHINA, G.F., *Russian Treasure Troves of the 12th and 13th Centuries,* Moscow, 1954

MAKAROVA, G.I., *Cloisonné Enamel in Old Russia,* Nauka, Moscow, 1975

MAKAROVA, G.I., *Nielloing in Old Russia,* Moscow, Nauka, 1986

MONGAIT, A.L., *Old Ryazan,* Moscow, Nauka, 1955

RIBAKOV, B.A., *Applied Art and Sculpture: Collected Articles on the History of Russian Art,* 1951

RIBAKOV, B.A., *Handicrafts of Old Russia,* Moscow, 1948

RIBAKOV, B.A., *Paganism in Old Russia,* Moscow, Nauka, 1987

UVAROV, A.S., *Antiquities Catalogue,* Moscow, 1907

VASILENKO, V.M., *Russian Applied Art, Iskusstvo,* Moscow, 1977

ZABELIN, I.E., *Family Life of the Russian People in the 16th–17th Centuries,* 3 vols, Moscow, 1990

Russian Enamel Catalogue, Moscow, 1962

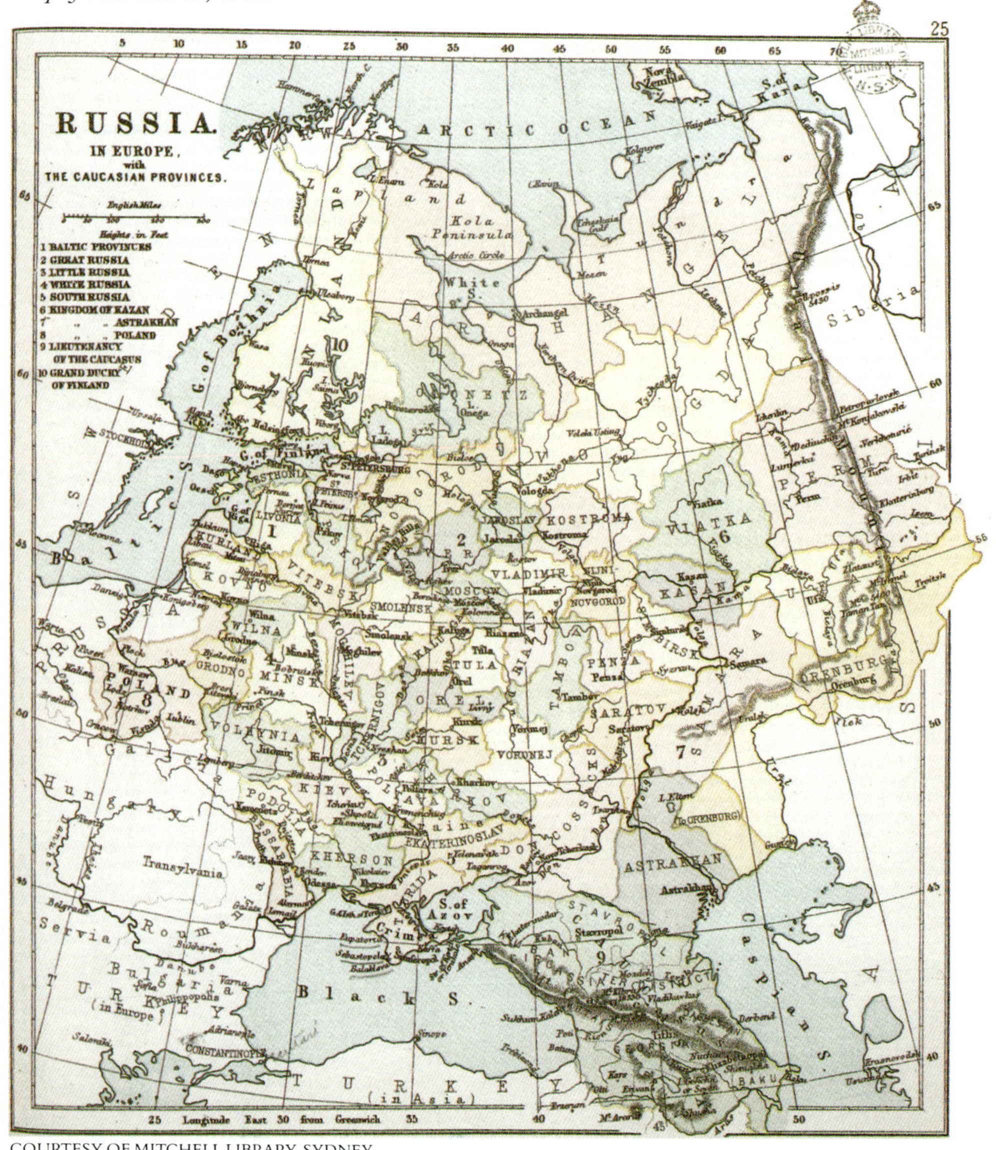

RUSSIA, 1898

COURTESY OF MITCHELL LIBRARY, SYDNEY

GLOSSARY

almandite a purplish-red garnet

barm necklace

basma hand-stamping of images onto thin sheets of metal

bezel a raised flange holding a stone, especially in a finger ring

bratina loving cup; metal bowl-shaped cup, often ceremonial in function

carnelian a red variety of chalcedony, semi-transparent, often used in jewellery

cartouche a panel, usually containing an inscription, which has an elaborately decorated frame

chalcedony a kind of quartz with a waxy lustre, variously coloured, usually greyish or milky; comprises agate, sardonix, cat's eye, jasper, carnelian and chrysoprase

charochka small wine vessel

chasing relief patterns raised by means of a hammer or punch

chrysolite a green or yellow silicate of magnesium and iron, of glassy lustre and granular structure

chrysoprase a golden green variety of very hard, lustrous mineral, in the same family as emerald and aquamarine

cloisonné a technique of enamelling in which cells or cloisons are built up on a thin sheet of metal by attaching metal wire or fine strips of metal fixed edgewise; the cells are filled with finely powdered glass paste, which is then fused to the metal in a furnace; as the enamel shrinks on melting and cools with a concave surface, more has to be poured in and the process repeated; finally the surface is levelled and the whole is smoothed and polished

discos a liturgical dish of the Orthodox Church, used during the sacrament of the Eucharist

dvoichatky double earrings

Empire-style the term applied primarily to the style of furniture, dress and decoration which started in Paris after the French Revolution and spread through Europe

filigree openwork decoration made out of fine threads of silver or gold

grivna necklace made of twisted wire

hallmark a series of symbols stamped on an article of gold or silver to denote that it conforms to one of the legal standards

kolt crescent shaped pendant worn near the temples

korchik metal ladle based on an ancient Russian prototype

lamellate composed of thin plates or scales

locket a small hinged metal case for holding a picture, lock of hair, etc, usually hung from a necklace or ribbon

lost wax process the process whereby a model is carved in wax then placed in a mould and heated causing the wax to melt and run out. Molten metal is then poured into the mould

moss-agate a type of agate (a variety of chalcedony) with moss-like markings

niello a black compound of silver, lead, copper and sulphur used to fill incised decoration on silver

oklad frame or setting for icon

panagia pectoral image

pouncing metal surface hammered with fine dots to give a powdered or matt effect

riza chasuble, used to decorate an icon

rose-cut a style of cutting a gemstone so that it resembles a symmetrical rose

vyaz ancient style of calligraphy in which all the letters are connected to form an even, unbroken pattern

zern a decorative technique using small grains of metal to create a raised design on a metal or enamelled object

Art Exhibitions Australia Limited

Board of Directors

James B. Leslie, A.O., M.C., *Chairman*
Norman K. Baker
Jean A. Battersby, A.O.
Franco Belgiorno-Nettis, C.B.E., A.M.
Edmund Capon
Betty Churcher, A.M.
Michael Darling
Ann Lewis, A.M.
The Hon. Mr Justice John S. Lockhart
Alan McGregor, A.O.
Robert S. McKay
Robert Edwards, A.O., *Chief Executive*

Management

Carol Henry, *General Manager*
Graham Jephcott, *Business Manager*
Belinda Nemec, *Administrative Officer*
Jill Davies, *Accountant*
Lorraine Wright, *Secretary*
Nicole Aubertin, *Office Assistant*

Exhibition logistics

Exhibition design

Trevor and Esther Hayter, Architects & Designers

Catalogue design and production

Minale, Tattersfield, Bryce & Partners Pty Limited
International Design Consultants,
Sydney, Brisbane, Australia
Michael Bryce, Philip Whiting, John Holt,
Pat Williams, Nicole Feuz

Transportation

Hasenkamp Internationale Transporte, Cologne
Department of Administrative Services

Security

Australian Protective Service

Promotions

Lindley Mitchell Pty Limited